D1273018

3

BARGAINING BEHAVIOR
An International Study

BARGAINING BEHAVIOR:
An International Study

Donald L. Harnett
Graduate School of Business
Indiana University

L. L. Cummings
Graduate School of Business
University of Wisconsin

1980

dame publications inc.

P.O. Box 35556
Houston, Texas 77035

HD30.23
H366

© DAME PUBLICATIONS, INC. 1980

All rights reserved. No part of this publication may be
reproduced, stored in a retrieval system, or transmitted,
in any form or by any means, electronic, mechanical, photo-
copying, recording, or otherwise, without the prior written
permission of the publisher.

Library of Congress No. 320-79-67421 ISBN 0-931920-14-0
Printed in the United States of America.

To our families

APR 6   1988

PREFACE

The discovery of our mutual interests in bargaining behavior as a mechanism for making decisions occurred in the Fall of 1964. We came to the realization of these mutual interests from different perspectives; Harnett as an economist and statistician and Cummings as an organizational behavioralist and management scholar. The initial bond for these interests was a commitment to experimentally demonstrate the role of structure, information, and personality in determining variations in bargaining behavior.

Over the ensuing fourteen years, we have come to develop additional common perspectives as these pertain to the analysis of bargaining behavior. We feel that three of these are noteworthy and hope that each will be evident in what follows. First, our work has moved from an examination of student to managerial samples. This was generated by our desire to provide an increasingly realistic perspective on bargaining as a form of decision making. Second, over time our analyses have become more complex. We have moved toward studies examining the interaction effects of environmental or structural factors and personality and demographic characteristics as determinants of bargaining behavior. Over the span of our research we also have broadened the range of dependent variables which we have attempted to explain. Our domain of interest has expanded to include measures of bargaining aspirations and intentions, strategies of behavior during bargaining, monetary gain achieved through bargaining, and several affective responses to these processes and results. Third, while our sampling of bargainers was initially narrow (Midwestern university students), the scope of bargainers studied expanded to encompass managers from both the private and public employment sectors and from not only the United States but Europe, Japan, and Thailand.

We feel that the breadth of focus across several interacting bargaining determinants, the expansive nature of the bargaining behaviors and responses to be examined, and the international scope of the study each add a contribution to the knowledge of bargaining and, more generally, of decision making.

We have been extremely fortunate to have the cooperation and collaboration of several persons and institutions in conducting the program of research reported here. Without this help, the work would have been impossible. We wish to gratefully acknowledge the following persons for their assistance in facilitating the collection of data:

> Professor Leo Ahlstedt, Finnish Institute of Management
> Professor Henri Claude de Bettignies, The European Institute of Business Administration
> Professor A. J. Eccles, Manchester Business School
> Dr. William Haberle, Indiana University
> Dr. Kichiro Hayashi, Institute for International Studies and Training (Japan), now at McMaster University, Canada
> Dr. Choop Karnjanaprakorn, Thailand National Institute for Development Administration
> Professor W. G. McClelland, Manchester Business School
> Mr. Yuthasar Na Nagara, Thailand Management Association
> Dr. Howard Schaller, Indiana University
> Dr. Salvadore Teresi, The European Institute of Business Administration
> Professor Hugo Van Hassel, Catholic University of Louvain
> Dr. Jose' M. Veciana Verges, Escuela Superior de Administracion y Direccion de Empresas, now at the Autonomous University of Barcelona

To obtain access to managerial samples, we were very fortunate to have the cooperation of the following institutions and their management education programs. Without exception, the cooperation and assistance provided were generously offered and highly competent. We are most grateful to:

> Escuela Superior de Administracion y Dirección de Empresas (Spain)
> The European Institute of Business Administration (France)
> Finnish Institute of Management
> Indiana University, School of Business (U. S. A.)
> Institute for International Studies and Training (Japan)
> London Graduate School of Business Studies (England)
> Thailand Management Association
> Vervolmakingscentrum Voor Bedrijfsleiding of the Catholic University of Louvain (Belgium)

Of course, substantial funding was needed for a project of this scope. We wish to acknowledge the financial assistance provided by:

The Ford Foundation

The Business Research Committee, School of Business, Indiana University

The International Business Research Committee, School of Business, Indiana University

The School of Business Research Committee, University of Wisconsin-Madison

The Industrial Relations Research Institute, University of Wisconsin-Madison

We are indebted to two individuals for very special, substantial contributions to this research and this book. Dr. James Stevens, The European Institute of Business Administration (INSEAD), assisted in several of the data collections and was instrumental in performing several initial data analyses. We are especially grateful for his coolness under what at times were stressful conditions and for his insight as a keen observer of bargaining processes. Finally, Dr. W. Clay Hamner of Duke University was primarily responsible for the preparation of Chapter 2 of this book. We are most grateful to him for this substantial review of the relevant bargaining literature.

Donald L. Harnett
Larry L. Cummings

CONTENTS

1

RATIONALE AND
PREVIOUS EVIDENCE

This book reflects a decade of research focusing on the determinants, processes, and consequences of interpersonal bargaining as a method of decision making and on the personality profiles of decision makers. Two fundamental assumptions provide the rationale for our efforts. First, we believe that the essence of effective administration is the making and implementing of decisions. These processes constitute the critical elements in the management of organizations, without which the mere collection and analysis of data become a sterile and inefficient endeavor. Yet the actual process of deciding within a complex environment remains relatively understudied and little understood. Second, we believe that the understanding and improvement of decision making will be most enhanced through a multi-disciplinary perspective (Shull, Delbecq, and Cummings, 1970, Chapter 1). Exclusive foci through either economic or behavioral approaches to decision making capture only a part of the complexity and realism of decision making under complex conditions. Thus, our aim has been to combine the theories, methodologies, and findings of experimental economics and social psychology to increase knowledge relevant to decision making.

In addition to the above assumptions, two perspectives on the study of decision making guided our research. First, we see an urgent need for the systematic identification of the casual sequences which link the antecedents, processes, and consequences of decision making. Most of what is known about decision making has been derived from either case analyses, simulations, or mathematical models. Little systematic, experimental, empirical data exist to guide our efforts. Second, we see the need for the application of analytic and descriptive methods, versus the more typical perspective of normative, prescriptive approaches to the study of decision making. These two perspectives have led us to the use of experimental and quasi-experimental methods (Kenny, 1975) for the study of decision making. Later in this chapter we discuss the advantages of the use of these methods as they relate to both the goals of increased knowledge and applicability of this knowledge.

BARGAINING AS A DECISION-MAKING PROCESS

Bargaining and negotiating are frequently used ways of reaching decisions in a number of arenas of life. Examples abound in family relations; in business between buyers and sellers or their representatives; between countries which engage in bilateral negotiations concerning trade, armaments, knowledge, and human affairs; and among aggregations of countries (East-West, Arab-Israeli, Soviet-Chinese, developed-developing, and more generally, the haves and the have-nots). Even within these nation-blocs, one of the continuing concerns is to increase the within-bloc agreement and cohesion, through internal bargaining, sufficiently so that bilateral or dyadic negotiations are viable.

In all of these cases that surround and, to varying degrees, involve us, decisions must be reached within an environment composed of complex motivational tendencies. A large part of this complexity derives from the multiple and mixed motives which the parties bring into the bargaining setting (whether family, business, profession, nation) and which guide their behaviors within negotiations. Motivations toward self-interest and competition *against* the other party are nearly always coupled with motivations toward joint-interest and cooperation *with* the other party. In most of these complex, yet real, environments there exist no completely clear and agreed-upon rules of behavior or standards for decisions. In the pressure of this uncertainty, bargaining has become a socially acceptable, and even encouraged, method of reaching decisions about how, when, and with whom to behave. Thus, we see interpersonal bargaining as a process of social decision making. It serves the function of establishing operational values and of allocating scarce resources.

INCREASING IMPORTANCE OF BARGAINING

Bargaining will continue to increase in frequency and importance as a process of decision making. This arises from three factors which are becoming increasingly apparent to most individuals, organizations, and nations.

The first of these is the increasing *scarcity of the resources* needed and desired by humans. We can see the impact of this scarcity reflected in concerns over the protection of and access to environmental resources (air, water, space), over processed resources (food, energy sources), and over access to and maintenance of influence, prestige, and power (the Watergate affair, United Nations membership, or local issues like which country club has the best golf course). As scarcity of valued resources increases, the saliency and strength of motivations, both to compete and perhaps to cooperate, increase. Bargaining to increase the predictability and rationality of interaction during decision making becomes increasingly likely. Increasing scarcity is enhancing the likelihood that bargaining will be seen as a reasonable means of survival.

Secondly, humans and institutions are becoming increasingly *interdependent*. We are becoming aware that a single party (person, organization, state, nation) cannot garnish and preserve the resources sufficient to guarantee a long-run, viable achievement of its goals. Interdependence, in the face of scarcity, places a premium on the development and effective use of mechanisms or channels for communicating values, priorities, and tactics. Interpersonal and interinstitutional bargaining provides one means for such communication.

Thirdly, many methods, other than bargaining and compromise, of making decisions and resolving differences are *becoming increasingly costly and/or less viable in the long-run*. Organized conflict (e.g., war) has always been a dysfunctional mechanism for resolving differences. It has now become potentially catastrophic in consequences. These human and financial costs associated with the use of alternative conflict resolution methods enhance the necessity of alternative mechanisms and will increase the importance and frequency of the use of bargaining as a decision-making mechanism.

This increasing relevance of bargaining to all areas of our contemporary affairs will be masked as long as we view bargaining and negotiating in terms that imply win-lose postures wherein party A wins by causing party B to lose. Gradually, social scientists and managers are leaning toward the consideration of the value and the practicality of win-win solutions which are attainable through bargaining (Filley, 1975, Chapter 2). The identification of the environmental conditions and bargaining strategies which increase the probability of such win-win outcomes are crucial to effective social change and organizational management.

This broad, encompassing description of the relevance of bargaining in human affairs and the urgent need for alternative decision-making processes should not blind us to the necessity for careful, experimental studies which can aid in establishing the causal mechanisms underlying successful, conciliatory bargaining. These causal mechanisms between bargaining situations, bargainer personalities, bargaining strategies, and bargaining outcomes should be the focus of any efforts to improve bargaining skills and to discover more creative bargaining solutions.

We feel that this commitment to understanding bargaining via experimental and empirical procedures is a necessary and fruitful ingredient in the improvement of decision making in an increasingly complex environment.

In what is to come, we argue for the advantages of an experimental approach to the study of decision making under conditions of bargaining. We then develop the historical context from which our work was evolved. The specific empirical studies of informational and personality determinants which provided early leads for our work are then reviewed. Chapter 2 provides a comprehensive review of the structural and personality determinants of bargaining as well as the impact of strategic influences on bargaining. In Chapter 3 we develop the theme of the importance of the person in bargaining and present the empirical development of the personality measure used in our research. Chapter 4 presents the results of our research on personality across cultures. In Chapter 5 we develop the formal model of bargaining underlying our experimental design, describe the methodology employed and present international results on several bargaining parameters. Chapter 6 examines the role of the independent effects of personality and strategy in determining bargaining achievements as well as the association of personality and behavioral strategies in the bargaining situation. Finally, Chapter 7 provides an overview of the themes emerging from our research as well as identifying the constraints surrounding our work and several opportunities for future research.

THE CASE FOR AN EXPERIMENTAL APPROACH

The use of the experimental method for the generation of knowledge is widely accepted and developed in the physical and biological sciences. Within the last fifty years, social and behavioral scientists have recognized the importance and utility of experimentation in their quest for understanding social and behavioral phenomena. Only recently, however, has the study of business problems in general, and managerial decision making in particular, progressed to the stage where the application of the experimental method (both in the field and in the laboratory) can generate trustworthy and practical knowledge.

An experiment is simply a means for testing hypotheses regarding the relationships between two or more specified variables. It is important to emphasize that experimentation forces us to be explicit about the variables and relationships we wish to examine. The method encourages rigorous and convincing arguments because of this explicitness and clarity. In this sense, experimentation as a strategy for investigation stands in sharp contrast to intuition and personal persuasion as methods for solving managerial problems. The use of experimentation to study managerial problems does not, however, deny the utility of intuitive approaches under highly uncertain and ambiguous conditions.

Managerial decision-making problems usually involve a multiplicity of factors or variables, each requiring some degree of consideration in arriving at a decision. Academicians and executives are beginning to develop some degree of competence in building models to represent problems involving several variables and interrelationships among variables. From a practical viewpoint, however, these models (for example, operations research models of investment behavior, production scheduling, or personal recruiting) produce little useful information until the relationships among the variables are tested for validity and generality. The experimental method is a particularly appropriate means for accomplishing just this. Why is this the case?

First, experimentation allows the researcher to maintain control over the variables involved in the model of a problem. In contrast to observational methods, the goal of experimentation is to manipulate (vary) the variables assumed to be critical or most important and to control (hold constant) all other variables known or thought to influence the phenomenon in question. Holding certain variables constant helps clarify the nature of the relationships being examined and also facilitates concise interpretation of the resulting data.

In the social sciences, precise control of important factors may not always be possible or practical because the variables in question concern human behavior and because experimentation is done with human subjects. In some cases, randomization of subjects across the conditions of the experiment can be utilized as a substitute for actually controlling the differences between subjects. However, control can also be achieved in experimentation by matching subjects into two groups, one group being exposed to certain chosen variable(s) and the other not. For example, if we are interested in knowing the effects of a particular leadership style on the productivity of a group of operative workers (or the effects of a commission incentive system on the sales performance of a group of salesmen), we might expose two matched groups to two different styles of supervision and note the resulting differences in performance. Since we desire to explain any differences in performance as resulting from differing leadership behavior, we need to match our two groups on all other variables that might account for such differences (for example, level of education, type of task, ability, and monetary compensation systems). Thus, randomization and matching of subjects can serve as reasonable substitutes for control when studying managerial problems in which control is not feasible.

Second, experimentation as a method of knowledge generation forces the researcher to design studies so that the conditions under which knowledge has been acquired will be known precisely. This explicitness in design produces knowledge about the variables studied that has high generality. One argument frequently cited by those questioning the utility of the experimental method for the study of managerial problems is that the method yields results that cannot be generalized beyond the conditions surrounding the specific study in question. Therefore, goes the argument, since potential and present managers need to operate under a variety of different conditions, we should generate "practical" knowledge through intuitive methods and case studies. On the contrary, these methods normally tell the decision maker very little concerning the conditions under which the information has been produced. Actually, the decision maker is justified in generalizing such information only to very similar conditions. These may, indeed, be difficult to locate or even to identify.

Experimentation, on the other hand, allows the decision maker, in cooperation with the researcher, to design studies aimed at a basic understanding of the processes and behaviors underlying managerial problems. Generalization, even to apparently dissimilar conditions, thereby becomes less risky to the manager for two reasons: (1) the exact conditions under which the information was generated is available for consideration, and (2) the resulting knowledge concerns basic processes and underlying causes rather than merely manifest symptoms. Certainly not all "real-world" decision-making situations can be replicated in the laboratory; neither can the student nor the practitioner of administration have the opportunity to experience all cases. So there appears to be a significant range of managerial problems within which experimental methods of study are both more reliable (in the sense of control and explicitness of design) and practical (in the sense of generality of basic processes and causal relationships).

A third issue in the experimental study of managerial problems centers on the use of nonmanagers as substitutes for managers in such studies. One side of the argument is well represented by B. Alpert (1967) who states ". . . in relating the conclusions about behavior of nonbusinessmen to behavior of businessmen in the business situation, a distinct danger of bias exists in the sample." On the other hand, M. T. Orne (1965) has argued that ". . . once a subject has agreed to participate in a psychological experiment, he implicitly agrees to perform a very wide range of actions on request without inquiring as to their purpose, and frequently without inquiring as to their duration." This description of the psychological conditions surrounding participation in an experiment is not highly dissimilar from the conditions implicit in working for a real organization. As with real organizational employment, Orne suggests that the subject's performance in an experiment is a function of the total situation, which includes the experimental variables and the social and psychological characteristics of the experimental setting. Experimentation provides the researcher with a means for controlling these characteristics and thereby enhancing the generality of the results.

Two studies of managerial problems can be cited that support this line of reasoning. S. Siegel and D. L. Harnett (1964) found that industrial sales personnel (General Electric employees) responded similarly to college students in their bargaining processes and in the results they achieved. W. H. Starbuck and F. M. Bass (1967) have reported a similar result in an experiment involving risk-taking and the value of information in a new product introduction decision. They report generally comparable results in terms of basic decision-making processes from widely diverse samples—for example, high school juniors and seniors in an industrial management program, marketing professors, and county agricultural agents engaged in extension work. Alternative means can also be utilized to reduce problems of sample bias. The use of university executive program participants is increasing, and the practice of designing and implementing carefully controlled field (inplant) experiments has also been used to counteract such bias (Cummings, 1974.

A typical managerial problem that has recently been exposed to experimental investigation is that of sales forecasting errors and the role these errors play in the causation of business cycles. J. A. Carlson (1967) has developed a classroom experimental economy in which students simulated managers of business firms producing a consumer good. These "managers" made decisions regarding the degree of utilization of productive capacity and quantity of new capital equipment to order for future use in the face of uncertain sales forecasts. The experiment was developed to test the hypothesis that "aggregated forecasts of sales should tend to underestimate changes (of sales), no matter how carefully individual forecasts have been prepared." Results indicate that systematic forecasting errors continued for many forecasting periods despite the fact that the structure of the experimental economy was relatively simple. Thus, Carlson was able, through the use of experimentation, to illustrate that these basic forecasting errors could be predicted from microeconomic theory rather than by allusion to market complexities, uncertainties, and aberrations as causal phenomena. Again the logical tightness and conciseness of the experimental method permitted the testing of causal assumptions in an unequivocal manner.

Management has always been concerned with the pricing practices most conducive to profitability under different forms of market organization. V. L. Smith (1967) has designed a series of experiments to investigate one aspect of this problem. More specifically, he has investigated "the effect of discrimination, competition, and the relative number of rejected bids on the level of (price) bids tendered by subjects and the receipts (profits) of a monopolistic seller." Examples of markets possessing these characteristics are described by Smith as (1) the auction market for new Treasury bills; (2) the letting of contracts for transportation services where the demand for transportation is greater than the supply capacity of any single firm; or (3) the letting of material contracts where, again, the demand exceeds the capacity of any one supplier. Smith explicitly studied bidding behavior and price determination under two market structures: (1) price discrimination and (2) pure competition. In the laboratory, these conditions were "created" by instructions to the subject regarding the rules for accepting the subjects' bids under the two forms of market organization. The relative advantages of each market structure to the seller were established, and conciseness was attained regarding the relative role of the independent variables. This research by Professor Smith would be nearly impossible to conduct in a real-world market due to a lack of control over the primary causal variables.

Another important managerial problem that has been studied experimentally centers on the amount of test market information that would be desirable and economically reasonable prior to introduction of a new product into a market. Starbuck and Bass created an experimental situation where subjects (students and executives) were tested to ascertain (1) if they would undertake introduction of a new product when lack of information created uncertainty about the product's profitability; and (2) the maximum value they would place on information, which could be obtained from a test market, regarding the product's real market acceptance. The researchers were able to ascertain the role played by the importance of risk to the decision maker in introducing a product under varying conditions of uncertainty. As Starbuck and Bass point out, the experimental situation utilized to collect data on product introduction is highly adaptable to other business decision problems; for example, problems of financial investment in the stock market, problems of production management involving scheduling of production runs, and other problems of general business policy.

This approach perhaps can be summarized succinctly by quoting K. E. Weick (1965):

> ... even though a (real world) problem is reformulated and transposed, it will retain its relevance to natural organizations if the experimental situation retains some properties of the setting, task and participation association with natural organization ... Because laboratory experimentation is much more flexible than most persons realize, the laboratory can be adapted to exceedingly complex and ambiguous problems. At the same time, many organizational problems are encumbered with extraneous and superfluous details. These details can be removed with little effect on generality. It is this continual balance between altering the method and losing control and altering the problem and losing validity that accounts for much of the drama of organizational experimentation (p. 254).

HISTORICAL DEVELOPMENT

Economists and mathematicians have long been interested in theories of bargaining as they relate to economic decision making in general. As early as 1881 Edgeworth suggested that in price-quantity negotiations a contract will be reached which maximizes joint payoff. This solution, which corresponds to the one suggested by Pareto in 1909, is traditionally referred to as being "Pareto optimal" (i.e., no other solution is better for *all* participants in the negotiations). Such a solution was suggested by Schumpeter in his introduction to Zeuthen's work (1930), as well as by Stigler (1952), who used the "all-or-none" form of bargaining.[1] The most complete treatment of the general bargaining problem was presented by Von Neumann and Morgenstern in 1947 in their treatise, *The Theory of Games and Economic Behavior*. Their solution corresponds to the division of maximum joint profits.

Despite general agreement on the quantity to be exchanged in economic bargaining, traditional analysis has provided little theory for determining the division price and resulting division of profits in such negotiations. There are however, several general approaches which suggest a process by which agreement is reached, if not a specific solution.

---

[1] In "all-or-none" bargaining a single offer is made which must either be accepted in its entirety or rejected.

Hicks (1935) analyzes the problem in terms of concession bargaining in the labor market. The concession of each party will depend on the cost of a strike resulting from a refusal to concede as compared with the loss in profit from a concession. Each party will make a concession when the cost of the concession would be less than the cost of the strike resulting from a refusal to concede. Thus, the highest wage rate possible for a union would be at that contract associated with a strike of the same length for both employer and union, for at any higher rate the employer would lose more via a concession than he would through a strike.

Zeuthen's (1935) solution is in terms of the risk necessary to change the price beyond the point at which a settlement is worth more than a conflict. The sacrifice to reduce the claims of an opponent is measured in terms of the probability of conflict to which they are willing to expose themselves if an ultimatum is maintained. In Zeuthen's approach each party should increase its demands until the loss resulting from the potential conflict exceeds the maximum profitability which it thinks its opponent will make by opposing this demand.

The general model developed by Nash (1950) results in a solution which is the only one satisfying the following "reasonable" assumptions: (1) invariance with respect to utility transformations, (2) Pareto optimality, (3) independence of irrelevant alternatives, and (4) symmetry. The unique solution under these four conditions maximizes the product of the participants' utility functions. If utility is assumed to be linear in money, this solution corresponds to an equal division of maximum joint profits. A fifty-fifty split of maximum joint profits was suggested by Pigou in 1908, and also corresponds to the solution specified by Schelling (1960) as the apparent one. Schelling, however, is one of the few researchers to explicitly stipulate that his solution depends on the fact that the "value of the game" be known to the participants.

Harsanyi (1956) shows that Zeuthen's solution is mathematically equivalent to the Nash model and also supplies a "plausible psychological model for the actual bargaining process." Harsanyi further develops the Zeuthen concession model by considering the expected utility of conceding when the subjective probability of an opponent's conceding is known.

In the Raiffa (1953) arbitration scheme, it is suggested that the negotiations proceed in discrete steps which improve each player's position until a solution is reached along the Paretian optima. The solution developed by Raiffa is identical to Nash's for linear utility functions, although the approaches are quite different. Raiffa's "negotiation curve," leading to the unique arbitration value along the Paretian optima, would satisfy all the Nash conditions except for the independence of irrelevant alternatives.

Despite the extensive historical development of various theories about the resolution of bargaining in economic settings, the scope of traditional economic and mathematical analysis was not sufficient to eliminate a variety of alternative hypotheses. Missing were experimental analyses of bargaining behavior. It was not until the 1950s that developments in game and conflict theories provided the means to construct theories of bargaining which are testable by the use of experimental procedures.

FOURAKER-SIEGEL: RESEARCH AND EXTENSIONS

The use of experimental procedures to study economic decision-making is generally regarded to have its origins in the extensive theoretical and experimental research published in 1960 and 1963 by L. E. Fouraker, an economist, and the late S. Siegel, a psychologist. In their own words, Siegel and Fouraker employed "... the methods of experimental social psychology in the study of behavior which has been considered in the theoretical province of economics." (1960, p. 72).

In their first book, *Bargaining and Group Decision Making* (1960), Siegel and Fouraker investigated various forms of the market situation usually referred to as bilateral monopoly, where a single buyer must negotiate a price and quantity agreement with a single seller. In general, their experiments supported the theoretical proposition that contracts will be negotiated at the quantity maximizing joint payoffs, but the price agreement at this quantity is indeterminate. A considerable portion of the Siegel-Fouraker research was directed toward studying some of the influences on the variability in negotiated contracts. Siegel and Fouraker concluded that there are a number of different variables which can influence bargaining behavior, including the amount of profit involved, the amount of information each bargainer has about the potential rewards an opponent can receive, and each participant's level of aspiration. They attribute much of the variability in their research results to personal differences among the participants.

In their second book, *Bargaining Behavior* (1963), Fouraker and Siegel extended their analyses of bilateral monopoly bargaining to include the price leadership case.[2] In addition, they studied oligolopolistic[3] bargaining using price and quantity adjuster models using both two and three sellers. As was the case in their first book, Fouraker and Siegel were interested in the effects of information as well as personal differences. We will not attempt to review all of the numerous aspects of research contained in the two books by Fouraker and Siegel. In some cases we will refer to specific results when they are relevant to the development of the research reported in this book. We will focus our review of their research on the two major influences upon bargaining as reported by Fouraker and Siegel; namely information effects and personal differences.

----

[2] Under price leadership, one party names the price at which the exchange will take place, while the other party names the quantity to be exchanged at this price.

[3] Oligopoly is the marked structure characterized by having only a few sellers.

The Effect of Information

In one of their initial sets of experiments, Siegel and Fouraker were interested in determining the effect of information on the quantity agreement among bilateral monopoly bargainers. Three experimental information conditions were used: (1) *complete-complete* information (C-C), where both bargainers had the other's payoff table, (2) *complete-incomplete* (C-I), where one bargainer had the opponent's payoff table and the other did not, and (3) *incomplete-incomplete* (I-I), where neither bargainer had the opponent's payoff table. Bargainers with complete information were told the amount of information given their opponent; the bargainers with incomplete information were given no indication of their opponent's information level.

The results of this experiment confirmed the Siegel-Fouraker hypothesis that increasing information will reduce the variability about the joint maximizing quantity. While 75 percent of the contracts negotiated under C-C fell exactly on the joint maximizing quantity, only 47 percent of the C-I contracts fell at this point, and only 36 percent of the I-I contracts were concluded at this quantity. In addition, Siegel-Fouraker report that contracts were concluded notably more rapidly under the C-C condition than under the other two conditions.

One of the Siegel-Fouraker interests regarding information was in its effect on bargaining strength. Schelling (1960) has argued that if two bargainers have different amounts of information, the bargainer with less information often will receive a greater share of joint payoff than the bargaining position would indicate. This follows from Schelling's hypothesis that the less informed bargainer's lack of knowledge of what is fair or reasonable will generally induce this person to concede more slowly than the more informed opponent. A more completely informed opponent may feel obligated to concede in order to avoid a stalemate, especially when this bargainer realizes that the opponent has the saving grace of ignorance. Schelling suggests that when the possibility of a fifty-fifty split is obvious, then there is a "moralistic" force toward such a solution. The results of the C-I condition in the Siegel-Fouraker experiments were in the direction predicted by Schelling, although not statistically significant (perhaps because of the small sample size).

Our own research has indicated support for the Schelling hypothesis. One of these studies [see Harnett, Hughes, Cummings (1968)] investigated the effect of information on bargaining in a manufacturer-wholesaler-retailer channel. In this research, the effect of information on the wholesaler was studied by using three information levels: *incomplete* information where participants knew only their own payoffs, *partial* information where the wholesaler had the opponent's tables but they did not have the wholesaler's, and *complete* information where everyone was fully informed.

The results of this study supported the Schelling hypothesis that greater information often places the bargainer at a disadvantage. The amount of profit earned by the manufacturer and the retailers decreased significantly from the partial information condition (where only the wholesaler had information) to the complete information condition (where they had full information). Analysis of the bidding process in this experiment suggested that uninformed bargainers generally required a more protracted period of negotiations, during which they presumably attempted to gain insight about the bargaining position of their opponent.

A second of our studies (Harnett and Cummings, 1972) focused on the effect of a broader interpretation of information (to include the ability to communicate) in the bargaining triad shown in Figure 1.1.

A number of different experimental conditions were examined using this paradigm. Condition 1 was a "no information" variant, wherein both B and C were furnished with only their own profit tables. They were not given any information concerning A's profit function. For this condition, as well as conditions 2, 3, and 4, Bargainer A was given "complete information;" i.e., these participants had their own profit table plus a copy of B's and C's tables. In condition 1, no communication was allowed between the bargainers. Condition 2 was identical to condition 1 with the exception that both B and C were given complete information; i.e., Bargainer A's profit table as well as their own. Condition 3 added communication to the system by allowing short written notes (at most five per bargainer) to be passed between any two of the bargainers. The content of the communications was unrestricted beyond not allowing bargainers to reveal their identity or to make threats or to suggest a division of profits after the experiment. In condition 4, one additional variable, what we call a power factor, was added by informing Bargainers B and C that if negotiations lasted until the time limit, they would have the final bid. Bargainer A could then only accept or reject; no counter offer was allowed. For conditions 1, 2, and 3, Bargainer A possessed the power of final bid.

The results of this study indicate that adding information and communication

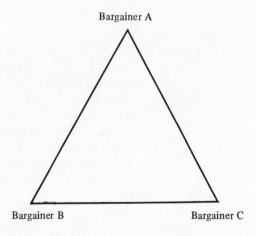

Figure 1.1   Bargaining Triad

to the bargaining system seems to support the Schelling hypothesis of the harmful effect of being overinformed. The ability to receive (or not to receive) and the ability to send (or not to send) communications were crucial variables in explaining behavior. For example, informed bargainers communicating with an uninformed adversary tended to pass information about their own payoffs presumably hoping that such information would encourage the opponent to make more reasonable demands. Uninformed bargainers did not typically seek information, almost as if they knew that such information would weaken their relative position. As a bargainer receives information, norms of equity, sharing, reasonableness, and perhaps equality begin to influence this person's motivation.

In these studies, the power inherent in the possession of the terminal bid apparently outweighed the negative influence of information for completely informed bargainers. That is, the effect was similar to a *reduction* in information, and participants with this power appeared to be more confident of their bargaining position. Thus the Schelling hypothesis may be only conditionally true, depending on the bargainer's power position.

In addition to its effect on the bargaining outcome, information was found to be related to a number of process variables in bargaining. For instance, the average initial asking levels were significantly less for completely informed bargainers in both of the studies described above. The number of bids required to reach a solution was also significantly lower under complete information. In general, bargainers under complete information seemed to take a more realistic opening position, yield rather slowly, and reach a solution in a relatively few number of bids.

Although the studies reported above generally indicate support for the Schelling hypothesis, other research has suggested that information may *increase* bargaining strength in some circumstances. For example, in Fouraker and Siegel's (1963) own research on price leadership bilateral monopoly, they found that increasing the amount of information to the price leader (the seller in their case) significantly increased this person's bargaining strength. An important difference between their earlier study, in which they explicitly tested the Schelling hypothesis, and their price leadership study is that in the latter experiment the structure of the model placed the price leader in a decidedly weaker bargaining position. This study and the results of our own research described earlier on the power of the terminal bid, suggest that the effect of information may not apply uniformly across all negotiations but rather be dependent on certain characteristics of the bargaining situation and its participants. An experiment designed to investigate the differential effect of information is described in the final section of this chapter.

Certainly some of the equivocal results regarding the effect of information can be attributed to personal differences among the bargainers. In fact, Siegel and Fouraker concluded (1960, p. 69) that "personal characteristics of the bargainers seem to be the main determinants of differential payoff and price in bilateral monopoly bargaining."

The Effects of Personal Differences

One personal variable studied by Siegel-Fouraker was the negotiation process used by their subjects. They characterized each bargainer in terms of the strategy this person seemed to use in attempts to achieve a price-quantity agreement with the opponent. The strategies they observed led them to identify three specific bargaining types, or what might be called "signaling strategies": cooperator, individualistic, and rivalistic. Cooperators seemed interested in maximizing the sum of joint profits, individualists in maximizing their own profits, and rivalists (or competitors) in maximizing the difference between their profit and that of their rivals. Of course, not every bargainer could be classified into one of these three groups, and different bargainers might use quite different strategies in arriving at the same price-quantity agreement. In addition they found that the structure of the bargaining game influenced the proportion of each type of bargainer. In fact, Siegel-Fouraker were able to induce specific types of bargaining strategies by altering the reward structure of the negotiation exercise.

In a follow-up study designed to look at additional properties of negotiated solutions under price leadership bilateral monopoly, Harnett (1967) found that a fifty-fifty split of maximum joint profits was often achieved under complete information even when such a solution had nonequilibrium properties making it difficult to attain. This research suggested a fourth bargaining type in addition to the three described by Fouraker and Siegel (the cooperator, the rivalist, the individualist)—namely, the equalizer. Such a person generally believes that since the "fair" solution to the game is an even split of profits, a fifty-fifty split solution should prevail. The bidding signals by such a bargainer might be a series of different offers all of which yield a fifty-fifty division of rewards. This result agrees with the numerous research findings in which participants reject anything less than an even division of joint payoff when the value of the game is known.

Most researchers on bargaining behavior would agree that the structural variables of information and the type of paradigm under investigation represent only two of many possible influences on the division of profits in a bargaining situation. Individual differences among bargainers, such as attitude toward conciliation, risk-taking propensity, experience in the negotiation process, and financial needs all would be expected to be factors in determining how one person goes about negotiating with another person, and hence would appear to be major determinants of differential payoffs. Unfortunately, little success has been achieved in experimental research in uncovering relationships existing between such individual differences and bargaining success. Research efforts by Dolbear and Lave (1966), Gallo and McClintock (1965), and Pilisuk, Potter, Rapoport, and Winter (1965) have had little success in attempting to relate bargaining behavior to personality characteristics of subjects. Sherman (1966) did find a relationship between risk-taking propensity and subject choices among various forms of the Prisoner's Dilemma game.

In their research on a manufacturer-wholesaler-retailer channel, Harnett,

Cummings, and Hughes (1968) also studied the effect of risk-taking propensity (RTP) on bargaining. In this study, risk taking was measured by an instrument developed by Kogan and Wallach (1964). The instrument consists of twelve choice dilemmas each of which describes a hypothetical situation in which the subject is asked to indicate the lowest probability of success he or she would tolerate and still recommend that the risky alternative be taken by a central person in the incident. Extensive use of the instrument has been made in the study of the influence of group processes on individual risk-taking propensity [Wallach and Kogan (1965); Wallach, Kogan, and Ben (1962); Wallach, Kogan, and Burt (1965)], but the relationship between an individual's risk-taking propensity and this person's behavior in risky situations has received relatively little attention.

Harnett, Cummings, and Hughes (1968) did not find any significant relationship between RTP and the profit earned by a participant. The data did suggest, however, that under complete information a relationship exists between RTP and the initial asking level—the greater the risk-taking propensity, the lower the initial asking level; and under incomplete information an inverse relationship was found between RTP and yielding behavior—the more risky the person, the less this person yielded. Thus, in this study it appears as if the more risky strategy was to take a moderate opening stance and be reluctant to yield from that position.

In a follow-up study to the symmetrical bargaining triad described earlier, Harnett and Cummings (1972) investigated not only the effects of information and communication, but also the influence of several personality variables in an asymmetric triad. The situation studied is presented in Figure 1.2. Both bargainers B and C must come to an agreement with A before a solution is reached. Bargainers B and C did not compete directly with one another.

Again, the Kogan-Wallach (1964), instrument was used to measure risk-taking propensity. Also each bargainer was asked three questions, just prior to the first offer. These were aimed at determining expectations and aspirations regarding earnings in the experiment to follow. Subjects were asked (1) how much they thought they would earn in the two-hour session, (2) what would be a "fair" amount to earn, and (3) the lowest amount considered acceptable payment for participating. Finally, a semantic differential instrument developed by Scott

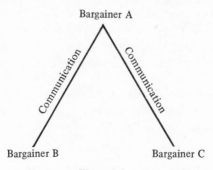

Figure 1.2

TABLE 1.1. Harnett and Cummings (1972) Results

	Bargainer B (With Information) (n = 11)	Bargainer C (Without Information) (n = 11)	Significance
Profit Earned	$ 3.86	$ 4.46	$p < 0.05$
Initial Asking	$ 5.01	$ 6.81	$p < 0.001$
Number of Bids	8.00	11.55	$p < 0.01$
Amount Yielded*	$ 0.99	$ 2.00	$p < 0.03$

*Amount Yielded = second bid minus profit earned. This holds for all conditions.

(1967) was used post-experimentally to determine, for each participant, this person's attitude toward (1) the bargaining task, (2) me (the bargainer) at the task, (3) my (the bargainer's) earnings, and (4) the other members of the bargaining group. Five different experimental conditions were conducted in this research, only one of which will be elaborated on in the discussion below.

Some of the most interesting results in this research were where Bargainer B had information, C had no information, and where there was no communication between B and C. The data of this condition strongly support the predictions described above relating to the Schelling hypothesis. Evidence of a more realistic attitude on the part of Bargainer B includes the fact this bargainer generally asked for less profit on the first bid, required fewer offers to complete an agreement, yielded less during the negotiations, and, in addition, earned significantly less profit for the session. Bargainer A was thus able to bargain more successfully with the opponent who had the greater amount of information. A summary of these results is shown in Table 1.1.

A number of interactions are especially interesting. We found that the relationship between duration of bargaining and amount earned by Bargainer B or C is significantly moderated by the presence or absence of information. Giving Bargainer B information of the sort described above changes the direction of the relationship between earning and number of bids. For bargainers operating without information, (C), there was a negative relationship r = −0.469 while for bargainers in the B role, there was a positive relationship r = +0.538. These correlations are significantly different at $p < 0.05$. Thus, it appears that naive (uninformed) bargainers start their bidding high in terms of profit to themselves. The longer they negotiate, the less favorable the outcome in terms of attained earnings. On the other hand, knowledgeable bargainers start lower in their bidding (at more realistic levels), and the more they negotiate the more they tend to raise their attained earnings.

The relationship between risk-taking propensity (RTP) and the number of bids actually shifts direction as the amount of information changes. Bargainers in position C showed a positive relationship between RTP scores[4] and the number

[4]The higher the RTP score, the less the propensity to take risks.

of bids during bargaining, r = +0.366, while those in the B role showed a negative relationship, r = −0.526; the difference is significant at p < 0.05. So when information regarding Bargainer A's potential payoffs is available, high risk-taking bargainers tend to start higher, generate fewer bids, and, as we noted earlier, have their first, naive bids accepted.

Information also significantly moderated the relationship between RTP and the difference between what a bargainer expected to earn (EE) and the actual earnings (AE). Bargainers without information (C position) exhibited a negative relationship between their RTP scores and the difference EE − AE, r = −0.521. When information is not available risk-taking bargainers thus tend to "give" from their expectation levels during the negotiations. The opposite was true of bargainers operating with information (B role), as they showed a positive relationship between RTP scores and EE − AE, r = +0.418. This difference is significant at p < 0.05.

We were interested in the question of how well the amount of profit an individual earned could be predicted from information gathered prior to this person's participation and from the number of bids made. To explore this question, we ran a stepwise multiple regression analysis on the B and C bargaining roles, using data gathered on the other participants' RTP and their preexperimental expectations about earnings (how much they expected, what they thought was fair, and the lowest they would accept). Because of the small sample size, the F-ratio in a number of cases was not significantly different from zero. We will report the multiple R for all variables entered in the regression analysis, cautioning the reader concerning overly positive interpretations of their predictive value.

As can be seen in Table 1.2 for Bargainer B (with information) the variables entered the stepwise regression in the following order: lowest amount of earnings perceived as acceptable, risk-taking propensity, how much the bargainer expected to earn and what he thought would be fair earnings. The R attained was approximately 0.75. It should be noted that for Bargainer C (without information), less variance in profit was accounted for (R = 0.5639) and the predictor variables entered the stepwise regression in a different order (risk-taking propensity, perceived fair earnings, expectations, and lowest acceptable earnings). The fact that RTP entered the stepwise regression first and accounted for greater variance in the dependent variable under the less structural condition (no information) is consistent with our earlier findings [Harnett, Cummings, and Hughes (1968).]

TABLE 1.2. Stepwise Multiple Regression on Profit Earned in
Harnett and Cummings Study (1972)

With Information		Without Information	
Variable	R	Variable	R
1. Lowest acceptable	0.6323	1. RTP	0.3837
2. RTP	0.7442	2. Perceived fair earnings	0.5468
3. How much expected	0.7450	3. How much expected	0.5598
4. Perceived fair earnings	0.7496	4. Lowest acceptable	0.5639

Level of Aspiration

Siegel and Fouraker (1960, p. 70) conclude that "level of aspiration is an important determinant of differential payoff, and thus of price, in bilateral monopoly bargaining." Their studies provided strong support for the hypothesis that the member of the bargaining pair who has the higher level of aspiration will negotiate a contract yielding the larger share of the joint payoff when bargaining with a rival having a lower aspiration level.

Siegel and Fouraker suggested that their lack of success in confirming the Schelling hypothesis might have occurred because of a differential effect of information on payoffs which can be attributed to the aspiration level of their subjects. They reasoned that subjects with complete information and relatively high aspirations (i.e., greater than their opponents) might tend to negotiate contracts in opposition to the predictions made by Schelling. If approximately half of their subjects had aspiration levels higher than the aspiration level of their opponent, this tendency might account for the equivocality of their results.

Experimental studies investigating the interaction effect of information and aspirations on bargaining behavior have produced conflicting results. Research by Messick and Thorngate (1967) indicated that information about the opponent's payoff table provided the means for bargainers to compare their own rewards with those of their opponents, and hence resulted in an increase in competitive interaction. Quite the opposite tendency was reported by Guyer and Rapoport (1969) who found that bargainers tend to be more cooperative under complete information than under incomplete information.

In one of the few studies which tested, albeit indirectly, the effect that information has on aspiration level, Liebert, Smith, Hill, and Keiffer (1968) concluded that ignorance is a bargaining advantage only when one's opponent is also bargaining in ignorance. They suggested that informed subjects can always neutralize an opponent's strategy by responding to such a strategy in kind.

Holmes, Throop, and Strickland (1971) found that negotiators with high levels of aspiration had higher opening bids, had lower concession rates, and earned more in the settlements that negotiators with low levels of aspiration. A significant correlation between the opponent's offers and the subject's offers was present in Yukl's research (1972), but this significant correlation was not present when the subject's aspiration level was partialed out. This result seems to confirm the hypothesis shared by Kelley, Beckman, and Fisher (1967), Harsanyi (1962), and Pruitt and Drews (1969) that prenegotiation expectations often determine the form and outcome of negotiations, and that the decisions of each negotiator are relatively independent of the opponent's actions.

Harnett and Hamner (1973) used a 2×2 fractorial design to provide a more extensive test of the interaction between information and aspiration levels. Bargainers in a bilateral monopoly setting were classified (by a pre-experimental questionnaire) into either high or low aspirations, depending on whether they said they expected to earn more or less than the fifty-fifty split of maximum joint profits. Half the participants bargained under complete information, the other half under incomplete information.

The results of this study suggest that complete information provides a more "realistic" perspective for each bargainer in setting an aspiration level. In general, among those bargainers whose initial aspiration levels (measured prior to the negotiations) were below the fifty-fifty split point of the payoff table, the lowest initial aspiration levels were among those who had incomplete information rather than complete information; among those buyers whose initial aspiration levels were above the fifty-fifty split point on the payoff table, higher initial aspiration levels were found under incomplete information than under complete information.

Thus, the effect of giving additional information appears to be to raise the aspiration level of a low-aspiration participant, and to lower the aspiration level of a high-aspiration participant. The Harnett-Hamner research also indicated that this effect on aspiration level resulted in a similar effect on bargaining strength (profit earned); that is, bargainers with low aspirations tended to gain strength with additional information, while those with high aspirations tended to lose strength with additional information.

SUMMARY

We have examined research on two major determinants of differences in both the processes and results of bargaining; information and certain personality variables. This work provided the background within which our research, as reported beginning in Chapter 3, was designed and conducted. Of course, these are not the only two determinants which have been shown to influence bargaining behavior, nor do they represent the only determinants studied by Siegel and Fouraker, and in our own research. The literature review presented in Chapter 2 will reflect a broader spectrum of research organized into the following categories: (1) structural influences, (2) individual differences, and (3) strategic differences. These represent what we view as the three major determinants of bargaining behavior.

By *structural influences* we mean those characteristics which are inherent to the bargaining situation. Siegel and Fouraker identified a number of such influences in their two books, including:

1) the number of participants,

2) the form of the negotiations (either "one-shot" or repeated transactions),

3) the symmetry among the participants in terms of the payoff they can receive, and the magnitude of the payoff difference between the various possible agreements, and

4) the amount of information provided each participant about the payoff the opponent will receive for each possible agreement.

We will use the term *individual differences* to mean the characteristics of the individuals who are participating in the negotiations. For instance, the research reviewed earlier in this chapter suggests that variations in behavior may occur because of the influence of:

1) personality differences, such as attitudes toward risk taking, conciliation, and trust,
2) cultural differences,
3) occupational differences,
4) age and sex differences, and
5) bargaining experience differences.

Finally, we suggest there are differences in bargaining because of various *strategic aspects*, such as:

1) differences in opening bids,
2) differences in the number of concessions and the size of each concession,
3) the number and frequency of offers and counter offers, and
4) differences in the pattern of offers and counter offers (e.g., signaling strategies).

2

THE INFLUENCE OF STRUCTURAL, INDIVIDUAL, AND STRATEGIC DIFFERENCES

W. Clay Hamner
Duke University

Social scientists are interested in studying bargaining processes as they relate to the behavior of people since the timely management of conflict has great consequences for organizational effectiveness. While there are many approaches to handling conflict and conflict resolution (e.g., handing conflict to a panel of judges, forming a coalition, taking conflict to court, withdrawing from the situation, etc.), settlements of disagreements between parties usually involve some sort of bargaining, whether implicit or explicit. The process of bargaining can be defined as interaction that occurs when two or more persons attempt to agree on a mutually acceptable outcome in a situation in which their order of preferences for possible outcomes is negatively correlated. Since interpersonal negotiation bargaining is a common method of reaching conflict resolution, it is receiving greater emphasis in the research of behavioral scientists who are interested in conflict and conflict resolution in various environments.

According to many conflict theorists the problem of human conflict is not its elimination, but an understanding of it for better predictions of human behavior. Much research during the past 20 years has focused on determining what structural and individual difference variables determine the process (strategy) by which conflicts are resolved, and how the strategy used in a given situation affects the outcome of the bargaining session. Chapter 2 will review the experimental literature from the last 20 years on the effects of structural, individual, and strategic differences on the bargaining outcomes.

Although there are many types of bargaining games which can be used for the study of interpersonal conflict, the two games which have been studied most extensively are the Prisoner's Dilemma (PD) game[1] and the bilateral monopoly bargaining game. While both of these game settings are well suited for studying situations in which there is a mixture of mutual and opposed interest, PD game settings are somewhat more structured in that bargainers are not allowed to coordinate their strategies and agreements in advance (McClintock, Strand, and Gallo, 1963). Instead, both parties choose their strategies simultaneously, with the outcome determined by the result of the joint move. Bilateral monopoly bargaining games, on the other hand, are less structured and hence tend to more truly represent the negotiation process found in many real settings (e.g., union-management negotiations and buyer-seller purchasing agreements). Because our interest in this book is primarily on bilateral monopoly bargaining games, the literature on PD game results will be reported only when these findings help to interpret bilateral monopoly bargaining studies, or when they have direct bearing on the study of the effects that structural, individual, and strategic differences have on bargaining outcomes.

STRUCTURAL DIFFERENCES AND BARGAINING OUTCOMES

Although many of the bargaining studies over the past 20 years have produced consistent findings, several results and theoretical positions seem, on the surface, to be inconsistent. The main purpose of this section is to report on differences in the results of bargaining outcomes which have been attributed to structural considerations. The structural effects reviewed include: (1) the number of participants in the bargaining game and their role obligations, (2) the external pressure placed on the bargainers to reach agreement, (3) the size of the reward offered, (4) the power structure of the bargaining game, (5) the information given to the bargainers, and (6) the amount and types of communication allowed during the bargaining game.

The discussion of each of these structural variables will include three major points. First, an examination of the *points of controversy* surrounding how differences in the structural variable might affect the bargaining outcome. Following this, a general discussion of the *experimental results* which shed light on the controversy will be presented. Finally, a *detailed experimental study* dealing with the controversy will be presented in order to give the reader an appreciation of the methodology which has been used to examine the controversy in question. An attempt will be made to select a study which shows the type of experiment typically conducted, with a detailed discussion of both the operational definitions of the variables involved and the findings which resulted.

---

[1] In PD games, each of two players is given the option of either cooperating (C) or competing (D). The joint choices of the players lead to four possible outcomes on each trial—CC, CD, DC, and DD. The outcomes are so arranged that the interests of the two players are partly cooperative and partly opposed, (e.g., see McClintock, Strand, and Gallo, 1963).

Number and Role Assignments of the Parties to the Disagreement

Points of Controversy. Most studies dealing with bargaining resolutions have been limited to dyadic interactions. Several researchers have questioned the generalizability of bargaining studies which have been limited to dyadic interactions. Generally, their reservations about these studies have centered around one of three points of controversy. First, while most studies place the subject in a decision-making situation where this person interacts only with one opponent, several researchers (e.g., see Walton and McKerzie, 1965) point out that many real world bargainers (e.g., union-management negotiators) are essentially representing a constituency and must bargain with their constituents as well as the bargaining opponent; therefore, dyadic bargaining studies may not be generalizable to these particular settings. Frey and Adams (1972), for example, state: "In conceptualizing most bargaining situations, one should look upon them as much more than just two individuals who negotiate with each other . . . a negotiator's behavior cannot be adequately explained by the variables of the dyadic bargaining process alone (p. 345)."

A second point of controversy deals with the ability of the parties to the conflict to turn to a third party for guidance in a stalemated situation, since many real-world bargaining situations (e.g., union-management negotiations, real estate purchases, stock purchases, etc.) have explicitly defined the influence which third parties can potentially introduce to a bargaining situation. A third party refers to any nonparticipant to the bargaining outcome whose role in the conflict is to facilitate the resolution or control of conflict between primary disputants (Bartos, 1967, Kerr, 1954).

It is generally argued (Blake, Shepard, and Mouton, 1964; Elkouri and Elkouri, 1960; Kerr, 1954; Prassow and Peters, 1970; Pruitt and Johnson, 1970) that the extent to which a third party is successful in resolving bargaining impasses is often determined, in part, by the power granted the third party; i.e., the amount of pressure the third party might bring to bear upon the parties to force closure. On a continuum of increasing power, third party intervention is characteristically classified into one of the following categories: (1) conciliation and mediation, (2) fact-finding, (3) voluntary arbitration, and (4) compulsory arbitration. *Conciliation and mediation* consist of those responses by a third party made with the intention of enabling both parties to overcome mutual distrust in order to bring about agreement or compromise. Under conditions of conciliation and mediation, the decision-making responsibility of mutual accommodation remains internalized within the bargaining dyad. *Fact-finding* involves the third party in an investigative role, with an obligation to explore the issues causing conflict and report each party's respective position relative to a bargaining settlement regarding the specific bargaining impasse. Under *compulsory arbitration*, the arbitrator is given power to make the final determination in a stalemated bargaining situation by contractual arrangement or a judicial ruling, whereas under *voluntary arbitration*, the arbitrator's decision must be voluntarily accepted by the parties.

While there is much agreement among the researchers that the design of bargaining studies should be expanded to include the role of a third party, there is much controversy surrounding the effectiveness of each of the preceding modes of third party intervention. Podell and Knapp (1969) concluded that evidence concerning the contribution of a third party has remained anecdotal and controversial. Many writers theorize that the presence of a third party enhances the bargaining process and fosters a greater sense of urgency for the bargainers to settle their disputes (Chamberlain, 1965; Landsberger, 1955). Bok and Dunlop (1970), among others (for example, see Adams, 1976; Bartunek, Benton, and Keys, 1975; Wall, 1976), disagree and argue that third party interventions, especially when compulsory, tend to undermine the willingness of the parties to bargain conscientiously over their difference.

A third point of controversy centering around the use of a dyadic bargaining paradigm to study the bargaining process is the criticism by some writers that many real-world bargaining situations involve more than two parties. For example, when a person chooses to buy a car, other dealers can be tried if dissatisfied faction exists with the potential bargaining agreement reached with the first dealer. Even though this criticism of the bilateral monopoly bargaining paradigm is often cited, few studies have been reported which look at multiple party bargaining situations. In addition, the effects of more than two parties can be estimated by simulation and experimental manipulations.

Experimental Results. As noted previously, few studies have examined the bargainer as a representative of a group rather than as a single individual. In the few studies which have dealt with the role assignment of the bargainer (individual vs. group representatives), conflicting results have been reported. Some evidence indicates a lack of differences between group representatives and individual bargainers (Druckman, 1967), some evidence is ambiguous with respect to the influence of representation (Vidmar, 1971; Druckman, 1971), and other findings show that group representation is detrimental to cooperation in terms of the opening bid, concession rate, or agreements reached (Hermann and Kogan, 1968; Lamm and Kogan, 1970; Druckman and Zechmeister, 1972). Walton and McKersie (1965) contend the reason the individual bargainer tends to be more favorably inclined toward making the concessions than are their constituents is because bargainers are generally better acquainted with the other party's priorities and hence are more realistic about the difficulty of achieving concessions from the other party.

Benton (1972) has shown that a representative's willingness to make concessions depends, in part, on the extent of his accountability ;i.e., the extent of his constituent's ability to reward or penalize him for his actions—the more accountable the bargainer, the less cooperation is extended to the bargaining opponent. Frey and Adams (1972) found that representatives who know they are not trusted are unwilling to make concessions when the other bargainer is conciliatory and willing to make concessions when they are exploitative. Pruitt (1974) concludes that when the results of the Frey and Adams study are combined with findings from similar studies, there can be little doubt that the behavior of the representative is a joint function of the behavior of the constituents and the behavior of the other negotiator.

As mentioned earlier, third parties often intervene in bargaining, either as a result of being called in by the bargainers or on their own initiative. However, only a few experiments dealing with the effect that third party intervention has on bargaining outcomes have been performed in the past few years. Among the first researchers to investigate the impact of third party intervention, within the context of experimental simulations, was McGrath and his colleagues (McGrath, 1966; McGrath and Julian, 1962; McGrath and Julian, 1963; Vidmar and McGrath, 1967). One of the major conclusions resulting from these studies was that for a mediator to be successful, this person should focus the group on its task sufficiently early and should refrain from displaying negative interpersonal affect.

Podell and Knapp (1969) also examined bargainers' willingness to accept a solution offered by a mediator once a bargaining deadlock had been reached. Their study simulated a labor-management wage negotiation with the subjects assuming the role of labor and a research assistant assuming the role of management. Once a deadlock was reached due to the "hard line" position taken by "management," the experimenter induced the subject to accept mediation. In final stages of the study, the subject was offered exactly the same concession on two different issues, one of these offers coming directly from the subject's opponent, and the other coming through the mediator. The findings indicate that suggested concessions attributable to the mediator were more readily accepted by the subjects than comparable concessions offered by the subject's opponent. Pruitt and Johnson (1970) found similar results and concluded that it was because the mediator helps the bargainer to save face. If bargainers concede on their own, they fear that they will appear weak, but they can rationalize the concessions by expert council.

A few studies have examined the effect of more than one type of intervention by a third party on bargaining behavior. Johnson and Pruitt (1972); Urban (1973); Johnson and Tuller (1972); Bigoness (1974); and LaTour, Houlden, Walker, and Thibaut (1976), employing either a simulated collective or distributive bargaining game, sought to determine the impact of the anticipation of alternative modes of third party intervention had upon concession making in negotiation. The results of each of these studies generally confirm that negotiators faced with a binding decision (arbitration) made larger and more frequent concessions than those faced with a nonbinding decision (mediation). An interpretation of these findings could be that bargainers view binding arbitration as a high pressure condition and the greater the external pressure placed on bargainers, the greater the tendency to concede early in order to avoid the external threat.

In the LaTour, *et al.* study, the researchers examined the spontaneous preference of individuals in conflict for different dispute-resolution procedures arranged along a continuum of decreasing third-party intervention. By matching subject preferences for the features of ideal methods of conflict resolution with the judgments of law students, it was found that the average person preferred arbitration over mediation and bargaining procedures. This was especially true when outcomes were noncorrespondent, when a standard was available and when there was time pressure.

The third point of controversy noted in the previous section was that most bargaining studies were bilateral monopoly studies with little effort being made to study the case where a person can bargain with more than one party in order to reach an agreement. The only set of triadic bargaining studies which can be found[2] has dealt with the "truel" (Cole, 1969), which is based on the concept of a three-person conflict (PD) setting. Studies using the truel as a paradigm have couched their results in terms of the coalition formation literature rather than the bargaining outcome literature (e.g., see Caplow, 1959; Caplow, 1956), and thus are beyond the scope of this review. It appears, therefore, that researchers have failed to adequately examine the important structural effects of three or more participants on the agreements reached in a bargaining setting.

An Experimental Example. Johnson and Tullar (Johnson and Tullar, 1972) tested the impact of various third-party intervention modes on bargaining behavior both prior to and after intervention. The styles of intervention investigated in their study were: nonbinding suggestion (mediation), binding decision (arbitration), selection of the better of the bargainers' own proposals (govplan), or no third-party intervention. These authors also divided the bargaining subjects into two "need to save face" groups in order to see if those who felt a high need to save face would be less likely to reach an agreement prior to intervention than those who felt a low need to save face.

The experiment made use of a modified version of a collective bargaining simulation developed by Bass (1966). The task involved face-to-face bargaining between the two subjects in a dyad. The 104 male undergraduate union versus management negotiators bargained over five issues simultaneously; medical plan, wages, cost of living, pay differential, and vacation plans. The instructions given to the subjects indicated that if after 12 minutes from the beginning of the negotiation an agreement had not been reached, the negotiation would stop and the third party intervention would take place. In the no-intervention group, the subjects were stopped after 12 minutes to rethink their position and then returned to the bargaining process for an additional 6 minutes. All bargainers were assessed a penalty for each minute of elapsed time it took to reach agreement. The subjects were apparently not paid, but participated in the experiment as part of a class requirement.

In order to manipulate the face-saving condition, a video tape and voice re-

---

[2]The Harnett and Cummings studies (Harnett, Cummings, and Hughes, 1968; Harnett and Cummings, 1972; Harnett, Hughes, and Cummings, 1968) all examined three-party bargaining and were discussed in Chapter 1.

corder were utilized. In the high need to save face condition, the equipment was presented and it was explained that a training film was being developed on "novice bargaining" to be used in various classes in the area. There was also a TV monitor present so that the subjects could see themselves as they were being filmed. In the low face-saving condition, the equipment was not present. This manipulation was pretested by the authors and it was found that the presence of the equipment resulted in the subject being considerably more concerned with self-presentation.

The main results of the Johnson and Tullar study are shown in Figure 2.1. The interaction of the dependent measures indicated that when there was a high need to save face, bargainers were more conciliatory when no intervention was anticipated. When there was a low need to save face, those expecting arbitration were closer to reaching agreement.

The authors conclude that when the need to save face is strong, bargainers are more willing to let an outsider come in and resolve the conflict. The expectation of any outside intervention appears to decrease the likelihood of agreement prior to that intervention. Parties appear even willing to allow the possibilities of forced compliance to a third party's demands. When there is a low need to save face, those expecting arbitration expend considerable effort in order to avoid intervention and settle things on their own.

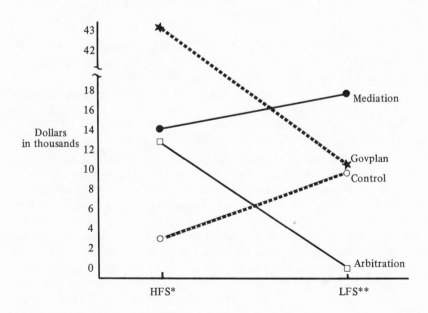

Figure 2.1 Mean difference (in dollars) between pairs immediately prior to intervention (Trial 6). Adapted from Johnson and Tullar[1972, p. 324]. (*High need to save-face group and **low need to save-face group)

Another interesting finding shown in Figure 2.1 is that the bargainers who did not expect to receive outside help if they failed to reach agreement were closer to reaching agreement after the first 12 minutes than were the bargainers who expected third party intervention. The only exception to this finding was the low need to save face group which faced binding arbitration. It, therefore, appears that much more research in both field and laboratory settings is needed before we make recommendations concerning the need for outside intervention as a means of increasing the speed at which agreements will be reached in negotiation settings.

External Pressure Placed on the Bargainers to Reach Agreement

Points of Controversy. It has often been contended that since the bargaining situation places negotiators in a dilemma in which they must weigh the value of agreement against the costs of not reaching agreement, it is plausible that the effects of concession making will, in part, depend on the pressures to reach agreement. While many studies are conducted under low pressure to reach agreement conditions (i.e., there is little time pressure and/or no monetary penalty for failure to reach agreement), other studies have greater amounts of pressure placed on the bargainers. As Hamner (1974) has pointed out, it may be misleading to compare bargaining outcomes when the studies involved placed different situational pressures on the bargaining subjects.

Experimental Results. According to Kelley (1965), negotiations tend to fill up all the available time. Bartos (1965) predicted that the less time a bargainer has, the greater should be the concession rate since a high concession rate will lead to a faster agreement than a low concession rate. Komorita and Barnes (1969) and Smith and Anderson (1975), found a lower number of trials to reach agreement were directly related to the pressure placed on the subjects. Pillisuk and Skolnick (1968) and Yukl (1972) also found that when there was high pressure to reach agreement, more concessions were made by the subjects.

Bass (1966) and Pruitt and Drews (1969), however, found that high pressures placed on the bargainers did not lead to a higher concession rate as predicted. Hamner (1974), using a monetary penalty condition rather than a time pressure condition, found that the manipulation of pressure to reach agreement had a highly significant effect on the bargaining behavior of the subjects. He found that bargainers reacted to increased pressure by yielding more per trial, taking fewer trials to reach agreement, and reaching agreement more often. With the exception of the Bass (1966) and Pruitt and Drews (1969) studies (where the subjects were either stopped prematurely or were not bargaining for money), the results of the studies cited leave little doubt that pressure applied to bargainers under bilateral monopoly conditions have marked effects on their bargaining behavior.

An Experimental Example. In a two-person monopoly bargaining game, Komorita and Barnes (1969) tested the effects of unilateral and multilateral pressures to reach agreement in two related experiments. Eighty subjects in Experiment I were assigned the role of a buyer and were led to believe that they were paired with subjects in another room assuming the role of a seller. They were told to assume that the seller was asking $100 for a hypothetical commodity and had rejected an offer of $50. The subjects were given 12 trials to reach agreement and if an agreement was reached, the subjects earned from $.05 to $5, depending upon their success in bargaining with the other person. The eighty subjects in Experiment II were given the same instruction. However, they consisted of buyer-seller dyads who actually bargained with each other.

Experiment I was a 2 × 2 × 2 factorially designed experiment, where Factor A represented the subjects' pressure to reach agreement—either $0 agreement price cost per trial or $2 agreement price cost per trial, Factor B was the opponent's cost ($0 or $2), and Factor C was the concession rate of the opponent (either 100% or 50% of that made by the subject). Experiment II consisted of a 2 × 2 factorial design with Factor A representing buyer's penalty and Factor B the seller's penalty.

The results of Experiment I indicated that a bargainer under pressure to settle will tend to yield more. Conversely, a bargainer led to believe that the other party is under pressure to settle, will yield less. The data also suggested that a firm strategy (50% concession rate) is likely to be effective only against a party who is under pressure to settle, and may evoke resistance and less yielding if the other party is not under such pressure.

The results of Experiment II indicated that pressures to reach agreement when mutually applied increased the rate of concessions and, therefore, decreased the number of trials to reach an agreement. Under unequal costs, however, the bargainer with the higher cost presumably was under greater pressures to reach an agreement, and was placed in a weaker bargaining position. Accordingly, the party with the handicap made more concessions and settled for a lower outcome than the party without such handicap.

While there appears to be general agreement in the literature that the situational pressure to reach agreement has an effect on bargaining behavior, the results of this study by Komorita and Barnes add another dimension to these findings. It also appears that the relative pressure of the bargaining parties also has an important effect on the effectiveness of the bargainer's strategy for reaching agreement.

Reward Magnitude and Bargaining Behavior

Points of Controversy. Many studies of interparty conflict (e.g., Johnson and Ruller, 1972; Chertkoff and Conley, 1967; Chertkoff and Baird, 1971) have asked the subjects to bargain over hypothetical outcomes with no actual monetary rewards accruable to the bargainers themselves. Several authors (see Pruitt, 1974, for example) when examining the generalizability of the results of these studies have questioned the seriousness with which a bargainer negotiates over imaginary money. Recently there has been a considerable interest given to examining the situational variable of reward magnitude as it affects decision-making behavior in negotiation settings.

Experimental Results. McClintock and McNeel (1966a; 1966b; 1967) found that subjects receiving low rewards were found to compete more in a PD game than those receiving high rewards. Gallo (1966) used a modification of the Deutsch and Krauss (1962) trucking game and found that subjects playing for imaginary money lost heavily on the average, whereas subjects playing for real money won an average of $4.96 over the course of 20 trials. Gumpert, Deutsch, and Epstein (1969) found that subjects in a PD game playing for imaginary money competed less than subjects playing for real money. Radlow, Weidner, and Hurst (1968) found just the opposite in that subjects playing for real money competed less than subjects playing for imaginary money. Evans (1964) and Wrightsman (1966) found that there was no difference in the level of cooperation of a PD game when subjects played for imaginary rewards or when they played for actual rewards.

Oskamp and Kleinke (1970) found no differences in the effects that five different reward schedules had on cooperation in a PD game. Hinton, Hamner, and Pohlen (1974) had subjects bargain using payoff tables which yielded profit from $0.01 to $10.00 for a total joint profit over 18 decision periods of $24.00. They found that there was no difference in either the level of cooperation as measured by the rate of concession and the opening bid or in the payoffs received in a bilateral monopoly bargaining game when subjects' reward magnitudes varied. While the studies dealing with imaginary versus real money payoff tables yield conflicting results [e.g., see Wrightsman, O'Conner, and Baker (1973)], the results of the Oskamp and Kleinke (1970) and the Hinton, Hamner, and Pohlen (1974) studies suggest that the bargaining behavior of subjects is fairly constant across various reward schedules.

One conclusion which can be drawn from these studies is that when subjects have some personal interest in the bargaining outcomes [e.g., see Gallo (1966)], they tend to be more serious about reaching a mutually rewarding agreement than subjects who do not have a personal interest in the bargaining outcomes. Therefore, some personal incentive scheme (money, points toward grade, etc.) is necessary, but the magnitude of the incentive does not seem to make a difference in the relative settlement of dyadic conflict. This conclusion is supported by the results of a study by Kelley (1966). The negotiating parties were teams of two or three college students. Two teams, one acting as buyer and the other as seller, had to reach agreement about the price of five commodities. Each team knew its own payoff for every price on each commodity but not the other team's payoffs. In the *low* incentive condition, these payoffs represented hypothetical points (no *personal* reward condition) and in the *high* incentive condition, each team member was paid 1¢ per point made by his team and an extra point on his final examination grade for every 10 points made beyond a certain base level (*personal* reward condition). The results showed that subjects in the personal reward condition reached more agreements than did the subjects in the no personal reward condition.

An Experimental Example. As noted earlier, Hinton, Hamner, and Pohlen (1974) tested the effect of various reward magnitudes on agreements reached in a managerial negotiation game. The experimental setting was comprised of a buyer and a seller, each attempting to maximize his individual return on investment in a fixed sum bargaining setting. The 24 male graduate students negotiated over certain types of market information supposedly worth from $1,000 to $1,000,000 in future company profits. The commission fee to the buyer and seller of the information was equal to .001 percent of the organization's profit or from $.01 to $10.00 for a total joint profit over the 18 decision periods of $24.00. The subjects were allowed five minutes to reach each decision, and if they failed to reach a decision during that period of time, they earned no money for that decision period. In the process of collecting the data, each dollar value was rotated against each form of information, and each subject was rotated against the other subjects, so that each individual decision was essentially unique.

The findings of this study revealed that the bargainers opening bid ($r = -.01$) and concession rate ($r = -.01$) did not correlate significantly with the amount of potential profit in a particular decision period. The results show that the opening bid and the concession rate of the bargainer were crucial in reaching mutually rewarding agreements over a period of time regardless of the magnitude of the potential earnings. By partialling out the number of agreements reached and concession rate, it was found that the correlation between the opening bid and profit earned was highly significant ($r = .59$, $p < .001$). Likewise, when the number of agreements reached and the opening bids are partialled out, the correlation between the concession rate and the profit earned was also highly significant ($r = .64$, $p < .001$). Therefore, it appears that the strategy used by the bargainer, and not the situational variable of reward magnitude, determined the bargaining success of the subjects in this experiment.

Differences in Reward Magnitude as Power in Bargaining Settings

Points of Controversy. In the earlier discussion of the experimental results of the Komorita and Barnes (1969) study, it was reported that the bargainer who faces less pressure to reach agreement held an advantage (and, therefore, had potentially more bargaining power) than the opponent who faced more pressure to reach agreement. A similar argument could be made concerning the relative range of the payoffs available to the bargainer and his opponent. Thibaut and Kelley

(1959) state that the difference in ranges of payoffs between two bargaining partners will determine the relative *power* one bargainer has over another. "Generally, we can say that the power of A over B increases with A's ability to affect the quality of outcomes attained by B" (Thibaut and Kelley, p. 101). Several similar positions have been independently advanced proposing that power can be defined in terms of social interaction (Adams, 1965; Blau, 1964; Emerson, 1962; Harsanyi, 1962; Homans, 1958). According to social interaction theory then, power is the ability to affect the expected outcomes of an opponent, where the magnitude of power of one person over another is measured by the relative range of the bargaining outcomes each controls (Cartwright, 1965).

Since many bargaining parties in real world situations have unequal resources and, therefore, unequal power, the question is often raised concerning the impact of this situational difference on the bargaining behavior of the parties concerned. The assumption which appears most reasonable is that the party with more power (as indicated by the relative wealth) would have an advantage in bargaining. However, several writers have raised the question, "Is the person who is the 'strongest' with respect to initial resources actually the weakest?" This phenomenon, referred to as the "strength is weakness" effect, has been predicted by theories which deal with coalition formation (Camson, 1961) as well as theories which deal with three-person negotiation problems (Cole, 1969). For example, if a land developer has purchased all the land for a housing project except for a one-acre plot in the middle of the development, the owner of that plot of land would probably have more relative bargaining power than the land developer. The major point of controversy, therefore, is in what situations does having more resources give one more bargaining strength and in what situations is it a handicap.

Experimental Results.   Even though power as determined by the relative difference in potential reward magnitude has received considerable theoretical attention in the bargaining literature, very few studies have been reported which actually test the effect that the structural differences in payoff tables have on bargaining outcomes. The traditional assumption in the majority of bargaining studies has been that an equal power relationship exists between the bargaining opponents. The literature has virtually ignored the phenomenon of "strength is weakness" and "weakness is strength" in two-party bargaining settings. The common belief is that the person who controls the greater amount of rewards is more powerful than the opponent and, therefore, would earn more money. However, this may not always be the case. Morgan and Sawyer (1976) and Messé (1969) found strict equality was highly preferred in some circumstances. The power assumption was supported by Messé (1971) who found that equity was preferred in a bargaining game where inputs on a prior task were equal to the ratio of the payoff table at the equity point.

The way one reacts to an obvious difference in power may depend on how the opponent with the greatest amount of power uses the power. Komorita (1965) found that if a person has greater power, and in the absence of other forms of communication, this power must be used if the bargainer wishes to influence the other's behavior. If both parties have equal power, then Komorita, Sheposh, and Braver (1968) found that if one party relinquishes the use of this capability and makes unilateral concessions, the other party will tend to reciprocate this behavior.

The bargainer with the greater magnitude of rewards generally feels more powerful, and will often act accordingly. Rosen and Crow (1964) found that unequal power acquisition tended to increase the incentive of aggressive actions. Similar findings have been reported by Thibaut and Faucheux (1965); Thibaut (1968); Smith and Seginski (1970); and Zechmeister and Druckman (1971). Deutsch and Krauss (1962) developed a trucking game in which they found that a unilateral power position was detrimental to cooperation. Deutsch (1969) and Deutsch, Canavan, and Rubin (1971) reported similar results. Deutsch (1969) concluded "as the size of conflict increases (as measured by the difference in the range of the payoffs between the two players),[3] the bargainers experienced significantly greater difficulty in reaching a cooperative agreement . . . resulting in significantly poorer bargaining outcomes or lower joint pay" (p. 1090).

Hamner and Baird (1978) designed a study to determine the effectiveness of various amounts of relative power on bargaining behavior. Three amounts of power—less than opponent, equal to opponent, and greater than opponent—were manipulated in a bilateral monopoly paradigm under relative amounts of pressure to reach agreement and under various strategy conditions. A relatively advantageous power condition led to better outcomes for the subjects than did the relative disadvantageous condition. The results indicated that a bargainer facing an opponent who is at a disadvantage due to a difference in relative potential earnings has a better chance of reaching an agreement by being conciliatory.

Therefore, it appears that even though the bargainer with the greater resources believes to have more power, and acts accordingly, this belief may actually be detrimental to reaching an agreement unless the other party also views the bargainer as having more power [as in the Messé (1969) study]. In those cases where the other party is unaware that the first bargainer has greater resources and in the cases where the other party views his own weakness as a strength, then the power of the first bargainer tends to be detrimental to reaching an equitable agreement.

An Experimental Example. Drawing on equity theory, which states that persons should be satisfied with a distribution of rewards proportional to the individual's differential contribution or inputs, Messé (1971) tested the effect of an unequal reward schedule on bargaining behavior under various prior input-ratio conditions. The 80 male subjects were asked to bargain in pairs. In each pair, the reward structure (see Table 2.1) of one person was always one-half of that of the other. Notice that the payoff table has three salient agreement points: Outcome C would provide equal rewards, Outcome E would provide the maximum product

[3] Parentheses added.

TABLE 2.1   Payoffs in Each Outcome of the Bargaining Board

Reward Structure	Outcome								
	A	B	C[a]	D	E[b]	F	G	H	I[c]
Side 1: High	$1	$1.50	$2	$2.50	$3	$3.50	$4	$4.50	$5
Side 2: Low	$2.50	$2.25	$2	$1.75	$1.50	$1.25	$1	$ .75	$ .50

Source: Messé [1971, p. 289].
[a]The equality outcome.
[b]The maximum product outcome.
[c]The maximum sum outcome.

reward, and Outcome I would provide the maximum joint reward.

Prior to beginning the bargaining process, each pair of subjects worked for varyingly lengths of time on a pretask (essay writing assignments). In ten pairs, both subjects worked for 80 minutes; in five pairs, one subject worked for 80 minutes and the other for 60 minutes; in five pairs, one subject worked for 70 minutes and the other for 50 minutes; in ten pairs one subject worked for 80 minutes and the other did not perform the pretask. In each case, the subject who had worked longer was assigned to Side 1, which contained the high reward payoffs. Note that equity theory predicts that different outcomes should be dominant, depending on differences between pair members with respect to time worked on the pretask. In the eighty-eighty condition, equity theory would predict an equal split solution would dominate. However, the "reward is strength" proposition would predict that Side 1 should do much better than Side 2 (Outcome E, for example) since Side 1 "obviously" has twice as much power. The "strength is weakness" hypothesis, however, would suggest that in the eighty-eighty condition, Side 1's outcome would range between Outcome A and Outcome D, but certainly no greater.

The frequencies of the agreed-upon outcomes in each input condition is shown in Table 2.2. All but five of the pairs settled on an agreement ranging from the equal outcome to the maximum product outcome. In the equal prior input (eighty-eighty) condition, notice that 70 percent of the pairs agreed on an equal split agreement which tends to support the predictions made by equity theory and the "strength is weakness" hypothesis. Only in those cases where Side 2 could

TABLE 2.2   Frequencies of Agreed-Upon Outcomes in Each Input Condition[a]

Input Condition (min.)	Outcome								
	A	B	C	D	E	F	G	H	I
80-80	0	0	7	0	1	0	0	1	1
60-60	0	0	1	4	0	0	0	0	0
70-50	0	0	1	3	0	0	1	0	0
80-40	1	0	1	2	6	0	0	0	0
80-0	0	0	1	3	2	3	1	0	0

[a]From Messé (1971), p. 289.

be sure that Side 1 had earned the better agreement (80-40 and 80-0) did the weaker bargainers give in to the more powerful position.

While there are many questions still unanswered by the literature on the effect of unequal power on bargaining outcomes, one conclusion seems to be clear—relative differences in reward magnitude does have a tremendous effect on bargaining behavior. Therefore, it appears that the majority of studies which use symmetrical payoff tables may not be generalizable to the real world settings where unequal power prevails.

Amount of Information and Bargaining Outcomes

Points of Controversy. Just as different amounts of pressure to reach agreement and different amounts of reward magnitude between the bargaining partners can have an impact on their relative bargaining power, it can be argued that the amount of information one has about the opponent's reward structure can also affect the relative bargaining power. Until recently, most bargaining theories have ignored this problem by assuming that all participants have the same amount of information.

There are at least two alternative hypotheses concerned with the effect of additional information on bargaining behavior. The "information is weakness" hypothesis, attributed to Schelling (1960) states that if two bargainers have different amounts of information, the bargainer with incomplete information (knowledge of only one's own payoffs) will receive a greater share of joint profits (i.e., will have more bargaining power or "strength") than will a bargainer who is completely informed. The informed bargainer may temper his or her demands to avoid a stalemate, especially if upon realizing that the opponent has less knowledge about what a "fair" agreement would be.

The second hypothesis, which has been labeled the "reality of aspiration" hypothesis (Harnett and Hamner, 1973), was developed from the research of Siegel and Fouraker (1960). In a test of the Schelling hypothesis, Siegel and Fouraker designed an experiment where each subject with complete information faced a subject with incomplete information. This experiment did not yield significant support for the Schelling hypothesis, although the results were in the predicted direction. Siegel and Fouraker suggested that their lack of success in confirming the Schelling hypothesis might have occurred because of a differential effect of information on payoffs which can be attributed to the aspiration level of their subjects. They reasoned that subjects with complete information and relatively high aspirations (i.e., greater than their opponents) might tend to negotiate contracts in opposition to the predictions made by Schelling. If approximately half of their subjects had aspiration levels higher than the aspiration level of their opponent, this tendency might account for the equivocality of the results.

To illustrate the differential effect of information on aspiration levels under this second hypothesis, consider two incompletely informed bargainers having equal power (i.e., symmetrical payoff tables) who must negotiate an agreement over the division of a fixed reward. Assume, for the moment, that one of these bargainers has an aspiration level which is higher than the fifty-fifty split as a "fair" solution, then one would expect the additional information to tend to reduce this bargainer's aspiration level. This same "moralistic" tendency toward the fifty-fifty split should raise the aspiration level of a bargainer whose original expectations are below the point representing a fair solution. Therefore, information can reduce or increase a bargainer's strength depending on whether the "reality" of the information is above or below the bargainer's present aspiration level.

Experimental Results. Experimental studies investigating the effects of information on bargaining behavior have produced conflicting results. Research by Messick and Thorngate (1967) indicated that information about the opponent's payoff table provided the areas for bargainers to compare their own rewards with those of their opponents, and hence resulted in an increase in competitive interaction. Yukl (1974) and Smith and Emmons (1969) found that subjects conceded more when they had no information about the opponent's payoff table than when they had complete information.

Liebert, Smith, Hill, and Keiffer (1968) concluded that ignorance is a bargaining advantage only when one's opponent is also bargaining in ignorance. They suggested that an informed bargainer can always neutralize an opponent's strategy by responding to such a strategy in kind. When two bargainers both have complete information, Siegel and Fouraker's (1960) research, as well as numerous other studies, indicated a strong tendency for bargaining agreements to fall at the fifty-fifty split of joint payoffs. As noted earlier, the bargaining literature also suggests that when both parties have incomplete information, there will be a greater variability of agreements, and that one of the major determinants of differential payoffs will be the bargainer's aspiration level. The interaction between the amount of information and the level of aspiration was studied by Harnett and Hamner (1975, 1973) and a discussion of this work is presented in the next section.

An Experimental Example. Hamner and Harnett (1975) conducted a study designed to test the possible interaction effect between a bargainer's aspiration level (an individual variable) and the relative amount of information available to the bargainer (a structural variable). In this study, 160 male subjects participated in a bargaining game in which a buyer and a seller must reach agreement on the price of a fictitious commodity which is to be exchanged between them. Each bargainer was given a set of instructions describing the negotiation process, as well as a payoff table indicating the profit he could earn for all possible agreements he and his opponent might negotiate. The payoff tables (Table 2.3) gave no advantage to either bargainer since they were completely symmetrical. A bargainer could earn as low as $0 to as high as $7.91 with a profit of $2.87 representing the fifty-fifty split of maximum joint payoffs.

TABLE 2.3 Buyers Payoff Table

Price	\multicolumn{19}{c}{Quantity}																		
	1	2	3	4	5	6	7	8	9	10	11	12	13	14	15	16	17	18	19
110	210	250	285	300	320	341	389	512	558	573	576	582	598	608	628	631	633	710	791
115	200	237	270	287	310	330	374	487	526	538	539	543	557	564	581	583	583	650	711
120	190	224	255	274	300	319	359	462	494	503	502	504	516	520	534	535	533	590	631
125	180	211	240	261	290	308	344	437	462	468	468	465	475	476	487	487	483	530	551
130	170	198	225	248	280	297	329	412	430	433	428	426	434	432	440	439	433	470	471
135	160	185	210	235	270	286	314	387	398	396	391	387	393	388	393	391	383	410	391
140	150	172	195	222	260	275	299	362	366	363	354	348	352	344	346	343	333	350	311
145	140	159	180	209	250	264	284	337	334	328	317	309	311	300	299	295	283	290	231
150	130	146	165	196	240	253	269	312	302	293	280	270	270	256	252	247	233	230	151
155	120	133	150	183	230	242	254	287	270	258	243	231	229	212	205	199	183	170	71
160	110	120	135	170	220	231	239	262	238	223	206	192	188	168	158	151	133	110	0
165	100	107	120	157	210	220	224	237	206	188	169	153	147	124	111	103	83	50	0
170	90	94	105	144	200	209	209	212	174	153	132	114	106	80	64	55	33	0	0
175	80	81	90	131	190	198	194	187	142	118	95	75	65	36	17	7	0	0	0
180	70	68	75	118	180	187	179	162	110	83	58	36	24	0	0	0	0	0	0
185	60	55	60	105	170	176	164	137	78	48	21	0	0	0	0	0	0	0	0
190	50	42	45	92	160	165	149	112	46	13	0	0	0	0	0	0	0	0	0
195	40	29	30	79	150	154	134	87	14	0	0	0	0	0	0	0	0	0	0
200	30	16	15	66	140	143	119	62	0	0	0	0	0	0	0	0	0	0	0

The sellers in this experiment were treated as a control group against which the buyer's performance could be compared—that is, they were all given incomplete information and their aspiration levels were not controlled. For the buyers there were two treatment conditions: (1) incomplete information, where the buyer had only his own payoff table, and (2) complete information, where the buyer had the seller's table as well as his own. In addition, after reading the instructions and seeing the payoff table(s), each buyer was asked, "How much money do you expect to earn during the bargaining session today?" This information was used to classify bargainers into a high and low aspiration group, high if the stated amount was greater than $2.87 and low if the amount was less than $2.87.

This 2 × 2 factorial study was designed to test the authors' Information-Aspiration Model of bargaining behavior. This model suggested that complete information should induce a more "realistic" perspective for each buyer in setting his aspiration level. In general, the model states that bargainers with low aspiration levels will tend to gain strength with additional information, while those with high aspiration levels will tend to lose strength with additional information.

The results of this study supported the information-aspiration model in that the low aspiration buyers had a higher mean aspiration level under complete information than under incomplete information, while the high aspiration buyers had a lower mean aspiration level under complete information than under incomplete information. Likewise, the completely informed buyers earned more money than the incompletely informed buyers in the low aspiration group, and less in the high aspiration group.

This study thus offers one potential explanation for the conflicting results found in the literature concerning the effect of different amounts of information on bargaining behavior—additional information increases the bargaining strength of negotiators whose estimation of a fair outcome is unrealistically low, but reduces the bargaining strength of the negotiators whose estimation of the fair outcome is unrealistically high. Once again, it appears that the situation in which the bargainer is participating is a contributing factor in determining bargaining behavior.

Communication and the Bargaining Outcome

Points of Controversy. In bargaining settings, communications between negotiators can take place either in a direct or in an indirect form. Direct communication is straightforward, across-the-table where words are used in their dictionary terms. Indirect or tacit communication is more subtle or circuitous—the kind found in signals, information conferences, and messages carried by intermediaries or mediators (Pruitt, 1971). Most laboratory studies have used a tacit communication process where the only form of communication allowed was recorded offers and counter offers.

The lack of opportunity for verbal communication is a source of criticism of experimental studies since many real-world bargaining sessions allow verbal communication. According to Druckman (1971), communication may serve to change the definition of the bargaining situation from that of a "game" to a serious undertaking. It can be argued that when people are bargaining face-to-face they will gain a greater appreciation for the other party's position and, therefore, much more cooperation will be the result because the intensity of the conflict will be reduced. However, as Rubin and Brown (1975) point out:

> A well-known adage concerning the value of communication in a broad range of conflict situations states that 'If you can get the parties to communicate with one another, their conflicts will resolve themselves.' This maxim has a familiar ring in bargaining, too, being typical of the sort of curative that both naive observers and armchair diagnosticians readily prescribe for the amelioration of conflict. Yet if one puts such advice to empirical test, one is likely to find that its applicability is somewhat limited— for experimental research as well as day-to-day bargaining incidents make it quite clear that *the mere availability of communication channels provide no guarantee that they will be used or used effectively* (p. 92).

Experimental Results. The studies which have been reported have yielded conflicting findings concerning whether bargaining behavior is different under direct versus tacit communication conditions. When communication is not allowed, early trial behavior takes on informational value (Pilisuk, 1965; Terhune, 1968; Liebert, Smith, Hill, and Keiffer, 1968). When communication is allowed, the greater the frequency or amount of communication, the greater is the level of cooperation (Deutsch, 1958; Deutsch, 1960; Loomis, 1959; Scodel, Minas, Ratoosh, and Lipetz, 1959; Radlow and Weidner, 1966; Shomer, Davis, and Kelley, 1966, Swennson, 1967, Voissemand Sistrunk, 1971). Wichman (1970) and Ellis (1965) found that of various combinations of one-way versus two-way, written versus oral, and face-to-face communication conditions, only two-way, face-to-face, oral communication increased the level of cooperation.

Bixenstine, Levitt, and Wilson (1966) and Caldwell (1976) predicted that it was not the ability to communicate per se which was important, but the information about the intended choice of moves in bargaining strategy that produces more cooperation. Ellis (1965), in a study of interdepartmental bargaining, found the way in which bargainers used their opportunity to communicate affected the extent to which competitiveness decreased. When departments used their communication opportunities to explain how the opponent could cooperate and why this was the best mutual strategy to follow, competitiveness decreased significantly. Loomis (1959) reported similar results. Gahagan and Tedeschi (1968) found that the cooperation level was higher in bargaining trials that immediately followed communication for the subjects who received highly credible messages than for the subjects who received less credible messages. Evans (1964) investigated communication of promises which had different levels of enforceability and found that cooperation level decreased with decreases in enforceability.

Based on the results of their study, Krauss and Deutsch (1966) argued that communication which takes place prior to the bargaining session is more important than that which takes place during the bargaining session. Structured pretrial communication where subjects were instructed to communicate about a fair solution resulted in a higher joint payoff than both unstructured pretrial communication and unstructured communication during the bargaining session. Bass (1966) and Druckman (1968) also found that certain types of prenegotiation communications served to increase cooperation. If the communication was with the bargaining opponent, then cooperation was enhanced. However, communication among teammates to plan a formal bargaining strategy did not enhance cooperation over a condition where no prior coordination was permitted. These results generally indicate that bargainers act differently when they are allowed to directly communicate with their bargaining partners. The findings show that bargainers working in a direct communication condition cooperate more than in a tacit communication condition; and prior direct communication leads to higher levels of cooperation than direct communication during the bargaining session. It should be noted, however, that most of these studies used either a PD paradigm and/or used the level of cooperation as a measure of bargaining outcome. Future research, using a bilateral monopoly bargaining game and using the agreements reached as the measure of bargaining outcome, is needed for further understanding of the influence of the communication upon the bargaining process.

An Experimental Example.   Krauss and Deutsch (1966) have argued that while bargaining without explicit communication is unrealistic, it may be just as unrealistic to assume that communication will always enhance conflict resolution. It is often the case, they argue, that conflicting parties can communicate threats as well as offers of conciliation, and communication can, under certain conditions, serve to intensify conflict instead of ameliorating it.

In the experiment conducted by Krauss and Deutsch, 66 female Bell Telephone laboratory employees were paired at an experimental task which consisted of a two-person electromechanical bargaining game. In their "trucking game" [see Deutsch and Krauss (1962) for details], the participants play the roles of owner-drivers of trucking firms which carry merchandise over a road from a starting point to a destination. Their profits (paid in imaginary money) were based on the time it took them to complete a trip—the shorter the time, the greater the profit. If they took too long, they could lose money (again imaginary). Their routes are shown in Figure 2.2. One player (Acme) traveled from the left to the right, and the other (Bolt) from right to left. One section of their main route was common to both—the middle segment labeled "one lane road." This section was only wide enough for one truck to go through at a time. Therefore, in order to use the main route efficiently, the players must work out some method of sharing the one-lane section. As the map indicates, the subjects can use the alternate route

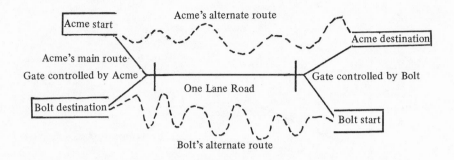

Figure 2.2   A Subject's "Road Map." From Krauss & Deutsch [1961], p. 573.

without any coordination with the other party. However, its length was such that the player would take a substantial loss on that trial. Each player also had control of a gate, which they would use to prevent the other player from passing that point on the main road. Subjects played the game for a total of twenty trials.

Following practice trials, subjects were given one of two types of communication orientation. In the *Untutored Pretrial Communication* (UPC) condition, subjects were told that they would be required to talk to each other *before* each trial, they were told that they could talk about anything they wanted to—but that it would be necessary that they say something to each other before each trial. In the *Tutored Pretrial Communication* (TPC) condition, subjects were told that, prior to each trial, they were to make proposals which were fair, both to themselves and the other player. In both conditions, subjects could communicate during the trials.

The results of these two treatment conditions (UPC and TPC) were compared with the results of a Permissive Communication (PC) treatment condition used in a previous study (Deutsch and Krauss, 1962). Subjects in the permissive communication conditions, like subjects in the present experiment, were allowed, but not compelled, to communicate during the trials. The mean transformed value (due to skewness in the distribution of payments) for the three communication orientations in three trial blocks are plotted in Figure 2.3. These results show that the pretrial communication conditions (TPC and UPC) resulted in higher payoffs than the PC condition. In addition, the tutoring instructions calling for a positive solution proposal (TPC) were significantly superior to the untutored pretrial condition which supposeldy would allow subjects to communicate threats as well as offer conciliations.

While this experiment shows that the type of verbal communication allowed the subjects makes a difference in the bargaining outcome, it fails to show that explicit communication in a bargaining experiment yields superior results (in terms of joint payoffs) than bargaining studies where only implicit communication is allowed. In addition, since this experiment was conducted using imaginary

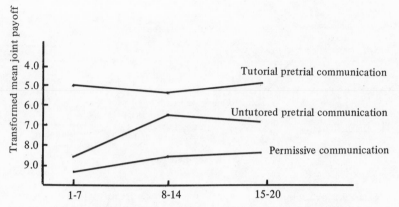

Figure 2.3 Trial Block. Transformed mean joint payoff in the three trial blocks (the lower the value of the transformed payoff, the better the outcome for the players). From Krauss and Deutsch [1966], p. 575.

money, one cannot help but question the generalizability of these results based on the previous discussion about the impact real versus imaginary rewards have on bargaining results. Further research needs to be conducted to determine if bargaining studies which allow only implicit communication (in the form of bids and counterbids only) yield different results than bargaining studies which allow various types of explicit communication.

Summary

The findings reported in this section indicate that structural differences in bargaining settings can lead to inconsistent findings among bargaining studies. We have shown that a bargainer's concession-making behavior varies with: (1) group versus individual representation, (2) amount of external pressure to reach agreement, (3) changes in the size of the potential reward, (4) relative differences in the reward magnitude of the bargaining pair, (5) amount of information available to the bargaining pair, and (6) the type and amount of communication allowed. It can be argued, therefore, that a comparison of any conflicting bargaining results should examine the differences in the bargaining structure as one of the possible underlying causes for the inconsistencies. As shown in the results of several studies, the interaction of the bargaining structure with both the individual and dynamic or strategic differences must also be examined.

INDIVIDUAL DIFFERENCES AND BARGAINING OUTCOMES

A consideration of major importance in the area of bargaining behavior centers around the personal characteristics of successful bargainers. It seems reasonable to suggest that if a certain "type" of individual is a better bargainer (as measured by the bargaining outcome) than other "types" of individuals, then the selection of that type of individual for a bargaining role would be advised. Also, it would be useful information to have if an organization (e.g., an automobile agency) were interested in teaching an individual how to be a successful bargainer.

The main purpose of this section, therefore, is to examine personal differences among various groups of potential bargainers to see if differences in the results concerning bargaining outcomes can be attributed to individual differences in the bargaining groups being studied. The individual difference effects being reviewed consist of: (1) differences in attitudes and personality makeup; (2) cultural differences; (3) differences in aspiration levels; (4) age, sex, and race differences; and (5) differences in the prior bargaining experience of the bargainers. Variations in each of these individual difference variables have been suggested as a possible explanation for why differences in bargaining results have been found.

Personality and Bargaining Behavior

Points of Controversy. While many bargaining researchers are quick to point out the need to study the individual differences of bargainers in explaining the outcome reached by bargainers, few studies have actually tested the bargaining behavior of different personality types. As Rubin and Brown (1975) point out, these studies have not only been few in number, but also have been extremely diverse in form. The assumption of most researchers is either: (1) by random assignments of subjects to the various treatments, the various personality types are equally distributed to each treatment condition, and, therefore, the differences in outcomes are probably not due to individual differences among the subjects; or (2) the subjects in the sample are so homogeneous (e.g., undergraduate social-psychology majors) that there is probably very little difference in the personality makeup among the subjects being studied. Nevertheless, in order to have generalizability of bargaining study results to the "real world", it seems imperative that an examination be made of how various personality traits affect bargaining behavior.

Two basic research questions can be asked about personality types and bargaining behavior. First, what impact do differences in personality have on bargaining behavior? Second, under what circumstances will a particular personality type do substantially better than others in terms of the final agreement?

While several investigators have argued against individual difference explanations, some experimental work points toward personality correlates of bargaining behavior (Druckman, 1967). The next section, which reviews the experimental results concerning the personality correlates of bargaining behavior, presents preliminary evidence to show that under certain circumstances (i.e., in certain *situations*), personality differences have a great impact on bargaining behavior.

However, as the review section will show, more research is needed before detailed prescriptions about personality makeup and bargaining behavior can be made.

Experimental Results. Marlowe, Gergen, and Dobb (1964) conclude from their research that the subject's personality definitely affected his/her behavior in their bargaining situation. Deutsch (1962) reported that authoritarians tended to be less trusting of other players and, therefore, made more uncooperative choices than did nonauthoritarians. Marlowe (1963) found that passive, dependent subjects were inclined to respond to cooperative behavior with cooperation. Lutzker (1960) and McClintock, Gallo, and Harrison (1965) reported that internationally-minded subjects were more cooperative when compared to political isolationists.

Goffman (1956) argues that there is a pervasive need in our culture to save or restore face, that this need is especially urgent during or after an agressive interchange, and that persons will attempt to satisy this need even at the cost of considerable personal sacrifice. Several researchers have shown that the need to maintain face increases conflict in interpersonal bargaining. Brown (1968, 1977), for example, has obtained experimental evidence that shows when subjects with a high need to save face encounter a hostile act, they are more likely to retaliate than were those subjects with a low need to save face. Similarly, Deutsch (1960) found that when there was a high need to save face, bargaining situations are viewed as more competitive than when there is a low need to save face. Findings reported by Tjosvold (1974) indicate that when a high-powered bargainer is intimidated by another whom he sees as less powerful, he will probably experience a threat to face, which is likely to lead to increased competitiveness. As noted previously, Pruitt and Johnson (1970) and Johnson and Pruitt (1972) said that mediators help the negotiators to save face, and therefore, should relieve the sense of personal weakness that is inherent in a conflict setting. Johnson and Tullar (1972) found that when there was a high need to save face, bargainers were more conciliatory when no intervention was anticipated, but when there was a low need to save face, those expecting arbitration were more conciliatory.

Faucheany and Moscovici (1968) found in a bargaining situation that high self-esteem subjects behave more exploitatively than low self-esteem subjects. Pepitone (1964) and Pepitone, *et al.* (1967) found the high self-esteem subjects tended to take advantage of the bargaining situation when possible. According to Pepitone's theory, a person will behave congruently with his self-evaluation in authorizing himself to accept rewards, rewarding himself in direct proportion to his self-esteem. Faucheany and Moscovici (1968) found that the high self-esteem subject will exploit conciliatory and generous acts.

Hatton (1967) and Worchel (1967) found that subjects who had a negative orientation toward their opponent yielded less than subjects who had a positive orientation toward their opponents. Similar findings were reported for such personality traits as need-for-power versus need-for-approval (Terhune, 1968), hostility and dominance versus dependency and submission (Wilson and Robinson,

1968, Geis, 1964), authoritarianism (Ashmore, 1969), cognitive complexity (Driver, 1976), risk-avoidance (Crow and Noel, 1976), high versus low Machiavellianism, and high versus low dogmatism (Druckman, 1967). Krauss (1966) found that the effect of one's personal attitude toward an opponent was stronger than the structure of the bargaining paradigm in determining bargaining behavior when the attitude was strongly anchored to self-esteem.

A series of studies by Terhune (1968, 1970) and Terhune and Firestone (1967), shows the relationship of a bargainer's need orientation and bargaining outcomes. Terhune administered (to subjects in these studies) the Thermatic Appreception Test. This test measures a persons needs for achievement, power, and affiliation. Only subjects strong in one of these three categories were used as subjects. The results showed that when bargainers bargained in a short period of time, bargainers who had a high need for achievement made a greater number of cooperative choices than bargainers in the other two categories, regardless of the opponent's level of cooperation. The high-need-for-affiliation bargainers were only cooperative when the opponent was cooperative, and the high-need-for-power bargainers were consistenly noncooperative. When Terhune allowed bargainers to negotiate for a longer period of time, these differences tended to disappear.

The importance of situational parameters as the primary source of interpersonal or intergroup conflicts has been stressed by Blake and Mouton (1962) and Sherif and Sherif (1965). Blake and Mouton (1962) coined the term "psychodynamic fallacy" to refer to the incorrect attribution of interpersonal behavior to the personalities of individuals. Druckman (1971) in a review of conflict studies from 1965-1970, concluded that "While several of these studies have demonstrated relationships between pre-experimentally assessed attitudes and behavior in dyadic conflict settings (e.g., see Crowne, 1966; Druckman, 1967), the evidence in general indicates that subject variables are not strongly predictive of conflict resolution behavior." This failure to obtain significant relationships between personality meausres and bargaining behavior also has been noted by Terhune (1968, 1970), Bartos, and Bixenstine and Blundell (1966), Slack and Cook (1973), and Hermann and Kogan (1977).

Walton and McKensie (1967, 1965) said that the correlation between personality and a competitive orientation in collective bargaining would be "highly significant if the more important contextual factors were controlled" (p. 194). This prediction that structural variables may "swamp" the effect of individual difference variables was supported by findings in studies by Pilisuk, et al. (1965) and Bixenstine and Blundell (1966). They found that while personal dispositions predict early trial behavior, later in the bargaining session structural characteristics of the interaction overwhelmed initial predispositions.

Other researchers have suggested that personality variables interact with structural variables to influence bargaining behavior. Terhune (1968), Douglas (1962), and Bixenstine and Blundell (1966) found that when communication between opponents was allowed, dispositional influences were stronger throughout the bargaining session. Druckman (1971) suggested that increasing the pressures on the bargainers and providing them with more information would serve to mitigate against any negative pre-experimental assessed attitudes and lead to certain prominant solutions.

Knapp and Podell (1968) claimed that the failure to obtain significant relationships between attitude scales and bargaining behavior in many studies (as noted previously) was probably due to the fact that these investigators used a homogeneous college population and did not obtain clear and large differences between criterion groups. Bartos (1967), Modelski (1970) and Turk and Lefcowitz (1962) each suggested that perhaps executives who bargain for a living might also be made up of the same personality types. Druckman (1971) said "Indeed the similarities among representatives as a function of their role per se may be a more important source for their behavior than whatever dimension of differences might exist between them" (p. 531).

Even though a large number of studies have examined the effect of personality differences on bargaining behavior, it appears that we have only begun to "scratch the surface." Several important issues need to be resolved before we can determine what effect these differences play in the bargaining process. First, are certain personality types better bargainers than others? Second, what interaction effects among structural and personality variables are important discriminators of bargaining outcomes? Third, are people who bargain for a living so similar in personality makeup that this individual difference characteristic is unimportant as an independent variable in bargaining studies, even though it would be very important in selecting bargainers?

An Experimental Example. Druckman (1967) designed a 2 X 2 X 2 factorial experiment with 15 replications in each cell in order to assess the relative contribution of personality and situational variables in determining conflict resolution. The subjects were assigned to either a union (employee) role or company (employer) role on the basis of their scores on a 24-item attitude scale which measured their identification with the union and management.

Subjects had to score in the upper and lower quartiles of the labor-management scale distribution to be eligible for participation.

The first variable in the 2 X 2 X 2 design represented a *prior strategy* condition where the two bargaining teams (or individuals) were separated into different rooms for approximately 40 minutes. In the *planned strategy* condition, the bargainers (either as a team or an individual) were asked to spend the time to plan their bargaining strategy and develop a set of points defining the rationale or arguments for the position they would take on each issue. In the *joint study* condition, the bargainings (either as a team or as an individual) were told not to take a rigid position, but instead to use the 40 minutes to learn as much as possible about company and union perspectives. The time was to be spent studying the issues in order to gain understanding of both points of view and not to plan any strategy for bargaining.

The second variable in the design represented a *group* versus an *individual* role assignment. Some subjects debated their position as an employer or employee (individual) in a simulated nonunionized company, while others were members of teams and representatives of labor or management organizations.

Whereas the first variable represented a strategic difference and the second variable represented structural difference, the third variable in the design represented a personality or prior individual difference.[4] In order to see whether personality made a difference, bargainers were chosen on the basis of extreme scores on a modification of the Dogmatism Scale devised by Rokeach (1960). Subjects had to score in the upper and lower quartiles of the modified Dogmatism Scale distribution to be elibible for participation. The following items are typical of the scale:

High Dogmatic	Low Dogmatic
I feel quite justified in sticking to a position that I feel strongly about even in the face of strong opposition.	If progress is ever to be made in this world, we must encourage cooperation between conflicting political and religious groups.
One must be as critical as possible of the ideas of one's opponents.	A leader should look to his opponents for good ideas as well as to his supporters.

In order to attain enough subjects at the extreme of both the union-management scale and the Dogmatism Scale, the questionnarie was administered to 850 students from undergraduate psychology classes.

The subjects were given a nonzero-sum collective bargaining game devised by Campbell (1960) which was modified for this experiment. Both sides received issues on a form, each arranged with the position of the union and company. Below each position on the scale, the estimated cost to the company in thousands of dollars for the duration of the contract was listed. An example of an issue scale is as follows:

Company	0	10	20	30	40	50	60	70	80	Union
	(0)	(4)	(8)	(12)	(16)	(20)	(24)	(28)	(32)	

The scale range for each issue was as follows:

Issues	Company Position	Union Position
Wages	No raise	$.16 raise per hour
Off-job training	No vocational school payment	80% tuition fees paid by company
Hospital plan	20% premium payment	100 premium payment by company
Paid vacation	2 weeks for 1 year of service (no increase for more years)	3 weeks for 10 years of service (now 3 weeks at 25 years)

[4]The Druckman study is one of the most sophisticated studies and is one of the few studies which includes all three classes of variables (structural, individual, and strategic) in the design. The major weakness in the design was that the subjects were not paid.

Subjects were allowed to bargain for 30 minutes. In order for a contract to be settled, agreement had to be reached on each of the four issues. The results indicated that strategy experience before bargaining led to a hardening of positions as reflected in measures of agreement and amount of yielding. Bilateral study experience, on the other hand, resulted in faster agreement and more yielding on the part of bargainers. These results appeared to be a function of prenegotiation experience apart from the effects of group commitment per se. In this study, whether bargainers represented groups or themselves did not have a significant effect on bargaining behavior.

The modified Dogmatism Scale was predictive of conflict resolution. Regardless of prenegotiation experience or role assignment, high dogmatics were more resistant to compromise than low dogmatics in terms of yielding behavior and number of agreements reached. A postnegotiation question revealed that high dogmatics viewed compromise as defeat more than low dogmatics.

Druckman says that implications of this study are clear. First, professional bargainers should learn the positions and merits of both vantage points prior to entering the negotiation sessions. Second, efforts aimed at reducing conflict have a better chance of succeeding if carried out by people who are more collaborative in interpersonal relations and who do not view compromise as defeat.

Regardless of whether one accepts Druckman's interpretation of the implications of his study, it seems clear that researchers need to design studies which include these three classes of independent variables. We especially need more research on the impact of personality makeup on bargaining behavior.

Cultural Differences and Bargaining Behavior

Points of Controversy.   Most studies dealing with resolving bargaining conflict assume that the parties to the conflict share similar values and orientations but have different positions due to the role they are in. As Porat (1970) and others have pointed out, the assumption that bargainers are similar in all but role assignments may no longer be valid. With the increase of international business and the growth of multinational companies, the cultural differences may influence the bargaining process even though the same basic issues are being resolved (e.g., labor-management problems, automobile sales, etc.). Therefore, for investigators to take the results of studies conducted on subjects from English-speaking cultural backgrounds (primarily North American) and generalize behavior to other cultures may be premature and lead to errors and undesirable results. The main point of concern centers around a lack of information rather than conflicting results in the bargaining literature.

Experimental Results.   Porat (1970) examined cross-cultural behavioral differences in a conflict resolution situation in five Western European countries (Denmark, Spain, Sweden, Switzerland, and the United Kingdom). A union-management negotiation exercise was the basis for the data provided by the managers in the five countries. The results show that the Spanish negotiators, at least those who reached agreement, were the least flexible (i.e., they deviated the least from a pre-planned group strategy) and were the most successful in balancing the competitive and cooperative issues. They ended up with the lowest average cost to the company and the highest gain to the union—followed by the United Kingdom, Switzerland, Denmark, and Sweden. The Swedish bargainers were the most flexible (i.e., they deviated the most from their pre-planned group strategy). The findings point to a relationship between the countries economic and social environment and behavior in conflict situations. Porat suggests that differences between the countries advise against collapsing of samples of geographic proximity or assumed cultural similarities.

Maxwell and Schmitt (1975) found that with Norwegian negotiators, a pacifist strategy (total cooperation in a PD setting) led to a cooperative strategy on the part of the opponent. However, in the United States, a pacifist strategy tended to enhance a competitive strategy on the part of the opponent.

Sawyer and Geutzkow (1965) also speaking about international negotiators, discussed the "national character" of the negotiator and maintained that different nations have different strategies of negotiations. Bartos (1967) said, "Whether these differences are due to unique personal idiosyncrasies of the negotiators or to characteristics shared by a whole nation, it is perhaps clear that standard sociological variables such as sex, age, nationality, race, religion, and personality should be related to such variables of negotiation as toughness" (p. 484). Bartos (1965, 1967) found that Caucasions were softer than Japanese as bargainers, well adjusted subjects scoring high on the California Personality Inventory tended to be softer than "poorly adjusted" ones who scored lower, and older bargainers were softer than younger ones. Bartos (1967), said that until researchers are willing to isolate these individual difference variables, especially as they confound cultural differences, the optimal strategies for international negotiations will be impossible to define.

Druckman, Benton, Ali, and Bagur (1976) tested bargaining behavior of subjects from three cultures—India, Argentina, and the United States—and found that Indians negotiated longer, were more competitive, were more symmetrical in their competitiveness, and had larger discrepancies in their settlements than did either the Argentineans or the Americans.

Whereas there are those who have compared the impact of formal structure on collective bargaining in a number of countries (Summers, 1965) and studied its impact upon national aggregates of economic indexes (Gaston, 1959; Oxnam, 1965) and studied the development of union-management relationships in various countries (Dufty, 1965; Kannappass, 1963; Shearer, 1964), only the work of Bartos (1967, 1975), Druckman, *et al.* (1967), and Porat (1970) have attempted to examine the impact of cultural differences on bargaining styles and outcomes.

An Experimental Example. As noted previously, Porat (1970) examined how cultural differences among managers from Denmark, Spain, Sweden, Switzerland,

and the United Kingdom affected bargaining behavior in a union-management negotiation exercise. The 260 managers were given a nonzero-sum union-company bargaining simulation task very similar to the one used by Druckman (1976) as previously discussed. The specific task was modified by Bass (1966) from the original Campbell (1960) game and was used to examine the differential effects of cultural affiliations, operational goals, strategy, and role perceptions on the behavior in the negotiation period.

The subjects were randomly assigned to either a union or management position and were to bargain over five issues: a hospital and medical plan, wages, an adjustment scale for increases in cost of living, night shift differential, and vacation pay. The subjects were all middle-level managers participating in a manager's workshop in their respective countries and were given the instructions in their own language.

The subjects were given 40 minutes in which to bargain. A cost of $1,000 per minute of negotiating time was equally taxed to both the union and the company, until agreement was reached on all five issues and the contract signed by both parties. Under the conditions of the simulation, each side had to make decisions on its competitive versus cooperative approach to the negotiation. The competitive aspect was emphasized by the company's need to hold concessions to a minimum in order to retain a competitive position in the textile industry. The union on the other hand, had to obtain a wage and benefit settlement equal to or better than the community average to satisfy and consolidate its membership. The need to cooperate was emphasized by the interest of both parties to reach an agreement quickly in order to reduce the penalty associated with lengthy negotiations.

In their efforts to resolve the conflict, each negotiating pair had to reach agreement on two levels. One was to determine the total cost of the settlement and the other was to determine how it would be distributed among the five individual items. These results are shown in Table 2.4.

Porat suggests that several of the variations in the results shown in Table 2.4 can be attributed to cultural differences resulting from economic and historical reasons. First, the general salary level in the country must have had some influence on the amount allocated to the wage item. Sweden, which has the highest relative wage rate ($1.64 per hour at the time of the study) of the five countries, reached the lowest average settlement on wage items ($26,667). Conversely, Spain, with the lowest wage rate ($0.42 per hour at the time of the study), obtained the highest wage settlement ($38,000).

In all five samples, the percentage allocated to the three fringe benefit items was lower than results of the same simulation in the United States (Porat, 1969). According to Porat, this may be attributed to the different levels of welfare services supplied by the State—nationalized health benefits are more common in the five European countries while benefits for night shift and vacation are lower than in the United States, reducing the company participation in all three areas.

In this study, those negotiators who deviated least from their group strategies (Spain and the United Kingdom) also achieved the higher settlements, even after

TABLE 2.4   Summary Results of the Negotiations[d]

Item	Denmark	Sweden	Switzerland[a]	United Kingdom	Spain[a]
Cost of Settlement and Negotiations					
No. of negotiating pairs	16	12	19	59	24
No. of deadlocks	0	0	1	0	4
Average					
1. Negotiating time[b]					
(min.)	30.6	32.7	28.4	23.1	17.8
2. Settlement cost[c]					
($1,000)	63.8	53.4	63.8	63.8	65.7
3. Cost to company					
($1,000, 1 + 2)	94.4	86.0	92.2	86.9	83.5
4. Gain for union					
($1,000, 2 − 1)	33.2	20.7	35.4	40.7	47.9
% Distribution of Settlement Items					
Wages	57.1	50.0	57.8	51.2	57.9
Sliding pay scale	19.6	21.9	19.2	27.6	22.8
Hospital and medical plan	14.7	19.8	13.1	13.0	10.9
Night shift differential	5.7	6.9	6.0	6.0	5.0
Vacation pay	2.9	1.6	3.8	2.2	3.4
Total	100.0	100.0	100.0	100.0	100.0

[a]The results exclude the deadlocks.
[b]Statistically significant differences between the means at p = .05 were found among the following samples: Spain versus Denmark, Sweden, Switzerland, and United Kingdom versus Denmark, Sweden.
[c]Statistically significant differences between the means at p = .05 were found between Sweden versus United Kingdom, Denmark.
[d]From Porat (1970), p. 446.

negotiation time cost. Conversely, the Swedish union negotiators, who indicated the greatest deviation between their actual and planned strategy, ended up with the lowest gain to the union. Also, the deviation from a planned strategy did not help in reaching a quicker settlement.

It thus appears that cultural differences, especially in areas where union-management roles are involved, influence the goals and strategies used to reach a settlement. It would be interesting to know whether or not a different bargaining task would have resulted in the same cultural differences being observed. Also, would payment for agreements reached have changed the results? Regardless of the answers to these questions, this study points out the need for additional cross-cultural bargaining research, both with bargaining opponents from the same nations and from different nations bargaining with each other.

Aspiration Level and Bargaining Outcomes

Points of Controversy.   A number of researchers contend that some bargainers enter a negotiation with information about what the various agreements will mean to them, and sometimes with information about what the various agreements will mean to the opponents. In many cases there is no clearcut goal for a bargainer. Liebert, Smith, Hill, and Keiffer (1968) suggested that bargainers set a reasonable goal for themselves, and most of the individual's bargaining behavior is thus directed toward reaching this goal.

While there is disagreement in the literature concerning the effect that other individual difference variables will have on bargaining behavior, there seems to be little disagreement about the effect that the aspiration level of the bargainer will have on the process and results of negotiations.

Schelling (1960) describes the bargaining process as a coordination of expectations in order to reach a mutually acceptable outcome. What is acceptable, according to Morgan and Sawyer (1967) depends not only on your own aspirations, but also on the aspirations of your opponent. Since bargaining is usually done with incomplete information about the opponent's reward structure, a bargainer's estimate of what the other expects is usually imprecise, and so expectations usually change over the course of interaction (Siegel and Fouraker, 1960). The central problem, according to Kelley (1966) is to find out what the other's expectations are while concealing your own. That is, if you know what an opponent will take, you can represent this as exactly the most you will give, and thus obtain the most favorable outcome possible.

Experimental Results. Holmes, Throop, and Strickland (1971) found that negotiators with high levels of aspiration had higher opening bids, had lower concession rates, and earned more in the settlements than negotiators with low levels of aspirations. Support of these findings were reported by Walton and McKersie (1965), Kelley (1966), Pruitt (1962), Pruitt and Lewis (1975), Ikle and Leites (1962), Sawyer and Guetzkow (1965), Harsanyi (1962), Stevens (1963), Siegel and Fouraker (1960), Fouraker and Siegel (1963), and Crowne (1966). A significant correlation between the opponent's offer and the subject's offer was present in Yukl's research (1972, 1974), but this significant correlation was not present when the subject's aspiration level was partialled out. This result seems to confirm the hypothesis shared by Kelley, Beckman, and Fisher (1967), Harsanyi (1962), and Pruitt and Drews (1969) that prenegotiation expectations often determine the form and outcome of negotiations, and the decisions of each negotiator are relatively independent of the opponent's actions.

Hamner and Harnett (1974) studied the effect of the bargainer's goal on his bargaining performance and satisfaction. Specifically, they examined whether Locke's (1969) theory—that one's goal has a direct motivational effect on his task performance, and Ilgen and Hamstra's (1972) theory that satisfaction with one's performance is a function of the difference between actual performance and performance goals, and also a function of the difference between actual performance and performance of a reference person (in this case the bargaining opponent)—will hold in a competitively structured bargaining task as well as in the more common independently structured task. Their results supported both theories.

Studies have also been reported which examined the level of aspiration set by the bargainers. Schelling (1960) states that if two bargainers have complete information, then there is a moralistic responsibility for a fifty-fifty agreement. This focal point solution, according to Schelling, will be the goal of the bargainer and will be the agreement most often reached. Support of this hypothesis has been reported by Leventhal, Allen, and Kelamelgar (1969) and Smith (1970). They found that when members of a dyad have equal inputs, an individual member usually attempts giving about an equal division of rewards to the coworker. However, when there are unequal inputs in a complete information bargaining setting, the focal point shifts, such that members allocate rewards in accordance with perceived input contributions (Land, Messe, and Phillips, 1971, Leventhal, Michaels, and Sanford, 1972; Leventhal and Michaels, 1969).

When there is incomplete information, the subject's aspiration level will be "less realistic" than the focal point solution suggested by Schelling (Schelling, 1960; Siegel and Fouraker, 1960; Hamner and Harnett, 1975; Harnett and Hamner, 1973). Yukl (1974) found that complete information subjects set higher goals on the average than incomplete information subjects. As noted in an earlier section, Harnett and Hamner (1975, 1973) in a test of their Information-Aspiration Model, found no significant difference between the aspiration levels of the incompletely and completely informed bargainers. When the bargainers who had low aspiration levels in each information condition were compared to bargainers with high aspiration levels, they found that bargainers with low aspiration levels earned more money under complete information than did bargainers under incomplete information conditions; however, bargainers with high aspiration levels earned more under incomplete information conditions than bargainers under complete information. In addition, low aspiration level subjects earned significantly less than high aspiration level subjects regardless of the amount of information.

These findings are highly consistent. Bargainers outcomes are effected by their pre-negotiation aspiration level. Researchers should make every effort to examine the effect of this individual difference variable on their bargaining results. Also, more studies need to be performed testing the interaction effect of the subject's aspiration level with structural variables (such as amount of information on the bargaining outcome).

An Experimental Example. As previously mentioned, Hamner and Harnett (1974) designed a study to determine the effect that goals have on performance and that performance has on reported levels of satisfaction in a bargaining task. The hypotheses tested in this study were developed from the literature on individual task performance as well as bargaining behavior. The specific hypotheses tested included:

H_1: The higher a bargainer's goal, the better will be his bargaining outcomes.

H_2: A bargainer whose outcome exceeds his goal will be more satisfied than a bargainer whose outcome is less than his goal.

H_3: A bargainer whose outcome exceeds his opponent's outcome will be more satisfied than a bargainer whose outcome does not exceed that of his opponent.

The 160 male subjects participated in an interdependent bargaining task similar to that used by Hamner and Harnett (1975) which has previously been described. In this task, a buyer and a seller must reach agreement on the price and quantity of a fictitious commodity. Each bargainer was given a set of instructions describing the negotiation process, as well as a payoff table indicating the profit he could earn for all possible agreements he and his partner might negotiate. The payoff tables were completely symmetrical, thus giving no advantage to either bargainer. The payoff table ranged from $0 to $7.91 with a profit of $2.87 representing the fifty-fifty split. If a bargainer reached agreement within the one hour time limit, he was paid (in cash) an amount equal to the profit shown on his payoff table.

Just before making his first price-quantity offer, each buyer was asked "How much money do you expect to earn during the bargaining session today?" At the end of the bargaining session, the buyers were asked to complete a self-report measure of satisfaction. Due to the interdependent nature of the bargaining task, the sellers in this experiment were treated as the control group, and only the buyer data were analyzed.

In order to test the stated hypothesis, the following measures were obtained: (1) *outcome level* where outcome is defined as the amount of money earned by each subject, (2) *goal set* which is the amount of money each subject expected to earn during the bargaining task, (3) *performance satisfaction* as measured by the self-report measure mentioned previously, (4) *goal-performance discrepancy* which is the degree to which the outcome level achieved differed from the goal set, and (5) *perceived earnings* of the bargaining opponents. This last estimate was used to classify the buyers as either perceiving that they earned more or less than their bargaining partner.

The data of this study were consistent with the hypothesis stated. Bargainers who set high goals for themselves performed better on the task than those who set low goals ($2.92 vs. $2.54). In addition, buyers who exceeded their goals performed better, on the average, than buyers whose performance did not exceed their goals ($2.87 vs. $2.65).

In order to test hypothesis two, a 2 X 2 factorial design was employed. Factor A was two levels of goal-performance discrepancies, where subjects were classified as either earning less than their goals or more than their goals. Factor B was two levels of partner's earnings, where subjects were classified as perceiving themselves as either earning less than or more than their bargaining partner. The results indicated that there was little difference in the satisfaction among individuals who exceeded either their goal, or exceeded their reference person's performance, or did both. The least satisfied bargainers by far were those who failed to exceed either of the two comparison points. This result seems to suggest that many individuals may have a flexible standard of reference for satisfaction in a bargaining situation—either exceed their personal goal or exceed the performance level of their bargaining opponent, but not necessarily both. Hamner and Harnett argued that in a bargaining task, beating one's opponent becomes a goal which is just as important, if not more important, than exceeding the original goal.

Most level of aspiration bargaining studies are designed to test the impact of the goals or level of aspirations on bargaining behavior. The study reviewed here takes the process one step further and examines how two different goals (absolute earnings and relative earnings) affect bargaining behavior and also the satisfaction with bargaining behavior. The results support the previous findings. If the findings of this study and those of other researchers reviewed are supported in additional bargaining studies, we should be able to predict more sufficiently the level of performance and satisfaction expected in a bargaining task from an examination of individual and group goals.

Other Individual Difference Variables

Points of Controversy. We previously found that individual differences such as personality, cultural background, and level of aspiration differentially affect bargaining outcomes. It is also possible that other individual differences within the same culture can have an impact on the bargaining process. For example, age, sex, race, and past bargaining experience should have some impact on the goals and strategies used by subjects. However, since most studies use a homogeneous sample (predominantly while male college students from behaviorally oriented classes), then one cannot help but raise a point of controversy—are these results generalizable to other settings where people of different backgrounds must bargain with one another?

Experimental Results. As noted, most of the individual difference variables examined in the bargaining literature have been either personality, cultural, or aspiration type variables. There are a scarcity of bargaining studies which have dealt with other individual difference variables. These studies have examined the effect of the sex, age, race, or past bargaining experience of the subject on his/her bargaining behavior.

Joseph and Willis (1963) found that the effects of sex differences on game behavior interacted with the intensity of a conflict of interest. Vinake (1969) and Lirtzman and Wahba (1972) claim that females are probably more compliant and responsibe to the demand characteristics of the situation than are males. Kelley (1965); Joseph and Willis (1963); Leventhal and Lane (1970); Steiner

(1960), and Smith, Vernon, and Tarte (1975) found that females were more cooperative than males.

Zechmeister and Druckman (1971) found that females were only more cooperative under high conflict conditions. They found no sex differences under low conflict conditions. Grant and Sermat (1969) and Gregovich (1968) found that there was no significant effect on bargaining behavior due to sex. They did find, however, that frequency of criterion choices were dependent upon the interaction between the sex of the subject and the sex of the opponent. They found that mixed pairs cooperated more than bargaining pairs of the same sex. Deutsch, Canavan, and Rubin (1971) found that subjects were more competitive when they were opposite in sex from the experimenter than when they were the same sex. Kanouse and Wiest (1967) and Rapoport and Chammah (1965) found that bargaining behavior was not affected by the sex of the subject, sex of the partner, or any combination of these variables.

While a few of the above studies report significant, albeit conflicting, effects due to the sex of the bargainers, most studies have failed to reveal any relationship between sex of the bargainers and bargaining behavior. These include Marlowe (1959); Lutzker (1960); Minas, Scodel, Marlowe, and Rawson (1960); Wilson and Bixenstine (1962); Bixenstine, Potash, and Wilson (1963); and Pilisuk, Skolnich, and Overstreet (1968).

Sampson and Kardush (1965) examined the effect of age, sex, social class, and race on conflict resolution behavior. Using 72 homogeneous pairs of pre-teenage subjects, they found that age and sex interacted, in that older males were more cooperative than younger males, while older females were less cooperative than younger females. Black children were more cooperative than were white children across all other treatment conditions. Harford and Cutter (1966) found that white subjects (ages 6-12) became more cooperative when they began negotiating with a black opponent after having previously negotiated with a white opponent, than when they began negotiating with a second white opponent. With adult female subjects, Wrightsman, et al. (1973) found that game responses were not affected by the race of the bargaining opponent.

Wilson and Wong (1965, 1968) compared levels of cooperation in pairs of students of Caucasion ancestry and pairs of students of Japanese ancestry, using a modified PD game. Results showed that Japanese-American subjects were more cooperative against their Japanese-American partners than Caucasion subjects were against their Caucasion partners. Uijio and Wrightsman (1967) examined conflict resolution behavior using a PD game in which 80 Japanese-American and Caucasion female subjects played against another female, either of the same or different ethnic group. They found no significant differences in the level of cooperation of either group in any of the treatment conditions.

Just as with race, sex, and age variables, the findings of the effect that the prior experience of the bargainer has on negotiation behavior have been conflicting in nature. Most bilateral monopoly bargaining studies use naive subjects who have never bargained previously over the commodity in question and who will be allowed to bargain only once. Many of these studies recognize the problem of generalization to professional bargainers, but few studies have attempted to compare the results of naive bargainers to those of experienced bargainers.

Dorris (1972), for example, warned about the danger of bias in relating the conclusions about behavior of nonbusinessmen to behavior of businessmen in the business situation. On the other hand, Hamner, *et al.* (1974) argued that the description of the psychological condition in an experiment is quite similar to the conditions implicit in working for a real organization. They suggested that an experimental setting includes not only the experimental variables but the social and psychological characteristics of the total situation as well. Therefore, by controlling these characteristics in the experiment, the researcher can enhance the generality of the result.

Bartos (1967) said, "Specifically, it does not seem profitable to conduct simple experiments with subjects who are not professionals and generalize from their behavior to that of professionals . . ." (p. 495). Many researchers are beginning to conduct experiments using professionals in order to overcome this possible limitation to bargaining studies (see e.g., Porat, 1970).

Siegel and Harnett (1964) found that industrial sales personnel responded similarly to college students in bargaining experiments, and, therefore, concluded there is no difference in decision-making behavior between college students and mature organizational personnel. However, an argument still can be made that the mature personnel in this study were not "experienced" in the sense that they did not engage in similar decision tasks in their job assignment.

While most bilateral monopoly bargaining researchers use one-decision experiments, most PD game studies use repeated trial designs. The results of these studies [see Druckman (1971a) for a review] indicate that previous dyadic experience affects later cooperative behavior. Generally, the experience level of the subject is confounded with a treatment effect and, therefore, it is difficult to separate the effect of the experience from the treatment manipulation. Studies which have separated the effect of experience per se from type of prior experience (McClintock and McNeel, 1967; Harrison and McClintock, 1965; Galli, 1966; Conrath, 1970) have found that prior experience per se increased the level of cooperation in a PD type game. In the only bilateral monopoly bargaining study reporting repeated trials, Hinton, Hamner, and Pohlen (1974) found that experience of 18 separate bargainer partners did not influence the level of cooperation or the percentage of profit earned when later trial decisions were compared to earlier trial decisions.

There has been little evidence presented which would indicate that age, sex, or race have a significant effect on bargaining behavior of adults. Most studies reported use either a PD game or use children for subjects. Studies using adult subjects and/or bilateral monopoly bargaining games have failed to show any relationships between age, sex, and race of the bargainers and their bargaining behavior. The individual difference variable which needs to be examined more closely is that of the prior experience of the bargainer. Since researchers are generally interested in generalizing their results to nonstudent, experienced bargainers, this problem needs to be carefully studied in future research.

An Experimental Example. One study designed to determine if experienced bargainers negotiate differently than college students was conducted by Hamner, Kim, and Heid (1974). They predicted that if their study supports the bargaining results of the Siegel and Harnett (1964) study, then the generalizability of the multitude of the bargaining studies using college students as subjects can be upheld.

To test the major hypothesis that the results of bargaining studies using college students are representative of the bargaining behavior of experienced negotiators, the present study compared the bargaining behavior of naive subjects (college students) against the bargaining behavior of experienced bargainers (purchasing agents). The experienced purchasing agent is a person who bargains, through a process of "bidletting" and counterbidding, for a living. The experimental paradigm also examined the effect of different levels of pressure to reach agreement and goal-setting behavior so that the results could be compared to the studies (mentioned previously) which used only naive college students as subjects.

Sixty-four bargaining dyads (128 subjects) participated in a bilateral monopoly bargaining task in which a buyer and seller must reach agreement on the price of a fictitious commodity which is to be exchanged between them at a wholesale price. The experimental design was a 2 X 2 X 2 factorial design with unequal cell frequencies. Factor A was two levels of goals; with *low* goals being defined as having a goal lower than the median goal leval and *high* goals being defined as having a goal higher than the median goal level. Factor B was two levels of pressure to reach agreement; with *low* pressure being defined as allowing the subjects 30 trials to reach agreement, and high pressure being defined as a five percent per trial penalty on trials 21 to 30. Factor C was prior experience.

Each bargainer was given a set of instructions describing the negotiation process, as well as a payoff table indicating the profit he could earn for all possible agreements he and his partner might negotiate. Prices on the payoff schedule ranged in 10-cent steps from $5.00 to $13.30, while payoffs ranged in 10-cent steps from − $2.00 to $6.30.

The results indicated that the level of experience of the bargainer had no impact on his opening bid or his concession rate. However, the experienced bargainer did take fewer trials to reach agreement. This last finding indicates that the buyers and sellers in the experienced bargaining condition were more responsive to the opponent's concessions and tended to respond in kind, while the inexperienced bargainers were less sensitive to their opponent's concession, and this took longer to reach agreement. This resulted in the experienced bargainers earning more than the naive bargainers.

The pressure to reach agreement and the level of goal treatment conditions resulted in findings which support the previous research. Subjects with high goals had higher opening bids than subjects with low goals and took longer to reach agreement. Subjects facing high pressure conceded more per bid, and reached agreement faster than subjects under low pressure.

One surprising finding was that high goal, naive subjects earned less (since fewer reached agreement) than low goal naive subjects, but high goal experienced subjects earned more than low goal experienced subjects. This finding seems to show that the initial goal of the experienced bargainer has a greater effect on his bargaining behavior than it does for a naive bargainer. This would seem reasonable, since the inexperienced bargainer would be less confident in his initial goal than a bargainer with prior experience.

These findings indicated that purchasing agent bargainers appeared to be more flexible and realistic than college student bargainers, probably as a result of their past experience with other bargainers. However, while the *magnitude* of difference was present, the *trend* in the findings concerning the impact of goal setting and pressure to reach agreement on bargaining behavior was generally in the same direction of that shown in previous research. Thus, while experience does seem to make a difference, the generalizability of experiments with college students as subjects is generally upheld.

Summary

This section reviews the effect of differences in: (1) attitudes and personality; (2) culture; (3) aspiration levels; (4) age, race, and sex; and (5) prior bargaining experience. Variations in these variables among individuals have often been suggested as possible explanations for the inconsistencies among bargaining results.

To date, very little consistent evidence has been presented which would link differences in personality makeups to differences in bargaining outcomes. Several important issues need to be resolved before we can determine what effect these differences play in the bargaining process. First, are certain personality types better bargainers than others? Second, what interaction effects among structural and personality variables are important determinants of bargaining outcomes? Third, are people who bargain for a living so homogeneous in personality make-up that this becomes unimportant as an issue to study?

Very little work has been done to compare the influence that cultural differences have on bargaining styles and outcomes. Generally, the results of these few studies suggest that bargainers from different cultural backgrounds tend to bargain differently. Much more research is indicated before conclusions and generalizations can be made.

The findings on the influence of the bargainer's aspiration level on his bargaining outcomes are highly consistent. Bargaining outcomes are affected by prenegotiation aspirations. The higher the bargainer's aspiration level, the greater are his earnings (e.g., see Hamner and Harnett, 1974). Studies testing the interaction effect of the subject's aspiration level with structural variables on the bargaining outcomes are now needed.

TABLE 2.5 Summary of Individual Differences in Background and Personality
that Appear to Lie at Opposite Ends of the Sensitivity to the
Opponent Continuum

High Sensitivity to Opponent	Low Sensitivity to Opponent
Older children and college students	Young children
Blacks	Whites
Females	Males
Low risk-takers	High risk-takers
Externals	Internals
Abstract thinkers	Concrete thinkers
Persons high in need for affiliation and power	Persons low in need for achievement
Cooperative	Competitors
Persons low in authoritarianism	Persons high in authoritarianism
Persons high in internationalism	Persons low in internationalism
Persons high in machiavellianism	Persons low in machiavellianism
Normal personalities (e.g., nonparanoids)	Abnormal personalities (e.g., paranoids)

Source: Adapted from J. Z. Rubin and Bert R. Brown, *The Social Psychology of Bargaining and Negotiation*, New York: Academic Press, 1975, p. 194.

Little evidence has been presented to link the age, sex, or race of the bargainer to differences in bargaining outcomes. The prior experience of the bargainer needs to be studied in more detail so that the generalizability of bargaining studies can be determined. However, the few studies reported tend to uphold the generalizability to the business world of studies using naive students.

Even though Rubin and Brown (1975) agree with this reviewer that the studies which have examined the impact of individual differences on bargaining behavior present numerous contradictory findings, they have summarized how they think the research findings are leaning. Their summary is presented in Table 2.5.

According to Rubin and Brown, the bargainer who is highly sensitive to his opponent (high interpersonal orientation) is reactive to the opponent's cooperativeness or competitiveness, to the distribution of power, and the dependence in the relationship. Moreover, he pays close attention to the other persons adherence and deviation from norms of equity, exchange, reciprocity, and so forth. The bargainer with a low interpersonal orientation, on the other hand, is more sensitive to the situational factors rather than the individual or strategic difference of his opponent. His main interest seems to be in maximizing his own gain, regardless of how his opponent fares.

STRATEGIC DIFFERENCES AND BARGAINING OUTCOMES

In the material presented so far, bargainers have been treated as if they were alone in the bargaining setting, where the bargaining outcome was determined by the situation and the individual makeup of the bargainer, i.e., his personality, level of aspiration, and cultural background. According to Pruitt (1972); Kelley, Beckman, and Fischer (1967); and Hamner and Yukl (1977), such an approach can account for numerous findings. However, the dynamic process of interaction between the parties to the bargaining conflict must also be examined in order to explain and predict bargaining outcomes.

While individual differences among bargainers and situational differences among studies help explain a significant amount of the findings reported by bargaining researchers, the dynamics of the bargaining interaction itself should also account for a large percentage of the variance in the outcomes reported. That is, once the bargaining session is underway, the bargainer's outcome will be significantly influenced by (1) the flexibility in adjusting to developing situations and (b) by the commitment or lack of it to an initial bargaining plan previously developed [e.g., see Bass (1966)].

A bargainer can enter the bargaining process with no prior plan (this is the argument made about naive subjects) and react to the situation that presents itself. Or else, the bargainer can develop tactics and/or strategies to be used as a bargaining plan.

A *bargaining tactic* is a position or maneuver to be taken at a specific point in the bargaining process. A *bargaining strategy* consists of a series of bargaining tactics to be used throughout the bargaining process. It implies a commitment to a long-range position to be taken with the bargaining opponent from initial contact.

This section of the chapter will present evidence concerning four major theories dealing with strategies of concession making. The four strategies reviewed are: (1) Siegel and Fouraker's (1960) "tough" strategy, (2) Bartos' (1967) and Komorita's (1972) "moderately tough" or "intermediate" strategy, (3) Osgood's (1962) "soft" strategy, and (4) Schelling's (1960) "fair" strategy. Each of these strategies can involve a series of tactics to be used against the bargaining opponent, including (1) "hard" versus "soft" initial offer tactic, (2) "many small" versus "few large" concessions tactic, (3) bluffing tactic, and (4) "last clear chance" tactic. A definition of each of the tactics involved in implementing a specific concession-making strategy is presented in the discussion of that strategy.

Individual Strategies

Points of Controversy. One of the key problems facing a bargainer in a conflict situation is what type of concession-making strategy is most effective. For instance, is it better to concede less often or more often than your opponent? Making many concessions can be effective in the sense that they may lead to agreement sooner and may reduce tension. However, such an agreement may be disadvantageous in terms of the payoff to the party making the larger number of concessions. Therefore, each negotiator must face the dilemma of whether to risk not reaching an agreement in order to reach an advantageous agreement.

This section of the chapter investigates major theories dealing with strategies of concession making. Two of these theories, the Siegel and Fouraker (1960) "level of aspiration" model and the Osgood (1959) "graduated reciprocation in tension reduction" model make apparently inconsistent predictions about what type of concession-making strategy is most effective. Osgood (1962) describes his concession-making model in terms of an arms race, a series of reciprocal initiatives in which each side alternatively contributes to international "tension" and distrust. His suggestion for a solution to this type of a situation is for an "arms race in reverse," with each side alternatively taking tension-reducing initiatives. To produce such a reversal, it is necessary for one side to adopt a policy he called *graduated reciprocation in tension reduction*. This can be defined as a "soft" strategy of bargaining. Osgood's model suggests the following guidelines:

1 Unilateral initiatives must not reduce the capacity to inflict retaliation on an opponent.

2 Unilateral initiatives must be graduated in risk according to the degree of reciprocation obtained from the opponent.

3 Unilateral initiatives should expect and invite reciprocation in some form.

4 Unilateral initiatives must be continued over a considerable period.

Osgood implies his proposal is valid when (1) the two parties have equal power, (2) the parties are stalemated or moving away from a range of acceptable solutions (high initial position tactic), and (3) the two parties are facing mutually applied high pressure to reach agreement. He says that in this situation one side should initiate concessions which are small in magnitude (many small concessions tactic). Osgood's reasoning is that a negotiator will fail to make concessions because the opponent is distrusted. A person who makes unilateral concessions will thereby remove the main obstacle to this opponent's concession making. Gouldner (1960) thinks that our culture emphasizes giving back to others an equivalent measure of what has been received from them. This reciprocity, according to Gouldner, helps to stabilize the social relationship.

Siegel and Fouraker (1960), on the other hand, argue that a negotiator should make a concession only if the opponent makes no concession. If success is experienced, i.e., the opponent makes a generous offer, a negotiator should not make a concession. This reasoning is based on the changing level of aspiration of the bargainer where success is assumed to raise one's level of aspiration, and failure to lower it. Therefore, a negotiator's demands reflect this person's level of aspiration. The implication, then, is that a negotiator who wants to maximize payoffs should make few, if any, concessions when the opponent is conceding (few small concessions tactic).

Siegel and Fouraker describe a typical pattern of bargaining as one where a bargainer opens negotiations at a high level, usually the highest level of expectancy (high initial position tactic). The bargainer soon learns, by the rival's early bids, that it probably will be necessary for concessions to be made before agreement can be reached. According to the Siegel and Fouraker model, as negotiations progress, the succession of bids seem to (1) give experience to the bargainer, enabling him to establish a realistic level of aspiration, and (2) also enable the bargainer to find means by which concessions could be made to the opponent (e.g., by bluffing and presenting "last clear chance" concessions) without making offers below the aspiration level. Aspiration levels should be modified as negotiations continue, although subjects are assumed to begin the bargaining with an a priori minimum level of expectancy. If his opponent makes no concessions, then Siegel and Fouraker suggest that concessions should be made until the bargainer's level of aspiration approaches, or coincides with, the bargainer's minimum expectancy. On the other hand, if a bargainer's rival is making discernable concessions, then the bargainer should modify the maximum concession willing to be made, raising the level of aspiration to a higher, more advantageous level.

Siegel and Fouraker's recommendation for success in bargaining is that a bargainer should follow the "toughness" principle first presented by Fellner (1949). This principle suggests that a bargainer who wants to make a relatively higher payoff than the opponent should (a) open the negotiation with a high request, (b) have a small rate of concession, (c) have a high minimum level of expectation, and (4) be unyielding.

It thus appears that both of these theories recommend that once the opponent is no longer making concessions (a stalemate), then a bargainer must begin making concessions. Both theories also imply that bargainers should start high in the initial stages of bargaining in order to allow the bargainers room to make concessions. The basic differences in the two models are (1) the motive for concession making, and (2) the prediction of the rival's reaction to the bargainer's concession.

For Siegel and Fouraker (1960), the motive of the bargainer is to "maximize his personal total profit" (p. 2). Siegel and Fouraker predict that concessions in general will not be reciprocated but instead will raise the level of aspiration of the opponent and increase this person's demands. Osgood, on the other hand, sees concession making as a method of gaining trust and enticing reciprocity so that equality can be maintained.

The Siegel and Fouraker models and the Osgood model represent extreme bargaining positions concerning concession making strategies. Several additional strategies have also gained some prominence. Komorita (1969, 1972, 1967) and Bartos (1967) both follow the basic assumption that it pays to be tough in bargaining, but there is a limit to this principle. They suggest a position somewhere between a tough and soft approach may prove to be an optimal strategy in terms of the payoff it produces. A *moderately tough* strategy, they contend, will lead to a relatively superior outcome since it will induce more concessions than an *extremely tough* strategy, thus decreasing the chances of not reaching an agreement, but at the same time lead to a relatively superior outcome.

Schelling (1960), on the other hand, proposes a position which more closely follows the logic of Osgood. Schelling reports that bargainers often realize that there is one agreement which dominates the possible solutions, and that bargainers will settle at this solution since it represents that which is *fair* to both parties. In the case of symmetrical payoff tables, the fair solution is a fifty-fifty split, the midpoint of the payoff table. From the viewpoint of equity theory, bargainers should readily agree once the prominent, fair solution is identified. The bargainer following the fair strategy should not attempt to "bluff" the opponent, but instead should make a large initial offer, and a few large concessions up to the point where the prominent solution is reached. If communication is allowed, the bargainer should point out the fact that this is the equitable solution and stay at this point until agreement is reached.

Pruitt (1972) states that unfortunately there are many different standards of fairness and equity, and wishful thinking is fully capable of determining the standard chosen by an individual. Hence, bargainers often disagree about what alternatives are fair and equitable and may spend considerable time and energy debating the matter. In a later article, Pruitt (1975) noted that when there is disagreement about the future of a fair solution, bargainers are often tempted to employ distributive tactics in order to force the other party to accept an alternative that person considers unfair and, therefore, the relationship may be impaired.

It appears, therefore, that there is much disagreement about what strategy will be most effective in reaching mutually acceptable outcomes over a long period of time. In terms of relative positions, the *tough* and *moderately tough* positions will be defined as "tougher" strategies and the *fair* and *soft* strategies will be defined as "softer" strategies. The next part of this section will examine the research dealing with the effectiveness of each of these strategies.

Experimental Results.   Numerous experiments have examined the impact of one party's behavior on the other's level and pattern of behavior. These studies have used either a bilateral monopoly setting or a related setting (e.g., Deutsch and Krauss' [1962] trucking game), or a PD game setting. The review of the experimental results will be divided into two parts: (1) the effect of various concession-making strategies in a bilateral monopoly bargaining setting, and (2) the effect of various concession-making strategies in a PD game setting. Results from both of these studies will be useful in determining the full extent of our knowledge about strategic differences and bargaining outcomes.

Concession-making strategies in bilateral monopoly settings.   Bartos (1967) says the real test of the effectiveness of various bargaining strategy positions is to look at the payoffs received when subjects used the strategies suggested. "The important question is what a tough negotiator's payoff is on the average: considering not only the payoff he makes when he succeeds, but also the payoff he receives when the negotiation breaks down; does he still come out ahead of the negotiator who makes concessions readily?" (p. 5).

In his studies, Bartos reportes support for both the Osgood and the Siegel and Fouraker theories. "We are thus drawn to the conclusion that, in our negotiations, the subjects tended to respond to high offers by making high demands, while at the same time reciprocating concession by concession" (p. 14). However, those subjects who made large concessions tended to make a somewhat lower payoff than the negotiator who made small concessions. "Concession making helps as well as hinders obtaining high payoff; in our experiments, the hindrance was somewhat larger than the help" (p. 19).

Bartos concludes his research by saying that the negotiator who wishes to make a higher than average payoff is well advised to make fewer concessions than the opponent, but that one should avoid being extremely uncooperative because by so doing, the negotiator is drastically reducing the chances of reaching an agreement. He seems to be making an argument for less than a "pure" tough strategy and more of an argument for a "moderately" tough strategy. He argues, as does Osgood, that the negotiator must consider the future payoffs as well as the present one. Such a position is well stated by Morgan and Sawyer (1967) who theorize that, "Wise persons, however, do not treat every encounter like a used-car transaction where they never expect to see others again; friends, instead, also take care that the other obtains an outcome sufficiently rewarding so that he is willing to interact again" (p. 40).

Stevens (1963) argued that in the early stage of negotiation, a concession is often viewed as a sign of weakness, and may elicit tough behavior in return. On the other hand, in later stages, when both parties are anxious to reach agreement, one party's concession often elicits a return concession from the other party, who "hopes to start an 'arm-in-arm' progression of reciprocal concessions toward agreement" (p. 106). Liebert, Smith, Hill, and Keiffer (1968) found that the first trial behavior was affected by the other negotiator's first bid, but the subsequent behavior of the subject was unaffected by the opponent's concession rate.

According to the Osgood theory, the subsequent behavior of the bargainer who makes unilateral concessions for a period of time should affect the opponent's concession rate. This period should gain the trust of the opponent and thereby remove the main obstacle to the opponent's concession making. However, for Osgood's proposal to be valid, there must be a period of time where no concessions have been made and both parties must have equal power. Studies which are not conducted under these conditions are not an adequate test of the Osgood proposal.

Pilisuk and Skolnick (1968) support the position that the Osgood proposal must be tested under equal power conditions when they commented on the unequal power studies of Rosen and Crow (1964) and Deutsch and Krauss (1962). Rosen and Crow (1964) found that unequal power acquisition tended to increase the incentive of aggressive actions. Deutsch and Krauss (1962) developed a trucking game in which they found that a unilateral power position was detrimental to cooperation. Pilisuk and Skolnick (1968) said, "Both of these studies were related more to the converse of the Osgood proposition—that is, to the effects of acquiring unilateral power rather than to the effects of unilateral conciliation" (p. 122).

To test the Osgood principle, Pilisuk and Skolnick compared a matching strategy and a conciliatory strategy against a control group of subjects who played each other. Their hypothesis was that the conciliatory strategy when combined with a chance to communicate, would produce the greatest amount of cooperation. They simulated an arms race, where the subjects were rewarded on a relative basis, for converting missiles to factories. In the matching strategy condition, the experimenter conceded three missiles on the first trial (unilateral concession), and thereafter the number of missiles the subject showed on trial n was revealed as the number shown by the opponent on trial $n + 1$. In the conciliatory strategy condition, the experimenter conceded three missiles on the first trial, and thereafter one missile less than the subject showed on trial n was revealed as the number shown by the opponent on trial $n + 1$. The results indicated: (1) that both matching strategies and conciliatory strategies, with or without prior honest expression of intentions (bluffing versus no bluffing), increased cooperation, and (b) that the communication opportunity tends to be used deceptively in the control condition, reducing cooperation.

Pilisuk and Skolnick found that a subject's behavior on the first trial may be predictive of cooperation on later trials. They reported support for the Osgood proposal in that combining small, consistent, unilateral overtures of good intentions with an honest prior announcement of moves did apparently produce markedly more cooperation than was found in a control group. But they found only a marginal increase over the rate found in a comparable matching strategy. They suggest perhaps the best strategy is a combination strategy, one that uses conciliatory moves in the beginning and then switches to a tit-for-tat strategy. Also, "it does not appear to be absolutely necessary to give a public announcement or to let adversaries know the overall plan of the strategy, or even for the adversary to perceive the strategy accurately in order for the strategy to be effective" (p. 133).

Although the Pilisuk and Skolnick research lends support to Osgood, it is not conclusive evidence either for Osgood or against Fouraker and Siegel (1963). First, it does not compare a "tough" strategy to either the conciliatory or matching strategy. Second, it is predicted that almost any preprogrammed strategy would be superior in terms of payoff to a control group, where subjects represent a mixture of strategies and nonstrategies. Third, even the most cooperative subjects ended up with more missiles than the experimenter—to the extent that the experimenter on the last block of trials could not have retaliated had the subject become aggressive. This is clearly in violation of Osgood's GRIT proposal. Fourth, the subjects are "doubly" punished for disarming more than the experimenter, and in the control group, "doubly" punished for disarming more than the opponent. This almost assures the control group will not cooperate as much, since a subject will be doubly punished for excessive concessions.

Chertkoff and Conley (1967) said two of the main tactics of a tough bargainer should be a high opening offer and an infrequent concession rate. Siegel and Fouraker (1960) support this view that the best bargainer should be the one who opens negotiations with a high request and who has a small concession rate. Osgood

(1959), although not against a tough initial position, warned that it may lead to a stalemate, heighten tension, and lower trust and, therefore, lead to no agreement. Chertkoff and Conley (1967) found that with a high initial offer, the experimenter did better with an infrequent movement rate than with a moderate movement rate. With a moderate opening offer, the experimenter did about equally as well with a moderate as an infrequent concession rate.

Pilisuk and Skolnick (1968) found that subjects in the control group lied about the number of missiles they had. Chertkoff and Baird (1971) tested the "big lie" tactic by hypothesizing that the more a bargainer exaggerates the minimum concession limit (break-even point) and the more often this false break-even point is stated, the more successful the bargainer will be. They also tested the hypothesis that if a bargainer had the last clear chance to agree or not, the tendency is to yield to the demands of the opponent. Schelling (1960) states. "In the bargaining the commitment is a device to leave the last clear chance to decide the outcome with the other party, and in a manner that he fully appreciates; it is to relinquish further initiative having rigged the incentives so that the other party must choose in one's favor" (p. 37).

Chertkoff and Baird (1971) found that the more extreme a bargainer's statement about her/his break-even point, the more successful was the bargainer, i.e., her/his opponent yielded more, and it took the bargaining pair fewer trials to reach agreement. Subjects yielded more often when they went second rather first. Chertkoff and Baird suggest the "tougher" bargainer was more successful because he/she was taking advantage of the other bargainer who worked under a philosophy of equity (Adams, 1965) or distributive justice (1958), and because the subject's level of aspiration was lowered by the extremely high break-even point claimed by her/his opponent. Unfortunately, the findings by Chertkoff (1967, 1971) are not conclusive. First, Chertkoff did not compare his results to a group using Osgood's increased concession rate. Second, the concessions made by the stooge were independent of the subject's concessions which is not the proposal of either Osgood or Siegel and Fouraker. Osgood proposes that a person should concede greater amounts than are received in concessions in order to break a stalemate; and Fouraker and Siegel suggest there is no need to concede when the opponent is conceding. Third, Chertkoff's subjects received no pay, but were working for hypothetical money. Gallo, Funk, and Levine (1969) found that subjects playing for real money were more cooperative than subjects playing for points. Chertkoff and Baird (1971) found 23 of 51 subjects in the "last clear chance" group refused to agree to the stooge's demands, and gave up a ten dollar profit. One cannot help but wonder if the subjects would have refused to agree had real money been at stake. Fourth, in the Chertkoff and Conley (1967) study there was no apparent stalemate, and no pressure to reach agreement—two necessary ingredients for a test of the Osgood proposal.

Komorita's research over the past ten years has shed some light on the Osgood versus Fouraker-Siegel controversy. Komorita and Brenner (1968) hypothesized that as the magnitude of concessions become larger during the course of negotiations, one of the parties may feel that the expected gains from obtaining an advantageous bargain may outweigh the expected losses of not reaching an agreement. "Hence it is plausible that Osgood's model may be valid only when the expected losses from not reaching an agreement far outweigh the expected gains" (p. 19f). In the Komorita and Barnes (1969) study, this point is extended by stating that it is plausible that Siegel and Fouraker's model is valid only when the expected losses are very small or nonexistent.

Komorita and Brenner's study had two experimental conditions. In Condition 1, agreement was necessary to win money and in Condition 2, agreement was not required to make money. The independent variable was the rate of concession making as manipulated by the experimenter; the dependent variable was the mean offer of subjects on the last trial. They found (1) that the concessions by the subjects were inversely related to concessions by the experimenter, (2) a firm bargaining strategy increased the probability of reaching an advantageous agreement, but reduced the probability of reaching a "fair" agreement, and (3) a strategy of making a unilaterally "fair" offer (fifty-fifty split) initially and remaining firm thereafter led to the least amount of yielding. The shortcomings of this research were that (a) very few subjects reached agreement, (b) only 12 trials were allowed, which may have been too few for their subjects to make enough counter offers to be indicative of how cooperative they were, and (c) the concession rate by the experimenter was not independent of the subject's concessions during the "trust" phase. Komorita and Brenner conceded either 10 percent, 50 percent or 100 percent as much as the subject on each trial. "Thus a small value of c (concession magnitude) reflects a 'tough' bargainer who makes small concessions, while a large value of c reflects a 'soft' bargainer who makes relatively large concessions" (p. 16). Osgood's theory calls for unilateral concessions in the initial bargaining stages. Komorita and Brenner's study covered only Osgood's maintenance phase.

Komorita and Brenner conclude that when agreement is not required to earn money, and an agreement at some "fair" price level is desired, (a) a strategy of reciprocating concessions is not significantly different from a firm bargaining strategy, and (b) it is better to be moderately firm than extremely firm. One cannot help but wonder when bargaining would be initiated without the goal of reaching ag agreement; and also one cannot help but assume that the agreement should be the ultimate dependent variable, not the last offer made. Similar findings have been reported by Esser (1975), Esser and Komorita (1975), and Komorita and Esser (1975).

Two interesting results of the Komorita and Brenner research centered around the post-experimental questionnaire and the "fair" offer condition. The results of the post-experimental questionnaire revealed that a person who yields the least is likely to be viewed as "bad" but strong. The "fair" offer condition resulted in the least yielding by the subject. Komorita and Brenner state that the main implication of this result is that an important variable which should be explored in future research is the effects of the initial offer as well as the rate of concession.

They also report that this result indicates that one should start at a level from which one can make fairly large concessions.

Benton, Kelley, and Liebling (1972) and Yukl (1974a, 1974b) tested the effect of the initial offer as well as the concession magnitude on the outcomes of bargaining. In the Benton, *et al.* (1972) study, subjects faced either (1) an extremely tough initial bid and a tough concession strategy (E initially demanded the largest possible share of available money and maintained this demand during the entire interaction), (2) an extremely tough initial demand followed by a moderately tough concession strategy [E initially demanded the largest possible share and slowly reduced the demands to a moderately tough ($2.00 for E versus $.70 for S) position], or (3) a moderately tough initial position and a tough concession strategy (E initially demanded $2.00 vs. $.70 for S) and maintained this demand throughout. These results showed that making extreme initial demands and reducing them when necessary was found to be more effective in achieving monetary gain. It should be noted, however, that 30 percent of the bargainers did not reach agreement in this "best strategy" condition. The results of this study do not tell us how the tough and moderately tough positions would have compared to a softer strategy by E.

Yukl (1974b) drawing on his earlier work (1972, 1974a) used a 2 × 3 factorial design with two levels of concession magnitude (large versus small) and three levels of initial offer (hard, moderate, and soft) to test the effect of various concession-making strategies on bargaining behavior. The results of this study indicated that subjects had lower aspirations and made a more favorable initial and final offer when the opponent made a hard initial offer than when the opponent made a soft initial offer. The subjects made a more favorable final offer, had lower aspirations, and perceived the opponent to be tougher when the opponent made small concessions than when the opponent made large concessions. Therefore, the results of this study would tend to suggest that a tough strategy is superior. However, since the S's final offer and not the agreement price was presented, it appears premature to draw this conclusion.

Cann, Esser, and Komorita (1973), drawing on the research that concludes that it pays to be tough, tried to examine the limit of this principle, i.e., "Does it always pay to be tough, and how tough should one be?" They state that studies in which the opening offer has been varied indicate that a more competitive offer leads to a better agreement and designed a study to test whether or not this principle holds under various "toughness" conditions. In this study, the subjects were given one of three initial offers (extremely tough, − $30 profit; tough, $0 profit; or moderately tough, + $10 profit) followed by one of three concession strategies in a uniform condition (moderately tough, 75 percent; soft, 100 percent; or extremely soft, 175 percent) or a two-stage concession-strategy condition (initially tough, 20 percent concession rate until a stalemate was reached, a single concession which placed the subject at the point he would have been under the uniform condition, and then a uniform strategy thereafter, i.e., 75 percent, 100 percent, or 175 percent).

The results indicated that with a moderately tough opening offer, an initially tough concession rate is more effective, whereas the higher opening offers were effective only when paired with the more cooperative concession rate. The results also showed that there are definite limits on the effectiveness of a tough strategy. The combination of a tough opening offer and a competitive concession rate was not the most effective strategy; a more moderate strategy proved superior.

As reported earlier, Bartos (1965) study found support for a tough approach to bargaining. The author agrees that his study may not do justice to a test of the Osgood theory since there was no pressure to reach agreement for the subjects. Bartos says that the less time a bargainer has, the better a strategy of concession making will be. "Thus our interpretation of the finding that concession making is an unprofitable policy has to be qualified: had the subjects had much less time in which to reach an agreement, concession making might have been a profitable strategy" (Bartos, 1965, p. 25).

Komorita and Barnes (1969) found support for Bartos' hypothesis that pressures affect concession making. They found that (1) concession making and the number of trials to reach agreement are directly related to pressures placed on reaching agreement, (2) mutual pressures to reach agreement evoke reciprocated concession making, and (3) a firm bargaining strategy evokes greater concessions only if the other party is under pressure to settle.

These authors interpret their findings as supporting Osgood's model to the extent that pressures to reach agreement, mutually applied, resulted in greater concessions and more rapid agreement. When there was minimal pressure to reach agreement, Siegel and Fouraker's model was supported. They also reported that a moderately "tough" strategy was not significantly different than a matching strategy in terms of the *last offer* made. This research project was an improvement over other tests of the Osgood model in that there was a cost penalty which put pressure on each dyad to settle. However, there was no stalemate condition. Many of the same shortcomings reported for the Komorita and Brenner (1967) research are present in this experiment. First, the subjects only interacted for 12 trials. The dependent variable was the last offer, not the agreement. Very few subjects accepted an offer by the experimenter prior to the end of the experiment. Second, the "soft" condition was a matching strategy, without a period of unilateral concessions (trust phase) as called for by Osgood.

Pruitt and Drews' (1969) experiment investigated the effects of time pressure, elapsed time, and the other negotiator's rate of concession on four aspects of bargaining behavior. These aspects included: (1) the level of demand, which was defined as the value of the current offer, (2) the size of concession, which was the extent to which a subject's current offer departed from his previous offer, (3) the subject's goal, which was defined as the minimum level to which he aspired, and (4) the extent of bluffing, which was the difference in the current offer and the subject's goal.

Pruitt and Drews say it is necessary to study the "perennial dilemma that faces negotiators between taking a 'tougher' or 'softer' approach" (p. 44). A tougher approach implies making more extreme demands, bluffing more, and making fewer concessions. A softer approach implies the opposite. They also state that in moderation each position seems to have its virtue. Assuming that an agreement will be reached, a moderately tough approach seems instrumental to getting more for oneself out of the agreement. The higher a bargainer's demands and the more slowly concessions are made, then according to the hypothesis of Pruitt and Drews, the less likely it is the opponent's minimal goal will be overshot, i.e., concessions made beyond the point to which the opponent would eventually be willing to retreat.

Using a Siegel and Fouraker payoff table, Pruitt and Drews found that on the first trial, increased time pressure resulted in less ambitious goals, lower levels of demand, and less bluffing. The level of demand and amount of bluffing were reduced over subsequent trials, but the goals remained unchanged. Their findings revealed that despite apparent awareness of the concession rate of the opponent, that variable had no effect on the subject's bargaining behavior. Only time pressure had an effect on early demands and bluffing. They found few subjects actually reached agreement. Therefore, they admit the weakness of the study and say their findings may be confounded by allowing only six trials. Another weakness noted by the authors was instructing the subjects that the partners' payoff table was symmetrical. This, according to Siegel and Fouraker (1960) is the same as a complete-information situation and "When both bargainers are negotiating with complete information, the result is almost invariably a fifty-fifty split of the joint payoff" (p. 70). Concerning the six-trial limit, Pruitt and Drews (1969) said, "Perhaps people gather information at first in a negotiation and only apply it to their behavior later"(p. 59). In any case, one cannot help but question the validity of a study on bargaining behavior where few subjects actually reached agreement.

Concession strategies in prisoner's dilemma (PD) game studies. In addition to the bilateral monopoly situations, the effects of concession making have been studied in Prisoner's Dilemma game settings. Studies which have attempted to examine preprogrammed strategies and their effect on cooperation in a PD setting include:

1   Total unilateral cooperation (extremely soft): The preprogrammed strategy is set to cooperate on every trial regardless of bargainer's actual moves (Rapoport and Chammah, 1965; Solomon, 1960).

2   Total unilateral defection (extremely tough): The preprogrammed strategy defects on every trial (Solomon, 1960).

3   Random feedback: The preprogrammed strategy cooperates (C) (soft) or defects (D) (tough) according to a random schedule without regard to the bargainer's behavior (Bixenstine, 1963; Marlowe and Dobb, 1964).

4   Matching strategies: Matching may be a function of the bargainer's present choice or previous choice (tit-for-tat). Cooperation is thus a function of the bargainer's own performance (Komorita, 1965).

5   Partial reinforcement strategy (moderately tough): The preprogrammed

strategy responds at one probability level if the bargainer's choice is a cooperative one, and at another probability level if the choice is a defective one (Komorita, 1965).

If Osgood's theory holds in these types of settings, then these studies should have found the bargainer's cooperation to be highly correlated with the stooge's cooperation. Komorita (1965) found a matching strategy conducive to cooperation. In total unilateral cooperation, Rapoport and Chammah (1965) found about half the subjects take continuous advantage of the stooge while the other half completely cooperated. Scodel (1959), Sermat (1964), and Vanden Heuvel (1968) found a tit-for-tat strategy produced more cooperative behavior than a strategy which deviates from reciprocity. Solomon (1960) found the conditional cooperative strategy (matching) led to cooperative behavior by the bargainer.

Bixenstine, Potash, and Wilson (1963) and Sermat (1964) found no effect on the subject's strategy based on the stooge's behavior. Scodel (1962), however, found that a strategy of 10 competitive moves, and then cooperative moves over the next 40 trials led to more cooperation than did unconditional cooperative moves. Swingle and Coady (1967) found no significant difference between the number of cooperative responses between groups exposed to unconditional cooperative partners versus those with unconditional competitive partners. However, unconditionally competitive partners were less favorably evaluated and tended to be less desirable as a future partner. In terms of Osgood's Phase II maintenance stage, the unconditionally cooperative strategy may prove superior in a long-term relationship.

McClintock, Harrison, Strand, and Gallo (1963) compared subjects playing against programmed opponents whose level of cooperative responding was either 85 percent, 50 percent, or 15 percent. These authors found no significant difference among the number of cooperative responses made in these groups. These findings were later supported by Komorita (1965) who found that subjects who faced a 75 percent cooperative strategy did not cooperate more than subjects who faced a 25 percent cooperative strategy.

Oskamp (1971), using a PD setting examined the effect of shifts in cooperativeness of a simulated other upon the subject's cooperation and found that a sequential change in other's behavior from low to high cooperativeness induces greater cooperativeness than either a shift from high to low or a pattern of high unchanging cooperativeness. These findings were not duplicated when live, freely interacting opponents were used causing Oskamp to conclude that these results are due to a tendency for live opponents to behave more variable than a programmed strategy. Rubin and Brown (1975) suggested that Oskamp's results show that subjects may actually come to view themselves as more capable of influencing the behavior of a simulated adversary than a real one. Of course, the more parsimonious explanation is that a statistical relationship is possible when there is systematic variance between two variables, but is not possible when there is no systematic variance. Thus, if there were no pattern to the strategy used by either or both opponents, then no systematic relationship would be possible.

The only strategy which seems to induce cooperation in a mixed-motive game is the "tit-for-tat" or matching strategy. Sermat (1970) says that a tit-for-tat strategy can be viewed as "fair play" since a player who adopts this strategy neither exploits the other nor allows himself to be exploited (assuming they start from equal positions). A subject who tries to gain advantage over such a player will be frustrated by his responses. This may explain why a prolonged tit-for-tat strategy tends to elicit increasing amounts of cooperative behavior (Sermat, 1967).

Unfortunately, the tit-for-tat strategy, while meeting the requirements of Osgood's Phase II maintenance requirement, does not meet his Phase I stalemate requirements of concession making. Osgood says in the Phase I stage, a person should "lead" (not follow) by making small unilateral concessions, and when reciprocated by the opponent, an even greater concession should be made. Wilson (1969), using a PD game with programmed strategies, concluded that his quest for a strategy which would induce high levels of cooperation must be considered a failure. He hypothesized that tit-for-tat would be superior, but it was not. Wyer (1969) concluded that when subjects faced an opponent, they tended to choose cooperatively when they expected their partner to do so, and that the tendency to make uncooperative choices was due to a lack of trust, rather than to a desire to exploit the partner for personal gain. However, Wyer's later results (Wyer, 1971) did not uphold these findings when he used a simulated partner.

Komorita and Meckling (1967) and Pruitt and Kimmel (1977) hypothesized that if an individual strongly expected a cooperative response from the other person, the effects of a disconfirmation of his expectation ought to be greater than if the expectation was not as strong. This is especially true, according to Pruitt and Kimmel, if the bargainer also has a "goal" of cooperation. However, the findings indicated that the low expectation group required a larger number of trials than did the higher expectation group for reconciliation after betrayal. Komorita, Sheposh, and Braver (1968) interpreted their study on power and cooperation as showing that when two adversaries both have threat capabilities (equal powers), and if one party relinquishes the use of this capacity, the other party will tend to reciprocate this behavior. This interpretation according to the authors, is consistent with the Osgood model and his prediction that benevolent moves will lead to reciprocation.

Komorita (1972) reported that even though there has been considerable evidence refuting Osgood's proposal (Crow, 1963; Bartos, 1967; Caggiula, 1964; Komorita and Brenner, 1967), he believes that "earlier studies both supporting and refuting the theories proposed by Osgood and by Siegel and Fouraker are quite equivocal" (p. 2). He states that in none of the cases has the research been based on a long history of competitive acts where both sides are deadlocked. He reports a study by Komorita and Koziej (1970) that, given a stalemate, tested under what conditions a conciliatory act was perceived as a sign of weakness and met with exploitation as implied by Siegel and Fouraker, and under what conditions it was likely to be perceived as "honest" or "fair" and be reciprocated as implied by Osgood. Two situational variables on cooperative choices were investigated: (a) the length of the competitive stalemate prior to conciliatory acts, and (b) the consequences or cost to the party initiating such acts. The dependent variable was the amount of cooperation on the last block of trials.

In this experiment, Komorita and Koziej made a conciliatory move "deliberately" large and dramatic so that it would be "salient and distinctive." There were three phases in this simulated PD game: (a) Extinction phase where the experimenter made ten consecutive competitive moves (D), (b) Repentance phase where the experimenter made consecutive cooperation (C) choices matching the number of the cooperative choices made by the subjects in Phase I, and (c) Reconciliation phase where the experimenter played either a "tit-for-tat" strategy for 60 trials or a martyr strategy such that whenever the subjects made five consecutive D choices, the experimenter made a C choice and then went to a "tit-for-tat" strategy. A second experiment was also run by Komorita (106) slightly changing the experimenter's behavior during the three phases. It was hypothesized that the martyr conditions would evoke a higher level of cooperation under high costs than under low cost conditions.

Komorita found that there was no significant difference in the martyr or tit-for-tat strategy. The conclusion was that it may pay to be tough against a tough person, but not necessarily against a cooperative person because a tough strategy against a cooperative person may subsequently evoke a tough strategy in return. Komorita stated that he would hypothesize that the Siegel and Fouraker's proposal is valid at the initial and intermediate stages of negotiation, but that Osgood's proposal is valid in the later stages when the negotiations are deadlocked for an extended period of time.

Of all the research found on the Osgood, Siegel-Fouraker debate, this study by Komorita is one of the best attempts at replicating the Osgood setting. However, several aspects of this research should be noted: (1) There was no attempt to simulate a Siegel-Fouraker strategy, i.e., in Phase III, to make small conciliations (C choices) only while the subject is playing D for an extended period of time, then play D when the subject is predominately playing C. No comparison can be made directly, since neither tit-for-tat nor martyr represent a Siegel-Fouraker strategy; (2) While tit-for-tat would represent Osgood's Phase II maintenance theory, a martyr strategy would never be recommended by Osgood since he proposes that one not leave himself vulnerable over an extended period of time, (3) There is no cost for a stalemate (D-D condition). The payoff matrix shows that when both subjects and opponents compete, they receive a zero payoff. Normally one would expect a negative cost for being stalemated, (4) The percentage of cooperation is used as the dependent variable. Again, the real test of a strategy would be the payoff one receives. No mention of which subjects received the highest payoff was given. As Harsanyi (1962) observed, "in the absence of a theory yielding determinate predictions as to the *outcome* (underlining added), even the mere description of many social situations in a satisfactory way becomes impossible" (p. 145).

While there is some disagreement as to which of the four concession-making strategies leads to superior outcomes, it appears that two general findings are consistently reported in the literature. First, there is a limit to the amount of toughness an opponent will tolerate before terminating the bargaining session. Secondly, bargainers expect concessions to be made throughout the bargaining process and, therefore, bargainers should open with an initial bid large enough to allow room for concession making. In the following section, we will review two studies in detail which have attempted to build on the research reviewed in this section in order to design experiments which will allow us to draw more conclusions about the effectiveness of various concession-making strategies.

Experimental Examples. Using the ideas gained by examining some of the experimental designs described above, Hamner (1974) and Dorris (1972) tested the effects of various bargaining strategies on bargaining outcomes, Hamner (1974) stated that there appears to be several reasons why findings in the literature which support various bargaining positions are not necessarily contradictory. First, few of the experiments reported tested the extreme posititions (tough versus soft) against each other. Instead, the results of the programmed strategy tested were usually compared to a control group. Second, the evidence seems to suggest that the effectiveness of a given strategy may depend on the pressure to reach agreement—with a tough strategy being more effective under low pressure (e.g., see Komorita and Brenner, 1967) and a softer strategy being more effective under high pressure (e.g., see Komorita and Barnes, 1969). Third, since many of the studies used the last offer as a measure of the bargainer's success and not the settlement price, there is some question as to whether or not the strategy tested would have led to a superior outcome.

The purpose of the study by Hamner was to determine, once a stalemate in a negotiation session had been reached, if there was a bargaining style which led to a distinctively superior outcome. The four bargaining styles replicated in a stalemated bilateral monopoly paradigm, under both high and low pressure to reach agreement conditions, were "tough," conciliatory or "soft," "intermediate" or moderately tough, and "fair." There were 12 subjects in each of the 2 X 4 factorial cells. The 96 subjects were male undergraduate business students who volunteered to participate in order to fulfill part of a course requirement.

Subjects received both a set of instructions appropriate for their given role and a payoff table showing only their profits. The instructions informed the subject that he would be exchanging offers about the wholesale price of a product with a subject in an adjoining room. The product was unnamed, but was said to retail for approximately $13.30. Ostensibly, one member of the bargaining pair acted as buyer and the other as seller. In actual fact, the subject was always the seller and the experimenter played the role of the buyer, making a programmed set of offers.

The payoff schedule showed the possible prices at which the product could be exchanged and the profit associated with each price. Prices on the schedule ranged in 10-cent steps from $5.00 to $13.30, while payoffs ranged in 10-cent steps from − $2.00 to $6.30. Subjects were paid in cash at the profit level associated with the price on which agreement was finally reached.

"Low pressure to reach agreement" was defined as allowing the subjects 30 trials to reach agreement without penalty. If, after 30 trials, subjects had failed to reach agreement, they received a zero payoff. "High pressure to reach agreement" was defined as allowing the subject 20 trials to reach agreement with no penalty, and thereafter imposing a penalty of 5 percent per trial to both sides.

In addition to the pressure condition, subjects faced either a tough, moderately tough, soft, or fair strategy, in the manner described below. Each of the programmed strategies was designed (on the basis of pilot studies) to induce both a stalemate phase and a trust phase in the bargaining session. The feedback program was as follows:

1 *Stalemate Phase*: The experimenter opens the bidding at the maximum possible payoff and makes no concessions on the first five trials.

2 *Trust Phase*: The experimenter makes a concession of two units on each of the next five trials. A unit was defined as a 10-cent increment on the payoff table.

3 *Strategy Phase*: Starting with trial eleven, the behavior of the experimenter varied according to the operational definition of each of the strategies being tested as described below.

A *tough strategy* was defined as one that, starting on trial eleven, has a concession rate of one unit for every two units (50 percent) of concession made by the subject.

An *intermediate strategy* was defined as one that, starting on trial eleven, has a concession rate of three units for every four units (75 percent) of concession made by the subject.

A *soft strategy* was defined as one that, starting on trial eleven, has a concession rate of one unit for every unit (100 percent) of concession made by the subject.

A *fair strategy* was defined as one that, starting on trial eleven, makes a single concession to the midpoint of the bargaining range and no concessions thereafter.

The results of this study indicated that: (1) a soft strategy resulted in significantly higher payoffs in both pressure conditions, (2) the subject conceded significantly more under high pressure conditions than under low pressure conditions, (3) the subjects who faced a soft strategy opponent responded with a higher concession rate in both pressure conditions, (4) the probability of not reaching an agreement was significantly greater when a tougher strategy was used (as measured by the number of "last clear chance" offers refused), and (5) the subjects who faced a tougher opponent took significantly more trials and reached significantly fewer agreements than did subjects who faced a softer opponent. These results, combined with those of Komorita (1972) and Komorita and Koziej (1970) indicate that a conciliatory strategy is superior in a *stalemated* negotiation under both high and low pressure conditions.

Hamner interpreted this finding as showing that while a tough strategy is superior when agreements are reached, it is an inferior strategy overall because fewer agreements are reached and it takes longer to reach agreement when agreements are reached. One plausible explanation offered for these results was that bargainers believe that if they accept the tougher opponents' offer, they will be earning considerably less than their opponent. Therefore, for many subjects, the utility of saving "face" may be greater than the utility of the money given up. Thus, they choose not to reach agreement rather than reach an inequitable agreement. Goffman (1956) argues that there is a need to save or restore face during an aggressive interchange, and that persons will attempt to satisfy this need even at the cost of considerable economic sacrifice. Brown (1968) and Organ (1971) obtained experimental evidence which supported this theory in a bargaining setting.

While Hamner (1972) pointed out some of the weaknesses of bargaining studies which show support for the superiority of one concession-making strategy over another, Dorris (1972) says that a real test of strategy effectiveness must be tested in the "real world" and not in a laboratory setting. He states that a review of experiments shows that the reason a cooperative (soft) strategy is ineffective can be attributed to variables in the laboratory setting itself. These variables, Dorris contends, include (a) instructions which either tacitly or explicitly encourage exploitation, suspend reciprocity norms, and make "unconditionally cooperative" behavior uncomprehensible, and (b) experimental conditions that conceal the player's identities and severely restrict normal channels of communication and social influence.

A field study was designed to remove these factors (Dorris, 1972). The 65 subjects were rare coin dealers who were offered a chance to buy a small collection of rare coins from a "naive," "unconditionally cooperative" seller. Two theoretical variables were manipulated by the seller's explanation of why he was selling the coins: (a) whether or not a "moral" appeal was made and (b) whether or not information was given to the dealer indicating that a prior dealer had been exploitative or fair toward the seller.

In this 2 X 2 factorial design (Type of Appeal X Prior Dealer's Behavior), the subject's task was one which regularly occurs in the course of his daily business. He was offered the opportunity to buy a small collection of coins by the experimenter, who enacted the role of a male college student wanting to sell the coins he had inherited from his grandfather. Eight coins were offered for sale. These coins were kept in separate clear plastic envelopes, each of which had a label stapled onto it indicating the type of coin, and an abbreviation of its condition. All of the coins were Lincoln pennies with a total retail price of about $45.

An empty envelope was used to vary the factor of the prior dealer's behavior. Since all nine envelopes were given to the dealer in a "Sucrets" box, he was forced to notice the empty one first, since it was always on top. The coin seller then explained that he had sold the missing coin to another dealer, and by reading the label on the empty envelope, the subject learned that the prior dealer had been either *fair* ($15 for a penny worth $30 retail) or *exploitative* ($15 for a penny worth $140 retail).

Comments made by the coin seller before giving the coins to the dealer determined whether the subject received a "moral" or "neutral" appeal. Since the coin seller made it quite clear that he had no idea of what the coins might be worth, the dealer was lead to believe that he had the opportunity to buy the coins as cheaply as he desired. The coins were never sold to the dealer. In the *moral* appeal, the seller explained that he needed to sell the coins to get some money to help pay for some school books and that he was going to sell them to this dealer on the basis of recommendation of another customer, an acquaintance of the seller. In the *neutral* appeal, the seller explained that he simply had some coins that he wanted to sell because he was not interested in becoming a collector. In both appeals, the seller's ignorance of the coins' value and his desire to sell them to this dealer were clearly indicated.

The results indicated that the moral appeal was found to elicit higher bids than did the neutral one ($13.63 vs. 8.72, $p < .0001$). This difference was attributed by Dorris to considerable helping behavior by the moral-appeal dealers combined with some exploitative attempts by the neutral-appeals dealer.

The time lapse from the point at which the dealer was given the coins until he made his first price offer was longer following the moral appeal (392 seconds) than after the neutral appeal (238 seconds). Moral-appeal dealers also made more comments giving more information about the coin sold to the prior dealer, about the coins he offered for sale, and other alternatives for receiving more money for the coins than did the neutral appeals dealers.

If the prior dealer had been exploitative, the dealer gave more information about the coin that had been sold to the prior dealer than if the prior dealer had been fair ($p < .0001$). Also when talking to a seller who had been exploited, dealers made fewer comments which degraded the value of his remaining coins than they did to sellers who had previously received a fair price for the one coin ($p < .06$).

When the results of the Hamner (1974) and Dorris (1972) studies are compared, it appears that there are at least two occasions where a soft strategy is met with reciprocity—after a stalemate has been reached and after a moral appeal has been made. Much more research is needed, but these two studies combined with those previously examined would lead one to believe that the type of strategy most effective would vary with the situation and the individual makeup of the parties involved.

Summary

Research has been reported which supports both the position that a tougher concession-making strategy and the position that a softer concession-making strategy leads to superior bargaining outcomes. Support for the position that a softer approach to bargaining yields more agreements, yields a higher payoff, or yields a greater concession rate by the opponent has been reported by Bartos (1967); Pilisuk and Skolnick (1968); Komorita, Sheposh, and Braver (1968); Hamner (1974); Dorris (1972); and Pruitt and Lewis (1977). Support for the position that a tougher approach yields more agreements, yields a higher payoff, or yields a greater concession rate by the opponent is reported by Bartos (1965), Pruitt and Drews (1969), Chertkoff and Conley (1967), Chertkoff and Baird (1971), and Komorita and Barnes (1969).

When the studies which support the various positions are compared, differences in the bargaining situation can be seen (e.g., prior stalemate, pressure to reach agreement, last offer versus agreement price, etc.). Therefore, the next phase of studies examining the effectiveness of various bargaining strategies needs to include the systematic studies of situation and strategy interactions in order to determine *under what conditions* various strategies are most effective.

CONCLUSIONS

It is apparent from this review that a large number of situational, individual, and strategic variables affect dyadic conflict behavior. The attempted integration of these results in this chapter should serve to suggest directions for future research. This review has attempted to measure the progress made to date with the hope that future research will begin to answer many of the questions raised in this review.

In addition, it is hoped that this review, which has identified variables which need to be examined, will only be the first step toward the eventual construction of a model which links the various situational, individual, and strategic variables together into a network of relationship. By so doing, we can begin to overcome the criticism of laboratory research on bargaining behavior. As Patchen (1970) pointed out:

> This obviously presents a serious scientific problem. On the one hand, there is a temptation—especially in the laboratory—to study one, or a few isolated variables as they affect conflict and cooperation. Such studies are often useful but it is usually hard to know how the results are affected by other important but unspecified variables, nor is it usually easy to see how the results of many studies concerning many apparently disparate variables may be fitted together.

Strauss (1978) answers the skeptic who believes bargaining takes place in too many unique settings or with too many different personalities to ever allow integrative theory or model construction. Strauss says:

In a historical perspective, structural conditions . . . do change, and therefore new types of negotiation contexts do evolve—while old ones may disappear. . . . This means that old contextual properties of negotiation may
disappear, while new ones emerge and while their combinations with each
other also change. The changes brought about by 'the workings of history'
do not at all signify that a general theory of negotiation is impossible.
They only mean that no such theory can ever predict all the future permu-
tations of negotiation contexts (p. 244).

Hopefully, this chapter has begun to identify a strategy for looking at bargaining
variables in a way that they can be logically integrated in order to achieve a general theory of negotiation.

3

THE PERSON IN BARGAINING

WHY PERSONALITY?

Leads from Previous Work

Our interest in the influence of personality on bargaining behavior began in 1967 when we discovered that the behavior of bargainers was only partially explained by several experimental variables which we had studied in our early research (Harnett, Hughes, and Cummings, 1968). In these initial studies this unexplained variance seemed to be associated with the bargainer's willingness to take a risk. This general proposition was tested in an experiment wherein 78 subjects acted as monopolistic sellers and monopsonistic buyers in a simulation of a manufacturer-wholesaler-retailer relationship (Harnett, Cummings, and Hughes, 1968). Several interesting results emerged from this early study. First, risk-taking propensity did not directly effect the amount of profits earned by a bargainer nor was the influence of risk taking propensity on results influenced by the amount of information available to a bargainer. Second, risk propensity did impact bargaining processes. Specifically, risk propensity and willingness to yield during bargaining were negatively related. Third, this relation between risk proneness and tenacity was influenced by the amount of information about an opponent's payoff structure available to a bargainer. The less the information available (the less the structure provided by the environment), the greater the effect of risk proneness. In fact, we found that risk-taking propensity influences bargaining tenacity *only* in the absence of information. Fourth, since we found no significant relationship between risk-taking propensity and final profit, the amount a bargainer yields is not independent of this person's original aspirations. High risk takers must tend to start with low initial offers. To test the strength of this relationship we ran a regression analysis between risk-taking propensity and the magnitude of the second offer. The results of this analysis showed that the relationship between risk proneness and the bargainer's second offer (which we labeled "aspiration level" in that research) was less than the relationship of risk proneness and tenacity or yielding.

This brief review of these two early studies in our research program indicated to us that the examination of personality as a potentially important determinant of bargaining behaviors should be a component of our work thereafter. Given the cross-cultural and comparative nature of our research after 1967, personality differences among executives was to become a significant focus in their own right.

The Person Concept in Understanding Bargaining

While our early research focused only on risk proneness, several studies have examined the relation of other personality concepts to bargaining behaviors. In addition to the literature reviewed in Chapter 2, the role of personality characteristics in bargaining has been the subject of several studies. These studies are briefly reviewed here because they played a significant role in the early development of the personality assessment instrument utilized in our post-1967 research. Shure and Meeker (1967) note this influence and provide a brief description of linkage between these studies and the development of the Personality/Attitude Schedule (PAS).

Lutzker (1960) found that pairs of bargainers high on "internationalism" bargained more cooperatively than those high on "isolationism." McClintock, Harrison, Strand, and Gallo (1963) and Marlowe (1963) obtained similar findings when "isolationist" and "internationalist" bargainers were bargaining against bargainers instructed to behave cooperatively. In addition, Marlowe (1963) reported that extremely cooperative and noncooperative bargainers differed from one another on need aggression, need autonomy, need abasement, and need deference. The noncooperatives were higher on the first two needs and the cooperatives were higher on the latter two. Deutsch (1960) found that bargainers low on authoritarianism tended to be trusting and trustworthy while high authoritarians tended to be capricious and untrustworthy.

Again, of particular importance in the context of the personality instrument used in our research, Vinacke (1969) reviewed several experiments which studied the effects of personality (and other) variables on bargaining behavior. Several general personality dispositions were found to relate to various indices of bargaining, psychopathology, attitudes and traits, and motives. In particular, the following specific traits have been found to be influential: authoritarianism

(Smith, 1967), dogmatism (Druckman, 1967), propensity to trust (Wrightsman, 1966), levels of ascendance (Fry, 1965), level of aspiration (Kahan, 1968), and machiavellianism (Christey and Geis, 1970).

Overall, these studies, as well as the approximately 200 experimental studies cited by Rubin and Brown (1975), indicate that several personality characteristics, not risk proneness alone, are relevant to our understanding of bargaining behavior. Thus, in 1969 we began our search for a personality assessment instrument that would, or could be made to, represent a broad range of personality characteristics. We applied three criteria in our search. Ideally the instrument should be designed for explicit use in advancing understanding of bargaining behavior. Secondly, the instrument should assess a broad range of personality characteristics rather than focusing on a single dimension of the person. Thirdly, the characteristics assessed should contain dispositions toward behaviors that are generally assumed to differ across cultural groupings. It was with these criteria in mind that we searched the published literature on cross-cultural personality studies and the bargaining literature for an appropriate instrument or instruments.[1] Before describing our specific choice, modification. and psychometric testing of an instrument, it is important to review several studies which have reported data on personality comparisons across cultures and nationalities.

The Person Concept in Cross-Cultural Comparisons

The basic proposition underlying the cross-cultural examination of personality is that the culture within which a person is socialized, educated, and reinforced exerts a significant influence on that person's basic personality as reflected in attitudes and dispositions. This proposition has been examined numerous times in the literature. We will review several of the studies reporting such relations. These studies also provide the background rationale for the development of the personality assessment instrument reported later in this chapter.

Simple Comparative Studies

In this section, we will review the findings of several descriptive and correlational studies reporting cultural differences in personality characteristics, attitudes, and desires.

A series of studies have reported differences among South African populations on personality characteristics that are relevant to the sociopolitical climate of that country. Bloom (1960) reported differences between white and nonwhite

---

[1] Of course, an alternative strategy would have been to develop such an instrument. This would have taken us well beyond the scope of our intended research program and, fortunately, was not necessary as we shall note momentarily.

college students within South Africa. The following five questions were presented to 94 students of white, black, Indian, and other nonwhite backgrounds:

1. If you could change yourself in any way you liked, in what way would you like to change?
2. What sort of person do you most despise?
3. What sort of person do you most admire?
4. What is your highest secret ambition or goal?
5. Give a rough sketch of what sort of person you expect to be in ten years' time.

The predominant theme of the answers of the whites was a wish for a higher standard of living and a better family life. The nonwhites were mainly concerned with social and political change for the total system within which they live.

Mann (1962) had white and nonwhite South African students write stories in response to seven standard anecdotes, each posing a social choice. The non-white students expressed themes inclined more toward community service (vs. private, individual interest), public welfare (vs. individual religious scruples), and full democracy for all citizens. These differences were attributed to both cultural and social stratification differences between the white and nonwhite samples.

Botha (1971) reported a study on South African and Arabic (mostly from Beirut) students' motives for achievement. Results indicated that female South African students were more achievement oriented than Arabic females. "Fear of failure" scores were higher for the Arabic than for the South African sample and below what is typically found with North American samples. Males and females did not differ on either characteristic in either sample.

Three studies have focused on comparisons of Indian samples with those from other countries. Singh, Huang, and Thompson (1962) studied Indian, American, and Chinese (National) students attending an American university. They found that the American students exhibited more self-centered characteristics while the Indian and Chinese students were more society-centered. The Chinese and Indian students exhibited greater aesthetic orientations while the Americans were more theoretical in their interests. The Indian sample was more politically conscious and economically oriented than either the American or Chinese samples. Both the Indian and Chinese students were more authoritarian than the American students. The American students seem to wish for a flexible and many-sided life, while the Indian and Chinese students preferred to enjoy life through group participation and expressed greater concern for the quality of interaction with others.

Kanekar and Mukerjee (1971) explored differences on four personality variables across three subcultures within India (Marathi speaking, Bengali speaking, and Tamil speaking). All subjects were male college graduates holding white collar jobs, predominantly in the public sector. The four personality characteristics measured were extraversion, neuroticism, authoritarianism, and misogyny. No significant differences were found across the three groups on neuroticism, authoritarianism, and misogyny. There were significant differences on extraversion.

Carment (1974) found Indian male students to be more conservative than Canadian males (English speaking) in a gambling situation and in a situation where outcomes were dependent on skill. Carment reports that the overall approach of the Indians was similar to that of individuals with low achievement drive, high fear of failure and a belief in the external control of reinforcement.

Several studies have compared the personality characteristics of white Americans with samples from other, perhaps contrasting, cultures. Mason (1967) administered the California Psychological Inventory to 49 junior high school students, including 26 American Indians, 13 Caucasians, and 10 Mexican Americans, all of whom had been characterized as culturally disadvantaged. Sex differences were found to be stable across all three samples with the females responding consistently negatively across all 18 subtests of the CPI. Ethnic group differences for males indicated that the Mexicans and Indians had lower social pressures than the Caucasians. Flexibility scores were lower for the Mexican males but the Mexican males were higher on social responsibility, tolerance, and intellectual efficiency.

Choungourian (1970) examined the personality differences of Lebanese and American students across six dimensions of personality; i.e., orality, anality, sexuality, aggression, independence, and achievement. Equal numbers of males and females were included in each sample. The Americans showed more orality and sexuality. The Lebanese showed greater aggression. American males showed greater sexuality than Lebanese males while Lebanese males exhibited greater aggression than American males.

Schneider and Parsons (1970) studied the differences between Danish and American student samples on locus of control of reinforcement. Samples consisted of 124 male and 148 female Danish students and 116 male and 108 female American students. No differences were found between the males and females in either sample. In addition on four of five dimensions of locus of control, the Danish and American samples did not differ. Only on belief of internal vs. external control over success in leadership positions was there a significant difference, with the Americans scoring in the more internal direction.

In a study designed to investigate whether the risky shift, frequently observed in group decision making, is a function of a cultural value favoring risk, Carlson and Davis (1971) compared Ugandan and United States students on two tasks. On both tasks, the Ugandans made more conservative decisions. In addition, the Ugandans did not exhibit the risky shift usually found with American samples and as found with the American sample in the Carlson and Davis (1971) study.

Concha, Garcia, and Perez (1975) reported a comparison of the cooperation vs. competition of 96 Anglo- vs. Cuban-American students. The Anglo-Americans cooperated to a significantly greater degree than did the Cuban-Americans. In addition, as age increased within each sample cooperativeness increased. The authors attribute the differences in competitiveness to social reinforcement for competitive or aggressive behavior in the Cuban community. Furthermore, Concha *et al.* argue that as Cuban children, in the United States, become acculturated to the American culture they learn that cooperation is a necessary factor for advancement.

In a field experimental analysis of the conformity and anticonformity of American vs. Chinese students, Meade and Barnard (1973) found that Americans showed a much greater tendency toward anticonformity than did the Chinese; that is, the Americans did not shift their opinions in the direction of a majority opinion as often as did the Chinese. However, when the Americans did shift, the magnitude of their opinion changes were greater than those of the Chinese.

In a comparative study of levels of achievement motivation across four developing countries and Britain, Melikian, Ginsberg, Cuceloglu, and Lynn (1961) found that British male students scored lower on achievement motivation than any of the other student samples. In order of need for achievement, from highest to lowest, were Afghanistan, Brazil, Saudi Arabia, Turkey, and Britain. Only in Afghanistan were males and females significantly different with the males scoring higher on achievement motivation.

In a comparative study of the Bahamas, Thailand, and the Philippines, Lefley (1972) found that while Thais expressed honor and pleasure in associating with authority figures, both Filipinos and Bahamians indicated discomfort in the presence of authority. Thais and Filipinos responded with anger to interpersonal aggression while Bahamians expressed suppression and impulse control. Both Filipinos and Thais place greater emphasis on wealth and money as an important value. The greatest problem in life was perceived as economic by 60 percent of the Filipinos, 57 percent of the Thais, but only 13.7 percent of the Bahamians, who named internal psychological conflict as the major source of anxiety in life.

In summary, we can characterize most of these simple studies as descriptive and not focused on a systematically derived set of personality characteristics. Most studies compare a limited range of cultures or nationalities and nearly all depend on students as subjects. Clearly, the knowledge gained from these studies is not cumulative across studies because of the lack of a commonly employed personality instrument. Finally, the personality assessment questionnaires (or interviews in a few cases) that were used were not examined for similarity of factor structure across nationality groupings. There have been a few studies which have examined this question. We now turn our attention to these.

Factor Comparison Studies

Cattell and Warburton (1961) examined the stability of the factor structure of the Sixteen Personality Factor Questionnaire between 604 American and 204 British male and female university undergraduate students. They derived the second-order factors of anxiety and extraversion-introversion by factoring the correlations among first-order factors. Cattell and Warburton concluded from the similarity they found between these factors across the two samples that there was confirmation of the appropriateness of using the concepts of anxiety and extraversion-introversion in these cultures. They further concluded that they were dealing with the same genus but different species, for dominance was more heavily weighted in the extraversion measure in Britain, while dispositional timidity played a larger role in the anxiety measure in the American sample.

Cattell (1965) reported a study designed to determine the personality factor structure of the High School Personality Questionnaire (HSPQ) and simultaneously to check on cross-cultural consistency. He administered the HSPQ to 209 boys and girls (age twelve to fourteen) in Australia and to a matched sample of 296 in the United States. The fourteen scales of the test were intercorrelated and factored separately in each sample. An independent rotation of the five emergent factors yielded four factors matched across cultures. These were the same factors as recognized in adults: extraversion-introversion; anxiety-adjustment; cortertiapathemia; and independence. Cattell concluded that the primary practical utility of the results of this study was the weights derived, making it possible to get scores from the HSPQ on second-order factors as exvia and anxiety.

Comrey, Meschieri, Misiti, and Nencini (1965) administered an Italian version of an English-language factorially developed personality test to 507 Italian males and females, about half of whom were university students. Factor analysis was used to select the items best defining each of the 28 personality dimensions measured. The total scores of these item groups were intercorrelated along with two control scales: age and sex. The resulting correlation matrix when factor analyzed produced a factor solution with substantial similarity to the factor solution for a previously tested American sample. The factors that emerged in both cultural samples were hostility, compulsion, neuroticism, dependence, and social desirability. However, the authors state that the correspondence between the factors was "not perfect."

Kikuchi and Gordon (1966) identified the Survey of Interpersonal Values (SIV) scales of support, conformity, recognition, independence, benevolence, and leadership by means of an item factor analysis on an American sample. Twenty-four items from a translated version of the SIV were administered to 132 Japanese college students, and the results factor analyzed. Five factors emerged from the orthogonally rotated factor matrix with only a few items having their largest loadings on a factor other than the ones originally hypothesized. The results of the factor analysis indicated that the constructs incorporated in the SIV do emerge as factors in the Japanese culture. The majority of the items in the translated version of the test instrument had their principle loadings on the same factors as did the corresponding original items. After determining that the translated scales were reliable, independent, and meaningful, evidence regarding construct validity was obtained by correlating the scales with those of two other personality tests and comparing the mean scores of groups which differed in known respects relevant to the characteristics measured by the instrument.

Gordon (1967) reported a multinational study of the SIV involving student samples tested in Hong Kong, Taiwan, India, Japan, Samoa, the Philippines, and the United States. The author used Q-typing for identifying personality types and describing individuals and groups. Trait level data were obtained for the samples where each group had some distinguishing characteristic. The mean trait scores of these groups were then intercorrelated. Finally, the resultant correlation matrix was factor analyzed and rotated to simple structure with use of the varimax criterion, and the emergent factors were used to identify the personality types. The resultant three factors, which accounted for 95.4 percent of the variance, were found to distinguish clearly among the cultures. The Oriental student samples had interpersonal values in common which differentiated them from their American counterparts. Also, clustering by nationality appeared within the Oriental grouping.

Jamison and Comrey (1969) reported a study comparing the factor structure similarity of the Comrey Personality Scales (CPS) between a British and an American sample. Their samples consisted of 250 male and female American university students and 232 male and female British university students. The version of the CPS administered to the two samples was designed to measure seven factors: shyness, dependence, empathy, neuroticism, compulsion, hostility, and socialization. Each of these seven factors was made up of six to nine factored homogeneous item dimensions (FHID), defined as several items developed to measure the same variable and shown to be homogeneous through actual data analysis. The total scores for the 52 FHIDs were intercorrelated, and the resulting matrix factor analyzed and the factors rotated to simple structure. The emergent factors were dependence, empathy, neuroticism, socialization, compulsion, hostility, and shyness (which split into two factors in both samples). The factor loadings in the British and American factors were correlated. Jamison and Comrey found a high correlation between the British and American factor structures, six of the eight factors having a correlation of over .85. Significant differences did exist, however, in the mean FHID and factor scores between the two samples.

Apparent by omission in both the simple and factor comparison studies are investigations of instruments which have been explicitly and systematically designed to assess personality dimensions hypothesized to relate to bargaining behavior. In addition, studies sampling adult, managerial populations are also notably absent. We now turn our attention to the original development, our modification and use of such an instrument involving such samples.

OUR MEASURES OF PERSONALITY

In this section, the Personality-Attitude Schedule (PAS) as originally reported by Shure and Meeker (1967) is presented. In this section, our adaptation and revision of the instrument is presented. In that section, we will focus on the process used in revising and psychometrically testing the PAS and present the version of the instrument used in our research.

Development of the Personality-Attitude Schedule

Shure and Meeker (1967) developed the PAS in response to the need to find and synthesize a number of existing attitude and personality scales that would prove predictive of behavior in bargaining settings. In constructing the PAS Shure and Meeker proceeded through a series of steps.

First, 24 personality scales were selected for their assumed relation to bargaining behavior. These 24 scales are presented in Table 3.1.

Second, these 24 scales were factor analyzed using the principle axes solution and retested using a normal varimax program. The factor sample consisted of 247 freshman and sophomore college males. Six factors were interpreted but not named at this stage.

Third, additional interpretation was conducted by examining the individual test items. Factor scores were estimated for all subjects and these six estimates were then correlated with all test items. Groups of items with high correlations on *only* one of the six factors were identified. These items were thereby considered appropriate to represent a single scale and the content of these items was used in the further interpretation of the factors.

Fourth, additional items were eliminated by the Wherry-Gaylord method (Jones and Shure, 1965). According to Shure and Meeker (1967, p. 237) this procedure selects that subsample of items yielding the highest correlation coefficients between the items and the factors. One hundred twenty-nine of the most promising remaining items were identified to represent the six factors.

Fifth, these 129 items were then factor analyzed, following the same procedure as in step two, based on data from a sample of 544 freshman and sophomore students. Twenty-seven items exhibited low loadings on all of the six emerging factors and were eliminated, resulting in a 102 item, six scale PAS.

Sixth, the PAS scales were interpreted and labeled in terms of the items assigned to each by the above steps.

The scales were labeled and described as follows (Shure and Meeker, 1967, pp. 240-241):

> a. *Aggressive militarism (factor I).* High scorers emphasize reliance on use of force, threats, power, and armed strength as national policy in dealing with foreign powers; they de-emphasize trust and understanding as a foundation for negotiations. They advocate the use of arms to intervene by force, to threaten to attack, and to counterattack, and are willing to fight physically and suffer fatalities for "what is right.". . .
>
> b. *Conciliation versus belligerence in interpersonal relations (factor II).* High scorers advocate responding to the needy and less fortunate (or even to unfriendly, quarrelsome, provocative, and hostile persons) with understanding, help, and friendliness. They urge admitting their own wrongs, and refuse to use threats or belligerent means or to be motivated by revenge.

TABLE 3.1   Original 24 Scales Underlying the Shure-Meeker
Personality-Attitude Schedule[1]

1. Adorno, Frenkel-Brunswik, Levinson, and Sanford (1950)
   a. California F scale (F)

2. Brim (1954)
   a. Extremity-confidence scale (EC)

3. Guilford, Christensen, Bond, and Suttom Human Interest Tests
   (1953)
   a. Material risk (RM)
   b. Physical risk (RP)

4. Thurstone Temperament Schedule (1951)
   a. Stable (S)
   b. Active (A)

5. Rotter, Seeman, and Liverant (1962)
   a. Internal/external control scale (IE)

6. Levinson (1957)
   a. Internationalism scale (IN)

7. McCord and McCord (1960)
   a. Integratist conscience scale (IC)

8. Gladstone Interpersonal Scales (1955)
   a. Belligerence in general (G1)
   b. Belligerence under threat (G2)
   c. Pacification in general (G3)
   d. Pacification under threat (G4)
   e. Tendency to feel threatened (G5)
   f. Self-assertiveness (G6)
   g. Competitiveness (G7)

9. Gladstone International Scales (1955)
   a. Belligerence in general (G8)
   b. Belligerence under threat (G9)
   c. Pacification in General (G10)
   d. Pacification under threat (G11)
   e. Tendency to feel threatened (G12)

10. Putney and Middleton (1962)
    a. General items (P1)
    b. Provocation level for nuclear attack (P2)
    c. Nuclear fatalities acceptable (P3)

[1] From: Shure and Meeker, 1967, pp. 234-235.

Instead they advise a diplomatic and constructive response guided by considerations of humanitarianism and cooperation. . . .

c. *Authoritarian nationalism versus equalitarian internationalism (factor
III).* High scorers exhibit the authoritarian personality and values, ethno-
centrism (outsiders seen as inferior, envious, and threatening), nationalism
(American idealized, emphasis on national honor and sovereignty), and a

policy of military strength that may lead to "fortress American" isolationism or military imperialism. Their ideology reflects autocratic and moralistic orientations to child-rearing, over-idealization of parents, who are seen as strong authorities requiring obedience and respect, and an emphasis on work rather than leisure. They exhibit little capacity for, and an avoidance of, self-awareness; they deny aggressiveness to friends, fear expressing weakness, and desire to submit to a powerful authority. . . .

   d. *Risk avoidance (factor IV)*. High scorers are unadventuresome, exhibit a low activity level, and are unwilling to expose themselves to dangers or to hazard risks of either a material or physical character. . . .

   e. *External versus internal control (factor V)*. . . . High scorers believe that events are controlled by external forces (fate, chance, events). Low scorers believe that they can exercise some control over the events around them.

   f. *Suspiciousness versus trust (factor VI)*. High scorers are characterized by paranoid-like traits of selfishness, projection of hostility, excitability, and terseness. Low scorers are characterized by a trusting, unselfish, calm, and optimistic orientation. . . .

Shure and Meeker presented some norm data on the six scales as well as inter-correlations among the scales, scale reliabilities (split-half), and scale validities (1967, pp. 243-246). Briefly, they found that the intercorrelations among the scales were generally small, ranging from $-.27$ to $.34$ with the majority less than $|.15|$ and with a mean coefficient equal to $|.16|$. Split-half reliability coefficients for the scales are reported as ranging from $.48$ to $.87$, with a mean of $.73$. The $.43$ coefficient was reported for Scale V (external versus internal control) and may have been due to the small number of items composing the scale. In terms of validity, two studies are reported. Shure, Meeker, Moore, and Kelley (1966) found scores on scales II, III, and IV to be related to payoffs in a bargaining game. Bargaining pairs composed of high conciliators, equalitarians, or risk avoiders earned more than pairs of low conciliators, authoritarians, or risk seekers. In addition, suspicious bargainers were less generous and trusting bargainers were more generous to their opponents. Crow and Noel (1965) found the scale scores of Navy recruits were significantly related to behavior in an international, military simulation game. Individuals high in aggressive militarism prefer high risk alternatives, while those high in authoritarian nationalism prefer higher levels of military response.

ADAPTATION OF THE PAS[2]

Two purposes were sought in our adaptation of the PAS. First, we modified the instrument to narrow its focus upon those dimensions of personality dealing

[2] This section is based on more detailed reports found in Cummings, Harnett, and Schmidt (1972, 1973).

explicitly with the interpersonal aspects of bargaining (vs. the international). Second, we analyzed the stability of the factor structure of the PAS across heterogeneous language samples and employment sector samples. This second purpose was an important requirement for our use of the PAS in the research reported in Chapters 4 and 7. That is, there we will make comparisons of personality findings across language and employment groupings of executives and such findings call for interpretation within the light of the evidence concerning the factor stability of the PAS.

Modification of the PAS

The original 102-item PAS scale was reduced to a 58-item version by eliminating Scales I (aggressive militarism) and III (authoritarian nationalism versus equalitarian internationalism). This reduced the PAS to 64 items. An additional six items were eliminated because they were judged inappropriate for middle and upper level managerial samples as studied in our research. The resulting 58-item adapted PAS is presented in Table 3.2.

The four scales used and the item numbers from Table 3.2 associated with each scale are as follows:

	Scale	Items Numbered
I.	Conciliation vs. belligerence:	1, 3, 5, 7, 9, 11, 13, 15, 17, 18, 20, 22, 24, 26, 27, 28, 29
II.	Risk avoidance vs. risk taking:	30, 31, 32, 33, 34, 35, 36, 37, 38, 40, 41, 42, 44, 45, 46, 48, 49
III.	External vs. internal control:	50, 51, 52, 53, 54, 55, 56, 57, 58
IV.	Suspiciousness vs trust:	2, 4, 6, 8, 10, 12, 14, 16, 19, 21, 23, 25, 35, 39, 43, 47

TABLE 3.2   Adapted Personality/Attitude Schedule

The items below are a study of what people think about a number of social questions. The best answer to each statement is *your personal opinion*. Many different points of view are covered; you may find yourself agreeing strongly with some of the statements, disagreeing just as strongly with others, and perhaps uncertain about others. Whether you agree or disagree with any statement, you can be sure that many other people feel the same way you do.

For each statement circle with your pencil the number which best fits your reaction according to how much you agree or disagree with it. Please mark every one, using the following scheme:

7: I agree very much	3: I disagree a little
6: I agree pretty much	2: I disagree pretty much
5: I agree a little	1: I disagree very much

If you are really completely neutral about an item, or if you are completely uncertain how you feel about an item, or if you don't understand it, mark *4*.

1   When someone has been nasty to you, you should try to understand what's bothering him, so that you can be helpful.

$$1 \quad 2 \quad 3 \quad 4 \quad 5 \quad 6 \quad 7$$

2   Even people who appear friendly to you may be unreliable because they are mainly concerned with their own interests.

$$1 \quad 2 \quad 3 \quad 4 \quad 5 \quad 6 \quad 7$$

3   We should always help those who are in need, even if they are very unfriendly to us.

$$1 \quad 2 \quad 3 \quad 4 \quad 5 \quad 6 \quad 7$$

4   Some people just have it in for you.

$$1 \quad 2 \quad 3 \quad 4 \quad 5 \quad 6 \quad 7$$

5   There are some people who can't be trusted at all.

$$1 \quad 2 \quad 3 \quad 4 \quad 5 \quad 6 \quad 7$$

6   In quarrels with other people we should make a point of admitting it when we're wrong.

$$1 \quad 2 \quad 3 \quad 4 \quad 5 \quad 6 \quad 7$$

7   Even nations that appear friendly to us may be unreliable because they are mainly concerned with their own interests.

$$1 \quad 2 \quad 3 \quad 4 \quad 5 \quad 6 \quad 7$$

8   We should always feel responsible for helping others less fortunate than ourselves.

$$1 \quad 2 \quad 3 \quad 4 \quad 5 \quad 6 \quad 7$$

9   Most people are not always straightforward and honest when their own interests are involved.

$$1 \quad 2 \quad 3 \quad 4 \quad 5 \quad 6 \quad 7$$

10 There is nothing more satisfying than doing something which pleases another person.

    1   2   3   4   5   6   7

11 A surprising number of people are cruel and spiteful.

    1   2   3   4   5   6   7

12 Doing favors for people who aren't in a position to return them is a waste of time.

    1   2   3   4   5   6   7

13 You are likely to have some personal enemies that you don't even know about.

    1   2   3   4   5   6   7

14 When you quarrel with someone you should make an especial effort to understand his point of view.

    1   2   3   4   5   6   7

15 You should not have anything to do with people who are hostile to you.

    1   2   3   4   5   6   7

16 When someone has said something to hurt you, it is not good to pay him back, even if the things you say about him are perfectly true.

    1   2   3   4   5   6   7

17 Doing something to please a person who doesn't like you can give you a lot of satisfaction.

    1   2   3   4   5   6   7

18 Most activities are more fun when you compare your own abilities with other people's.

    1   2   3   4   5   6   7

19 It is not worthwhile to make compromises and give your own preferences in order to make peace with a personal enemy.

    1   2   3   4   5   6   7

20 You shouldn't be modest if it leads people to underestimate your abilities.

    1   2   3   4   5   6   7

21 When you are engaged in a personal dispute, you shouldn't do favors for people who won't take your side.

    1   2   3   4   5   6   7

22 It is extremely upsetting to be more poorly dressed than most of the people you associate with.

    1   2   3   4   5   6   7

23 We should try to get people from other countries to visit us and explain their points of view.

1   2   3   4   5   6   7

24 You should not have anything to do with people whom you don't approve of.

1   2   3   4   5   6   7

25 We should be completely frank in telling other people about our own shortcomings and mistakes.

1   2   3   4   5   6   7

26 When people are uncooperative, the most effective way to get them to do what you want is to use threats.

1   2   3   4   5   6   7

27 It's a good idea to know the problems and worries of people around you, so that you can be helpful.

1   2   3   4   5   6   7

28 In spite of occasional lapses, most people are pretty trustworthy.

1   2   3   4   5   6   7

The next series of questions are about your likes and dislikes, preferences and habits in everyday life. There are no right or wrong answers to these questions; one answer can be just as good as some other answer.

INSTRUCTIONS: For each question, circle with your pencil either number 1, 2, or 3 for the answer that fits you best.

> If your answer is *Yes*, circle number 1.
> If you cannot decide, circle number 2.
> If your answer is *No*, circle number 3.

29 Do you like to wager with very small stakes just for the kick you get out of gambling?

1   2   3

30 Would you like to do stunt flying in an aerial circus?

1   2   3

31 Would you like to dive from a high spring-board?

1   2   3

32 Do you like to play games when money is at stake?

1   2   3

33   Would you like to ride with dare-devil drivers?

1   2   3

34   Do you often alternate between happiness and sadness?

1   2   3

35   Do you drive a car rather fast?

1   2   3

36   Would you like to drive a "hot-rod" in a race?

1   2   3

37   Do you like to bet money on athletic events?

1   2   3

38   Do you often feel impatient?

1   2   3

39   Do you like to invest money in a promising invention?

1   2   3

40   Would you like to be a test pilot?

1   2   3

41   Would you like to run river rapids in a motor boat?

1   2   3

42   When you are emotionally upset, do you tend to lose your appetite?

1   2   3

43   Would you like to work as a flying trapeze acrobat in a circus?

1   2   3

44   Would you like to ride out a storm in a small boat?

1   2   3

45   Would you be willing to take a chance by accepting a job you know nothing about?

1   2   3

46   Does it irritate you to be interrupted when you are concentrating?

1   2   3

47   Do you usually work fast?

1   2   3

48   Do you like to drive a car rather fast when there is no speed limit?

1   2   3

49   Would you like to go on the first rocket-ship expedition to the moon?

1   2   3

This series of items attempts to find out the way in which certain important events in our society affect different people. Each item consists of a pair of statements, one of which has the number *1* in front of it and the other the number *2*. In the case of each item, read both statements *carefully* and select the one statement of each pair (*and only one*) which you more strongly *believe* to be the case as far as you are concerned. Indicate your choice by placing a circle with your pencil on the number of the statement which you believe to be more true. There are no right or wrong answers to this questionnaire. For every item there are large numbers of people who pick *1* and large numbers who pick *2*.

I more strongly believe that

50   1   if I make an effort, I can get people I like to become my friends.

    2   no matter how hard you try, some people just don't like you.

51   1   people's misfortunes usually result from the mistakes they make.

    2   sometimes I feel that I don't have enough control over what happens to me.

52   1   in the long run, people get the respect they deserve in this world.

    2   unfortunately, an individual's worth often passes unrecognized no matter how hard he tries.

53   1   some guys are born to take orders and others are born to give them.

    2   in the long run the guy with more ability ends up giving the orders.

54   1   I could usually tell whether I had done well or poorly on a test as soon as I had finished taking the test.

    2   I often felt I couldn't predict which grade I would get on a test.

55   1   if one gets the right teacher, he can do well in school; otherwise he has trouble.

    2   the grades a person gets in school are up to him.

56   1   I often can't understand how it is possible to get people to do what I want them to.

    2   getting people to do what you want takes hard work and patience.

57   1   getting a good job depends partly on being in the right place at the right time.

    2   if you've got ability, you can always get a job.

58   1   people are lonely because they don't know how to be friendly.

    2   making friends is largely a matter of being lucky enough to meet the right people.

Factor Structure of the Adapted PAS

Two factor analytic studies of the adapted PAS were conducted. The first derived and tested the factor structure across three language groupings of executives of nine nationalities. The second derived and tested the factor structure across two employment sector groupings.

Cross Language Factor Study

The subjects used in this study were managers from the following nations: Belgium, Denmark, England, Finland, France, Greece, Spain, Switzerland, and the United States. At the time of data collection the respondents, all of whom were managers employed in middle and upper level positions in private enterprises, were enrolled in executive development courses in the countries identified above.

The PAS was administered under one of three different translation-language conditions. The first category of respondents consists of those managers whose native language was English and who received the English language version of the PAS. This category of managers is designated as the *EngL-EngQ category*. The second category of respondents consists of those managers whose native language was not English, but who were bilingual and received the English version of the PAS. This category is designated as the *nonEngL-EngQ category*. The third category of respondents consists of those managers whose native language was not English and who received the PAS translated into the respective native language (Danish, Finnish, Flemish, French, Spanish, and Greek). This category of managers is designated as the *nonEngL-nonEngQ category*.

Selected demographic characteristics of the managers in each of the three categories, as well as the sizes of each group, are as shown in Table 3.3.

The PAS was translated from its English language version into the required languages by means of the partial use of a back-translation procedure advocated by Brislin (1970) for its applicability to cross-cultural research. (The Brislin paper appeared subsequent to the development of our instrument.) For each country in which the questionnaire was administered, a native of the country translated the PAS questions from the English language version into his native language. This person was instructed to concentrate on translating the meaning of the questions, rather than on a word-by-word literal translation. This translated version of the instrument was then independently translated back into English by another native of the country where the questionnaire would be administered. The two translaters were then brought together and instructed to resolve jointly any difference in the two English language versions. Finally, the questionnaire for each country was carefully reviewed by a third native of the target country who was familiar with the backgrounds of the prospective managerial respondents. Copies of the translated questionnaire are included in Appendix A.

Responses from each of the three categories of respondents were factor analyzed by use of the same procedure employed by Shure and Meeker (1967) in

TABLE 3.3 Demographic Characteristics[1]

| | Category | | |
Sample Characteristics	EngL-EngQ	NonEngL-EngQ	NonEngL-NonEngQ
Number	181	93	172
Mean age	40.0	37.0	35.3
SD	6.3	5.7	7.6
Mean number years business experience	17.1	12.7	11.4
SD	6.3	5.8	5.4
Mean number years experience in present firm	11.9	8.7	7.3
SD	7.2	5.1	5.8
Mean number years formal education beyond age 18	3.8	4.1	3.9
SD	1.8	2.0	2.6
Mean number years residence in present location	37.7	23.0	33.3
SD	10.9	15.6	10.1

[1] Bivariate subsample method used for missing data.

the original development of the PAS.[3] For each category, this involved constructing a correlation matrix for the 58 PAS item scores. The resulting matrix was then factored by use of the principal axes solution and rotated by means of a varimax program (Kaiser, 1958).[4] Although Shure and Meeker (1967) reported item loadings as low as .25, only item loadings of .4 or above are reported in our analysis, to permit clearer interpretation of the factors.

We will report the factors in order of the percentage of total variance and the percentage of total factor variance accounted for by each factor. The amount of variance explained by each of the first seven factors across the three categories is shown in Table 3.4. These data (i.e., variance explained) cannot be compared with the Shure and Meeker (1967) findings, since comparable analyses were not reported in that paper. Table 3.5 shows the number of each item loading on each of the first seven factors extracted in our analysis. This table also shows the factors across the three categories (EngL-EngQ, nonEngL-EngQ, and nonEngL-nonEngQ). Tables 3.6 through 3.9 report our first four orthogonal factors for each category along with one of the PAS factors obtained in the Shure and Meeker (1967) cross-validation factor analysis. Table 3.10 reports the next three factors

[3] The correlation matrices for the different nonEnglish forms of the questionnaire were examined and found to be generally similar. The samples completing the nonEnglish versions were combined in order to generate a sample size sufficient for factor analysis.

[4] A STATJOB FACTOR 1 program was used on a UNIVAC 1108 computer.

TABLE 3.4 Variance Analysis by Factor: Rotated Factor Matrix Category

Factor	Percent of	Category		
		EngL-EngQ	NonEngL-EngQ	NonEngL-NonEngQ
I	factor variance	13.7	13.1	9.0
	total variance	9.1	9.7	6.0
II	factor variance	8.1	7.0	8.6
	total variance	5.4	5.2	5.8
III	factor variance	6.2	6.3	5.8
	total variance	4.1	4.7	3.9
IV	factor variance	6.0	5.7	5.6
	total variance	4.0	4.2	3.8
V	factor variance	6.0	5.5	5.5
	total variance	3.9	4.1	3.7
VI	factor variance	5.1	5.1	5.4
	total variance	3.4	3.8	3.6
VII	factor variance	4.9	5.0	5.1
	total variance	3.3	3.7	3.4
Above seven	factor variance	50.0	47.7	45.0
factors	total variance	33.2	35.4	30.2

TABLE 3.5 Item Numbers by Factor and Corresponding Shure-Meeker Factor Designates[1]

Factor	Category		
	EngL-EngQ	NonEngL-EngQ	NonEngL-NonEngQ
I	[C-B] 1, 7, 13, 15, 24, 27, 29	[C-B] 1, 4, 7, 9, 15, 20. 22, 27, 28, 29 [S-T] 8, 16, 25	[R-A] 31, 32, 37, 41, 42, 44
II	[R-A] 31, 34, 37, 41 42, 44	[R-A] 31, 32, 34, 37 41, 42	[C-B] 1, 8, 9, 11, 18, 28, 29
III	[S-T] 2, 6, 8, 10	[S-T] 19 [R-A] 36, 49	[C-B] 20, 22 [S-T] 16, 25
IV	[C-B] 3, 9, 11, 18	[S-T] 2, 10, 12 [R-A] 33, 38	[R-A] 30, 33, 38
V	[R-A] 30, 33, 38	[C-B] 17 [R-A] 33, 38	[R-A] 36, 49
VI	[S-T] 16, 25 [C-B] 5	[E-I] 53, 56	[S-T] 2, 4, 14
VII	[E-I] 53, 56, 57	[E-I] 57 [S-T] 6, 8 [C-B] 3	[C-B] 5 [R-A] 40 [E-I] [C-B] 15

[1]The key to Shure-Meeker factors is as follows: [C-B] Conciliations vs. Belligerence; [R-A] Risk Taking-Risk Avoidance; [S-T] Suspiciousness vs. Trust; [E-I] External vs. Internal Control.

TABLE 3.6 Comparison of Three Language Samples and Shure-Meeker Scale: Factor 1

| | Shure-Meeker Conciliation-Belligerence | | Category | | | | | |
| | | | EngL-EngQ | | NonEngL-EngQ | | NonEngL-NonEngQ | |
Rank	Item	Loading	Item	Loading	Item	Loading	Item	Loading
1	1	-.63	29	.76	15	.85	31	.75
2	15	-.58	24	.75	7	.79	41	.75
3	7	-.56	15	.73	27	.69	32	.73
4	13	.53	28	.68	9	.63	42	.72
5	3	.50	7	.68	1	.59	37	.64
6	29	.50	27	.65	28	.56	44	.51
7	11	-.47	13	.65	24	.52		
8	17	-.46	1	.58	8	.49		
9	9	-.44			29	.48		
10	28	-.44			16	.45		
11	18	-.40			22	.44		
12	24	.38			20	.41		
13	5	.37			25	-.40		
14	27	.37						
15	22	.33						
16	26	-.29						
17	20	.28						
% factor variance	Not reported		13.7		13.1		9.0	
% total variance	Not reported		9.1		9.7		6.0	

TABLE 3.7 Comparison of Three Language Samples and Shure-Meeker Scale: Factor II

| | Shure-Meeker Risk Taking- Risk Avoidance | | Category | | | | | |
| | | | EngL-EngQ | | NonEngL-EngQ | | NonEngL-NonEngQ | |
Rank	Item	Loading	Item	Loading	Item	Loading	Item	Loading
1	44	-.60	31	.80	34	.81	28	.73
2	41	-.60	41	.75	42	.64	9	.65
3	34	-.57	37	.63	31	.58	26	.60
4	37	-.54	34	.62	37	.56	3	.59
5	42	-.51	42	.52	41	.52	11	.57
6	30	-.48	44	.45	32	.47	18	.56
7	32	-.47					29	.47
8	31	-.45					1	.45
9	45	-.44						
10	49	-.39						
11	40	-.38						
12	33	-.38						
13	36	-.37						
14	46	-.35						
15	38	-.29						
16	35	-.27						
17	48	-.22						
% factor variance	Not reported		8.1		7.0		8.6	
% total variance	Not reported		5.4		5.2		5.8	

TABLE 3.8 Comparison of Three Language Samples and Shure-Meeker Scale: Factor III

	Category							
	Shure-Meeker External vs. Internal Control		EngL-EngQ		NonEngL-EngQ		NonEngL-NonEngQ	
Rank	Item	Loading	Item	Loading	Item	Loading	Item	Loading
1	51	.67	2	.78	36	.77	25	.72
2	53	.63	8	.72	49	.77	16	.70
3	58	.68	6	.50	19	-.69	20	-.45
4	52	.58	10	.43			22	-.42
5	54	.54						
6	50	.47						
7	57	.45						
8	56	.43						
9	55	.37						
10	33	.25						
11	15	-.25						
% factor variance	Not reported		6.2		6.3		5.8	
% total variance	Not reported		4.1		4.7		3.9	

TABLE 3.9 Comparison of Three Language Samples and Shure-Meeker Scale: Factor IV

| | Shure-Meeker Suspiciousness vs. Trust | | Category | | | | | |
| | | | EngL-EngQ | | NonEngL-EngQ | | NonEngL-NonEngQ | |
Rank	Item	Loading	Item	Loading	Item	Loading	Item	Loading
1	2	.54	9	.67	2	.75	30	.77
2	12	.44	3	.64	12	.54	38	.73
3	14	.44	11	.63	10	.49	33	.69
4	4	.43	18	.44				
5	6	.43						
6	8	.41						
7	10	.40						
8	47	−.40						
9	35	−.38						
10	43	−.35						
11	19	−.35						
12	21	−.35						
13	16	.34						
14	25	.34						
15	39	−.33						
16	23	.32						
17	22	.28						
18	30	.27						
% factor variance	Not reported		6.0		5.7		5.6	
% total variance	Not reported		4.0		4.2		3.8	

TABLE 3.10 Comparison of Three Language Samples:
Factors V, VI, and VII

| | Category | | | | | |
| | EngL-EngQ | | NonEngL-EngQ | | NonEngL-NonEngQ | |
Rank	Item	Loading	Item	Loading	Item	Loading
			Factor V			
1	30	.80	33	.74	49	.86
2	33	.77	38	.73	36	.78
3	38	.72	17	.54		
% factor variance	6.0		5.5		5.5	
% total variance	3.9		4.1		3.7	
			Factor VI			
1	16	.60	53	.80	4	.76
2	5	−.57	56	.58	14	.68
3	25	.57			2	.41
% factor variance	5.1		5.1		5.4	
% total variance	3.4		3.8		3.6	
			Factor VII			
1	57	.76	57	.76	5	.77
2	53	.68	3	−.64	15	.48
3	56	.48	8	.51	40	−.40
4			6	.42		
% factor variance	4.9		5.0		5.1	
% total variance	3.3		3.7		3.4	

that emerged from our analysis. These factors appear to represent elaborations and subdivisions of the original Shure-Meeker factors.

The first seven factors that emerged from our factor analysis of the revised PAS accounted for 50.0 percent of the total factor variance and 33.2 percent of the total variance in the EngL-EngQ category (see Table 3.4). In the nonEngL-EngQ category, Factors I through VII accounted for 47.7 percent of the total factor variance and 35.4 percent of the total variance. The least amount of variance was accounted for in the nonEngL-nonEngQ category. Here the first seven factors accounted for 45.0 percent of the total factor variance and 30.2 percent of the total variance. Thus, as we move toward less similarity, in terms of language form of the PAS and native language of the sample, less variance of both types in the responses to the PAS is accounted for.

In comparing the item composition of the factor structures of the Shure-Meeker analysis with our analysis, we find that several of the Shure-Meeker factors divided into more differentiated factors (see Table 3.5). The conciliation vs. belligerence factor, for example, segmented into another factor indicative of a propensity toward helping others. Also the risk avoidance factor split into physical and monetary risk avoidance factors in each of the three categories analyzed. The suspiciousness vs. trust factor held up across all three of our categories, though a lesser number of items loaded on this factor in our analysis than in the Shure-Meeker analysis. However, the external control factor did not emerge as a distinct factor in any category. Table 3.5 indicates the items loading on each factor and the corresponding Shure-Meeker designation for each factor. Later (see Table 3.11) an attempt will be made to label these factors as derived from our analysis.

We will now analyze our results by factor and, where possible, compare them with the four factors presented by Shure and Meeker (1967).

1. Factor I. Table 3.6 shows Factor I as extracted in our analysis for each of the three categories and compares these factors with the Shure-Meeker factor of conciliation vs. belligerence.

For the EngL-EngQ category, all eight of the items (1, 7, 13, 15, 24, 27, 28, and 29) that loaded on Factor I also loaded on the Shure-Meeker conciliation vs. belligerence factor. Thus it appears that Factor I in this category refers to the dimension that Shure and Meeker have labeled "conciliation vs. belligerence". Factor I accounts for 13.7 percent of the total factor variance and 9.1 percent of the total variance of the EngL-EngQ category.

For the nonEngL-EngQ category, nine (out of 13) of the items (1, 7, 9, 15, 20, 22, 27, 28, 29) that loaded on our Factor I also loaded on the conciliation vs. belligerence factor. However, three of the items (8, 16, and 25) loading on this factor loaded on the Shure-Meeker suspiciousness vs. trust factor. Thus, factor I of the nonEngL-EngQ category, which accounts for 13.1 percent of the total factor variance and 9.7 percent of the total variance, again appears to tap the conciliation vs. belligerence dimension.

For the nonEngL-nonEngQ category, all six times (31, 32, 27, 41, 42, and 44) that loaded on Factor I also loaded on the Shure-Meeker risk avoidance factor. These items, which refer only to a physical risk concept, account for 9.0 percent of the total factor variance and 6.0 percent of the total variance of the nonEngL-nonEngQ category. Thus, when the questionnaire was translated and administered in a language other than English, the first factor to emerge from our analysis shifted. In addition, once again with the single exception of the nonEngL-EngQ, total variance and the amount of variance accounted for decreased as we move toward less similar forms of the PAS and more different samples.

2. Factor II. Table 3.7 shows Factor II as extracted from each of the three categories and compares these factors with the Shure-Meeker factor of risk avoidance.

For the EngL-EngQ category, all six of the items (31, 34, 37, 41, 42, and 44)

that loaded on Factor II also loaded on the Shure-Meeker risk factor with loadings greater than .40. The items loading on this factor are almost identical to
those that loaded on Factor I of the nonEngL-nonEngQ category. Factor II in
the EngL-EngQ category, for example, also refers to physical risk avoidance and
accounts for 8.1 percent of the total factor variance and 5.4 percent of the total
variance.

For the nonEngL-EngQ category, all six items (31, 32, 34, 37, 41, and 42)
that loaded on Factor II also loaded on the Shure-Meeker risk factor. As in the
previous category, this factor taps a physical risk avoidance dimension. Factor
II accounts for 7.0 percent of the total factor variance and 5.2 percent of the
total variance of the nonEngL-EngQ category.

As was true for Factor I, the nonEngL-nonEngQ category generated different
items loaded on Factor II. The eight items (1, 3, 9, 11, 18, 26, 28, and 29) that
loaded on Factor II of the nonEngL-nonEngQ category also loaded on the Shure-
Meeker conciliation vs. belligerence factor. However, it appears that these items
refer to helping behavior and satisfactions derived from exhibiting a helping attitude. This factor accounts for 8.6 percent of the total factor variance and 5.8
percent of the total variance of the nonEngL-nonEngQ category.

3. Factor III. Factor III as extracted in each of our categories is shown with
the Shure-Meeker external vs. internal control factor in Table 3.8. For the EngL-
EngQ category, the four items that loaded on Factor III (2, 6, 8, and 10) loaded
on the Shure-Meeker factor of suspiciousness vs. trust. Factor III of the EngL-
EngQ category accounts for 6.2 percent of the total factor variance and 4.1 percent of the total variance. For the nonEngL-EngQ category, Factor III consists
of items 36 and 49, both of which loaded on the Shure-Meeker risk avoidance
factor. In addition, item 19 from the Shure-Meeker suspiciousness vs. trust scale
also loaded on Factor III. This factor appears to be a segment of the physical
risk avoidance factor as it specifically refers to driving risk. Factor III accounts
for 6.3 percent of the total variance of the nonEngL-EngQ category. For the
nonEngL-nonEngQ category, Factor III is composed of items 20, 22, and 25
which loaded on the Shure-Meeker conciliation vs. belligerence factor. However,
item 16 loaded on the Shure-Meeker suspiciousness vs. trust factor. Factor III,
suspiciousness vs. trust, accounts for 5.8 percent of the total factor variance and
3.9 percent of the total variance of the nonEngL-nonEngQ category.

Clearly, Factor III is not easily interpretable in terms of the original Shure-
Meeker factor structures. It clearly does not fit the label "external vs. internal
control." Furthermore, there is no overlap in the items loaded across the three
categories. Thus, the external-internal control factor does not appear to hold up
across language differentials in the PAS format.

4. Factor IV. For each of the three categories, Factor IV and the Shure-
Meeker suspiciousness-trust factor are shown in Table 3.9.

For the EngL-EngQ category, items 3, 9, 11, and 28 loaded on Factor IV and also loaded on the Shure-Meeker conciliation vs. belligerence factor. As with Factor III of the nonEngL-nonEngQ category, this factor indicates a helping dimension. Factor IV accounts for 6.0 percent of the total factor variance and 4.0 percent of the total variance of the EngL-EngQ category. For the nonEngL-EngQ category, items 2, 10, and 12 loaded on Factor IV and were from the Shure-Meeker suspiciousness vs. trust factor. Factor IV, suspiciousness vs. trust, accounts for 5.7 percent of the total factor variance and 4.2 percent of the total variance of the nonEngL-EngQ category. For the nonEngL-nonEngQ category, items 30, 33, and 38 loaded on Factor IV; these items also loaded on the Shure-Meeker risk avoidance factor. However, these three items refer only to monetary risk rather than the general risk taking and risk avoidance factor. Factor IV accounts for 5.6 percent of the total factor variance and 3.8 percent of the total variance of the nonEngL-nonEngQ category. Again there appears to be considerable sample variability in the order of factor emergence and no overlap in the items across the three categories. Only the nonEngL-nonEngQ category appears similar to the original Shure-Meeker suspiciousness-trust factor.

5. Factor V. For the EngL-EngQ category, items 30, 33, and 38 loaded on Factor V (see Table 3.10). This is the same composition as Factor IV of the nonEngL-nonEngQ category as shown in Table 3.7. Factor V, monetary risk avoidance, accounts for 6.0 percent of the total factor variance and 3.9 percent of the total variance of the EngL-EngQ category.

For the nonEngL-EngQ category, items 17, 33, and 38 loaded on Factor V. Of these, items 33 and 38 are from the Shure-Meeker risk avoidance factor, and item 17 from the conciliation vs. belligerence factor. It appears that Factor V of this category measures primarily a *monetary risk taking-risk avoidance dimension.* This factor accounts for 5.5 percent of the total factor variance and 4.1 percent of the total variance on the nonEngL-EngQ category.

For the nonEngL-nonEngQ category, items 36 and 49 of the Shure-Meeker risk avoidance factor loaded on Factor V. As with Factor III of the nonEngL-EngQ category (see Table 3.8), this factor assesses a *physical risk avoidance* dimension, since both items refer to fast driving. This factor accounts for 5.5 percent of the total factor variance and 3.7 percent of the total variance of the nonEngL-nonEngQ category.

6. Factor VI. For the EngL-EngQ category, items 5, 16, and 25 loaded on Factor VI, as shown in Table 3.10. Items 16 and 25 are from the Shure-Meeker suspiciousness vs. trust factor, and item 5 is from the conciliation vs. belligerence factor. Factor VI appears to tap a *propensity for confrontation.* This factor accounts for 5.1 percent of the total factor variance and 3.4 percent of the total variance of the nonEngL-nonEngQ category.

For the nonEngL-EngQ category, items 53 and 56 from the Shure-Meeker external vs. internal control factor loaded on Factor VI. This factor accounts for 5.1 percent of the total factor variance and 3.8 percent of the total variance in the nonEngL-EngQ category.

For the nonEngL-nonEngQ category, items 2, 4, and 14 loaded on Factor VI, and were from the suspiciousness vs. trust factor. Factor VI, suspiciousness vs. trust, accounts for 5.4 percent of the total factor variance and 3.6 percent of the total variance of the nonEngL-nonEngQ category.

7. Factor VII. Factor VII as extracted in each of the three categories is shown in Table 3.10. Items 53, 56, and 57 from the Shure-Meeker external vs. internal control factor loaded on Factor VII of the EngL-EngQ category. This factor accounts for 4.9 percent of the total factor variance and 3.3 percent of the total variance of this category.

For the nonEngL-EngQ category, four items from three different Shure-Meeker factors loaded on Factor VII. Item 57 is from the Shure-Meeker external vs. internal control factor; items 6 and 8 are from the suspiciousness vs. trust factor; and item 3 is from the conciliation vs. belligerence factor. Factor VII of the nonEngL-EngQ category accounts for 5.0 percent of the total factor variance and 3.7 percent of the total variance. For this category, Factor VII is clearly not interpretable.

For the nonEngL-nonEngQ category, items 5, 15, and 40 loaded on Factor VII. Item 5 is from the Shure-Meeker conciliation vs. belligerence factor; item 15 is from the external vs internal control factor; and item 40 is from the risk avoidance factor. Factor VII accounts for 5.1 percent of the total factor variance and 3.4 percent of the total variance of the nonEngL-nonEngQ category. Again, Factor VII does not appear to be interpretable.

Discussion. Table 3.11 compares the seven emergent factors across the three language classifications. The results are only partially supportive of the generality of the Shure-Meeker PAS instrument. In each of the three classifications, conciliation vs. belligerence, risk taking vs. risk avoidance, and suspiciousness vs. trust emerged as identifiable factors.

However, certain important differences do emerge when these results are compared to the Shure-Meeker 1967 extraction. First, the internal-external control factor did not emerge in any of the samples, with the exception of the weak emergence as Factor VII in the EngL-EngQ category. Second, in each sample, the risk taking-risk averting factor differentiated into two components; namely, physical risk taking and monetary risk taking, and in each case the physical risk taking factor emerged prior to the monetary risk taking factor. This breakdown of the risk factor into subfactors seems to parallel the earlier results of Thurstone (1951) and Guilford *et al.* (1953) in the construction of the scale used by Shure and Meeker in their original work. Third, if one examines only the first three fac-

TABLE 3.11   PAS Factors Across Three Language Groupings

	Category		
Factor	EngL-EngQ	NonEngL-EngQ	NonEngL-NonEngQ
I	Conciliation vs. belligerence	Conciliation vs. belligerence	Physical risk taking
II	Physical risk taking	Physical risk taking	Helping
III	Suspiciousness vs. trust	Driving fast	Conciliation vs. belligerence
IV	Helping	Suspiciousness vs. trust	Monetary risk taking
V	Monetary risk taking	Monetary risk taking	Driving fast
VI	Confrontation	Job order giving	Suspiciousness vs. trust
VII	Job order giving	Not interpretable	Not interpretable

tors, it is only with the EngL-EngQ sample that the three Shure-Meeker factors (conciliation-belligerence, risk taking, and suspiciousness-trust) emerged. Thus the order of factor emergence was similar to that of Shure and Meeker only in the grouping where both native language and questionnaire were English. Four factors must be considered in order to pick up each of the three Shure-Meeker factors in the nonEngL-EngQ sample, while six factors are necessary in the nonEngL-nonEngQ sample. Thus, as we move toward more dissimilar conditions (in terms of the native language of the respondents and the language version of the questionnaire), the factor structure of the PAS increases in dissimilarity compared to the original Shure-Meeker instrument.

In general, the results reported here are mildly encouraging regarding the cross-cultural use (with the associated language differences) of the Shure-Meeker PAS instrument. The differences between the original PAS and the version reported here are largely ones of differentiation within the original factor structure. The risk taking-risk aversion factor consistently split into physical and monetary components. In two of the three samples, a factor labeled "helping" emerged as a differentiation of the original conciliation-belligerence scale.

Thus, three of four scales originally identified by Shure and Meeker emerged in each of the three subgroups; the three scales were measures of conciliation-belligerence, risk taking-risk avoidance, and suspiciousness-trust. The order in which the factors emerged differed across the subgroups. In addition, the risk taking-risk avoidance factor, as well as the conciliation-belligerence factor, segmented into subcomponents.

Cross Employment Sector Study

Our second factor study examined the structure of the PAS in two United States samples differing in the sector of their primary employment and career.

The adapted PAS was completed by 51 male executives in advanced management courses at Indiana University and Harvard University. The military officer group was composed of 66 majors and colonels attending courses at the Industrial College of the Armed Forces. These military officers held comparable administrative positions, in terms of organizational rank, to their private sector executive counterparts.

The relative equivalence of the military and private groups should be noted. The average age of the military officers was 44.5 years, and that of the private executives was 44.8 years. The average number of years experience in the military was 22.3 years, and the average number of years experience in business for the private executives was 20.1 years. The military officers averaged 5.5 years of formal education beyond age 18, while the private executives averaged 3.9 years.

The military and private executive groups were factor analyzed separately with the results presented in Table 3.12. The factor analytic procedure used for the 58 item PAS was equivalent to that used in the Shure-Meeker (1967) PAS cross-validation studies and the analysis reported in the previous section.

Table 3.13 presents a summary of the interpretations of the seven factors which, after extraction and rotation, were interpretable for either one or both samples.

Interpretation of Factors. The first factor extracted is interpreted as a conciliation versus belligerence factor in both the military and private executive groups and is principally defined by loadings of the PAS conciliation-belligerence items and on several suspiciousness-trust items (items 25, 8, and 12 for the military, and 16, 25, and 12 for the private executives).

The second factor is interpreted differently for the military officers and the private executives. For the military group, this factor is interpreted as being subject to fate in a passive manner or taking chances in a passive fate sense and is defined by loadings of the PAS risk-taking items 44 and 45, the internal-external control items 56, 55, and 58, and the suspiciousness-trust item 43. For the private executives, Factor II is interpreted as a risk-taking factor also, but it refers to the taking of risks involving an element of personal danger. The factor is defined by loadings of the PAS risk-taking items 31, 37, 41, 42, and 34.

The third factor extracted is also interpreted differently between the two groups. For the military group, this factor refers to the taking of risks involving an element of personal danger. It is essentially the same factor as Factor II for the private executive group and is defined by loadings of the PAS items 31, 41, 37, 32, 34, and 42. The third factor for the private executives is interpreted as conciliation-belligerence in relation to competitive and helping situations and is defined by loadings of the PAS conciliation-belligerence items 3, 9, 18, and 11, and the suspiciousness-trust item 19.

The fourth factor for the military group is interpreted as a risk-taking factor but specific to risks involving monetary stakes. This factor is defined by loadings of the PAS risk-taking items 30, 38, and 33. For the private executives, Factor

TABLE 3.12 Item Loadings and Rank by Factor and Group (Military and Private Executive)

	Factor I				Factor II				Factor III			
	Military		Private		Military		Private		Military		Private	
Rank	Item	Loading	Item	Loading	Item	Loading	Item	Loading	Item	Loading	Item	Loading
1	15	.87	27	.88	44	.78	31	.84	31	.80	3	.83
2	7	.85	29	.88	56	−.78	37	.77	41	.78	9	.82
3	29	.81	15	.87	55	−.71	41	.73	37	.67	18	.63
4	27	.80	7	.84	58	.65	42	.66	32	.65	11	.58
5	1	.76	13	.80	45	.58	34	.60	34	.62	19	.48
6	24	.75	17	.80	43	−.57			42	.58		
7	28	.75	24	.79								
8	17	.73	28	.75								
9	25	−.67	22	.69								
10	20	.60	1	.67								
11	5	.58	5	.63								
12	22	.56	16	−.61								
13	8	.50	25	−.51								
14	11	.49	18	.48								
15	13	.49	11	.47								
16	12	−.48	12	−.40								
% total factor variance[1]	19.0		19.7		8.9		6.9		7.8		6.3	
% total variance[2]	15.0		16.4		7.0		5.7		6.2		5.2	

[1] Sum of total factor variance for military sample = 56.2%; for private sample = 52.8%.
[2] Sum of total variance for military sample = 44.3%; for private sample = 43.9%.

TABLE 3.12 Continued

	Factor IV				Factor V				Factor VI				Factor VII			
	Military		Private		Military		Private		Military		Private		Military		Private	
Rank	Item	Loading	Item	Loading	Item	Loading	Item	Loading	Item	Loading	Item	Loading	Item	Loading	Item	Loading
1	30	.84	58	.86	36	.63	47	.87	14	.74	35	.76	47	.82	20	.72
2	38	.71	39	-.76	37	.42	2	.58	13	.68	32	.71	35	.66	56	-.67
3	33	.70					14	.49	16	-.47	55	.64	39	.55	26	-.60
4							8	.45							8	.42
5							6	.43								
6																
7																
8																
9																
10																
11																
12																
13																
14																
15																
16																
% total factor variance[1]	5.6		5.1		5.4		5.0		4.8		4.9		4.7		4.9	
% total variance[2]	4.4		4.3		4.2		4.1		3.8		4.1		3.7		4.1	

[1] Sum of total factor variance for military sample = 56.2%; for private sample = 52.8%.
[2] Sum of total variance for military sample = 44.3%; for private sample = 43.9%.

TABLE 3.13   Interpretations of the Factor Composition Based on Item Content

Factor	Military sample	Private executive sample
I	Conciliation-belligerence	Conciliation-belligerence
II	Refers to being subject to fate in a passive manner; taking chances in a passive fate sense	Taking risks involving an element of personal danger
III	Taking risks involving an element of personal danger	Conciliation-belligerence in relation to competition and helping
IV	Taking risks involving money, "gambling"	Not interpretable
V	Taking risks involving a car, speed; "Dragster Factor"	Suspiciousness-trust in interpersonal judgments
VI	Mercenary, hostility in interpersonal relations	Not interpretable
VII	Suspiciousness-trust relating to personal emotions; "moods"	Not interpretable

IV is not interpretable and only consists of loadings of the PAS internal-external control item 58 and the suspiciousness-trust item 39.

The fifth factor differentiated between the military officers and private executive groups. For the military officers, this factor is interpreted as taking risks involving speed with a vehicle and is defined by loadings of the PAS items 36 and 37. The fifth factor for the private executives is interpreted as suspiciousness-trust in interpersonal judgments and is defined by loadings of the items 47, 2, 14, 8, and 6.

The sixth factor for the military officer group is interpreted as mercenary, hostile interpersonal relations and is defined by loadings of the PAS suspiciousness-trust items 14 and 16 and the conciliation-belligerence item 13. For the private executives, this factor is not interpretable and consists of loadings of the PAS suspiciousness-trust item 35, risk-taking item 32, and internal-external control item 55.

The seventh factor is interpreted for the military officers as a suspiciousness-trust dimension relating to personal emotions or moods. This factor is defined by loadings of the PAS suspiciousness-trust items 47, 35, and 39. The seventh factor is not interpretable for the private executive group and consists of loadings of the PAS conciliation-belligerence items 20 and 26, internal-external control item 56, and the suspiciousness-trust item 8.

From this factor analysis of the military officer group and the private sector executive group, we see that the first factor is virtually identical in both groups. The conciliation-belligerence dimension accounts for a large proportion of the variance in these two groups. However, on the other factors, the military officers appear to manifest a different structural profile from that of the private executives. The military structure consists of dimensions of passive subjection to fate, three forms of risk taking, hostility in interpresonal relations, and moods of suspiciousness-trust. For the military officer group, risk avoidance versus risk taking is differentiated into risks involving personal danger, monetary stakes, and vehicular speed. The private executives' structure contains only a risk-avoidance versus risk-taking factor involving an element of personal danger. The other two factors that are interpreted for the private executives are conciliation versus belligerence in relation to competition and helping situations, and the factor of suspiciousness versus trust in interpersonal judgments.

What can we conclude concerning the factor similarity of personality in the two samples as assessed by the PAS? Two specific questions can be asked in this regard. First, which of the original four PAS scales as extracted by Shure and Meeker (1967) emerged in these samples? Second, what specific differences are evident between the two samples?

The *conciliation-belligerence* scale emerged in both samples and in both cases emerged first after rotation, thus accounting for the greatest amount of factor and total variance. This scale and the underlying personality construct appear to be similar and stable across the two samples. The *suspiciousness-trust* scale emerged in both samples but with slightly different item compositions. In the military sample the scale seems to be specific to mercenary hostility and to a general emotion tone or "mood" in interpersonal relations. In the private executive sample, the scale emerges in a less specific form with an item composition similar to the original Shure-Meeker PAS scale. The *risk taking-risk avoidance* scale emerges in both samples. However, this personality characteristic is more differentiated in the military than in the private sample. Risk taking in the private sample is focused, as an identifiable factor, on physical danger involving risk to physical well being. The *internal-external control* scale emerges only in the military sample. It does not emerge as an identifiable characteristic of the private executive sample.

In general, more interpretable factors are identifiable for the military officers than the private executives. In addition, there exists greater subfactoring or differentiation within the military sample.

Congruence among Factors. In the comparison of the factor structures obtained from the military and private executive samples, it is of interest to note the degree of statistical congruence between the respective factors. Since the same variables are used in both factor analyses, it is possible to determine the degree of agreement between like factors in each sample. This is accomplished by use of the factor weights to determine the coefficient of congruence between any two factors (Harmon, 1967, p. 270). This index takes the summations of the factor weights over the number of variables, given different samples, to yield a measure of agreement between factors. The coefficient of congruence can range from +1 in the case of perfect agreement, to zero when there is no agreement, to −1 in the case of perfect inverse agreement.

In this study we computed the coefficients of congruence for the first seven factors of each sample, respectively. As shown in Table 3.14 each of the seven factors from the military sample is compared with all of the factors from the private executive sample.

From the coefficient of congruence matrix, we see that Factor III of the military sample and Factor II of the private executive sample have the highest degree of agreement (Φ = .866). These two factors were previously defined by their loadings to be concerned with taking risks involving an element of personal danger. The next highest degree of agreement between factors is between Factor I of the military sample and Factor I of the private executive sample (Φ = .849). Both of these factors were defined by loadings on approximately the same items from the conciliation-belligerence and suspiciousness-trust scales of the PAS.

The seventh factor of the military sample and the sixth factor of the private executive sample have a moderate degree of agreement (Φ = .551) which is apparently due to the high loading of item 35 on both factors. Also the sixth factor of the military sample and the first factor of the private executive sample have a moderate degree of agreement (Φ = .416). As previously shown, both of these factors were defined by PAS conciliation-belligerence items.

Discussion. These results suggest moderate optimism regarding the factor similarity of personality across the military and private executive samples studied. Of course this conclusion is limited in generality to the constructs assessed by the Shure-Meeker PAS.

These results, however, when coupled with those reported earlier in this chapter, suggest caution when interpreting across samples in personality and attitudinal studies, since the number of interpretable factors, the content of factors, and the degree of differentiation within factors all differed slightly across samples. At the very least, these findings suggest that researchers should report the factor structure of their instruments on the samples studied when comparing attitudinal responses and personality profiles across heterogeneous samples.

TABLE 3.14   Coefficient of Congruence Matrix

Factors I to VII from private executive sample	Factors I to VII from military sample						
	I	II	III	IV	V	VI	VII
I	.85	−.01	.09	.04	.09	.42	−.11
II	.09	.40	.87	.04	.32	−.07	−.16
III	.34	−.18	.10	−.10	−.13	.11	−.07
IV	.09	.10	.08	.01	.11	−.05	−.28
V	.02	−.05	−.09	.05	.01	.25	.36
VI	−.07	−.08	.08	.01	−.04	.10	.55
VII	.20	.29	.04	.05	.10	.06	−.13

4

SIMILARITIES AND DIFFERENCES: CLUSTERS OF PERSONALITY

We know very little concerning differences in attitudes and personalities of managers which might be attributed to their national and cultural identities. While there have only been a few studies published on this topic, it is important to place our findings within the context of previous work.

Hall, de Bettignies, and Amado-Fischgrund (1969) have reported a study which describes differences among business managers from six European countries on a number of different variables. In that study, data are reported on the time taken to reach a top management position, the number of years of experience in various business functions, and the functional exposure thought to be most useful in the careers of these business managers. In addition, summary data are presented on the birthplace, age, social class, educational background, compensation, international business travel, and language skills of the 576 executive respondents. Their study did not investigate attitudinal or personality differences among the managers. An earlier study which did report differences in attitudes was conducted by Haire, Ghiselli, and Porter (1966). These researchers examined differences in attitudes about desirable leadership styles, appropriate definitions of the managerial role, and need satisfaction (motivation) by means of a questionnaire responded to by 3,641 managers from 14 countries in Europe, North America, South America, and Asia. These investigators found that the nationality of the managers accounted for 28 percent of the variation in answers to the questionnaire, with 72 percent of the variation being attributable to the differences among managers within a country. However, the countries tended to cluster together into cultural groups, with relatively large differences between the groups. Five clusters were identified: (1) the Nordic-European countries (Norway, Denmark, Sweden, and Germany); (2) the Latin-European countries (France, Spain, Italy, and Belgium); (3) the Anglo-American pair (England and the United States); (4) the developing countries (Argentina, Chile, and India); and (5) Japan (a separate category according to Haire, Ghiselli, and Porter). The results indicated a discrepancy between belief in an individual's capacity for leadership and initiative and attitudes about methods of leadership. Generally, across countries, managers indicated approval of participative management styles. Simultaneously, however, these same managers expressed little faith in the capacity of their subordinates for initiative and leadership.

More recently, Clark and McCabe (1970) used the basic questionnaire developed by Haire and his associates to examine the attitudes of Australian managers towards leadership. Their study indicated that the managers believed in participative management but had little faith in the capabilities of others. These findings are consistent with those of the Haire study. In addition, the Australian sample showed a configuration of managerial beliefs which was closer to the Anglo-American cluster than to any other.

Ajiferuke and Boddewyn (1970) have emphasized not only the small number of studies describing nationality and cultural differences in managerial personality but the absence, in 1970, of investigations examining the influence of culture and industrialization on managerial attitudes. Since the Ajiferuke and Boddewyn review, one study has been reported that is directed toward this issue. Cummings and Schmidt (1972) examined the relative influence of cultural background and degree of industrialization on the managerial beliefs of a sample of Greeks. The Greeks were as inconsistent as the managers studied by Haire, Ghiselli, and Porter (1966) and Clark and McCabe (1970). They displayed little belief in their subordinates' capacities for leadership and initiative while advocating the practice of participative management. On two beliefs (capacity for leadership and initiative and belief in internal control) the Greeks tended to cluster with a Latin-European cluster thereby suggesting a cultural explanation. On the other hand, regarding beliefs in sharing information with subordinates and participative management the Greeks clustered with the developing countries (Argentina, Chile, and India), thereby suggesting an industrialization explanation. Clearly, exclusive focus on either explanation is not warranted.

With this backdrop of the relatively little available knowledge, we now turn to the presentation of our findings on managerial personality. Our results will be presented under four general headings, each reflecting an important possible determinant of managerial personality differences. First, and most heavily, we will emphasize the role of *nationality* as a correlate of personality. Second, we will examine the data from two countries more intensely in an attempt to discover *within nationality* differences in personality. Third, data will be presented describing *employment sector* (private vs. public) differences in managerial personality

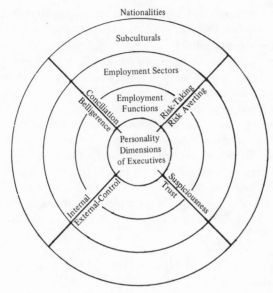

Figure 4.1

within two nationality samples. Finally, we will explore our data across national-ities for possible *employment function* (marketing, finance, etc.) differences in personality.

In each of these four cases, we will be examining variations in the four adapted PAS scales (see Chapter 3) across the indicated categorization of the managers. Figure 4.1 presents the general schema of the analysis and presentation of findings.

NATIONALITY AND PERSONALITY[1]

As cross-national contact among managers increases with the growing interde-pendence of corporate affairs, interpersonal behavior between executives of dif-ferent countries will play an increasing role in determining business effectiveness. As the trend toward multinationalism continues, it is crucial to improve our knowledge about the possible determinants of cultural differences in such behav-ior. We argue that one of these determinants is the basic attitudinal orientation of the executives toward others with whom they interact. Thus, this Chapter re-ports data on managers from eight geographical regions on the following four personality variables: (1) general tendency toward conciliation or belligerence in interpersonal situations, (2) tendency toward risk-avoidance or risk-taking, (3) belief in fate (external control of events) or self-determination (internal control),

[1] This section, and those to follow in this chapter, represent an extension and elabora-tion of partial results reported earlier in Cummings, Harnett, and Stevens (1971).

and (4) tendency toward suspiciousness or trust. These particular dimensions of personality are thought to be especially important in influencing *interpersonal behavior* in the managerial setting.

The purpose of this section is to describe the findings of a study designed to investigate the similarities and differences, on four dimensions of attitude, among managers from a variety of different countries. This study should not be interpreted as representing a complete description of the personalities of the managers studied. Nor do we claim that the men studied are representative of the total populations of the countries from which they come, or representative of all businessmen in their respective countries. We also caution that it is most important that the findings reported here should not be interpreted as favorable or unfavorable toward any particular national group, as we do not wish to convey value judgments through our findings. Rather, this study should be interpreted as an empirical description of selected attitudinal differences among the managers studied.

Sample and Research Method

Each of the executives included in this study were either presently or recently in an executive development course. In each case, the researchers collected the data to be reported by means of a questionnaire administered in conjunction with each program. The executives can be characterized as middle- and top-level managers in private business enterprises. Selected demographic characteristics of the executives are presented in Table 4.1.

A 58-item questionnaire adapted from the Personality Attitude Schedule (PAS) developed by Shure and Meeker was used to assess the attitudes of the managers (Shure and Meeker, 1967, pp. 233-252). The development and content

TABLE 4.1   Demographic Characteristics

Region	Number	Mean Age	Mean Number of Years of Formal Education Beyond Age 18	Mean Number of Years of Business Experience
Central Europe[a]	192	39.8	3.5	17.0
Greece	28	41.4	2.5	15.0
Japan	50	–	–	–
Scandinavia[b]	84	39.4	3.9	15.9
South Africa	264	31.2	3.9	8.9
Spain	124	35.0	3.8	11.1
Thailand	26	38.5	4.8	15.0
United States	23	42.3	4.0	16.8

[a]Includes executives from Belgium, France, Switzerland, and England.
[b]Includes executives from Denmark and Finland.

of the PAS adaptation used in our research was described in Chapter 3. This adaptation measures four dimensions of personality by means of 7-point and 3-point scales, as well as through forced-choice questions. As noted in Chapter 3, the four dimensions are:

1) conciliation vs. belligerence in interpersonal relations
2) risk avoidance vs. risk taking
3) external vs. internal control and
4) suspiciousness vs. trust.

As noted in Chapter 3, the questionnaire was translated from English into the relevant languages by the following procedure. A native of each country translated the questions from English into his native language, eliminating any completely irrelevant or meaningless questions. This translated version was then retranslated into English by an independent translator (again a native of the country in question). The two translators then discussed any differences in the two English versions, either agreeing on necessary changes or eliminating the question. Subsequent to this two-way translation, the questionnaire was adapted for local usage and carefully checked by a third native of the country who was intimately familiar with the backgrounds of the executives in question.

Findings

In general, rankings of the nationality groupings are not consistent across the four attitudinal scales; that is, the relationship of one nationality group to the others appears to be dependent on which attitude dimension is under consideration. For this reason, our discussion of the differences among regional groups will focus on each dimension separately.

Conciliation-Belligerence. The mean scores for the regional groups of managers on the conciliation-belligerence scale are shown in Figure 4.2. Notice that the average score for all regional groups falls above the midpoint (28) of the conciliation-belligerence scale. Hence, the average attitude in each case can be characterized as predominantly conciliatory rather than belligerent. Among the groups observed, the Spanish executives were the most conciliatory (58.0), while the South Africans were the most belligerent on the average (45.1).

It is important to recognize the fact that the average scores for a number of the nations shown in Figure 4.2 cluster too closely together for one to have much confidence that the differences in average scores reflect any real difference in conciliation. The Spanish and Greek managers form such a cluster, as do the Scandinavian, Central European, and Thai managers. On the other hand, a difference as large as that between the managers from Greece and Central Europe would occur, by chance, less than one time in ten, while a difference as large as

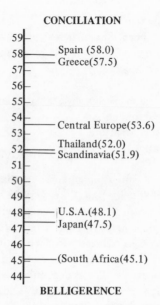

Figure 4.2   Conciliation-Belligerence Scale with a possible range of scores from –23 to 79.

that between Spain and the United States would occur less than once every 500 times by chance when there is no real difference between these managers.[2]

Risk-Aversion vs. Risk-Taking.   Figure 4.3 presents the average scores for the risk-aversion, risk-taking dimension. On this scale, the mean scores of all but one of the nationalities fall on the risk-aversion side of the scale's midpoint (32). The United States group (31.9) falls only slightly below the midpoint. While the Americans exhibited the highest tendency toward risk-taking, the Thai executives, as a group, were the most risk-averse.

Again, some of the differences among the average scores of the nationalities can be attributed to chance, while some indicate real differences in attitude toward risk. The difference between the Scandinavian, the Central European, and the Greek managers, for instance, is too small to justify a distinction of this scale. However, the difference between the Spanish and the Greek managers is large enough so that it could be expected to occur by chance less than one time in fifty if there was no real difference between these managers.

External Control vs. Internal Control.   The scores on generalized belief in fate or environmental determination vs. self-determination of events are presented in Figure 4.4. Note that average scores for all nationality groups, except two, were

[2]The statistical significance of the difference between the mean scores of the regions was computed throughout this section by using a two-sample t test.

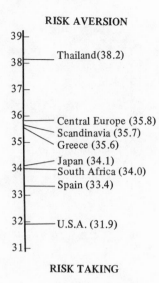

Figure 4.3 Risk-Aversion/Risk-Taking Scale with a possible range of scores of 16 to 48.

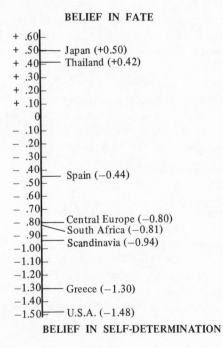

Figure 4.4 External vs. Internal Control Scale with a possible range of scores of –3 to 6.

SUSPICIOUSNESS

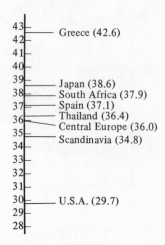

TRUST

Figure 4.5 Suspiciousness-Trust Scale with a possible range of scores from −12 to 76.

negative. This indicates a general tendency toward belief in self-determination. However, both the Japanese and Thai executives reported significantly different beliefs in the direction of belief in external determination or fate. This difference is, no doubt, heavily influenced by the differences in religious orientations between these two countries and the remainder of our samples (nonChristian vs. Christian). The United States managers recorded the most extreme belief in internal control (− 1.48).

A difference as large as that found between the score of the Spanish managers and the score of the managers from Central Europe would be expected to occur, by chance, less than 4 percent of the time if these managers had the same attitude, on the average. The difference between the scores of the Spanish and American managers would be expected to occur, by chance, less than one time in 500.

Suspiciousness vs. Trust. The scores of the managers on the suspiciousness-trust scale are shown in Figure 4.5. All but one of the nationality groupings fall on the suspiciousness side of the midpoint (32.0), the United States managers (29.7) being the only one below this point. The most suspicious group was the Greek managers, who had an average score of 42.6. A difference as large as that between Greece and Spain, or between Central Europe and the United States, would occur, by chance, less than one time in 50 if there were no real difference in their scores.

An Overview of Nationality Differences. In general, we found considerably more of the variability in our data attributable to individual differences than did

Haire, Ghiselli, and Porter (1966). While they report finding 72 percent of the difference in their scores attributable to individual differences within a nation, we found that on all four of our scales, the comparable percentage was 95 percent or more. This means that only about 5 percent of the variability in our observed scores was due to differences attributable to the fact that our managers came from the different nations. However, we hasten to add, that in all cases the percent of variability attributable to nationality differences is significantly different from zero at the $a = 0.05$ level.[3]

There are several interesting points to be noted when one examines Figures 4.2, 4.3, 4.4, and 4.5 in perspective. First, the United States managers had the lowest score on three of the four scales, and in each of these cases the mean score of the United States managers was considerably below the next highest ranking region. Thus, managers from the United States were, on the average, the most risk-taking, the most trusting of all nationality groups, and they also believed the most in internal control. Contrary to what might be one's *a priori* guess, the average score of the United States managers did not once fall adjacent to the Central European scores. Spanish managers scored highest on one of the four scales, having the most conciliatory attitude.

It is also interesting to note that on all four scales the nationalities seem to divide themselves into three sets of roughly comparable scores. On the conciliation-belligerence scale, for example, the scores of the Spanish and Greek managers are grouped together at the top of Fig. 4.2; Central Europe, Scandinavia, and Thailand comprise a second group in the middle of the scale; with the United States, Japanese, and South African managers forming a third group. On the risk scale, Central Europe, Scandinavia, and Greece seem to form a single group, with Thailand and the United States providing the psychological anchors for this scale. There are similar groupings for the control scale [(a) Japan and Thailand, (b) Central Europe, South Africa, and (c) Greece and the United States] and for the suspiciousness-trust scale [(a) Greece, (b) Japan, South Africa, Spain, Thailand, Central Europe, and Scandinavia, and (c) the United States].

Since we have indicated that differences among individuals account for approximately 95 percent of the variability in our data, one might ask whether the within-nationality variability differs from region to region. The Scandinavian and Central European groupings, for example, might be expected to contain more differences of opinion among the managers tested since these are the only two groupings consisting of more than one country. However, somewhat the opposite is true because on two of the four scales, Central Europe had the *lowest* within-region variability, and on the other two scales this group was in the middle on variability. Scandinavian managers also ranked in the lower half of the eight groups

[3]The percent and significance levels for the variabilities reported in this chapter were calculated using a one-factor analysis of variance. In this procedure, two measures of variability are calculated: (1) a within-nationality variability which measures the differences between individuals within a nationality, and (2) a between-nationality variability which measures the differences between the nationalities.

on all scales in their diversity of attitudes. The only nation with a consistently high variability of attitude was Greece, which had the highest within-nation variability on three scales and the second highest variability on the other. The United States managers showed the *largest* variability of attitude on conciliation-belligerence, and the *lowest* variability on the control scale.

Thus, we see that the degree of similarity or dissimilarity both among and within groupings seems to be dependent on the attitude under consideration, and that nationality differences appear to be only one, but perhaps the most important, determinant of differences in attitudes. This finding reinforces our previous conclusion as to the complexity of nationality differences and reemphasizes the need for caution in generalizing about such differences or even generalizing about the uniformity or diversity within any single group of executives. If we hope to understand such national differences and use this understanding to manage more effectively, then there must be continued research on the attitudes and behaviors of executives from diverse backgrounds and cultures. We begin this process by investigating several additional possible determinants of attitudinal differences; namely, differences within national groupings, across employment sectors, and across employment functions.

WITHIN NATIONALITY DIFFERENCES

We change our focus in this section to draw attention to the differences within two nationality groups, as opposed to differences between nationalities. Recall that in our overview of nationality differences we have indicated that there are differences in the variability within regions, and that this variability appears to depend on the attitude under consideration. To proceed one step further in this analysis, we present data which may be helpful in investigating whether these attitudinal differences are attributable to the subculture of the managers *within* a given country. These data concern Spanish and South African managers.

In Spain our questionnaire was administered to a total of 124 managers participating in executive development programs in three different subregions of Spain. The samples consist of 48 managers in Barcelona, 44 managers in Madrid, and 32 managers from Southern Spain (Alicante and Cordoba).

Our findings indicate a remarkable consistency to the mean scores across the three subregions of Spain in terms of their relationship to the other countries studied. On the conciliation-belligerence scale, for example, *all three* subregions of Spain fall in the same upper (i.e., highly conciliatory) portion of the scale used to indicate the differences among our national groups (Figure 4.2). Managers from Madrid were the most conciliatory (59.5), followed by the managers from Barcelona (57.6) and those from Southern Spain (56.6). From a statistical point of view, the differences between subregions is not large enough to be attributable to anything but random deviations.

TABLE 4.2   Attitudinal Differences Within Spain

	Con-Bel	Risk	Control	Sus-Trust
Madrid (n = 44)	59.5	33.7	−.23	34.7
Barcelona (n = 48)	57.6	32.1	−.56	37.0
Southern Spain (n = 32)	56.6	35.4	−.53	39.0

Risk differences among managers within Spain have the largest variability of the four scales, although all three subregional scores fall in the middle section of Figure 4.3. The most risk-taking attitude was among the managers from Barcelona (32.1), followed by the Madrid managers (33.3) and the managers from Southern Spain (35.4). The variability attributed to subnational differences, 5.9 percent, is large enough to conclude that there is a subnational influence on the risk-taking, risk-avoiding attitude.[4]

On the external-internal control scale, the three subnational groups from Spain again all fall in the same (upper) portion of the scale (i.e., a high belief in fate). All three scores would fall adjacent to one another if placed on our graph of the five regional groups (Figure 4.4). The Madrid managers had the highest average score in the direction of external control (− 0.23), followed by the Southern Spain managers (− 0.53) and the managers from Barcelona (− 0.56). The percent of variability attributable to subnational differences in this case does not differ significantly from zero.

The average suspiciousness-trust scores from the three Spanish subregions are all centered in the middle of the range of values shown in Figure 4.5, the highest (most suspicious) being the Southern Spanish managers (39.0), followed by the managers from Barcelona (37.0) and the Madrid managers (34.7). The differences among these subnational scores accounts for only about 3 percent of the total variability in scores.

In summary, we see in Table 4.2 that only on the risk dimenson of attitude did subnational differences account for a significant proportion of the variability of the scores within Spain. Thus, the variance within Spain cannot, in general, be attributed to differences in the attitudes of managers from different geographical regions within the country. On three of the four scales, Spain presents a relatively unified picture compared with intercountry differences.

In South Africa our questionnaire was administered to a total of 264 white executives from two subcultures, English and Afrikaan.[5] White South African executives tend to have been socialized in these two subcultures which are quite

---

[4] As was the case in our earlier national analysis, an analysis of variance was conducted to determine the percent of variability attributable to within-national differences as contrasted to between-national variability. Only on the risk scale was the amount of within national variability significantly different from zero at the 0.05 level.

[5] Additional details on the research underlying this comparison can be found in Cummings, Schmikl, and Blackburn (1977).

different in many respects. It is generally recognized that the English culture within South Africa has emphasized entrepreneurship, risk taking, political liberalism, and religious change more than has the Afrikaan culture. These differences are generally thought to be reflected in most dimensions of white South African society; e.g., economic, educational, and religious. On the other hand, thère exists little empirical evidence on specific personality and attitudinal characteristics to support these generally assumed macro differences.

Thus, our analysis was guided by the following hypotheses:

English speaking (first language) executives will be significantly
1) more conciliatory,
2) more risk prone,
3) more oriented toward belief in self-control and self-determination, and
4) more trusting toward others
than Afrikaan-speaking (first language) executives.

The within South African scores are presented in Table 4.3. While none of the differences is substantial, their direction is consistent with hypotheses 1, 3, and 4. The English sample is more conciliatory, expresses greater belief in internal control, and is more trusting. There is no difference in the risk proneness of the two samples. Quite obviously, from a statistical point of view, we must conclude that the two samples do not differ.

What explanations might be offered for the generally small differences between the Afrikaan and English South African samples? At least three possible reasons should be considered. First, all of the executives studied were involved in an educational program which emphasizes their similarities as managers and provides an intentional international perspective. This focus on the general managerial role and events external to Southern Africa and developments may tend to minimize within country differences.

Second, the two samples probably are not representative of the larger populations of white South African executives. The fact that they are pursuing postgraduate degrees indicates that they already have passed through motivation and ability filters that may homogenize initial differences based in their traditional and earlier cultures.

Third, cultural, religious, and language differences may not impact this partic-

TABLE 4.3   Attitudinal Differences Within South Africa

	Con-Bel	Risk	Control	Sus-Trust
English-South African Sample (n=85)	46.9	34.0	−.86	37.8
Afrikaan-South African Sample (n=179)	44.2	34.6	−.79	38.0

ular set of attitudes. There seems to be an increasing awareness among whites in South Africa that reconciling, or at least masking, their historic differences is an important ingredient for peace within, and even survival of, the present system in South Africa.

So, in conclusion, in neither of the cases of within nationality comparisons have we found substantial differences on the four personality dimensions. What holds true for a nationality clustering of executives seems to also hold true for subgroupings, based on location and subcultural identification, within that nationality. We have a much more solid basis for generalizations *within* the nationalities sampled than *between* them.

EMPLOYMENT SECTOR AND PERSONALITY

This section reports data on managers, within two countries (Belgium and the United States), from both the private and public or governmental employment sectors. We will examine the Belgian data first, followed by the data from the United States.

In Belgium

The Belgian managers were all Flemish-speaking and at the time the questionnaire was administered were all participating in a seminar given by the Management Training Center, University of Leuven, Leuven, Belgium.

The results comparing the attitudes of the private and public sector managers are shown in Table 4.4. Note that the average score of the Belgian public managers falls near one of the two extremes of attitude when compared with the national scores presented earlier (i.e., more conciliatory and more risk-avoiding), and they scored second only to Spain among the Western samples in their belief in fate. Differences in scores between the Belgian public managers and the average score of the national groups is large enough in these cases to be relatively sure that they would occur by chance fairly infrequently. Hence, we can conclude that the Belgian public managers are more conciliatory, have more of a tendency toward risk-aversion, and have more belief in external control than the average manager in our study. The difference between these managers on the suspiciousness scale is not large enough to draw a similar conclusion.

TABLE 4.4   Employment Sector Comparison : Belgian Private vs. Belgian Public

	Con-Bel	Risk	Control	Sus-Trust
Belgian Private (n=26)	56.0	36.0	−0.85	37.2
Belgian Public (n=22)	59.6	38.7	−0.59	36.3

slightly more risk averting. These differences are most likely due to chance variations. While exhibiting extreme belief in internal control and self-determination, the military officers are nearly identical to the private sector executives.

When we examine both the Belgian and United States comparisons there clearly emerges a suggestion, but certainly not a certainty, that employment sector within a nationality is associated with differences in personality across the four dimensions measured. These findings do seem to suggest that more extensive study of employment sector comparisons are warranted. We regard this aspect of our findings as a beginning point for such research.

EMPLOYMENT FUNCTION AND PERSONALITY

In order to investigate the relation between functional identification and attitudes, we were able to classify 358 of the executives in our total sample as belonging to one of the following four categories: (1) marketing and sales, (2) general management, (3) finance and accounting, or (4) production and engineering. The average score of these groups on each of the four PAS dimensions is shown in Table 4.6.

First note that the average scores by functional breakdown are less diverse than were the average scores by nationality groupings. On conciliation-belligerence, for example, the nationality scores range from a high of 58.0 (Spain) to a low of 45.1 (South Africa), while the functional scores range from a high of 54.9 (marketing and sales) to a low of 50.5 (engineering and production). The range of scores on risk, control, and suspiciousness-trust are similarly reduced. Although on all four scales only the difference between the two most extreme scores is large enough to warrant any confidence that these differences did not occur by chance, a number of interesting patterns did emerge from the data.[6]

Note that the scores for marketing-sales and production-engineering fall at one of the two extremes on three of the four scales. The marketing-sales executives exhibit relatively high conciliation; they are the highest risk takers and are

TABLE 4.6   Average Attitude Scores by Employment Function

	Con-Bel	Risk	Control	Sus-Trust
Marketing and sales (n=117)	54.9	34.1	−0.84	38.7
General management (n=148)	53.5	35.0	−0.81	36.1
Finance and accounting (n=36)	51.5	36.6	−1.09	37.1
Production and engineering (n=57)	50.5	34.5	−1.22	34.2

[6]The significance of the difference between the mean scores of the functions was calculated by a two-sample t test. Only the differences between the largest and smallest scores were significant at the 0.05 level.

The most interesting aspect of Table 4.4 is the distinct pattern found on three of the four scales, conciliation-belligerence, risk, and control. Most of the scores of the private managers (reported earlier) on all three of these scales fall between the scores of all other private managers and the scores of the public managers. The private managers studied in Belgium are thus less conciliatory than their public sector counterparts, but they are more conciliatory than most other private managers. They are more likely to take risks than the public managers, but less likely than most managers; and, finally, they tend to place less belief in fate than the public sector managers, but more than most of the private managers. The suspiciousness-trust scores do not fall in the same pattern, nor is it possible to draw similar inferences because of the closeness of these scores.

It thus appears that the attitudes expressed by the Belgian managers were dependent both on nationality and employment sector and that these influences acted in the same direction for both the private and public managers. In other words, the Belgian (private and public) managers studied are similar to one another in the sense that their average scores fall consistently on the same side of the average scores of all other managers studied (on three scales), yet they are consistently different in terms of the magnitude of the deviation of their scores away from the average score of most private managers. The implication we have drawn from this analysis is that there may be differences between managers, not only across national boundaries, but also across employment sectors within a given country as well. In order to add further light on this possibility, we will now report our comparison within the United States sample.

In the United States

The United States analysis compares the 23 private sector American executives included in the previous analyses with 74 United States military senior officers (lieutenant colonel rank and higher). The results of this comparison are presented in Table 4.5. The two groups differ substantially on only one of the four PAS scales: suspiciousness-trust. The military officers are more suspicious than are the private sector executives. However, when compared to most of the samples reported on earlier in this chapter, they remain toward the trusting end of the scale. Once again we see the possibly simultaneous influence of nationality and employment sector operating on personality as we did in the Belgian data. Table 4.5 also shows that the military officers are slightly more conciliatory and

TABLE 4.5 Employment Sector Comparison: United States Private vs. United States Military

	Con-Bel	Risk	Control	Sus-Trust
United States Private (n=23)	48.1	31.9	−1.48	29.7
United States Military (n=74)	50.4	33.3	−1.47	35.1

the most suspicious group of executives. On the other hand, the production-engineering executives are relatively low on conciliation; they score high on internal control and are the most trusting group. The fact that functional scores are specific to a particular dimension of attitude is illustrated by the fact that on the risk scale these two functions fall at adjacent positions.

Our findings on the managers' attitudes toward risk are consistent with the stereotype held by some people that marketing executives and sales personnel are generally relatively high risk-taking individuals, while managers in accounting and finance are more conservative. It may also be true that interpersonal conciliation is a more crucial determinant of effectiveness in marketing than in either production and engineering or accounting and finance. At least, it is likely that, in general, the interpersonal content of the former type of functional position is greater than that of the latter two types.

Of course, it is not clear from our data whether the association between the function of a manager and his attitude toward risk, conciliation, etc., is due to the socialization process inherent in working within a particular function, or due to the tendency of persons with a particular set of attitudes to move toward certain functions, or both.

CONCLUSIONS

In concluding their book in 1966, Haire, Ghiselli, and Porter emphasized that "we are ready . . . for a host of comparative studies of managerial attitudes and behavior that will lead us into a detailed understanding of the role of national and cultural traditions in shaping managerial strategy and style. Nothing seems clearer than the pressing need for data of this kind, and for the further understanding of comparative diversity in a world which, day by day, is growing rapidly smaller and more interdependent" (1966, p. 180-181). We feel that our findings have added to this stream of data and, hopefully, to understanding these data.

It will help to summarize and reflect upon our findings through the perspective of a simple model of possible causative factors leading to variations in the attitudes of the managers. There are at least four types of variables which could account for differences among the managers studied: (1) cultural values which are specific to either a single nationality or to a cluster of nationalities, (2) the degree of industrialization of the country from which a manager comes and within which he has been socialized, (3) the manager's functional identification, and (4) the employment sector of the social system within which the manager works. Any one or a combination of these factors might lead to differences in attitudes toward risk, conciliation, fate, and trust. As we noted earlier, these attitudinal differences may or may not, in turn, be associated with significant differences in the behavior of the managers. Thus, this simple diagnostic model would appear as follows:[7]

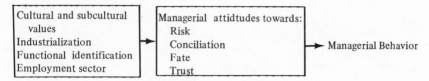

Our findings can be interpreted in terms of this model. First, we have found differences between the national groupings in our study, differences which probably can be associated with variations in *cultural values*. Our national groupings were found to have similarities with the north-south (Nordic-Latin) categories used by Haire, Ghiselli, and Porter in their study of managerial attitudes, although we found a higher percent of the variability attributable to individual differences than they did (95 percent vs. 72 percent). It is interesting to note that we did not find the similarity between the United States and English executives that Haire, Ghiselli, and Porter did, but, rather, we found the English to be similar to their neighbors across the channel (Belgium, France, Germany) and the Americans to be distinctly different from all other countries.

In neither Spain nor South Africa did we find substantial differences across geographical and cultural subgroupings within the country. Our hypothesis explaining this lack of expected differences is that the managerial role dominates any latent differences in basic personality dimensions. That is, being a manager attracts, socializes, and homogenizes persons such that other possible sources of differentiation are dampened.

Turning now to the factor of *industrialization* as a possible causative variable, two points seem clear. First, our data do not appear to support industrialization as a significant cause of differences in attitudes. For example, in comparing the United States and Central Europe to Greece and Spain, there is little evidence of a systematic relationship in attitudes. Secondly, it may well be that all of the countries sampled are of such a high degree of industrialization that not enough variance in degree of industrialization was sampled to allow a relationship to emerge. In other words, we doubt if we were able to attain a good test of the "industrialization hypothesis."[8]

[7]Other possible causative factors not examined here might be age of manager, type of industry, and managerial level. The diagram is not meant to imply an exhaustive listing.

[8]Industrialization does emerge as a stronger causal element when the leadership attitudes of one of the countries (Greece) are compared to more and less industrialized countries. See L. L. Cummings and S. M. Schmidt (1972). On the other hand, England has presented evidence that cultural factors (vs. technological factors) best fit personal value differences among American, Japanese, and Korean managers: See George W. England, "Personal Value System Analysis as an Aid to Understanding Organizational Behavior," *Exchange Seminar on Comparative Organizations* (Amsterdam: March 1970). For a general discussion of the role of cultural and other factors in comparative management studies, including an appeal for needed empirical data, see M. Ajiferuke and J. Boddewyn (1970).

As we have noted, *functional identification* appears to be weakly related to the four attitudes studied. Our findings indicate that one must be specific about the attitude in question.

Even though our findings should be interpreted only as a mere beginning, the *employment sector* differences within the Belgium sample are noteworthy. It is probably the case that cross-sector contact between private and public managers is increasingly becoming a necessary condition for conducting business. The quality of the interpersonal relations and understanding among managers from different employment sectors thereby becomes a crucial determinant of managerial effectiveness in both sectors. Hence, it becomes important to know more about the differences in attitudes of managers employed in the various employment sectors. We feel that our research is a step toward that end. We do not feel secure in inferring behavioral differences from these attitudinal differences; yet our data are at least consistent with some of the stereotypical differences often attributed to public and private sector executives. On the other hand, our comparison of the private with the military samples causes us to mellow our tendency to generalize and to exercise caution. Admittedly, it is true that considerable contact exists between the United States private and military sectors and that, in addition, employment mobility between the sectors is not infrequent. These forces might tend to reduce the personality differences due to selection and socialization processes that differentiate the two sectors. We now need studies on possible sector differences in additional countries and a movement·toward gathering of actual behavioral data in some systematic and, at least, semistandardized fashion.

We close on two notes: one of the *thrust*, inviting further research and speculation; and the other of *caution*, inviting conservatism in interpreting our findings. Dissimilarities among the regional groups on each of the four attitudes, all of which could be important determinants of managerial behavior, invite additional work on the causes underlying such differences as well as studies relating these attitudinal differences to behavior. Within-region variability and possible differences among the managers according to functional identification and employment sector also provide a thrust for further research and understanding. Yet, the excitement of discovering and interpreting such differences must be mellowed by noting that the limitations of our data collection procedures and the small number of observations in some cases mean that this study must be seen as descriptive, certainly not prescriptive or predictive.

We now turn our attention to an examination of the bargaining behaviors exhibited by the managers studied. Having done that, we will examine the relation between the personality results discussed in this chapter and bargaining behaviors in several of the samples.

5

THE BARGAINING MODEL, METHODOLOGY, AND CULTURAL RESULTS

As we have indicated, most researchers on bargaining would agree that personal differences among bargainers undoubtably account for a considerable portion of the variability in payoffs among bargainers. Nevertheless, there has been a scarcity of experimental research relating personality traits to bargaining behavior. Research efforts by Dolbear and Lave (1966), Gallo and McClintock (1965), and Pilisuk, Potter, Rapaport, and Winter (1965); found little support for the importance of personal differences. Sherman (1966) did find a relationship between risk-taking propensity and choices among various forms of the Prisoner's Dilemma game. Harnett, Cummings, and Hughes (1968) found a relationship between risk-taking propensity and the amount a bargainer yielded, but no relationship was found between risk and the amount of profit earned. In this same study they found that the less the amount of information a bargainer has about the opponent's reward structure, the more personality influences bargaining behavior.

One personal characteristic of special interest in the research reported here involves the effect of nationality differences on bargaining behavior. This type of analysis becomes increasingly important as the world becomes more international in character, and bargaining between individuals and firms of different nations, and their governments, assumes an increasing role in terms of world peace and prosperity. Our hope is to contribute to the small but growing stream of research reporting on cross-cultural aspects of bargaining behavior.

THE EXPERIMENTAL MODEL

In designing an experimental paradigm which would be suitable for our studies of international bargaining behavior we had to keep several factors in mind. First, we were anxious to use a model which would be interesting to study in its own right, independent of our cross cultural interests. This meant we wanted to use a model that would provide a somewhat new context for the study of bargaining. We did not wish to utilize a model which had been exhaustively studied previously. Secondly, we wanted to find a model which had no dominant (or obvious) solution, from either a mathematical or behavioral point of view, in order to allow individual differences to play as large a role in the bargaining as possible. Hence we could not use models with equilibrium points, and [following Schelling (1963)] we would probably not discover personal differences unless we held the bargaining under conditions of incomplete information. Finally, we hoped to use a fairly straightforward and easily understood situation, yet one which represented an interesting negotiation problem to the participants. The paradigm we chose was a bilateral monopoly model with the buyer and the seller in asymmetric roles.

Our bargaining monopoly paradigm involves bargaining between two business executives, representing the roles of a buyer and a seller, whose task is to agree on a single price and quantity for the exchange of a fictitious product between them. Participants were told the "profit" they would earn for every possible price-quantity agreement, but they were not told the profit their counterpart in the negotiations would earn (i.e., they bargained under incomplete information). In order to provide some measure of realism to the bargaining and to give an incentive for participants to take the experiment seriously, each person received a cash payoff corresponding to the amount of profit earned in the bargaining agreement.

The choice of a bilateral monopoly model for the present research represents an attempt to expand on the Fouraker-Siegel research, as well as our own findings in similar situations as reported in Chapter 1. Specifically, we were interested in investigating the effect of using parameters in the construction of the payoff tables which do not place the buyer and the seller in symmetric roles. Our general hypothesis is that both the process and the results of negotiations between a buyer and a seller will be significantly influenced by giving one of the bargainers a more favorable position from which to begin negotiations. In addition, we hypothesize that the amount of concessions by the bargainers will be, in part, a function of the slopes of their marginal cost and revenue functions. Both of these hypotheses are discussed more thoroughly below.

Theoretical Development

Most bargaining literature specifies the solution to the bilateral monopoly problem to be that quantity which maximizes the joint profit of the two bargainers. Joint profits are maximized when the marginal cost incurred by the bargainer who manufactures or acquires the product equals the marginal revenue derived by the bargainer who sells the product (after purchasing it from the first bargainer). Since we are only interested in the relationship between these two bargainers, the first will be denoted as the seller, and the second as the buyer. The derivation of the joint maximizing quantity can be demonstrated by considering the following simple model, in which marginal cost and marginal revenue are linear functions.

Let
    A = price axis intercept of the average revenue function
    A' = price axis intercept of the average cost function
    B = the slope of the average revenue function
    B' = the slope of the average cost function
    C = total cost
    P = price
    Q = quantity
    R = revenue
K, K' = constants

Suppose we assume that the total cost (C) to the seller of selling Q units is a second degree polynomial of the following form:

$$C = A'Q + B'Q^2 + K'$$

If C assumes the parabolic form shown above, then marginal cost, which is the first derivative of total cost, must be linear:

$$dC/dQ = A' + 2BQ$$

If we assume that total revenue (R) to the buyer is also parabolic, where

$$R = AQ - BQ^2 + K$$

then marginal revenue (dR/dQ) will have the following linear form:

$$dR/dQ = A - 2BQ$$

Since maximization occurs when marginal revenue equals marginal cost (assuming the second derivation is negative), then the joint maximizing quantity, Q_M, can be derived by setting the marginal functions equal and solving for Q.

$$dC/dQ = dR/dQ$$
$$A' + 2B'Q = A - 2BQ$$
$$Q_M = (A - A')/(2B + 2B')$$

If quantity is assumed determinate at Q_M, then the division of profits between the seller and the buyer will depend on the price they establish. Although some bilateral models consider price as indeterminate when both parties have equal bargaining power, the price usually accepted as most likely is the one yielding a solution which both participants regard as a draw, or a "fair" division of joint profits. As we indicated earlier this solution usually corresponds to a fifty-fifty split of joint payoffs. An equal split of maximum joint profit occurs when total profit to the seller equals total profit to the buyer, or when $PQ_M - C = R - PQ_M$. Thus, if we denote P_E as the equal split price, then

$$P_E = (R + C)/2Q_M$$

We are interested in two aspects of the general conclusions by Siegel and Fouraker concerning the main determinants of differential payoffs and price in bilateral monopoly bargaining under incomplete information. Our first interest involves the extent of the influence of certain characteristics of the payoff structure of the bargainers on their relative earnings. Secondly, we are interested in examining the influence of the nationality of the bargainers on the bargaining process and outcome.

In regard to the first of these interests, we suggest that the lack of any significant differences in average payoff between the buyers and sellers in the Siegel-Fouraker experiments can be attributed, at least in part, to the fact that their payoff matrices were symmetrical to the extent of yielding the same maximum payoff for both bargainers. Our contention is that this symmetry induces a measure of equality between the initial aspiration levels of the buyers and sellers, and it is this equality which leads to the similarity in average profits. In a related study, Chertkoff and Conley (1977) found that those bargainers opening with the more extreme offers did better in the negotiations. We thus hypothesize that for bargainers with unequal maximum payoffs, the bargainer with the more favorable position will have a higher aspiration level which, in turn, will result in bargaining behavior generating the larger profit.

Each bargainer's payoff in a negotiation process can be thought of as a function of the total amount of concessions made in yielding from an initial aspiration level. Fouraker (1957) has suggested that bargainers will make concessions by quoting price-quantity combinations along their own marginal function (cost or revenue), and equilibrium will occur at the point (on Q_M) where the marginal curves intersect. The price where marginal cost equals marginal revenue can be derived by substituting the quantity Q_M into the formula for either marginal function. Thus, if we denote the price at the intersection of the marginal functions as P_I, then

$$P_I = A - 2B \; \frac{A - A'}{2B + 2B'}$$

Although this solution results in maximum joint payoffs, it yields an equal split of these profits only if the slopes of the two marginal functions are equal (i.e., when $B = B'$). When $B > B'$ the marginal intersections solution will give the buyer the larger profit; when $B' > B$ the seller will earn more than the buyer. These two cases are illustrated in Figure 5.1.

Although Siegel and Fouraker reject the marginal hypothesis as a result of

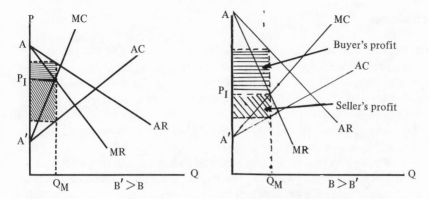

Figure 5.1. Asymmetrical marginal functions.

their 1960 experiments (in favor of the Fellner solution), their results do not preclude the possibility that the concessions the bargainers make will be at least partially influenced by the slope of their marginal functions. This influence, if there is any tendency for the bargainers to concede in amounts which are related to the slopes of their marginal functions, should favor the bargainer who will earn the larger profit at the marginal intersection solution. Thus, we hypothesize that when $B \neq B'$, there will be a tendency for the bargainer who has the steeper sloping marginal function to make the smaller total concession.[1]

Since the culture within which a person is socialized and educated presumably exerts a significant influence on his/her basic attitudes and dispositions, we might expect to find differences across national boundaries in bargaining behaviors. Unfortunately, systematic evidence regarding the nature of such differences is limited, so that our investigation is this area must be viewed as primarily descriptive. We do make one prediction, drawn from the commonly held belief that executives from the United States are generally more competitive than their counterparts from other countries. On this basis, we hypothesize that the bargaining between the United States executives will be more competitive in the sense that these participants will ask for higher payoffs at the beginning of the bargaining process, and that negotiations will take longer when compared to the executives from the other countries studied. This analysis of differences across cultures will be presented later in this chapter.

---

[1] It might be argued at this point that initial asking level and amount yielded are not independent, and that one would expect a larger concession rate from the bargainer who asks for a higher initial profit. We cannot disprove this argument, but rather point out that since the buyers do not know they are asking for an initially higher amount (i.e., they have incomplete information), there would seem to be little justification for arguing that this fact would influence their yielding pattern.

Methodology

A bilateral monopoly bargaining experiment was designed to test the hypotheses described above. This experiment was conducted in each of eight different countries–Belgium, England, Finland, France, Japan, Spain, Thailand, and the United States. The subjects for these experiments were administered the PAS (as described in Chapter 4)–at least one day prior to the experiments. As was the case with the PAS, all bargaining behavior instruments were administered in the native language of the country involved.

In each country the participating executives were divided, randomly, into an equal number of buyers and sellers. The buyers and sellers were then placed in separate rooms where they were seated by a master plan which (randomly) matched each seller with a specific buyer. As soon as all participants had found their assigned seats, each person was given a set of instructions describing the negotiation process and a payoff table showing the profit which could be earned for each possible price-quantity agreement. For each country the instructions given to the participants had been translated into the language being used at the seminar (i.e., Flemish, Finnish, Spanish, Japanese, and Thai), and the payoff tables had been converted to local currency at the official exchange rate (see Appendixes B and C).

After the participants were given sufficient time to read their instructions and ask questions (which were answered by a collaborator who spoke the native languages), the bargaining process was begun. The seller started the negotiations by writing his initial price-quantity offer on a sheet of paper. This sheet was then taken to the buyer, who had the option of either accepting the seller's offer or of making a counter-offer. If he made a counter-offer, this offer was taken to the seller who then had the option of accepting it or of making a new offer. This process of making offers and counter-offers continued until an agreement was reached (i.e., one party accepted the other's offer). The negotiations were conducted in silence, with no communication permitted between participants except for the written price-quantity offers and counter-offers. The participants were told that if they did not reach an agreement after 90 minutes of bargaining, the negotiations would end and neither person would earn any money.

Operational Definitions. The payoff matrices furnished the buyers and sellers were derived from the following parameters:

$$A = 270, B = 5, K = 65, A' = 0, B' = 10, \text{ and } K' = -200$$

For these values the joint maximizing quantity equals

$$Q_M = \frac{A - A'}{(2B + 2B')} = \frac{270}{10 + 20} = 9$$

For the parameters of this model $R + C = 2700$ when $Q = 9$, so that the equal split price is

$$P_E = (R + C)/2Q_M = \frac{2700}{18} = 150$$

Our model, as outlined at the beginning of this chapter, accomplishes the objective of not placing the buyer and seller in symmetric roles in terms of their maximum payoff or in terms of the slopes of their marginal (cost and revenue) functions. At the maximum payoff points this model gives the buyer the advantage as his profit can be as much as $1.75 larger than the seller's ($14.25 – $12.50). Our hypothesis is that this difference will give the buyers a bargaining advantage in terms of the amount of profit earned—i.e., the buyers average payoff will be significantly larger than the average payoff of the sellers.

In our model the slope of the seller's marginal cost function $(2B' = 20)$ is twice the slope of the buyer's marginal revenue function $(2B = 10)$. Thus, since we hypothesized that the bargainer with the steeper sloping function will concede the smaller amount, for the present research we hypothesize that the average concession by the sellers will be significantly less than the average concession by the buyers. We have operationally defined the amount a bargainer concedes to be the difference between his second offer and his final payoff. Each person's second offer was chosen over his first offer as his initial aspiration level because many of the participants automatically made their initial offer at the price-quantity representing their maximum profit; hence it was felt that this first offer was more of an exploratory bid rather than a meaningful asking level.

It is important to note that the two hypotheses outlined above lead to opposite predictions in terms of bargaining advantage—i.e., the first predicts an advantage to the buyer because of his more favorable starting position, while the second predicts an advantage to the seller because he had the steeper sloping marginal function. The advantage in the first case is expected to be at most $1.75, representing the difference in maximum attainable profits. In the second case, the maximum difference is represented by the seller's advantage at the point where marginal cost equals marginal revenue, which is $5.40 in the present model ($10.10 vs. $4.70). Viewed in this manner our experiment becomes a test of the relative influence of differences in maximum payoff versus differences in the slopes of the marginal functions. Based on the Siegel-Fouraker data, however, we have implicitly predicted that the influence of the maximum payoff differential will dominate by hypothesizing an overall bargaining advantage to the buyer.

BUYER-SELLER DIFFERENCES

For our analysis of buyer-seller differences we used data from 204 executives, 134 from continental Europe (Belgium, England, France, and Spain) and 20 from the United States. There were four dyads which did not reach an agreement within the allotted 90 minutes. Since we were not able to compute meaningful values on a number of the variables of interest for these participants (i.e., final payoff, amount yielded, number of bids) we decided to exclude these groups

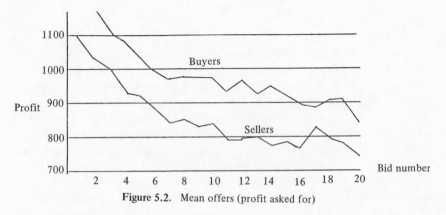

Figure 5.2. Mean offers (profit asked for)

from our analysis. Our findings for the remaining 196 participants (98 groups) are reported next.

Our initial hypothesis was that in the present model the buyer will have a bargaining advantage in terms of the amount of profit earned because this person has the higher maximum payoff. To test this hypothesis, we calculated the difference between the buyer's payoff and the seller's payoff for each of the 98 bargaining groups. A t-test for matched pairs was then used to test the null hypothesis that the population mean of these difference scores equals zero. The mean buyer-seller difference was $0.97, leading to rejection of the null hypothesis at $p < .005$ ($t = 3.104$). In order to present a more comprehensive picture of the relationship between the bids of the two participants, we have calculated the average offer by both buyers and sellers (i.e., average profit asked for) for the first twenty transactions. These data, shown in Figure 5.2, indicate a fairly constant difference between the mean bids of the buyers and the sellers. It thus appears that the buyer's larger maximum obtainable payoff does yield a bargaining advantage in the present bilateral monopoly model.

As Table 5.1 indicates, the average first offer by the buyer ($12.26) was $1.35 higher than the average first offer by the seller ($10.91), a difference which is significant at $p < .0005$ ($t = 3.567$). Thus, even on the first bid the buyer-seller difference was less than the maximum of $1.75, although many of the participants asked for their highest profit on the first offer. This first-offer difference, however, is larger than the buyer's advantage in final payoff (0.97), suggesting that the negotiation process has a moderating influence on the buyer's initial

TABLE 5.1 Buyer-Seller Difference Scores

Variable	Buyer-Seller Mean	t value	Significance
First Offer	$1.35	3.567	K
Payoff	0.97	3.104	< .005
Yielding	0.68	1.927	< .05

advantage. This moderating influence is the subject of our second hypothesis, concerning the amount conceded by the bargainers.

Our second hypothesis is that the average buyer-seller difference for the amount yielded (second offer minus final payoff) will be significantly greater than zero. That is, we have hypothesized that the seller will yield less than the buyer because $B' > B$. An interesting pattern occurred on the second bids in that the buyer-seller difference increased, to $1.65. The yielding difference of $0.68, which is significant at $p < .05$ ($t = 1.927$), supported our second hypothesis that the seller will yield significantly less than the buyers.

From the information in Table 5.1 and from our discussion thus far it is apparent that these data support our contention concerning the bargaining advantage of differences in maximum payoff relative to differences in the slopes of these marginal functions. In essence, we found that both of these factors influenced the process and results of the bargaining, but that the seller's advantage (due to the steeper sloping marginal function) was significantly less than the buyer's advantage. Hence, in general terms, we found that starting position is the more important factor in terms of relative impact on the bargaining outcome.

To conclude our analysis of the effects of the asymmetrical nature of the payoff tables, we examine the influences of these structural characteristics on the average price and quantity agreement. Recall that the Siegel-Fouraker data supported the Fellner hypothesis that agreements will be randomly distributed about the price and quantity reflecting an equal split of maximum joint payoffs. Our average negotiated price was $\bar{P} = 147.86$, which does not significantly differ from the equal-split price of $P_E = 150$. The average negotiated quantity was $\bar{Q} = 9.66$, which is significantly larger than the joint maximizing quantity of $Q_M = 9$ ($Z = 4.644$, $p < .0001$). Thus, the effect of the changes we introduced, as compared to the Siegel-Fouraker findings, was to move the negotiated quantity away from the joint maximizing quantity (and thus necessarily reduce total joint profits), but not to affect the negotiated price.

CULTURAL DIFFERENCES

One of our major interests is to investigate the effect of cultural differences on the process and results of negotiations. Ideally, we would have liked to compare and contrast the data from each country studied with all other countries, to determine what, if any, differences exist across nations. Because of the relatively small number of participants in most of our European groups, however, and the similarity of behavior across some of these groups, we decided to combine the data from Belgium, Finland, France, and Spain into a single group called "Europe." The groups included in our analysis are thus Europe, United States, Japan, and Thailand.

Our first cross-cultural interest involves the buyer-seller differences described earlier. Within the four groups studied, the managers from Thailand and Japan bargained in such a manner so as not to give a substantial advantage to the buyer. In these two countries the buyers seemed more willing to let their opponents set the pattern in the early phases of the negotiations, and were often content to more or less "match" the concessions made by the sellers from these countries. Thus, the impact of the asymmetrical nature of the payoff structure, shown to be significant for the data described in the last section, does not appear to be an important factor among the Thais and the Japanese. These data are shown in Table 5.2.

From Table 5.2 we see that the largest competitive advantage of the buyers over the sellers was in the United States ($1.94), and the lowest was in Japan, where the sellers earned an average of $0.11 more than the buyers. Thus, it appears that via the negotiation process the United States buyers were able to maintain, even increase, their initial structural advantage (which was $1.75). The Japanese and Thai bargainers, on the other hand, seemed to be striving more for equality in payoff, the result being a fairly even split in final profit between the buyers and sellers.

In the analysis below we will further elaborate on the differences between cultures by contrasting the bargaining patterns of the participants from the various areas studied. Since the data for the buyers are obviously not independent of the data for the sellers, we have chosen to analyze the results for only the buyers.

Our general expectation before conducting these experiments was that the United States executives would be the most competitive—i.e., they would tend to ask for the highest initial profits and they would take the most time and the largest number of bids to reach agreement. The executives from Thailand were hypothesized to be the least competitively oriented. Table 5.3 presents the data for this analysis.

The data in Table 5.2 and 5.3 generally support our expectation that the United States executives would be more competitive than their counterparts from other countries. For example, in the first row in Table 5.3 the highest average first offer was by the United States buyers ($13.15), while the lowest was by Japanese executives ($11.64), followed closely by the European executives ($11.85). This $1.30 difference between the United States/European participants is significant at $p < .025$, as is the United States/Japanese difference. Similarly, the average number of offers made by the United States participants (22.7) is

TABLE 5.2 Buyer-Seller Differences by Groups

	Buyer Profit	Seller Profit	Difference	p
United States	$8.26	$6.32	$1.94	$p < .001$
Europe	$7.63	$6.83	$ .82	$p < .001$
Thailand	$7.37	$7.25	$ .12	N.S.
Japan	$7.24	$7.35	-$ .11	N.S.

TABLE 5.3 International Comparison of Mean Scores for Buyers

Variable	United States	Europe	Japan	Thailand
First Offer	$13.15	$11.85	$11.64	$12.54
Yielding	$ 4.50	$ 3.79	$ 3.94	$ 4.25
Profit	$ 8.26	$ 7.63	$ 7.24	$ 7.37
Number of bids	22.70	15.10	19.50	13.30
Time to achieve agreement	71.92	61.75	76.13	55.50

significantly higher (p < .03) than the number of offers by the Europeans (15.1) and the Thais (13.3), but not significantly different from the average number of bids by the Japanese (19.5). Finally, although the United States executives did not take quite as long to reach agreement as did the Japanese participants, they did take significantly longer than the Europeans (p < .085) and the participants from Thailand (p < .05).

We did not expect differences to occur in the payoffs, as any additional competitive spirit assumed to exist for the United States buyers would be expected to be offset by a similar spirit among the sellers. We were thus somewhat surprised by the fact that the United States buyers had the largest average profit. Although this profit advantage by the United States buyers is not statistically significant (perhaps because of the relatively small sample size), these data may indicate that the United States buyers were more successful in using their structural advantage to earn higher profits than were their counterparts from other countries.

DISCUSSION OF BARGAINING RESULTS

The data in Table 5.3 indicate a number of important differences in bargaining behavior. For the initial offers as well as final profit, it appears that the United States (and to a lesser extent the European) buyers were much more competitively oriented than were the executives from Japan and Thailand. In interpreting this behavior, we might point out that when compared to the United States, most countries are more homogeneous in ethnic composition. This may mean, in the latter cases, that societal norms and standards of judgment lead to greater interpersonal sensitivity and empathy. Many societies are homogeneous enough to permit reliance on such standards or norms to establish social harmony.

Relative to the United States, for example, Japan has 1/25 the physical space and approximately half the population. This may well mean that the Japanese are more conscious of one another, and more sensitive to mutual evaluation. These two characteristics might be interpreted as suggesting that the range of behavior perceived as reasonable or acceptable is more narrowly defined by Japanese than by Americans. This lesser variance, in turn, may have been exhibited in the bargaining situation. Thus, it may be that the Japanese buyers, in contrast to the United States buyers, tried to exhibit more understanding of and deference to the demands of the sellers.

Overall, however, we are struck by the similarities in behaviors of the executives from the different nations. It is clear from our experiments that a majority of the variance in bargaining processes and results must still be attributed to personal differences other than cultural heritage. In Chapters 3 and 4, data were presented concerning differences in the personalities of the executives from the various cultures. In the next chapter we will investigate further the processes and results of bargaining across cultures including an analysis of the relation between personality differences and bargaining behaviors.

6

PERSONALITY, STRATEGY, AND ACHIEVEMENT IN BARGAINING

Our focus in this chapter is on five issues: (1) the offers and counter-offers made by subjects in bargaining, (2) how these offers and counter-offers form a strategy for negotiations, (3) how measures of personality which are assumed to be important in experimental bargaining research are related to the strategy chosen, (4) how strategies as well as personality variables are related to the subjects' payoffs, and (5) differences in bargaining between public vs. private sector bargaining samples. An overview of the relevant literature on these relationships is given below. Greater detail concerning these studies was described in Chapter 2.

BACKGROUND AND HYPOTHESES

Komorita and Brenner (1968) found that the higher a subject started in bargaining, the greater the payoff received. This finding was interpreted to imply that a negotiator should always start bargaining at a level from which fairly large concessions can be made. Previous research supports the conclusion that the most profitable subjects make smaller and fewer concessions in bargaining (Komorita and Brenner, 1968; Siegel and Fouraker, 1960). There is a debate in the literature, however, over whether the best strategy is to make a "few large" concessions or "many small" concessions. Pilisuk and Skolnick (1968) reported support for the Osgood (1959, 1962) proposal that many small concessions (conciliatory strategy) increases cooperation of the opponent and leads to the desired agreement. Chertkoff and Conley (1967) found the opposite tendency.

Bartos (1965) found that negotiators making higher than average payoffs made fewer concessions than their opponents, but they also avoided extremely uncooperative bidding presumably because such extreme behavior can drastically reduce the chances of reaching any agreement at all. This finding has also been reported by Komorita and Brenner (1968). Their research indicated that a strategy of reciprocating concessions was not significantly different from a firm bargaining strategy in terms of the yielding rate of the opponent.

Komorita and Barnes (1969) found support for an earlier Bartos hypothesis (1965) that time pressures increase concession-making. They found that (1) concession making and the number of trials to reach agreement are directly related to pressures to reach agreement, (2) mutual pressures to reach agreement evoke reciprocated concession making, and (3) a firm bargaining strategy evokes greater concessions only if the other party is under pressure to settle.

Pruitt and Drews (1969) investigated the effects of time pressure, elapsed time, and the opponent's rate of concession on four aspects of bargaining behavior. Using a Siegel and Fouraker (1960) payoff table, they found that increased time pressure resulted in less ambitious goals, lower levels of demand, and less bluffing on the first trial. The level of demand and amount of bluffing were reduced over subsequent trials, but the goals remained unchanged. Neither time pressure nor the opponent's rate of concession affected the rate of change in demand or the amount of bluffing, despite apparent awareness of the concession rate by the opponent. They also report that time pressure increased the number of concessions made. Liebert, Smith, Hill, and Keiffer (1968) found that the first trial behavior was affected by the other negotiator's first bid, but that subsequent behavior of the subjects was unaffected by the opponent's concession rate. Quite different findings were reported by Chertkoff and Conley (1967), and by Pruitt and Johnson (1970), who found that their subjects tended to make a large concession when the opponent made a large concession, and a small concession when the opponent made a small concession.

Based on the research reviewed above, our expectation was that subjects making the highest initial offers, those who made the fewest number of concessions, and those who conceded the smallest amount per concession would make the largest profit.

One interest we have had relative to our international bargaining data has been in classifying the strategies employed by our subjects. A number of bargaining strategies (or styles) have been identified in the literature as commonly used by subjects in a bargaining situation (Fouraker and Siegel, 1963; Komorita and Brenner, 1968; Osgood, 1959; Pruitt and Drews, 1969; and Siegel and Fouraker, 1960). For example, Fouraker and Siegel (1963) define a "tough" bargainer as one who makes a high opening offer followed by infrequent, small concessions. They predict that a tough approach will be successful because it tends to reduce the opponent's aspiration level. Komorita and Brenner (1968) found that a tough bargaining strategy increased the probability of reaching an advantageous agreement and reduced the probability of a "fair" agreement. Osgood's (1959) position is that a "soft" approach is optimal, especially in the case of stalemated negotiations, as concessions by one party should induce the other party to make similar concessions.

In addition to classifying subjects according to their bargaining styles, we are interested in identifying the payoffs generated by following these strategies. Since we regard our experiment as "low pressure" in that subjects were given ample time (1½ hours) to reach agreement, the literature reviewed above suggests that a tough strategy will yield the greatest payoffs. At the other extreme, the lowest payoff should go to the "fair" group since these subjects are aiming only at a "reasonable" profit level (we assume the other strategies are aimed toward *at least* that level). In addition, a "reasonable" approach to bargaining may well increase the aspiration level of an opponent who is unaware of the intentions of such an approach. The relative advantages of a soft strategy versus an intermediate strategy are more difficult to predict. We are inclined to follow the suggestion provided by Bartos (1965) and Komorita (1972) that a soft strategy will more likely result in a "bad" bargain, hence an intermediate strategy will be superior. We therefore hypothesize that the average payoffs of our subjects will be arrayed as follows:

$$\text{tough} > \text{intermediate} > \text{soft} > \text{fair}$$

A third purpose of this investigation is to study the relationship between certain personality measures and the subject's choice of an initial starting position, his choice of an overall strategy, and his payoff. The Shure and Meeker (1967) *Personality Attitude Schedule* (PAS) described in Chapter 3 was used to assess the four personality variables: (1) general tendency toward conciliation or belligerence, (2) tendency toward risk avoidance or risk taking, (3) belief in fate (external control of events) or self-determination (internal control), and (4) tendency toward suspiciousness or trust.

Although Shure and Meeker assumed these particular dimensions of personality to be important in bargaining behavior, we have indicated that most researchers have had limited success in establishing a relationship between personality variables and bargaining behavior. Based on our own research involving risk-taking propensity (Harnett *et al.*, 1968), we do not expect a subject's risk score to be related to the profit this person earns; that research did suggest, however, that subjects scoring the highest in risk avoidance tend to start higher and concede more during the bargaining than those subjects scoring highest in risk taking. Thus, we hypothesize that such will be the case in this study. We cannot make specific predictions about the relationship between bargaining behavior and the other three PAS variables. Although a generally held view of a "good" bargainer might be one who is relatively belligerent, internally oriented, and suspicious, we know of no evidence to support these contentions. In this study, we present results which describe the relationship between the four PAS measures and the subject's initial asking level, the bargaining strategy taken, and the final payoff.

Our fourth concern focuses on the interaction between the concession rates of the subjects in each bargaining pair. As we indicated in our literature review, there is conflicting evidence about the extent to which the strategy of one bargainer influences that of his opponent. We began our investigation of this interaction by determining the correlation between the concession pattern of each buyer and seller. These correlation coefficients are then used to categorize each bargaining pair according to whether concessions are positively related, negatively related, or have no relationship to one another. This information is then related to the bargainers' initial offers, the size of the concessions, the frequency of the concessions, and payoffs. Thus, we are examining the following issues:

1) the effects of personality on bargaining processes and payoff,

2) the effects of bargaining process on payoffs,

3) the development of a taxonomy of bargaining strategies and the relation between strategy and payoff, and

4) the patterns of concessions within bargaining dyads and the effects of these patterns on bargaining processes and payoffs.

The data analyzed in this chapter consist of the bilateral monopoly bargaining results from the 156 managers from five countries—Belgium, England, Finland, France, and Spain.

As we indicated earlier, one of our interests is to identify four different bargaining strategies (or types) and then investigate the relationship between these strategies and both the PAS scores and profit earned. This identification of the four types of strategies depends on operational definitions of both (1) initial asking level and (2) concessions. A subject will be defined as starting "high" if the average of this person's first two offers is within $1.00 of the maximum obtainable profit.[1] An "intermediate" initial asking level is one which is more than $1.00 away from the maximum, and more than $1.50 away from the midpoint of the bargainer's payoff matrix. Finally, we will define "fair" bids as those within $1.50 of the midpoint of the range.

As for concessions, we shall define a bargainer to be making a concession when an offer is made yielding this person a profit less than the lowest profit which could have been earned on any of the previous offers. A subject whose first offer is less than the maximum amount will be assumed to be making a concession on the first bid. Each subject's total concession is thus equal to the difference between the maximum possible profit and the final payoff. Subjects will be classified as making either (1) frequent or (2) infrequent concessions, depending on whether they make more or less than the median number of concessions for all subjects within their group. In a similar fashion, the size of each bargainer's

---

[1] We chose the average of the first two bids because we felt that for present purposes neither the first bid nor the second bid alone was representative of what we call initial asking level.

concessions will be classified according to whether this person gave up a large, moderate, or small amount per concession, on the average.

We can now describe our four bargaining strategies in terms of these definitions:[2]

1) *tough strategy*: start high, conceded infrequently and in either moderate or small amounts;

2) *soft strategy*: start high and make frequent, small concessions;

3) *intermediate strategy*: start at an intermediate position, and yield a moderate amount per concession;

4) *fair strategy*: either start at a fair position or move rapidly to this point, and then make small or zero concessions thereafter.

RESULTS

The subjects used to investigate these four issues were the 156 participants from Belgium, England, Finland, France, and Spain. As we indicated earlier, about five percent of the variability in the PAS scores from the European countries was attributable to regional differences; hence, we felt justified in combining subjects from the five countries on all four PAS scales. To satisfy ourselves that our data do not contain significant differences across countries on any of the variables being measured, we ran several analyses of variance tests (Treatment X Blocks design). The data indicate randomness for all effects involving nationalities and the two bargaining measures (initial offer and payoffs) as well as for the four PAS scales.

PAS and Initial Asking

Of the four PAS variables, we have predicted the direction of our anticipated results on only the risk variable—namely, that the more risk adverse subjects will tend to ask for higher initial profits and yield more than will risk takers. We tested the relationship between initial asking level and the PAS variables by dividing the subjects into those above the median (high) and those below the median (low) on each personality measure and then calculating the average initial asking level for each group. These results are presented in Table 6.1.

In Table 6.1, as predicted, those subjects classified as having the most tendency toward risk avoidance asked for a significantly higher profit than did those classified as low on risk avoidance ($p < .05$). Of the other three relationships,

---

[2]To avoid the possibility that our criteria for classifying a bargainer's strategy might (by definition) limit the range of payoffs he could earn, we categorized bargainers into strategies on the basis of only the first one-half of their offers.

TABLE 6.1   Initial Starting Position Classified by the PAS Scores

	High	Low	t	Significance
Conciliation	$12.05	$11.85	0.416	< .70
Risk avoidance	12.47	11.35	1.836	< .05
External control	11.51	12.45	1.793	< .10
Suspiciousness	12.19	11.68	0.962	< .35

only the external control values differed at a level approaching significance ($p <$ .10), with the subjects rated highest on external control making the lowest starting offers. The differences for the conciliation and suspiciousness scales are not significant, although it is interesting to note that the initial demands by the more suspicious subjects were an average of 51 cents higher than those of the more trusting subjects.

Bargaining Process and Payoffs

As indicated previously, we are interested in each bargainer's initial offer, the sequence of offers, the number of concessions made and the rate at which concessions are made, and how these behaviors are related to profit. The average number of offers made by each subject was just over fifteen (15.14). Concessions (i.e., an offer more favorable to the opponent than the previous best) were made on less than one-half of these offers, with the average number of concessions being 6.79. The average amount of profit given up per concession was $0.98. On the average, each buyer made $7.66. Only four of our bargaining groups failed to reach agreement in the allotted 90 minutes (they are excluded from this analysis); the remaining groups reached agreement in 61.31 minutes, on the average.

We analyzed the profit each subject earned relative to the number of concessions made, as well as to the average amount of profit given up per concession. These data are shown in Table 6.2. As anticipated, those subjects who made "frequent" concessions made significantly less profit ($p <$ .05) than did those

TABLE 6.2   Concessions versus Payoff

Profit	Frequency of Concession		Size of Concession[a]	
	Frequent (N=42)	Infrequent (N=36)	Few large (N=24)	Many small (N=27)
Mean payoff	7.33	7.96	7.32	7.61
t-Test	2.072 (p < .05)		1.06 (p < .30)	

[a]Size of sample (51) is less than 78 because in a number of cases it was impossible to classify a bargainer as clearly falling into one of the two groups.

subjects making "infrequent" concessions. Those subjects who made a "few large" concessions did not make significantly less profit than those who made "many small" concessions, although the difference between the two was in the predicted direction.

Using the definitions presented earlier for classifying each subject's overall bargaining strategy, we found that eighteen bargainers (23 percent) could be classified as following a "tough" strategy, 23 (29 percent) followed an "intermediate" strategy, fourteen (18.5 percent) followed a "soft" strategy, and thirteen (15.6 percent) followed a "fair" strategy. There were seven subjects (9 percent) who did not appear to fall into any one of our four categories; we have labeled these strategies as "others." An additional three subjects (4 percent) came to an agreement in such a short number of trials (less than five) that we hesitated to classify them as following any particular strategy.

The largest average time to reach agreement was taken by subjects in the "soft" category (72.8 minutes), followed closely by subjects in the "tough" group (71.1 minutes). The subjects in the "intermediate" and "fair" group took significantly ($p < .05$) less time (57.3 and 60.0 minutes, respectively), while the subjects in the "other" group took the shortest time (39.0 minutes). The "soft" group was the only one in which a majority of the subjects did not agree until within five minutes of the end of the allotted time (nine of fourteen took longer than 85 minutes).

In terms of the average profit earned by subjects employing the different strategies, we hypothesized that the "tough" strategy would be the most successful, followed by the "intermediate" strategy, then the "soft" strategy, and finally, the "fair" strategy. The data for this analysis are shown in Table 6.3.

As shown in Table 6.3, the predicted ordering of average profit for the four strategies was supported. While the difference between the payoffs for tough and intermediate is significant at $p < .10$, and the difference between soft and fair is significant at $p < .05$, the difference between intermediate and soft is not significant. The lowest profit earned was in the "other" category, primarily because subjects in this group were usually the most naive (or perhaps the most uninterested) bargainers; they generally started at a low asking level and/or yielded rapidly.

TABLE 6.3 Strategies vs. Profit

Strategy	Mean Payoff	t	p
Tough	$8.35		
		1.679	< .10
Intermediate	7.94		
		0.105	< .45
Soft	7.90		
		1.973	< .05
Fair	7.17		

TABLE 6.4   PAS Scores vs. Strategies

| Strategies | PAS Scores | | | |
| | Risk avoidance | | External control | |
	High	Low	High	Low
Tough	12	6	5	13
Intermediate soft or fair	22	28	29	21
χ^2		2.72 (p < .10)		4.84 (p < .025)

PAS, Bargaining Strategy and Profits

We suggested that a subject's PAS score might be related to his choice of a bargaining strategy. In general, we found little evidence of a pattern relating personalities and bargaining style. However, by dichotomizing our bargaining styles into two groups, one representing the "hard nosed" approach (the tough strategy) and the other representing the "softer" approaches (i.e., intermediate, soft, and fair) we did find a pattern relating to the risk and control scales. The number of subjects falling in each of these categories is shown in Table 6.4.

A chi-square analysis on these data indicates the null hypothesis of no relationship between the risk measure and our classification of strategies can be rejected at p < .10. Similarly, the hypothesis of no relationship for the control scale can be rejected at p < .025. It thus appears that the more highly risk adverse subjects and those scoring relatively high on internal control tend to take a tougher approach to bargaining.

In order to examine the relationship between our PAS measures and profit we classified each subject as falling either "high" or "low" on each of the four PAS scales depending on whether his score was above or below the median for that scale. The mean profits earned by subjects in these categories are shown in Table 6.5.

Again, the risk and control variables had the strongest relationship to our bargaining results. Contrary to our expectations, the more risk-adverse subjects made a higher average profit than did the risk-taking subjects, although this difference is significant only at p < .10. Those subjects believing the most in self control received a higher payoff than those believing in external control (p <

TABLE 6.5   PAS Scores versus Payoff

	High	Low	t	Significance
Conciliation	$7.75	$7.56	0.114	< .90
Risk avoidance	7.87	7.43	1.419	< .10
External control	7.35	7.96	2.713	< .001
Suspiciousness	7.54	7.82	0.971	< .35

TABLE 6.6 Intercorrelations for the Bargaining Variables (n=78)

Variable	Initial Offer	Size of Concession	Frequency of Concession	Payoff
Initial offer	1.00	−.62	.32	.31
Size of concession	....	1.00	−.35	−.48
Frequency of concession	....	....	1.00	−.10
Payoff	....	....	....	1.00
Mean	12.22	0.98	.47	7.66
S. D.	2.58	1.46	.20	1.51

.001). The differences on the conciliation and suspiciousness scales are not significant, although the more conciliatory and the more trusting subjects did earn slightly more profit.

In order to gain a better understanding of the interrelationship between our four measures of bargaining behavior, we have determined the correlation between these variables. These correlations, shown in Table 6.6, indicate that, as predicted, the higher a bargainer's initial offer, the higher his profit ($r = .31$, $p < .005$). Our hypothesis that the frequency of a bargainer's concession would be negatively correlated with the size of his payoff was not confirmed ($r = −.10$, n.s.). As predicted, the size of a bargainer's concession was inversely related to his payoff ($r = −.48, p < .001$). This implies that those bargainers who asked for high initial payoffs tended to make small concessions during the bargaining process, and those who asked for more moderate payoffs initially tended to make larger concessions. Since initial offers were positively correlated with frequency of concession ($r = .32, p < .005$), this means that those bargainers who started high tended to concede more often (not greater amounts) than the bargainers who started at a lower level. As one might expect, size and frequency of concession were inversely related ($r = −.35, p < .005$).

In an effort to determine the combined relationship of our bargaining variables plus the four PAS scores, to payoff, we ran a stepwise multiple regression analysis which included all of these variables with payoff as the dependent variable. As shown in Table 6.7, only three of the variables entered at a significant level of $p < .05$. It is interesting to note in Table 6.7 that only one of the four PAS measures (control) was among the significant variables. Also, notice that initial

TABLE 6.7 Stepwise Multiple Regression Model
(Payoff as Dependent Variable)

Order of Variable Entered	Multiple R	F Value	p
Size of concession	.48	25.4	< .01
Frequency of concession	.55	9.3	< .01
External vs. internal control	.58	3.6	< .05
Conciliatory vs. belligerence	.59	2.7	> .05
Suspiciousness vs. trust	.59	0.5	> .05
Risk avoidance vs. risk taking	.60	0.2	> .05
Initial offer	.60	0.1	> .05

offer was not one of the variables to enter significantly, despite the fact that we have previously shown this variable, by itself, to be significantly related to payoff. This is undoubtably due to the high correlation between initial offer and size of concession.

Bargaining Reciprocity

While investigating strategies, we also attempted to determine how many subjects appeared to be following a reciprocating concession-making strategy. A correlation analysis was run to determine the relationship between the amount of change in the buyer's asking level from one trial to the next, relative to the amount of change in his opponent's asking level over the previous two trials (these changes, which can be either positive or negative, were all measured in terms of the buyer's payoff). The resulting Pearson product-moment r values were generally quite low. Less than 20 percent were above 0.50, and only about one-third were above 0.20. One particularly surprising fact is that approximately 40 percent of the r values were negative in value, suggesting an inverse relationship between the changes in asking level of the buyers relative to the sellers. The negative r values were generally fairly small, however, over half being between 0 and − 0.20. Clearly the concessions of the sellers had a varying effect on the concessions of the buyers.

To study this effect in more detail, we classified each subject into one of three groups depending on whether his concessions were positively, negatively, or not significantly correlated with his opponent's concessions. Out of the 78 correlation coefficients for our bargaining pairs, 22 were significant in the positive directions, 23 were significant in a negative direction, and 33 were not significantly different from zero. Each of these three groups was then analyzed in the same manner in which the entire set of data was analyzed in Table 6.6 (i.e., to determine the relationship between the four bargaining measures). We note several interesting differences in these data, which are shown in Table 6.8. The most striking differences occur with the frequency-of-concession variable, where the correlations tend to change markedly from the positive group to the negative group. Those subjects who either ignore or react in a direction opposite to the concessions of their opponent are more likely to have a frequency of concession which is related to initial offer, and to have a higher relation (inverse) between size of concession and frequency of concession. Similarly, the variables "initial offer" and "size of concession" are seen to be significantly negatively correlated for the "no influence" and negatively influenced groups.

BARGAINING AND EMPLOYMENT SECTOR

In this section our focus is on a comparative analysis of two sets of data collected in Belgium, a private sector group (business executives) and a public

TABLE 6.8 Correlations of Bargaining Variables for Three Groups of Subjects

Variable	Positively Influenced (n=22)				No Influence (n=33)				Negatively Influenced (n=23)			
	IOF	SOC	FOC	PAY	IOF	SOC	FOC	PAY	IOF	SOC	FOC	PAY
IOF	1.00	$-.26^a$	.11	.09	1.00	$-.76^d$	$.34^b$	$.54^d$	1.00	$-.64^d$	$.49^c$	.17
SOC	..	1.00	$-.07$	$.59^d$	..	1.00	$-.34^b$	$.58^d$	..	1.00	$-.65^d$	$-.31^b$
FOC	..	..	1.00	$-.21$	..	..	1.00	$-.05$	..	..	1.00	.06
PAY	..	..	..	1.00	..	..	..	1.00	..	..	..	1.00

^{a}p < .10; ^{b}p < .05; ^{c}p < .01; ^{d}p < .001; IOF = Initial Offer; SOC = Size of Concession; FOC = Frequency of Concession; pay = payoff.

sector group (government employees). We were specifically interested in any differences in the vigor and effectiveness of the interpersonal bargaining behavior between these two groups. Based on our own conceptions of the stereotype of a public servant, especially for the government, we expected the private executives to bargain more aggressively and more successfully in the bilateral monopoly task.

For this experiment, 38 Flemish speaking Belgium executives participated, twenty from the private sector and eighteen from the public sector. The two groups did not differ significantly in terms of mean age, education, and years of experience. The data pertaining to these private and public executives are shown in Table 6.9.

Several interesting differences appear between the private and public executives. First, the private executives tended to begin bargaining with a more competitive initial offer. However, these private executives also tended to yield more, so the profit they earned was only slightly larger than that earned by the public executives ($7.35 vs. $7.15). The private executives took longer to reach agreement both in terms of the number of offers (14.10 vs. 8.11) and the duration of the negotiations (43.3 vs. 37.0 minutes). Thus, the private sector employees tended to begin bargaining from a more extreme stance, they tended to yield more in order to reach agreement, but they were only slightly more successful in terms of money earned. The public sector executives tended to start from a less selfish position, tended to yield less to reach agreement and to agree more quickly and with fewer exchanges, but they earned slightly less than their private counterparts.

In our analysis of the Belgium public and private executives we examined the personality (PAS) correlates of the initial offers, yielding, and final payoff. These data are shown in Table 6.10 in the form of a stepwise multiple regression output. Several interesting findings emerge from Table 6.10. First, it is apparent that the personality measures account for more of the variance (R^2) in the three bargaining behavior measures for the public executives than for the private executives. This is particularly the case with the two process measures: first offer, yielding. Second, the order in which the personality variables enter the regression differs between the samples. In the case of first offers and payoffs, the belief in internal-external control is particularly influential with the public executives; whereas with the private executives the dimension of suspiciousness vs. trust

TABLE 6.9 Bargaining Behavior Differences of Belgium Private and
Public Executives

	Private Executives	Public Executives	Significance Level
First offer	$10.70	$ 8.70	< .12
Payoff	$ 7.35	$ 7.15	NS
Yielding	$ 3.35	$ 1.55	< .07
Number of offers	14.10	8.11	< .15
Duration (minutes)	43.3	37.0	NS

TABLE 6.10 Stepwise Multiple Regression Relating PAS and Bargaining

Dependent Variable	Private Executives (N=20)			Public Executives (N=18)		
	Variable entered	F-ratio	R value	Variable entered	F-ratio	R value
First offer	S-T	3.361	.3967	Control	10.707	.6332
	C-B	2.537	.4794	C-B	7.435	.7056
	Control	1.687	.4902	Risk	5.049	.7209
	Risk	1.194	.4914	S-T	3.567	.7234
Payoff	S-T	5.162	.4721	Control	7.573	.5668
	C-B	3.235	.5280	Risk	4.480	.6115
	Control	3.006	.6004	S-T	3.373	.6477
	Risk	2.754	.6507	C-B	2.590	.6659
Yielding	C-B	7.265	.5362	S-T	8.162	.5812
	Risk	3.992	.5653	C-B	5.393	.6468
	Control	2.770	.5847	Control	3.502	.6548
	S-T	1.972	.5871			

seems dominant. In the case of the public executives the percentage of variance in the bargaining behaviors accounted for by the personality measures is high; e.g., 52 percent for first offer, 44 percent for payoff and 43 percent for yielding. A single personality dimension (internal-external control) in two cases accounts for more than 30 percent of the variance in each of the dependent variables. Thus, whereas the suspiciousness-trust dimension seems most dominant in relation to bargaining behavior for the private executives, the internal-external control dimension dominates in the case of the public executives.

SUMMARY AND CONCLUSIONS

Our findings indicate that the risk and control personality measures have the strongest relationship to the bargaining variables. In general, those subjects who were the most risk adverse and those who most strongly believed in internal control asked for the highest initial profits, tended to choose a tougher strategy and made significantly higher profits. Although the fact that most risk-adverse subjects tended to ask for high initial profits supports our earlier research in this area (Harnett et al., 1968), the present finding that risk avoiders tend to use a tough strategy, and make more profit, is not consistent with the earlier data. It thus appears that the risky approach in this study is to expose yourself to the possibility of being "compromised," or taken advantage of, by using some strategy other than a tough strategy.

As expected, subjects who made infrequent concessions make significantly greater profit than did those subjects who made frequent concessions. This re-sult supports the findings of Chertkoff and Conley (1967) in which they used a simulated bargaining opponent. Our finding that subjects who made few large concessions did not make higher profits than subjects who made many small concessions suggests that even in a "low pressure to reach agreement" experi-ment, the Osgood proposition is not disproved, contrary to the prediction made by Bartos (1965), Komorita (1971), and Pilisuk and Skolnick (1968). Our exper-iment, however, does not strictly conform to Osgood's model since he requires the two bargainers to have equal power, and for them to be stalemated, or to move away from a range of acceptable solutions. It may be that by giving our subjects an explicit time limit in which to reach agreement we were introducing more pressure than we thought.

Our calculations of the intercorrelations between the four measures of bar-gaining behavior indicated a significant positive relationship between the subject's initial offer and his payoff, and between his initial offer and the frequency with which he conceded. There was a significant negative relationship between initial offer and size of concession, between size and frequency of concession, and be-tween size of concession and payoff. In explaining differences among our sub-jects in terms of their payoffs, we found that two bargaining variables (size of concession and frequency of concession) and one personality measure (external versus internal control) entered significantly in a stepwise multiple regression analysis. These variables accounted for approximately 34 percent of the variation in payoffs.

Our data indicate considerable variability among our subjects in the extent to which their bidding pattern (strategy) was related to their opponent's pattern. In about 30 percent of our bargaining pairs there was a significant positive correla-tion between the sequence of concessions made by the two bargainers; another 40 percent were not significantly correlated; and perhaps most surprisingly, 30 percent of the correlations were significant in the negative direction. We also found that the subjects in these three groups differed in terms of the relationships between their initial offer, size of concessions, frequency of concessions, and payoff. In particular, we found that the subjects whose concessions had no rela-tionship, or an inverse relationship, to the concessions of their opponents had the highest correlations between initial offer and size of concession, between ini-tial offer and frequency of concession, and between size of concession and fre-quency of concession.

In terms of types of strategies used by the subjects, we found that the largest percent of our subjects employed what we have termed an "intermediate" strategy (29 percent), the next largest group being those using a "tough" approach (23.5 percent). There were approximately the same number of subjects using "soft" and "fair" as strategies (18.5 percent and 16.5 percent, respectively).

As predicted, those subjects classified as following a "tough" strategy earned the highest profit. It was surprising to find, however, that these subjects did not take any longer to reach agreement than did those in the "soft" group. The two strategies in which the bargainer is defined as starting at an asking level less than "high," the "intermediate" and "fair" groups, both took less time to reach agreement.

The fact that a tough strategy yielded the highest payoff gives support to the Siegel-Fouraker suggestion that the tougher the bargainer, the lower the resulting level of aspiration of the opponent, and therefore the higher the payoff predicted. However, the results of this study also support the Osgood proposal that a conciliatory (soft) strategy gains the trust of the opponent and does not result in a disadvantageous agreement or an exploitative strategy by the opponent. In fact, bargainers using any of the three strategies of "tough," "intermediate," and "soft" made more profit than the average of all subjects combined ($7.66). Only those subjects using a "fair" approach made less than this amount ($7.17). It is interesting to note that the average payoff to subjects using a "fair" strategy is very close to the payoff Schelling (1960) would predict as the "focal point" for the buyers, which is the mid-range of the payoffs to the buyer, or $\frac{1}{2}$ ($14.25 - 0$) = \$7.125.

This analysis is one of the first to compare strategies representing both the Osgood position and the Siegel-Fouraker position in a bilateral monopoly setting. Our results indicate that both styles of bargaining lead to a higher payoff than the mean for all subjects, and that both strategies require a longer time period before agreement is reached when compared to a fair or intermediate bargaining style. A partial explanation for the high profits yielded by these two approaches may be that both strategies start with a high initial asking level (IOF and PAY, $r = .31$). In fact, a high starting demand could explain both the longer time to reach agreement and the higher payoffs, if these subjects paced their concessions in terms of the time in which to negotiate (IOF and FOC, $r = .32$, IOF and SOC, $r = -.62$).

7

THEMES AND CONCLUSIONS

"Winning" in a conflict does not have a strictly competitive meaning; it is not winning relative to one's adversary. It means gaining relative to one's own value system; and this may be done by bargaining, by mutual accommodation, and by the avoidance of mutually damaging behavior (Schelling, 1960).

Our general orientation has been the study of bargaining as a decision-making mechanism among persons. This focus on interpersonal bargaining has been shaped by a concern for the effects of contextual and personality influences on the processes and results of bargaining. In this final chapter, we present what we consider to be the most important themes and conclusions emerging from our research. These integrative and closing comments are filtered by a tone of caution and conservatism. Many unsolved, perhaps unsolvable, problems and questions arose in the course of our research. These are confronted here as constraints on both the internal and external validity of our work. Wherever possible, we have attempted to solve the constraints by careful consideration of the benefits and costs of our decisions concerning design, analysis, and interpretation.

First, several themes are presented. These summarize the nature of our findings. The themes project our research onto the backdrop of previous work as reviewed in Chapters 1 and 2. Second, reservations and constraints are presented which condition the confidence that should be placed in our findings. Third, we draw conclusions concerning needs for research and future directions for efforts aimed at understanding bargaining behavior, its determinants, and its consequences.

THEMES

The Role of Information in Bargaining

One of the central themes throughout our research has been the significant role that information plays in the processes of negotiation and in determining the outcomes of bargaining. Early in our work we became interested in the strategic impact of ignorance; that is, in the impact that *not* knowing the needs and constraints of one's opponent has upon one's bargaining style and the results achieved. In addition, we were concerned with the role that knowledge by an opponent of his ignorance might have on bargaining. We have found that, indeed, the information structure of the bargaining situation does exert an important impact. Specifically, our research has produced four important findings relating to this theme.

First, we have generally confirmed the Schelling hypothesis; namely, that information can be a disadvantage to a bargainer. This is particularly the case where unequal information exists between bargainers, where the informed party knows that the other party is uninformed and where norms of equity or equality seem to be operating. Most strikingly, we have found that informed bargainers will attempt to use an available communication system to provide information concerning the payoff structure of the bargaining context *to* the uninformed bargainer. Presumably, the motive operating in such a situation is to induce the uninformed bargainer to lower his/her aspiration level and to take equity or equality considerations seriously.

Second, we found that whether bargainers possess information about the payoff structure of the bargaining situation influences the predictability of the bargaining outcome. Specifically, as discussed in Chapter 1, measures of a bargainer's expectations and personality are more predictive of the amount earned in bargaining in the presence than in the absence of information. In addition, the predictability of individual predictions shifts when one contrasts bargaining under information versus no-information conditions. Information seems to operate as a reality input into the bargaining process, resulting in a greater covariance of personal aspirations, expectations, and personality on the one hand and actual bargaining achievements on the other.

Third, we have discovered that the amount of information available to a bargainer concerning payoffs influences the impact that the bargainer's risk-taking propensity has on his/her success (money earned). We have found in two, separate studies that the impact of risk-taking propensity upon earnings is greater with less information. Our explanation of this is that, in general, the less structure available in the bargaining context, the greater the significance of the personal characteristics of the bargainer in influencing his/her behavior and the outcomes achieved.

Fourth, we have found strong evidence that the information available to a bargainer and the bargainer's aspiration level interact in influencing the bargaining process. Bargainers with relatively low aspiration levels prior to bargaining seem to gain bargaining strength when given information about their opponent's payoff structure while highly aspiring bargainers seem to lose strength with information. Our interpretation is that both types of bargainers adjust their aspiration levels (thus their behaviors) toward an intermediate ground when provided with the payoff structures of their opponents. Thus, information may serve to both raise and lower aspiration levels, depending on the initial discrepancy between a bargainer's a priori aspirations and the payoffs potentially available in the bargaining situation.

The Role of Personality in Bargaining

Our early research on United States subjects focused on one dimension of personality which we thought likely to influence bargaining behaviors; namely, risk-taking propensity. As we discussed in Chapters 3, 4, and 6, our later international research examined a much broader array of personality characteristics. Those international results will be summarized momentarily.

We have consistently found that a bargainer's risk-taking propensity impacts the processes that a bargainer uses in seeking his/her goals but does not show a significant relation to the results achieved in bargaining. Two primary themes summarize our findings. First, risk-taking propensity and willingness to yield are typically negatively related. Personalities characterized as high in risk taking show a reluctance to yield from an initial bargaining position. Clearly, in most bargaining situations, this can be seen as a risky strategy in that consistent and sustained refusal to yield can generate a stalemate resulting in a breakdown of negotiations. Second, as suggested earlier, we have found that this relation between risk-taking propensity as a personality characteristic and behavioral tenacity is influenced by the structure of the bargaining situation. In particular, we have typically found that risk proneness influenced tenacity only in the absence of information about the payoff structure confronting an opponent. Once again, our interpretation is that the reality of information about the opponent's situation dampens the reflection of the "pure" person in the bargainer's style of behavior. That is, as the payoff implications of a bargain are shared, norms of exchange, equity, and equality cause most bargainers to view the bargaining process within the context of self *plus* others *and* the situation facing them.

Importance of Careful Development of Measures

The development and refinement of an instrument to assess the personality characteristics of executives across cultures occupied a substantial portion of our research effort. Two major conclusions have emerged from this study of the *Personality/Attitude Schedule* (PAS).

First, the PAS, as refined and developed in our research program, was found to possess general, but not complete, factor structure stability across the three language groupings utilized. In each of the three language categories, the conciliation-belligerence, the risk taking-avoidance, and the suspiciousness-trust dimensions emerged as identifiable factors. The original internal-external control dimension did not emerge as an identifiable factor across the groupings. The risk taking dimension factored into two components in each of the language groupings: (a) physical risk taking, and (b) monetary risk taking.

Generally, as the language of the PAS used in our research became more dissimilar from the language of the original English of the PAS, the factor structure of the instrument decreased in similarity.

These results of the instrument development process are mildly encouraging regarding the cross-cultural use (with the associated language differences) of the original Shure-Meeker PAS instrument. The differences between the original version and the version of the PAS used in our work are largely ones of differentiation within the original factor structure.

Second, we found a less stable factor structure in the private executive versus military leader comparative study. One dimension (conciliation-belligerence) emerged as nearly identical across the two employment sector samples. The suspiciousness-trust dimension emerged in both samples but with slightly different item compositions. The risk taking dimension emerges in both samples also but is more differentiated in the military than in the civilian sample. The internal-external control dimension emerges only in the military sample.

So, it is clear that caution is needed when interpreting personality and attitudinal scores across samples in international research. The number of interpretable factors, the content of the factors, and the degree of differentiation within factors strongly suggest caution in interpreting our, as well as others', findings about personality comparisons across nationalities.

Managers' Personalities Across Cultures, Regions, and Employment Contexts

Our findings on management personality differences are quite rich and center on four themes. First, we can summarize our results concerning nationality differences on the PAS as follows by six conclusions:

1. Nationality differences of personality among executives appear to be specific to the personality dimension examined. The patterns of differences are not consistent across the four dimensions.

2. The executives scored as generally conciliatory (rather than belligerent), with the South Africans showing the greatest belligerence and the Spanish and Greeks exhibiting the strongest tendencies toward conciliation.

3. The executives generally fell on the risk averting end of the scale with the Thais being the most risk averting and the United States executives showing the greatest proneness toward risk.

4. Most executive groupings exhibited strong beliefs in internal control (self-determination) with the extreme exhibition of this belief being the United States sample. The Thai and Japanese executives were the only groups scoring relatively high on belief in external control (fate). Given the factor instability found for this dimension, caution is warranted in interpreting differences on this dimension.

5. Only the United States executives scored relatively high on the trust dimension. The remaining nationalities all exhibited strong tendencies toward interpersonal suspiciousness.

6. The United States executives exhibited an extreme position on three of the four scales. They were the most risk taking, the strongest believers in self-determination, and the most trusting.

Overall, it is important to note that only about five percent of the variability in the personality scores was due to nationality differences. However, in the case of each personality dimension, the percentage of variability attributable to nationality differences is significantly greater than zero ($p = .05$).

Second, we examined regional differences in personality within two of the nationality groupings. Within Spain we explored for differences among three regions within the country, finding the executives to be highly similar except for their risk-taking propensities. Spain presents a relatively unified picture compared with the intercountry differences. Within South Africa, the English and Afrikaan subsamples also did not differ significantly from one another, although the differences found were consistently in the predicted direction. We can conclude that in neither of the cases of within nationality comparisons have we found substantial differences on the four personality dimensions. We seem to have much firmer ground for generalizations *within* the nationalities sampled than *between* them.

Third, we explored the personality differences between the two employment sectors within each of two nationality groupings. We found that Belgian *public* sector managers were more conciliatory, more risk averting, and more fate-oriented than the average of all managers included in the total sample. The Belgian *private* sector managers, in contrast, scored between their public sector counterparts and the average of all managers in the total sample on three of the four PAS dimensions. Thus, the Belgian public and private managers studied are similar to one another in the sense that their scores fall consistently on the same side of the average scores for all executives studied. Yet, they are consistently different from one another in terms of the magnitude of the deviation of their scores away from the average score of most private managers. Within the United States comparison between the civilian and military managers, the two groups differ substantially only in that the military leaders exhibited tendencies toward greater interpersonal suspiciousness.

Finally, we examined differences in personality across employment functions within the total sample. The managers were categorized into one of four functions: general management, marketing and sales, finance and accounting, and production and engineering. The pattern that emerged indicates that the personality scores by functional breakdown are less diverse than were the average scores by the nationality groupings. However, the pattern of findings also confirms the general stereotype held of managers in the functional areas.

Bargaining Differences

Several findings summarize the themes of our research on this issue. While the nature of the bargaining situation gave the buyer an advantage, and while this advantage was utilized by the buyers in most of the nationality samples, the advantage was dissipated by the Thai and Japanese managers. In the other samples from Europe and the United States, the buyer did maintain the advantage inherent in the structure of the bargaining situation. The Japanese and Thai executives seem to strive for equality between the buyer and the seller roles. Of all the nationalities, the United States executives generated the largest differences in bargaining outcomes between the buyer and seller roles. In addition, of all the bargainers, the United States executives utilized the most competitive strategies while the Japanese and Thai executives were the least competitive and most cooperative.

We are generally struck, however, by the overall similarity of the bargaining behaviors of the executives from the different cultures. It seems clear from our results that most of the variance in bargaining processes and results must be attributed to differences other than nationality.

Determinants of Bargaining

Our findings on this issue are complex but can be summarized by discussing the relative importance of personality characteristics and situational factors as influences upon the bargaining processes and results. First, the personality variable having the most striking and consistent effect was the risk-taking propensity of the managers. Its strongest effect was upon the initial aspiration levels of the bargainers.

Second, we examined several strategic aspects of bargaining, both in terms of their consequences upon bargaining outcomes and in relation to their possible causes. Most noteworthy of our findings were that frequent concessions to an opponent, *regardless of their magnitude*, yielded less profit for a bargainer than infrequent concessions. When bargainers were classified according to four types of bargaining strategies, the total sample of managers was distributed as follows across the types:

23 percent followed a "tough" strategy,
29 percent followed an "intermediate" strategy,
10 percent followed a "soft" strategy, and
16 percent followed a "fair" strategy.

Third, the profit earned in bargaining was related to the strategy used. From most to least profit earned, the strategies were rank ordered as follows: tough, intermediate, soft, fair.

Fourth, risk-taking propensity and belief in internal versus external control were related to bargaining strategy with the risk averters and believers in internal control adopting the tougher bargaining strategies. In addition, the risk-averting bargainers earned more than the risk takers and the believers in internal control earned more than the believers in fate.

Fifth, one of the comparative analyses of the bargainers yielded a noteworthy difference. Within the Belgian sample, the private-sector executives tended to bargain more competitively, start with higher aspiration levels, yield more, utilize more bids, and take longer to reach agreement than did their public-sector counterparts. Personality variables were more predictive of the bargaining behavior of the public-sector executives than for their private counterparts.

CONSTRAINTS AND RESERVATIONS

In digesting our findings and interpretations, we are mindful of the need to comment explicitly upon some of the constraints of our work. While the cross-cultural aspects of our research program add a dimension of generalizability to our findings, the experimental nature of part of our methodology may well place constraints on the external validity of our research. We intentionally confronted the issue of the relevance of the experimental method and of findings derived therefrom in Chapter 1. We will not repeat that argument here except to emphasize that the choice was made in the interests of gaining the advantages of rigor, comparability of bargaining contexts and adaptability to analytical techniques. We do feel, in addition, that control of the conditions under which data are collected leads to increased, not decreased, generalizability of research findings.

Probably the major constraint operating on our research centers on the size and, perhaps, the representativeness of our samples. Clearly, there was an element of convenience of access operating in the selection of the samples. Due to the rather intensive nature of the interventions needed to collect both the bargaining and the personality data, we needed the full cooperation of the executive samples for an extended period of time. This requirement greatly constrained the number of available samples. Care was taken in terms of sample selection to assure as much sample similarity as possible on relevant demographic characteristics. As we have shown, our data indicate a reasonable degree of success in this regard.

The question of optimum sample size is nearly always a troublesome issue in "real world" research. We consciously attempted to optimize two objectives in selecting the sample sizes. First, we attempted to attain samples of size sufficient to apply appropriate analytical and statistical tests. This partially accounts for the differing sample sizes used with the different phases of our research program; e.g., instrument development versus experimental studies. Second, in the experimental phases of our research program, we could not exceed a sample size amenable to our experimental apparatus and technology. We also were constrained in this regard by our ability to study only a limited number of executives within the time available for access to these executives.

NEEDED RESEARCH

Three needs seem dominant to us as we review our work in the context of available knowledge on bargaining and personality as these relate to decision making.

First, clearly, the research reported here needs to be extended to additional cultures. It is important to know if our sampling of cultures was too homogeneous to discover the differences that would emerge across a broader spectrum of heterogeneity. Perhaps we should not expect to find large differences across cultures in the bargaining setting utilized in this research program. The bargaining situation studied here was explicitly selected to encourage differences to emerge and they, in general, did not. The general strategy used by the bargainers to approach the situation was basically similar across cultures. The demand characteristics of that situation may have dampened the emergence of differences. The general expectations toward competition, bargaining, and execution seemed similar across the samples. On the other hand, the differences among the countries *and* the clustering of the PAS scores did suggest that differences do exist among managers from different nations. These might well emerge in more distinct patterns from samples representing a wider spectrum of the world.

Second, this research needs to be extended to paradigms and settings that more closely approximate bargaining in enduring, interpersonal relationships. Of particular importance here is the need to insure that these extensions possess similar structural and processual characteristics as those of the bilateral monopoly bargaining context. This is the key to testing the external validity of our findings. It is not necessary to exactly model "reality" in the experimental setting. It is relatively unimportant to replicate each of the physical artifacts of the external world in an experimental setting. We have stated our position concerning the important trade-offs between internal and external validity in Chapter 1.

Thirdly, from the perspective of bargaining theory, there is a great need to extend the results attained here within the bilateral monopoly setting in the direction of other, more complex, bargaining models. An example of such a model would be the voting paradox wherein no logical solution exists which can be derived via analytical procedures. Yet, such dilemmas are, in fact, resolved behaviorally. Examining the differences in resolution strategies across cultures and samples should add significantly to our understanding of bargaining.

References

Adams, J. S., "Inequity in Social Exchange," in L. Berkowitz (Ed.), *Advances in Experimental Psychology*, Vol. 2, New York: Academic Press, 1965.

Adams, J. S., "The Structure and Dynamics of Behavior in Organization Boundary Roles," in M. D. Dunnette (Ed.) *Handbook of Industrial and Organizational Psychology*, Chicago: Rand McNally, 1967, 1175-1200.

Adorno, T. W., Frenkel-Brunswik, E., Levinson, D. J., and Sanford, R. N., *The Authoritarian Personality*, New York: Harper and Row, 1950.

Ajiferuke, M. and Boddewyn, J., "'Culture' and Other Explanatory Variables in Comparative Management Studies," *Academy of Management Journal*, 1970, Vol. 13, 153-163.

Alpert, B., "Non-businessmen as Surrogates for Businessmen in Behavioral Experiments," *The Journal of Business*, 1967, Vol. 40, 203.

Ashmore, R. D., "Personality-Attitude Variables and Characteristics of the Protagonist as Determinants of Trust in the Prisoner's Dilemma," unpublished manuscript, 1969.

Bartos, O. J., "Concession-making in Experimental Negotiations," in J. Berger, M. Zelditch, and B. Anderson (Eds.), *Sociological Theories in Action*, Boston: Houghton Mifflin, 1965.

Bartos, O. J., "How Predictable are Negotiations? " *Journal of Conflict Resolution*, 1967, Vol. 11, 481-496.

Bartunek, J. M., Benton, A. A., and Keys, C. B., "Third-party Intervention and the Bargaining Behavior of Group Representatives," *Journal of Conflict Resolution*, 1975, Vol. 19, 532-557.

Bass, B. M., "Effects on the Subsequent Performance Negotiations of Studying Issues or Planning Strategies Alone or in Groups," *Psychological Monographs*, 1966, Vol. 80, No. 614, 1-31.

Benton, A. A., "Accountability and Negotiations Between Group Representatives," *Proceedings*, 80th Annual Convention, *American Psychological Association*, 1972, 227-228.

Benton, A. A., and Druckman, D., "Constituent's Bargaining Orientation and Intergroup Negotiations," *Journal of Applied Social Psychology*, 1974, Vol. 4, 141-150.

Benton, A. A., Kelley, H. H., and Liebling, B., "Effects of Extremity of Offers and Concession Rate on the Outcomes of Bargaining," *Journal of Personality and Social Psychology*, 1972, Vol. 24, 73-83.

Bigoness, W. J., "The Effects of Alternative Modes of Third Party Intervention in Resolving Bargaining Impasses," Unpublished Doctoral Dissertation, Michigan State University, 1974.

Bixenstine, V. E., and Blundell, H., "Control of Choice Exerted by Structural Factors in Two-Person, Non-Zero-Sum Games, *Journal of Conflict Resolution*, 1966, Vol. 10, 478-487.

Bixenstine, V. E., Levitt, C. A., and Wilson, K. V., "Collaboration Among Six Persons in a Prisoner's Dilemma Game," *Journal of Conflict Resolution*, 1966, Vol. 10, 488-496.

Bixenstine, V. E., Potash, H. M., and Wilson, K. V., "Effects of Levels of Cooperative Choice by the Other Player on Choices in a Prisoner's Dilemma Game, Part I," *Journal of Abnormal and Social Psychology*, 1963, Vol. 66, 308-313.

Blake, R. R., and Mouton, J. S., "The Intergroup Dynamics of Win-Lose Conflict and Problem-Saving Collaboration in Union-Management Relations," in M. Sherif (Ed.), *Intergroup Relations and Leadership*, New York: John Wiley & Sons, 1962.

Blake, R. R., Shepard, H. A., and Mouton, J. S., *Managing Intergroup Conflict in Industry*, Houston: Gulf Publishing Co., 1964.

Blau, P. M., *Exchange and Power in Social Life*, New York: John Wiley & Sons, 1964.

Bloom, L., "Self Concepts and Social Status in South Africa: A Preliminary Cross-Cultural Analysis," *The Journal of Social Psychology*, 1960, Vol. 51, 103-112.

Bok, D. C., and Dunlop, J. T., *Labor and the American Community*, New York: Simon Schuster, 1970.

Botha, E., "The Achievement Motive in Three Cultures," *The Journal of Social Psychology*, 1971, Vol. 85, 163-170.

Brim, O. G., Jr., "Attitude Content-Intensity and Probability Expectations," *American Sociological Review*, 1954, Vol. 59, 68-76.

Brislin, R. W., "Back-Translation for Cross-Cultural Research," *Journal of Cross-Cultural Psychology*, 1970, Vol. 1, 185-216.

Brown, B. R., "The Effects of Need to Maintain Face on Interpersonal Bargaining," *Journal of the Experimental Social Psychology*, 1968, Vol. 4, 107-122.

Brown, B. R., "Face-saving and Face-restoration in Negotiation," in D. Druckman (Ed.), *Negotiations*, Beverly Hills, California: Sage Publications, Inc., 1977, pp. 275-299.

Caggiula, A. R., "The Reduction of Group Conflict," Unpublished Master's Thesis, University of Delaware, 1964.

Caldwell, J. D., "Communication and Sex Effects in a Five Person Prisoner's Dilemma Game," *Journal of Personality and Social Psychology*, 1976, Vol. 33, 273-280.

Campbell, R. J., *Originality in Group Productivity III: Partisan Commitment and Productive Independence in a Collective Bargaining Situation*, The Ohio State University Research Foundation, 1960.

Cann, A., Esser, J. K., and Komorita, S. S., "Equity and Concession Strategies," paper presented at the Midwestern Psychological Association Convention, Chicago, May, 1973.

Caplow, T. A., "A Theory of Coalition in the Triad," *American Sociological Reveiw*, 1956, Vol. 21, 489-493.

Caplow, T. A., "Further Development of a Theory of Coalition in the Triad," *American Journal of Sociology*, 1959, Vol. 64, 488-493.

Carlson, J. A., "Forecasting Errors and Business Cycles," *The American Economic Review*, 1967, Vol. 57, 462.

Carlson, J. A., "The Stability of an Experimental Market with a Supply-Response Lag," *The Southern Economic Journal*, 1967, Vol. 33, No. 33.

Carlson, J. A., and Davis, C. M., "Cultural Values and the Risky Shift: A Cross-Cultural Test in Uganda and the United States, *Journal of Personality and Social Psychology*, 1971, Vol. 20, 392-399.

Carment, D. W., "Risk-Taking Under Conditions of Chance and Skill in India and Canada," *Journal of Cross-Cultural Psychology*, 1974, Vol. 5, 23-34.

Cartwright, D., "Influence, Leadership, Control," in J. March (Ed.), *Handbook of Organizations*, Chicago: Rand McNally, 1965.

Cattell, R. B., "A Cross-Cultural Check on Second Stratum Personality Factor Structure: Notably of Anxiety and Exvia," *Australian Journal of Psychology*, 1965, Vol. 17, 12-23.

Cattell, R. B., and Warburton, F., "A Cross-Cultural Comparison of Patterns of Extraversion and Anxiety," *British Journal of Psychology*, 1961, Vol. 52, 3-16.

Chamberlain, N. W., *The Labor Sector*, New York: McGraw-Hill, 1965.

Chertkoff, J. M., and Baird, S. L., "The Application of the Big Lie Technique and the Last Clear Chance Doctrine to Bargaining," *Journal of Personality and Social Psychology*, 1971, Vol. 20, 298-303.

Chertkoff, J. M., and Conley, M., "Opening Offer and Frequency of Concession as Bargaining Strategies," *Journal of Personality and Social Psychology*, 1967, Vol. 7, 181-185.

Choungourian, A., "Lebanese and American Aspects of Personality: A Cross-Cultural Comparison," *The Journal of Social Psychology*, 1970, Vol. 81, 117-118.

Christe, R., and Geis, L., *Studies in Machiavellianism*, New York: Academic Press, 1970.

Clark, A. W., and McCabe, S., "Leadership Beliefs of Australian Managers," *Journal of Applied Psychology*, 1970, Vol. 54, 1-6.

Cole, S. G., "An Examination of the Power-Inversion Effect in Three-Person Mixed-Motive Games," *Journal of Personality and Social Psychology*, 1969, Vol. 13, 50-58.

Comrey, A., Meschieri, L., Misiti, R., and Nencini, R., "A Comparison of Personality Factor Structure in American and Italian Subjects," *Journal of Personality and Social Psychology*, 1965, Vol. 1, 257-261.

Concha, P., Garcia, L., and Perez, A., "Cooperation versus Competition: A Comparison of Anglo-American and Cuban-American Youngsters in Miami," *The Journal of Social Psychology*, 1975, Vol. 95, 273-274.

Conrath, P. W., "Experience as a Factor in Experimental Gaming Behavior," *Journal of Conflict Resolution*, 1970, Vol. 14, 195-202.

Crow, W. J., "A Study of Strategic Doctrines Using the Internation Simulation," *Journal of Conflict Resolution*, 1963, Vol. 7, 580-589.

Crow, W. J., and Noel, R. C., "The Valid Use of Simulation Results," *Western Behavioral Sciences Institute Report*, La Jolla, California, June 19, 1965.

Crow, W. J., and Noel, R. C., "An Experiment in Simulated Historical Decision Making" in M. G. Hermann (Ed.), *A Psychological Examination of Political Leaders*, New York: Free Press, 1976, 385-405.

Crowne, D. P., "Family Orientation, Level of Aspiration, and Inter-personal Bargaining," *Journal of Personality and Social Psychology*, 1966, Vol. 3, 641-645.

Cummings, L. L., Harnett, D. L., and Schmidt, S. M., "International Cross-Language Factor Stability of Personality: An Analysis of the Shure-Meeker Personality-Attitude Schedule," *The Journal of Psychology*, 1972, Vol. 82, 67-84.

Cummings, L. L., Harnett, D. L., and Schmidt, S. M., "Factor Similarity of Personality Across Private and Military Samples: An Analysis of the Personality-Attitude Schedule," *The Journal of Psychology*, 1973, Vol. 83, 215-226.

Cummings, L. L., Harnett, D. L., and Stevens, O. J., "Risk, Fate, Conciliation and Trust: An International Study of Attitudinal Differences Among Executives," *Academy of Management Journal*, 1971, Vol. 14, 285-304.

Cummings, L. L., and Schmidt, S. M., "Managerial Attitudes of Greeks: The Roles of Culture and Industrialization," *Administrative Science Quarterly*, 1972, Vol. 17, 265-272.

Cummings, L. L., Schmikl, E., and Blackburn, R., "White South African Managers: How Different Are They?", *Business Management* (Journal of the South African Association of Business Management), 1977, Vol. 8, 3-10.

Deutsch, M., "Trust and Suspicion," *Journal of Conflict Resolution*, 1958, Vol. 2, 265-279.

Deutsch, M., "The Effect of Motivational Orientation Upon Trust and Suspicion," *Human Relations*, 1960, Vol. 13, 123-140.

Deutsch, M., "Trust, Trustworthiness, and the F Scale," *Journal of Abnormal and Social Psychology*, 1960, Vol. 61, 138-140.

Deutsch, M., "Cooperation and Trust: Some Theoretical Notes," in M. R. Jones, (Ed.), *Nebraska Symposium on Motivation: 1962*, University of Nebraska Press, 275-320.

Deutsch, M., "Conflict and Its Resolution," paper presented at the 73rd American Psychological Convention, 1965.

Deutsch, M., "Socially Relevant Science: Reflections on Some Studies of Interpersonal Conflict," *American Psychologist*, 1969, Vol. 24, 1076-1092.

Deutsch, M., Canavan, D., and Rubin, J., "The Effects of Size of Conflict and Sex of Experimenter Upon Interpersonal Bargaining," *Journal of Experimental Social Psychology*, 1971, Vol. 7, 258-267.

Deutsch, M., and Krauss, R. M., "Studies of Interpersonal Bargaining," *The Jour-*

nal of Conflict Resolution, 1962, Vol. 6, 52-67.

Dolbear, F. T., Jr. and Lave, L. B., "Risk Orientation as a Predictor in the Prisoner's Dilemma," *Journal of Conflict Resolution*, 1966, Vol. 10, 506-515.

Dorris, J. W., "Reactions to Unconditional Cooperation: A Field Study," *Journal of Personality and Social Psychology*, 1972, Vol. 22, 387-397.

Douglas, A., *Industrial Peacemaking*, New York: Columbia University Press, 1962.

Driver, M. J., "Individual Differences as Determinants of Aggression in the Inter-Nation Simulation" in M. G. Hermann (Ed.), *A Psychological Examination of Political Leaders*, New York: Free Press, 1976, 337-383.

Druckman, D., "Dogmatism, Prenegotiation Experience, and Simulated Group Representation as Determinants of Dyadic Behavior in a Bargaining Situation," *Journal of Personality and Social Psychology*, 1967, Vol. 6, 279-290.

Druckman, D., "Prenegotiation Experience and Dyadic Conflict Resolution in a Bargaining Situation," *Journal of Experimental Social Psychology*, 1968, Vol. 4, 367-383.

Druckman, D., "The Influence of the Situation in Interparty Conflict," *Journal of Conflict Resolution*, 1971(a), Vol. 15, 523-555.

Druckman, D., "On the Effects of Groups Representation," *Journal of Personality and Social Psychology*, 1971(b), Vol. 18, 273-274.

Druckman, D., *Negotiations*, Beverly Hills, California: Sage Publications, Inc., 1977.

Druckman, D., Benton, A. A., Ali, F., and Bagur, J. S., "Culture Differences in Bargaining Behavior," *Journal of Conflict Resolution*, 1976, Vol. 20, 413-449.

Druckman, D., Solomon, D., and Zechmeister, K., "The Influence of Negotiator's Role and Negotiating Set on Children's Distribution of Resources," *Sociometry*, 1972, Vol. 35, 387-410.

Dufty, N. F., "The Evolution of the Indian Industrial Relations Systems," *Journal of Industrial Relations*, 1965, Vol. 7, 40-49.

Ellis, D. S., "An Analysis of the Differential Effects of Various Types and Degrees of Communication Opportunity on Conflict Between Groups," Unpublished Doctoral Dissertation, Purdue University, 1965.

Elkouri, F., and Elkouri, E. A., *How Arbitration Works*, Washington, D. C.: BNA Incorporated, 1960.

Emerson, R. M., "Power-Dependence Relations," *American Sociological Review*, 1962, Vol. 27, 31-41.

Erickson, B., Holmes, J. G., Frey, R., Walker, L., and Thibaut, J., "Functions of a Third Party in the Resolution of Conflict: The Role of a Judge in Pre-trial Conferences," *Journal of Personality and Social Psychology*, 1974, Vol. 30, 293-306.

Esser, J. K., "Effects of Prior Success or Failure on Subsequent Bargaining," Unpublished Doctoral Dissertation, Indiana University, 1975.

Esser, J. K., and Komorita, S. S., "Reciprocity and Concession-Making in Bargaining," *Journal of Personality and Social Psychology*, 1975, Vol. 31, 864-872.

Evans, H., "Effects of Unilateral Promise and Value of Rewards Upon Cooperation and Trust," *Journal of Abnormal and Social Psychology*, 1964, Vol. 69, 587-590.

Faucheany, C., and Moscovici, S., "Self-Esteem and Exploitative Behavior in a

Game Against Chance and Nature," *Journal of Personality and Social Psychology*, 1968, Vol. 1, 83-88.

Fellner, W., *Competition Among the Few*, New York: Alfred Knopf, 1949.

Fouraker, L. E., and Siegel, S., *Bargaining Behavior*, New York: McGraw-Hill, 1963.

Frey, R. L., and Adams, J. S., "The Negotiator's Dilemma: Simultaneous In-Group and Out-group Conflict," *Journal of Experimental Social Psychology*, 1972, Vol. 8, 331-346.

Fry, C. L., "Personality and Acquisition Factors in the Development of Coordination Strategy," *Journal of Personality and Social Psychology*, 1965, Vol. 2, 403-407.

Gahagan, J. P., and Tedeschi, J. T., "Strategy and the Credibiility of Promises in the Prisoner's Dilemma Game," *Journal of Conflict Resolution*, 1968, Vol. 12, 224-234.

Gallo, P. S., "Effects of Increased Incentives Upon the Use of Threat in Bargaining," *Journal of Personality and Social Psychology*, 1966, Vol. 4, 14-20.

Gallo, P. S., Funk, S. G., and Levine, J. R., "Reward Size, Method of Presentation and Number of Alternatives in a Prisoner's Dilemma Game," *Journal of Personality and Social Psychology*, 1969, Vol. 13, 239-244.

Gallo, P. S., and McClintock, C. G., "Cooperative and Competitive Behavior in Mixed-Motive Games," *Journal of Conflict Resolution*, 1965, Vol. 9, 68-78.

Gamson, W. A., "A Theory of Coalition Formation," *American Sociological Review*, 1961, Vol. 26, 373-382.

Gaston, V. R., "International Differences in the Strike Propensity of Coal Miners: Experience in Four Countries," *Industrial and Labor Relations Review*, 1959, Vol. 3, 389-405.

Geis, F., "Machiavellianism and the Manipulation of One's Fellow Man," paper presented at the 72nd Annual Meeting of the American Psychological Association, Los Angeles, 1964.

Gladstone, A. I., "The Possibility of Predicting Reactions to International Events," *Journal of Social Issues*, 1955, Vol. 2, 21-28.

Goffman, E., "Embarrassment and Social Organization," *American Journal of Sociology*, 1956, Vol. 62, 264-271.

Gordon, L. V., "Q-Typing of Oriental and American Youth: Initial and Clarifying Studies," *Journal of Social Psychology*, 1967, Vol. 71, 185-195.

Gouldner, A. W., "The Norm of Reciprocity: A Preliminary Statement," *American Sociological Review*, 1960, Vol. 25, 161-178.

Grant, M. J., and Sermat, V., "Status and Sex of Other as Determinants of Behavior in a Mixed Motive Game," *Journal of Personality and Social Psychology*, 1969, Vol. 12, 151-157.

Gregovich, R. P., "Sex Differences in the Prisoner's Dilemma Game," unpublished Doctoral Dissertation, University of Oregon, 1968.

Guilford, J. P., Christensen, P. R., and, N. A., and Sutton, M. A., "Technical Appendices to the Research Bulletin: A Factor Analysis Study of Human Interest." *Research Bulletin 53-11, Human Resources Research Center*, Lackland Air Force Base, San Antonio, Texas, 1953.

Gumpert, P. M., Deutsch, M., and Epstein, Y., "Effects of Incentive Magnitude on Cooperation in the Prisoner's Dilemma Game," *Journal of Personality and Social Psychology*, 1969, Vol. 11, 66-69.

Guyer, M., and Rapoport, A., "Threat in a Two Person Game," *Journal of Experimental Social Psychology*, 1970, Vol. 6, 11-25.

Haire, M., Ghiselli, E. E., and Porter, L. W., *Managerial Thinking: An International Study*, New York: John Wiley and Sons, 1966.

Hall, D., Bettignies, H. C., and Amado-Fischgrund, G., "The European Business Elite," *European Business*, 1969, Vol. 23, 45-55.

Hamner, W. Clay, "Effects of Bargaining Strategy and Pressure to Reach Agreement in a Stalemated Negotiation," *Journal of Personality and Social Psychology*, 1974, Vol. 30, 458-467.

Hamner, W. Clay, and Baird, L. S., "The Effect of Strategy, Pressure to Reach Agreement, and Relative Power on Bargaining Behavior," in H. Sauerman (Ed.), *Contributions to Experimental Economics*, Vol. V., Frankfurt, Germany: J.C.B., Mohr Tubigen, 1978.

Hamner, W. Clay and Harnett, D. L., "Goal Setting, Performance, and Satisfaction in an Interdependent Task," *Organizational Behavior and Human Performance*, 1974, Vol. 12, 217-230.

Hamner, W. Clay and Harnett, D. L., "The Effects of Information and Aspiration Level on Bargaining Behavior," *Journal of Experimental Social Psychology*, 1975, Vol. 11, 320-342.

Hamner, W. Clay, Kim, J. S., and Heid, D., "Bargaining Behavior: A Comparison Between Purchasing Agents and College Students," *Proceedings*, Midwest Meeting of the American Institute for Decision Sciences, May, 1974.

Hamner, W. C., and Yukl, G. A., "The Effectiveness of Different Offer Strategies in Bargaining" in D. Druckman (Ed.), *Negotiations*, Beverly Hills, California: Sage Publications, Inc., 1977, 137-160.

Harford, T. C., and Cutter, H. S. G., "Cooperation Among Negro and White Boys and Girls," *Psychological Reports*, 1966, Vol. 18, 818.

Harmon, H. H., *Modern Factor Analysis* (2nd ed., revised). Chicago: University of Chicago Press, 1967.

Harnett, D. L., "Bargaining and Negotiation in a Mixed-Motive Game: Price Leadership Bilateral Monopoly," *Southern Economic Journal*, April 1967, 33, 479-87.

Harnett, D. L., and Cummings, L. L., "Bargaining Behavior in an Asymmetrical Triad," in B. Lieberman (Ed.), *Social Choice*, Gordon and Beach, Inc., 1972.

Harnett, D. L., Cummings, L. L., and Hughes, G. D., "The Influence of Risk-Taking Propensity on Bargaining Behavior," *Behavioral Science*, 1968, Vol. 13, 1-11.

Harnett, D. L., and Hamner, W. Clay, "The Value of Information in Bargaining," *Western Economic Journal*, 1973, Vol. XI, 81-88.

Harnett, D. L., Hughes, G. D., and Cummings, L. L., "Bilateral Monopolistic Bargaining through an Intermediary," *The Journal of Business*, 1968, Vol. 42, 251-259.

Harrison, A. A., and McClintock, C., "Previous Experience Within the Dyad and Cooperative Game Behavior," *Journal of Personality and Social Psychology*, 1965, Vol. 1, 671-675.

Harsanyi, J. C., "Approaches to the Bargaining Problem Before and After the Theory of Games: A Critical Discussion of Zeuthen's, Hicks', and Nash's Theories," *Econometrica*, 1956, Vol. 24, 144-157.

Harsanyi, J. C., "Bargaining in Ignorance of the Opponent's Utility Function," *The Journal of Conflict Resolution*, 1962, Vol. 1, 29-38.

Hatton, J. M., "Reactions of Negroes in a Biracial Bargaining Situation," *Journal of Personality and Social Psychology*, 1967, Vol. 7, 301-306.

Hermann, M. G., and Kogan, N., "Negotiation in Leader and Delegate Groups," *Journal of Conflict Resolution*, 1968, Vol. 12, 332-334.

Hermann, M. G., and Kogan, N., "Effects of Negotiators' Personality on Negotiating Behavior" in D. Druckman, (Ed.), *Negotiations*, Beverly Hills, California: Sage Publications, Inc., 1977, 247-274.

Hicks, J. R., *The Theory of Wages*,London: Macmillan, 1935.

Hinton, B. L., Hamner, W. Clay, and Pohlen, M. F., "The Influence of Reward Magnitude, Opening Bid and Concession Rate on Profit Earned in a Managerial Negotiation Game," *Behavioral Science*, 1974, Vol. 19, 197-203.

Holmes, J. G., Throop, W. F., and Strickland, L. H., "The Effects of Prenegotiation Expectations on the Distributive Bargaining Process," *Journal of Experimental Social Psychology*, 1971, Vol. 7, 582-599.

Homans, G. C., "Social Behavior as Exchange," *American Journal of Sociology*, 1958, Vol. 63, 597-606.

Ikle, F. C., and Leites, N., "Political Negotiations as a Process of Modifying Utilities," *The Journal of Conflict Resolution*, 1962, Vol. 6, 12-28.

Ilgen, D. R., and Hamstra, B. W., "Performance Satisfaction as a Function of the Difference Between Expected and Reported Performance," *Organizational Behavior and Human Performance*, 1972, Vol. 7, 359-370.

Jamison, K., and Comrey, A. L., "A Comparison of Personality Factor Structure in British and American University Students," *Journal of Psychology*, 1969, Vol. 71, 45-57.

Johnson, D. F., and Pruitt, D. G., "Pre-intervention Effects of Mediation *vs.* Arbitration," *Journal of Applied Psychology*, 1972, Vol. 56, 1-10.

Johnson, D. F., and Tullar, W. L., "Style of Third Party Intervention, Face-Saving, and Bargaining Behavior," *Journal of Experimental Social Psychology*, 1972, Vol. 8, 319-330.

Jones, W. H., and Shure, G. H., "ITEMSEL—A Program to Select Items by the Wherry-Gaylord Method," *Behavioral Science*, 1965, Vol. 11, 80-82.

Joseph, M. L., and Willis, R. H., "An Experimental Analog to Two-Party Bargaining," *Behavioral Science*, 1963, Vol. 8, 117-127.

Kahan, J. P., "Effects of Level of Aspiration in an Experimental Bargaining Situation," *Journal of Personality and Social Psychology*, 1968, Vol. 8, 154-159.

Kaiser, H. F., "The Varimax Criterion for Analytic Rotation in Factor Analysis," *Psychometrika*, 1958, Vol. 69, 187-200.

Kanekar, S., and Mukerjee, S., "Personality Variables Among Three Communities in India," *The Journal of Social Psychology*, 1971, Vol. 84, 305-306.

Kanouse, D. E., and Wiest, W. M., "Some Factors Affecting Choice in the Prisoner's Dilemma," *Journal of Conflict Resolution*, 1967, Vol. 11, 206-213.

Kannappass, S., "Industrial Relations Problems in the Developing Indian Economy," *Industrial Relations Research Association*, 1963, Vol. 16, 76-88.

Kelley, H. H., "Experimental Studies of Threats in Interpersonal Negotiations," *Journal of Conflict Resolution*, 1965, Vol. 9, 79-105.

Kelley, H. H., "A Classroom Study of the Dilemmas in Interpersonal Negotiations," in K. Archibald (Ed.), *Strategic Interaction and Conflict*, Berkeley, California: Institute of International Studies, University of California, 1966.

Kelley, H. H., Beckman, L. L., and Fischer, C. S., "Negotiating the Division of a Reward Under Incomplete Information," *Journal of Experimental Social Psychology*, 1967, Vol. 3, 361-398.

Kenny, D. A., "A Quasi-Experimental Approach to Assessing Treatment Effects in the Nonequivalent Control Group Design," *Psychological Bulletin*, May, 1975, Vol. 82, 345-362.

Kerr, C., "Industrial Conflict and Its Mediation," *American Journal of Sociology*, 1954, Vol. 60, 230-245.

Kikuchi, A., and Gordon, L. V., "Evaluation and Cross-Cultural Application of a Japanese Form of the Survey of Interpersonal Values," *Journal of Social Psychology*, 1966, Vol. 69, 185-195.

Knapp, W. M., and Podell, J. B., "Mental Patients, Prisoners, and Students with Simulated Partners in a Mixed-Motive Game," *Journal of Conflict Resolution*, 1968, Vol. 12, 235-241.

Kogan, N., and Wallach, M. A., *Risk Taking: A Study in Cognition and Personality*. New York: Holt, Rinehart, and Winston, 1964.

Komorita, S. S., "Cooperative Choice in a Prisoner's Dilemma Game," *Journal of Personality and Social Psychology*, 1965, Vol. 2, 741-745.

Komorita, S. S., "Tacit Communication and Cooperation in a Two-Person Game," in Vol. III, *Workshop on Experimental Economics*, Frankfurt, Germany, 1972.

Komorita, S. S., and Barnes, M., "Effects of Pressures to Reach Agreement in Bargaining," *Journal of Personality and Social Psychology*, 1969, Vol. 13, 245-252.

Komorita, S. S., and Brenner, A. R., "Bargaining and Concession-Making Under Bilateral Monopoly," *Journal of Personality and Social Psychology*, 1968, Vol. 9, 15-20.

Komorita, S. S., and Esser, J. K., "Frequency of Reciprocated Concessions in Bargaining," *Journal of Personality and Social Psychology*, 1975, Vol. 32, 699-705.

Komorita, S. S., and Koziej, R., "Tacit Communication in a Prisoner's Dilemma Game," paper presented at the Midwestern Psychological Association Meetings, April, 1970.

Komorita, S. S., and Mechling, J., "Betrayal and Reconciliation in a Two-Person Game," *Journal of Personality and Social Psychology*, 1967, Vol. 6, 349-353.

Komorita, S. S., Sheposh, J. P., and Braver, L. S., "Power, the Use of Power, and Cooperative Choice in a Two-Person Game," *Journal of Personality and Social Psychology*, 1968, Vol. 8, 134-142.

Krauss, R. M., "Structural and Attitudinal Factors in Interpersonal Bargaining," *Journal of Experimental Social Psychology*, 1966, Vol. 2, 42-55.

Krauss, R. M., and Deutsch, M., "Communication in Interpersonal Bargaining," *Journal of Personality and Social Psychology*, 1966, Vol. 4, 572-577.

Lamm, H., and Kogan, N., "Risk Taking in the Context of Intergroup Negotiation," *Journal of Experimental Social Psychology*, 1970, Vol. 6, 351-363.

Landsberger, H. A., "Interim Report of a Research Project on Mediation," *Labor Law Review*, 1955, Vol. 6, 552-560.

Lane, I. M., Messe, L. A., and Phillips, J. L., "Differential Inputs as a Determinant in the Selection of a Distribution of Rewards," *Psychonomic Science*, 1971, Vol. 22, 228-229.

LaTour, S., Houlden, P., Walker, L., and Thibaut, J., "Some Determinants of Preference for Modes of Conflict Resolution," *Journal of Conflict Resolution*, 1976, Vol. 20, 319-356.

Lefley, H. P., "Model Personality in the Bahamas," *Journal of Cross-Cultural Psychology*, 1972, Vol. 3, 135-147.

Leventhal, G. S., Allen, J., and Kelamelgar, B., "Reducing Inequity by Reallocating Rewards," *Psychonomic Science*, 1969, Vol. 14, 295-296.

Leventhal, G. S. and Lane, D., "Sex, Age, and Equity Behavior," *Journal of Personality and Social Psychology*, 1970, Vol. 15, 312-316.

Leventhal, G. S., Michaels, J. W., and Sanford, C., "Inequity and Interpersonal Conflict," *Journal of Personality and Social Psychology*, 1972, Vol. 23, 88-102.

Leventhal, L. and Michaels, J. W., "Extending the Equity Model," *Journal of Personality and Social Psychology*, 1969, Vol. 12, 303-309.

Levinson, D. J., "Authoritarian Personality and Foreign Policy," *Journal of Conflict Resolution*, 1957, Vol. 1, 37-47.

Liebert, R. M., Smith, W. P., Hill, J. H., and Keiffer, M., "The Effects of Information and Magnitude of Initial Offer on Interpersonal Negotiation," *Journal of Experimental Social Psychology*, 1968, Vol. 4, 431-441.

Lirtzman, S. I. and Wahba, M. A., "A Managerial Myth: Differences in Coalition Behavior of Men and Women in Organizations," New York, 1972, (mimeo).

Locke, E. A., "What is Job Satisfaction?," *Organizational Behavior and Human Performance*, 1969, Vol. 4, 309-336.

Loomis, J. L., "Communication, the Development of Trust and Cooperative Behavior," *Human Relations*, 1959, Vol. 12, 108-118.

Lutzker, D. R., Internationalism as a Predictor of a Cooperative Behavior," *Journal of Conflict Resolution*, 1960, Vol. 4, 426-430.

Mann, J. W., "Race-Linked Values in South Africa," *The Journal of Social Psychology*, 1965, Vol. 58, 31-41.

Marlowe, D., "Some Personality and Behavioral Correlates of Conformity," Unpublished Ph.D. thesis, Ohio State Universtiy, 1959.

Marlowe, D., "Psychological Needs and Cooperation-Competition in a Two-Person Game," *Psychological Reports*, 1963, Vol. 13, 364.

Marlowe, D., Gergen, K. J., and Dobb, A. N., "Opponent's Personality, Expectation of Social Interaction, and Interpersonal Bargaining," *Journal of Personality and Social Psychology*, Vol. 3, 1966, 206-213.

Mason, E. P., "Comparison of Personality Characteristics of Junior High Students from American Indian, Mexican, and Caucasian Ethnic Backgrounds," *The Journal of Social Psychology*, 1967, Vol. 73, 145-155.

Maxwell, G. and Schmitt, D. R., *Cooperation: An Experimental Analysis*, New York: Academic Press, 1975.

McClintock, C. G., Gallo, P., and Harrison, A. A., "Some Effects of Variations in Other Strategy Upon Game Behavior," *Journal of Personality and Social*

Psychology, 1965, Vol. 1, 319-325.

McClintock, C. G., Harrison, A. A., Strand, S., and Gallo, P., "Internationalism-Isolationism, Strategy of the Other Player and Two-Person Game Behavior," *Journal of Abnormal and Social Psychology*, 1963, Vol. 6, 631-636.

McClintock, C. G., and McNeel, S. P., "Reward and Score Feedback as Determinants of Cooperative and Competitive Behavior," *Journal of Personality and Social Psychology*, 1966a, Vol. 4, 606, 613.

McClintock, C. G., and McNeel, S. P., "Reward Level and Game Playing Behavior," *Journal of Conflict Resolution*, 1966b, Vol. 10, 98-102.

McClintock, C. G., and McNeel, S. P., "Prior Dyadic Experience and Monetary Reward as Determinants of Cooperative and Competitive Game Behavior," *Journal of Personality and Social Psychology*, 1967, Vol. 5, 282-294.

McCord, W., and McCord, J., "A Tentative Theory of the Structure of Conscience," D. Willner ed., *Decisions, Values and Groups*, Vol. 1, London: Pergamon Press, 1960, 108-134.

McGrath, J. E., "A Social Psychological Approach to the Study of Negotiation," R. Bowers ed., *Studies on Behavior in Organizations: A Research Symposium*, Athens: University of Georgia Press, 1966.

McGrath, J. E., and Julian, J. W., *Negotiation and Conflict: An Experimental Study*, Technical Report No. 16, Group Effectiveness Research Laboratory, University of Illinois, 1962.

McGrath, J. E., and Julian, J. W., "Interaction Process and Task Outcomes in Experimentally-Created Negotiation Groups," *Journal of Psychological Studies*, 1963, Vol. 14, 117-138.

Meade, R. D., and Barnard, W. A., "Conformity and Anticonformity Among Americans and Chinese," *The Journal of Social Psychology*, 1973, Vol. 89, 15-24.

Melihian, E., Ginsberg, A., Ciiceloglu, D., and Lynn, R., "Achievement Motivation in Afghanistan, Brazil, Saudi Arabia, and Turkey," *The Journal of Social Psychology*, 1971, Vol. 83, 183-184.

Messe, L. A., "The Concept of Equity in Bargaining," Paper presented at the Meeting of the Peace Research Society, Ann Arbor, November, 1969.

Messe, L. A., "Equity in Bilateral Bargaining," *Journal of Personality and Social Psychology*, 1971, Vol. 17, 287-291.

Messick, D. G., and Throngate, W. B., "Relative Gain Maximization in Experimental Games," *Journal of Experimental Social Psychology*, 1967, Vol. 3, 85-101.

Minas, J. S., Scodel, A., Marlow, D., and Rawson, H., "Some Descriptive Aspects of Two-Person Non-Zero Sum Games: II," *Journal of Conflict Resolution*, 1960, Vol. 4, 193-197.

Modelski, G., "The World's Foreign Ministers: A Political Elite," *Journal of Conflict Resolution*, 1970, Vol. 14, 135-175.

Morgan, W. R., and Sawyer, J., "Bargaining Expectations and the Preference for Equality Over Equity," *Journal of Personality and Social Psychology*, 1967, Vol. 6, 139-149.

Nash, J. F., "The Bargaining Problem," *Econometrica*, 1950, Vol. 18, 155-162.

Organ, D. W., "Some Variables Affecting Boundary Role Behavior," *Sociometry*, 1971, Vol. 34, 507-534.

Orne, M. T., "On the Social Psychology of the Psychological Experiment with

Particular Reference to Demand Characteristics with their Implications,"
C. W. Qackman, and P. F. Secords, eds., *Problems in Social Psychology*,
New York: McGraw-Hill, 1965, 15.

Osgood, C. E., "Suggestions for Winning the Real War with Communism,"
Journal of Conflict Resolution, 1959, Vol. 3, 295-325.

Osgood, C. E., *An Alternative to War and Surrender*, Urbana, Illinois: University
of Illinois Press, 1962.

Oskamp, S., "Effects of Programmed Strategies on Cooperation in the Prisoners'
Dilemma and Other Mixed-Motive Games," *Journal of Conflict Resolution*,
1971, Vol. 15, 225-259.

Oskamp, S., and Kleinke, C., "Amount of Reward as a Variable in the Prisoner's
Dilemma Game," *Journal of Personality and Social Psychology*, 1970,
Vol. 16, 133-140.

Oxnam, D. W., "International Comparisons of Industrial Conflict," *Journal of
Industrial Relations*, 1965, Vol. 7, 149-163.

Patchen, M., "Models of Cooperation and Conflict: A Critical Review," *Journal
of Conflict Resolution*, 1970, Vol. 3, 389-407.

Peptione, A., *Attraction and Hostility*, New York: Atherton Press, 1964.

Pepitone, A., Fauchenx, C., Moscovici, S., Cesi-Biachi, M., Magistretti, G.,
Iacono, G., Asprea, A. M., and Villone, G., "The Role of Self-Esteem in
Competitive Choice Behavior," *International Journal of Psychology*, 1967,
Vol. 2, 147-159.

Pilisuk, M., Potter, P., Rapoport, A., and Winter, J. A., "War Hawks and Peace
Doves: Alternative Resolutions of Experimental Conflict," *Journal of
Conflict Resolution*, 1965, Vol. 9, 491-508.

Pilisuk, M., and Skolnick, P., "Inducing Trust: A Test of the Osgood Proposal,"
Journal of Personality and Social Psychology, 1968, Vol. 8, 121-133.

Pilisuk, M., Skolnick, P., and Overstreet, E., "Predicting Cooperation from the
Two Sexes in a Conflict Simulation," *Journal of Personality and Social
Psychology*, 1968, Vol. 10, 35-43.

Podell, J. F., and Knapp, W. M., "The Effect of Mediation on Perceived Firmness
of the Opponent," *Journal of Conflict Resolution*, 1969, Vol. 13, 511-520.

Porat, A. M., "Planning and Role Assignments in the Study of Conflict Resolution in Two Countries," Technical Report No. 28, Management Research
Center, University of Rochester, 1969.

Porat, A. M., "Cross-Cultural Differences in Resolving Union-Management Conflict through Negotiations," *Journal of Applied Psychology*, 1970, Vol. 54,
441-451.

Prassow, P., and Peters, E., *Conflict Resolution in Labor Relations*, New York:
McGraw-Hill, 1970.

Pruitt, D. G., "An Analysis of Responsiveness Between Nations," *Journal of
Conflict Resolution*, 1962, Vol. 6, 5-18.

Pruitt, D. G., "Indirect Communication and the Search for Agreement in Negotiations," *Journal of Applied Social Psychology*, 1971, Vol. 3, 205-239.

Pruitt, D. G., "Methods for Resolving Differences of Interest: A Theoretical
Analysis," *Journal of Social Issues*, 1972, Vol. 28, 133-154.

Pruitt, D. G., "Power and Bargaining," in B. Seidenberg, and A. Snadowsky, eds.,
Social Psychology, New York: Free Press, 1974.

Pruitt, D. G., and Drews, J. L., "The Effect of Time Pressure, Time Elapsed, and the Opponents' Concession Rate on Behavior in Negotiation," *Journal of Experimental Social Psychology*, 1969, Vol. 5, 43-60.

Pruitt, D. G., and Johnson, D. F., "Mediation as an Aid to Face-Saving in Negotiations," *Journal of Personality and Social Psychology*, 1970, Vol. 14, 239-246.

Pruitt, D. G., and Kimmel, M. J., "Twenty Years of Experimental Gaming: Critique, Synthesis, and Suggestions for the Future," *Annual Review of Psychology*, 1977, Vol. 28, 363-392.

Pruitt, D. G., and Lewis, S. A., "Development of Integrative Solutions in Bilateral Negotiations," *Journal of Personality and Social Psychology*, 1975, Vol. 31, 621-633.

Pruitt, D. G., and Lewis, S. A., "The Psychology of Intergrative Behavior," in D. Druckman (Ed.), *Negotiations*, Beverly Hills, California: Sage Publications, Inc., 1977, 161-189.

Putney, S., and Middleton, R., "Some Factors Associated with Student Acceptance or Rejection of War," *American Sociological Review*, 1962, Vol. 27, 655-677.

Radlow, R. M., Weidner, M. F., and Hurst, P. M., "The Effect of Incentive Magnitude and 'Motivation Orientation' Upon Choice Behavior in A Two-Person Non-Zero-Sum Game," *Journal of Social Psychology*, 1968, Vol. 74, 199-208.

Radlow, R. M., and Weidner, M. F., "Unenforced Commitments in 'Cooperative' and 'Noncooperative' Non-Constant-Sum Games," *Journal of Conflict Resolution*, 1966, Vol. 10, 497-505.

Raiffa, H., "Arbitration Schemes for Generalized Two-Person Games." In H. W. Kuhn and A. W. Tucker, eds., *Contributions to the Theory of Games*, Vol. 2, Annals of Mathematical Studies, 28, Princeton: Princeton University Press.

Rapoport, A., and Chammah, A. M., *Prisoner's Dilemma*, Ann Arbor, Michigan: University of Michigan Press, 1965.

Rokeach, M., *The Open and Closed Mind*, New York: Basic Books, 1960.

Rosen, J. R., and Crow, W. J., "Winsafe II: An International Simulation Study of Deterrence Postures," La Jolla, California: Western Behavioral Science Institute, 1964 (mimeo).

Rotter, J. B., Seeman, M., and Liverant, S., "Internal versus External Control of Reinforcements: A Major Variable in Behavior Therapy." In N. F. Washburne, ed., *Decisions, Values and Groups*, London: Pergamon Press, 1962, Vol. 2, 473-516.

Rubin, J. Z., and Brown, B. R., *The Social Psychology of Bargaining and Negotiations*, New York: Academic Press, 1975.

Sampson, E. E., and Kardush, M., "Age, Sex, Class and Race Differences in Response to a Two-Person, Non-Zero-Sum Game," *Journal of Conflict Resolution*, 1965, Vol. 9, 212-220.

Sawyer, J., and Guetzkow, H., "Bargaining and Negotiation in International Relations," in H. Kelman, ed., *International Behavior*, New York: Holt, Rinehart and Winston, 1965.

Schelling, T., *The Strategy of Conflict*, Cambridge: Harvard University Press, 1960.

Schneider, J. M., and Parsons, O. Z., "Categories of the Locus of Control Scale:

and Cross-Cultural Comparisons in Denmark, and the United States," *Journal of Cross-Cultural Psychology*, 1970, Vol. 1, 131-138.

Scodel, A., "Induced Collaboration In Some Non-Zero-Sum Games," *Journal of Conflict Resolution*, 1959, Vol. 6, 335-340.

Scodel, A., Minas, J. S., Ratoosh, P., and Lipetz, M., "Some Descriptive Aspects of Two-Person Non-Zero-Sum Games," *Journal of Conflict Resolution*, 1959, Vol. 3, 114-119.

Scott, W. E., "The Development of Semantic Differential Scales as Measures of 'Morale.' " *Personnel Psychology*, 1967, Vols. 20, 2, 179-198.

Sermat, V., "Cooperative Behavior In a Mixed-Motive Game," *Journal of Social Psychology*, 1964, Vol. 62, 217-239.

Sermat, V., "The Effect of an Initial Cooperative or Competitive Treatment Upon a Subject's Response to Conditional Cooperation," *Behavioral Science*, 1967, Vol. 12, 301-313.

Sermat, V., "Is Game Behavior Related to Behavior in Other Interpersonal Situations?," *Journal of Personality and Social Psychology*, 1970, Vol. 16, 121-132.

Shearer, J. C., "The Underdeveloped Industrial Relations of U. S. Corporations In Underdeveloped Countries," Industrial Relations Research Association, 1964, Vol. 17, 57-67.

Sherif, M., and Sherif, C. W., "Research on Intergroup Relations," in O. Klineberg and R. Christie, eds., *Perspectives in Social Psychology*, New York: Holt, Rinehart and Winston, 1965.

Sherman, R., "Individual Attitudes Toward Risk and Preference Between Prisoner's Dilemma Games," Unpublished manuscript, 1966.

Shomer, R. W., Davis, A. H., and Kelley, H. H., "Threats and the Development of Coordination: Further Studies of the Deutch and Krauss Trucking Game," *Journal of Personality and Social Psychology*, 1966, Vol. 4, 126.

Shull, F. A., Delbecq, A. L., and Cummings, L. L., *Organizational Decision Making*, New York: McGraw-Hill, 1970.

Shure, G. H., and Meeker, J. P., "A Personality Attitude Schedule for Use in Experimental Bargaining Studies," *The Journal of Psychology*, 1967, Vol. 65, 233-252.

Shure, G. H., Meeker, R. J., Moore, W. H., Jr., and Kelley, H. H., "Computer Studies of Bargaining Behavior: The Role of Threat in Bargaining," *Report No. SP-2196, System Development Corporation*, Santa Monica, California, 1966.

Siegel, S., and Fouraker, L. F., *Bargaining and Group Decision Making*, New York: McGraw-Hill, 1960.

Siegal, S., and Harnett, D. L., "Bargaining Behavior: A Comparison Between Mature Industrial Personnel and College Students," *Operations Research*, 1964, Vol. 12, 334-343.

Singh, P. M., Huang, S. C., and Thompson, G. G., "A Comparative Study of Selected Attitudes, Values and Personality Characteristics of American, Chinese, and Indian Students," *The Journal of Social Psychology*, 1962, Vol. 57, 123-132.

Slack, B. D., and Cook, J. D., "Authoritarian Behavior in a Conflict Setting," *Journal of Personality and Social Psychology*, 1973, Vol. 25, 130-136.

Smith, B. L., "Effects of Overpayment and Underpayment on Reallocation of Rewards." Unpublished Doctoral Dissertation, University of Mississippi, 1970.

Smith, N. S., Vernon, C. R., and Tarte, R. D., "Random Strategies and Sex Differences in the Prisoner's Dilemma Game," *Journal of Conflict Resolution*, 1975, Vol. 19, 643-650.

Smith, V. L., "Experimental Studies of Discrimination Versus Competition in Sealed-Bid Auction Markets," *Journal of Business*, 1967, Vol. 40, 56-84.

Smith, W. P., "Power Structure and Authoritarianism in the Use of Power in the Triad," *Journal of Personality*, 1967, Vol. 35, 64-90.

Smith, W. P., and Anderson, A. J., "Threats, Communication, and Bargaining" *Journal of Personality and Social Psychology*, 1975, Vol. 32, 76-82.

Smith, W. P., and Emmons, T. D., "Outcome Information and Competiveness in Interpersonal Bargaining," *Journal of Conflict Resolution*, 1969, Vol. 13, 262-270.

Smith, W. P., and Leginski, W. A., "Magnitude and Precision of Primitive Power in Bargaining Strategy," *Journal of Experimental Social Psychology*, 1970, Vol. 6, 57-76.

Solomon, L., "The Influence of Some Types of Power Relationships and Game Strategies Upon the Development of Interpersonal Trust," *Journal of Abnormal and Social Psychology*, 1960, Vol. 61, 223-230.

Stagner, R., *The Dimensions of Human Conflict*, Detroit: Wayne State University Press, 1967.

Starbuck, W. H., and Bass, E. M., "An Experimental Study of Risk-Taking and The Value of Information in a New Product Context," *The Journal of Business*, 1967, Vol. 40, 155-165.

Steiner, I. D., "Sex Differences in the Resolution of A-B-X Conflicts," *Journal of Personality*, 1960, Vol. 28, 118-120.

Stevens, C. M., *Strategy and Collective Bargaining Negotiations*, New York: McGraw-Hill, 1963.

Stigler, G. J., *The Theory of Price* (Revised Ed.) New York: Macmillan, 1952.

Strauss, A., *Negotiations: Varieties, Contexts, Processes and Social Order*, San Francisco: Jossey-Bass, 1978.

Summers, C. W., "Labor Relations in the Common Market," *Harvard Business Review*, 1965, Vol. 43, 148-160.

Swennson, R. G., "Cooperation in the Prisoner's Dilemma Game I: The Effects of Asymetric Payoff Information and Explicit Communications," *Behavioral Science*, 1967, Vol. 12, 314-322.

Swingle, P. G., and Coady, H., "Effects of the Partner's Abrupt Strategy Change Upon Subject's Responding in the Prisoner's Dilemma," *Journal of Personality and Social Psychology*, 1967, Vol. 5, 357-363.

Tegar, A. I., and Morchan, R., "The Agent, Team, and the Individual Factors in Negotiations." Unpublished Manuscript, 1972.

Terhune, K. W., "Motives, Situations, and Interpersonal Conflict within Prisoner's Dilemma," *Journal of Personality and Social Psychology Monograph Supplement*, 1968, Vol. 8, part 2, 1-24.

Terhune, K. W., "The Effects of Personality in Cooperation and Conflict." In P. G. Swingle (Ed.), *The Structure of Conflict*, New York: Academic Press, 1970.

Terhune, K. W., and Firestone, J. M., "Psychological Studies in Social Interaction and Motives (SIAM), Phase 2: Group Motives in International Relations Game," CAL Report VX-2018-5-2, March, 1967, Cornell Aero-
nautical Laboratory, Buffalo, New York.

Thibaut, J., "The Development of Contractual Norms in Bargaining: Replication
and Variation," *Journal of Conflict Resolution*, 1968, Vol. 12, 102-112.

Thibaut, J., and Faucheux, C., "The Development of Contractual Norms in a
Bargaining Situation Under Two Types of Stress," *Journal of Experimental Social Psychology*, 1965, Vol. 1, 89-102.

Thibaut, J., and Kelley, H. H., *The Social Psychology of Groups*, New York:
John Wiley and Sons, 1959.

Thurstone, L. L., "The Dimensions of Temperament," *Psychometrika*, 1951,
Vol. 16, 11-20.

Tjosvold, D., "Threat as a Low-Power Person's Strategy in Bargaining: Social
Face and Tangible Outcomes," *International Journal of Group Tensions*,
1974, Vol. 4, 494-550.

Turk, H., and Lefcowitz, M. J., "Towards a Theory of Representation Between
Groups," *Social Forces*, 1962, Vol. 40, 337-341.

Ueijio, C. K., and Wrightsman, L. S., "Ethnic-Group Differences in the Relationship of Trusting Attitudes to Cooperative Behavior," *Psychological Reports*, 1967, Vol. 20, 563-571.

Urban, T. F., "The Influence of Intervention Mode and Experience Upon Bargaining Behavior." Paper presented at the Midwest AIDS Conference, May,
1972.

Vanden, Heuvel, K., "Game Strategy as a Function of 'Partner's Strategy.' "
Unpublished Master's Thesis, University of Toronto, 1968.

Vidmar, N., "Effects of Representational Roles and Mediators on Negotiation
Effectiveness," *Journal of Personality and Social Psychology*, 1971, Vol.
17, 48-58.

Vidmar, N., and McGrath, J. E., *Role Structure, Leadership and Negotiation
Effectiveness* (Technical Report No. 6), Urbana: University of Illinois
Press, 1967.

Vinake, W. F., "Variables in Experimental Games: Toward a Field Theory,"
Psychological Bulletin, 1969, Vol. 71, 293-318.

Voissem, N. H., and Sistrunk, F., "Communication Schedules and Cooperative
Game Behavior," *Journal of Personality and Social Psychology*, 1971,
Vol. 17, 48-58.

Von Neumann, J., and Morganstern, O., *Theory of Games and Economic Behavior* (2nd ed.), Princeton: Princeton University Press, 1947.

Wall, J. S., Jr., "Effects of Constituent Trust and Representative Bargaining
Orientation on Intergroup Bargaining," *Journal of Personality and Social
Psychology*, 1975, Vol. 31, 1004-1012.

Wall, J. A., Jr., "Effects of Sex and Opposing Representative's Bargaining Orientation on Intergroup Bargaining," *Journal of Personality and Social
Psychology*, 1976, Vol. 33, 51-61.

Wallach, M., Kogan, N., "The Roles of Information, Discussion, and Consensus
in Group Risk Taking, *Journal of Experimental Social Psychology*, 1965,
Vol. 11, 1-19.

Wallach, M., Kogan, N., Bem, D. J., "Group Influences in Individual Risk Taking,

Journal of Abnormal and Social Psychology, 1965, Vol. 65, 75-86.

Wallach, M., Kogan, N., and Burt, R., "Can Group Members Recognize The Effects of Group Discussion Upon Risk Taking?," *Journal Experimental Social Psychology*, 1965, Vol. 1, 379-395.

Walton, R. E., and McKerzie, T. B., *A Behavioral Theory of Labor Negotiations*, New York: McGraw-Hill, 1965.

Walton, R. E., "Third Party Roles in Interdepartmental Conflict," *Industrial Relations*, 1967, Vol. 7, 29-43.

Weick, K. E., "Laboratory Experimentation with Organizations," in James G. March, ed., *Handbook of Organizations*, Chicago: Rand McNally, 1965, 194-260.

Wichman, H., "Effects of Isolation and Communication on Cooperation in a Two-Person Game," *Journal of Personality and Social Psychology*, 1970, Vol. 16, 114-120.

Wilson, K. V., and Bixenstine, V. E., "Effects of a Third Choice on Behavior in a Prisoner's Dilemma Game," Nebraska Psychiatric Institute, 1962 (mimeo).

Wilson, W., "Cooperation and the Cooperations of the Other Player," *Journal of Conflict Resolution*, 1969, Vol. 13, 110-117.

Wilson, W., and Robinson, C., "Selective Intergroup Bias in Both Authoritarians After Playing a Modified Prisoner's Dilemma Game," *Perceptual and Motor Skills*, 1968, Vol. 27, 1051-1058.

Wilson, W., and Wong, J., "Intergroup Attitudes and Strategies in Non-Zero-Sum Dilemma Games: I." Unpublished Manuscript, University of Hawaii, 1965.

Wilson, W., and Wong, J., "Intergroup Attitude Towards Cooperative and Competitive Opponents in a Modified Prisoner's Dilemma Game," *Perceptual and Motor Skills*, 1968, Vol. 27, 1059-1066.

Worchel, P., "Social Ideology and Reactions to International Events," *Journal of Conflict Resolution*, 1967, Vol. 11, 414-430.

Wrightsman, L. S., "Personality and Attitudinal Correlates of Trusting and Trustworthy Behaviors in a Two-Person Game," *Journal of Personality and Social Psychology*, 1966, Vol. 4, 328-332.

Wrightsman, L. S., Davis, D. W., Lucker, W. G., Gruininks, R. H., Evans, J. R., Wilde, R. E., Paulson, D. J., and Clark, G. N., "Effects of Other Person's Strategy and Race Upon Cooperative Behavior in a Prisoner's Dilemma Game," adapted from Wrightsman, L. S., O'Connor, J., and Baker, N. H., Cooperation and Competition: *Readings on Mixed Motives Games*, Monterey, California: Brooks/Cole, 1972.

Wyer, R., "Prediction of Behavior in Two-Person Games," *Journal of Personality and Social Psychology*, 1969, Vol. 13, 222-228.

Wyer, R. S., "Effects of Outcome Matrix and Partner's Behavior in Two-Person Games," *Journal of Personality and Social Psychology*, 1971, Vol. 7, 190-210.

Yukl, G., "Effects of Opponent Concessions on a Bargainer's Perception and Concessions," *Proceedings of the 80th Convention of the American Psychological Association*, 1972, Vol. 7, 229-230.

Yukl, G., "The Effects of Situational Variables and Opponent Concessions on a Bargainer's Perceptions, Aspirations, and Concessions," *Journal of Personality and Social Psychology*, 1974a, Vol. 29, 227-236.

Yukl, G., "Effects of the Opponent's Initial Offer, Concession Magnitude and Concession Frequency on Bargaining Behavior," *Journal of Personality and Social Psychology*, 1974b, Vol. 30, 323-335.

Zechmeister, K., and Druckman, D., "Determinants of the Resolution of a Conflict of Interest in a Simulation of Political Decision Making." Unpublished Manuscript, 1971.

Zeuthen, I., *Problems of Monopoly and Economic Warfare*, London: G. Routledge and Son, 1930.

Appendix A

PAS Questionnaire

1. English (U. S. A./England)
2. Flemish (Belgium)
3. Finnish (Finland)
4. French (France)
5. Greek (Greece)
6. Japanese (Japan)
7. Spanish (Spain)
8. Thai (Thailand)

English (U.S.A./England)

The items below are a study of what people think about a number of social questions. The best answer to each statement is *your personal opinion*. Many different points of view are covered; you may find yourself agreeing strongly with some of the statements, disagreeing just as strongly with others, and perhaps uncertain about others. Whether you agree or disagree with any statement, you can be sure that many other people feel the same way you do.

For each statement circle with your pencil the number which best fits your reaction according to how much you agree or disagree with it. Please mark every one, using the following scheme:

7: I agree very much	3: I disagree a little
6: I agree pretty much	2: I disagree pretty much
5: I agree a little	1: I disagree very much

If you are really completely neutral about an item, or if you are completely uncertain how you feel about an item, or if you don't understand it, mark *4*.

---

1 When someone has been nasty to you, you should try to understand what's bothering him, so that you can be helpful.

$$1 \quad 2 \quad 3 \quad 4 \quad 5 \quad 6 \quad 7$$

2 Even people who appear friendly to you may be unreliable because they are mainly concerned with their own interests.

$$1 \quad 2 \quad 3 \quad 4 \quad 5 \quad 6 \quad 7$$

3 We should always help those who are in need, even if they are very unfriendly to us.

$$1 \quad 2 \quad 3 \quad 4 \quad 5 \quad 6 \quad 7$$

4 Some people just have it in for you.

$$1 \quad 2 \quad 3 \quad 4 \quad 5 \quad 6 \quad 7$$

5 There are some people who can't be trusted at all.

$$1 \quad 2 \quad 3 \quad 4 \quad 5 \quad 6 \quad 7$$

6 In quarrels with other people we should make a point of admitting it when we're wrong.

$$1 \quad 2 \quad 3 \quad 4 \quad 5 \quad 6 \quad 7$$

7 Even nations that appear friendly to us may be unreliable because they are mainly concerned with their own interests.

$$1 \quad 2 \quad 3 \quad 4 \quad 5 \quad 6 \quad 7$$

8 We should always feel responsible for helping others less fortunate than ourselves.

$$1 \quad 2 \quad 3 \quad 4 \quad 5 \quad 6 \quad 7$$

9 Most people are not always straightforward and honest when their own interests are involved.

$$1 \quad 2 \quad 3 \quad 4 \quad 5 \quad 6 \quad 7$$

10   There is nothing more satisfying than doing something which pleases another person.

1   2   3   4   5   6   7

11   A surprising number of people are cruel and spiteful.

1   2   3   4   5   6   7

12   Doing favors for people who aren't in a position to return them is a waste of time.

1   2   3   4   5   6   7

13   You are likely to have some personal enemies that you don't even know about.

1   2   3   4   5   6   7

14   When you quarrel with someone you should make an especial effort to understand his point of view.

1   2   3   4   5   6   7

15   You should not have anything to do with people who are hostile to you.

1   2   3   4   5   6   7

16   When someone has said something to hurt you, it is not good to pay him back, even if the things you say about him are perfectly true.

1   2   3   4   5   6   7

17   Doing something to please a person who doesn't like you can give you a lot of satisfaction.

1   2   3   4   5   6   7

18   Most activities are more fun when you compare your own abilities with other people's.

1   2   3   4   5   6   7

19   It is not worthwhile to make compromises and give your own preferences in order to make peace with a personal enemy.

1   2   3   4   5   6   7

20   You shouldn't be modest if it leads people to underestimate your abilities.

1   2   3   4   5   6   7

21   When you are engaged in a personal dispute, you shouldn't do favors for people who won't take your side.

1   2   3   4   5   6   7

22   It is extremely upsetting to be more poorly dressed than most of the people you associate with.

1   2   3   4   5   6   7

23 We should try to get people from other countries to visit us and explain their points of view.

1   2   3   4   5   6   7

24 You should not have anything to do with people whom you don't approve of.

1   2   3   4   5   6   7

25 We should be completely frank in telling other people about our own shortcomings and mistakes.

1   2   3   4   5   6   7

26 When people are uncooperative, the most effective way to get them to do what you want is to use threats.

1   2   3   4   5   6   7

27 It's a good idea to know the problems and worries of people around you, so that you can be helpful.

1   2   3   4   5   6   7

28 In spite of occasional lapses, most people are pretty trustworthy.

1   2   3   4   5   6   7

The next series of questions are about your likes and dislikes, preferences and habits in everyday life. There are no right or wrong answers to these questions; one answer can be just as good as some other answer.

INSTRUCTIONS: For each question, circle with your pencil either number 1, 2, or 3 for the answer that fits you best.

If your answer is *Yes*, circle number 1.
If you cannot decide, circle number 2.
If your answer is *No*, circle number 3.

29 Do you like to wager with very small stakes just for the kick you get out of gambling?

1   2   3

30 Would you like to do stunt flying in an aerial circus?

1   2   3

31 Would you like to dive from a high spring-board?

1   2   3

32 Do you like to play games when money is at stake?

1   2   3

33   Would you like to ride with dare-devil drivers?

1   2   3

34   Do you often alternate between happiness and sadness?

1   2   3

35   Do you drive a car rather fast?

1   2   3

36   Would you like to drive a "hot-rod" in a race?

1   2   3

37   Do you like to bet money on athletic events?

1   2   3

38   Do you often feel impatient?

1   2   3

39   Do you like to invest money in a promising invention?

1   2   3

40   Would you like to be a test pilot?

1   2   3

41   Would you like to run river rapids in a motor boat?

1   2   3

42   When you are emotionally upset, do you tend to lose your appetite?

1   2   3

43   Would you like to work as a flying trapeze acrobat in a circus?

1   2   3

44   Would you like to ride out a storm in a small boat?

1   2   3

45   Would you be willing to take a chance by accepting a job you know nothing about?

1   2   3

46   Does it irritate you to be interrupted when you are concentrating?

1   2   3

47   Do you usually work fast?

1   2   3

48   Do you like to drive a car rather fast when there is no speed limit?

1   2   3

49   Would you like to go on the first rocket-ship expedition to the moon?

1   2   3

This series of items attempts to find out the way in which certain important events in our society affect different people. Each item consists of a pair of statements, one of which has the number *1* in front of it and the other the number *2*. In the case of each item, read both statements *carefully* and select the one statement of each pair (*and only one*) which you more strongly *believe* to be the case as far as you are concerned. Indicate your choice by placing a circle with your pencil on the number of the statement which you believe to be more true. There are no right or wrong answers to this questionnaire. For every item there are large numbers of people who pick *1* and large numbers who pick *2*.

I more strongly believe that

50   1   if I make an effort, I can get people I like to become my friends.

    2   no matter how hard you try, some people just don't like you.

51   1   people's misfortunes usually result from the mistakes they make.

    2   sometimes I feel that I don't have enough control over what happens to me.

52   1   in the long run, people get the respect they deserve in this world.

    2   unfortunately, an individual's worth often passes unrecognized no matter how hard he tries.

53   1   some guys are born to take orders and others are born to give them.

    2   in the long run the guy with more ability ends up giving the orders.

54   1   I could usually tell whether I had done well or poorly on a test as soon as I had finished taking the test.

    2   I often felt I couldn't predict which grade I would get on a test.

55   1   if one gets the right teacher, he can do well in school; otherwise he has trouble.

    2   the grades a person gets in school are up to him.

56   1   I often can't understand how it is possible to get people to do what I want them to.

    2   getting people to do what you want takes hard work and patience.

57   1   getting a good job depends partly on being in the right place at the right time.

    2   if you've got ability, you can always get a job.

58   1   people are lonely because they don't know how to be friendly.

    2   making friends is largely a matter of being lucky enough to meet the right people.

BELGIUM (FLEMISH)

Verhouding tussen persoonlijkheid en houdingen

De hiernavolgende standpunten vormen een studie over hetgeen de mensen denken aangaande een aantal sociale aangelegenheden.

Het beste antwoord voor elk standpunt is uw persoonlijke opinie. Vele verschillende gezichtspunten werden in beschouwing genomen; het is mogelijk dat u ten zeerste zult instemmen met sommige standpunten, en dat u andere even sterk zult afkeuren, en misschien zult u zich onzeker voelen over nog andere. Indien u in stemt of niet, met om het even welk standpunt, wees ervan overtuigd dat vele a dere personen uw opnie delen. Omring met uw potlood het nummer dat volgens u meest overeenstemt met uw mate van voor- of afkeur voor een bepaald standpunt. Doe dit voor elk standpunt aan de hand van volgend schema :

7. Ten zeerste akkoord	3. Lichtjes verschillend van opinie
6. Tamelijk akkoord	2. Tamelijk verschillend van opinie
5. Lichtjes akkoord	1. In het geheel niet akkoord.

Wanneer u werkelijk volledig neutraal staat tegenover een standpunt, of volled onzeker, of u begrijpt het in het geheel niet, omring dan 4.

Wanneer iemand onvriendelijk geweest is tegenover u, moet u trachten te versta wat hem dwars zit, zodat u hem zoudt kunnen helpen.

1 2 3 4 5 6 7

Zelfs mensen die u vriendelijk toeschijnen, kunnen onbetrouwbaar zijn, omdat ze hoofdzakelijk aan hun eigen belang denken.

1 2 3 4 5 6 7

We moeten altijd diegenen helpen die in nood zijn, zelfs als ze heel onvriendelijk zijn voor ons.

1 2 3 4 5 6 7

Sommige mensen willen u juist kwaad doen.

1 2 3 4 5 6 7

kunt geen vriendschap aanknopen met personen die u reeds bij de aanvang vijan-
ig gezind zijn.

1 2 3 4 5 6 7

r zijn mensen die men in het geheel niet kan betrouwen.

1 2 3 4 5 6 7

ij twist met andere personen zouden wij er moeten op staan te erkennen dat
e ongelijk hebben zo dit het geval is.

1 2 3 4 5 6 7

elfs landen die ons vriendelijk gezind schijnen te zijn, kunnen onbetrouwbaar
ijn, omdat ze hoofdzakelijk aan hun eigen belang denken.

1 2 3 4 5 6 7

ij zouden ons steeds verantwoordelijk moeten voelen om anderen te helpen die
r slechter aan toe zijn dan wijzelf.

1 2 3 4 5 6 7

e meeste mensen zijn niet altijd ronduit en eerlijk, wanneer hun eigen
elangen op het spel staan.

1 2 3 4 5 6 7

r is niets dat meer voldoening schenkt dan anderen een plezier te doen.

1 2 3 4 5 6 7

en verrassend aantal mensen zijn wreed en hatelijk.

1 2 3 4 5 6 7

unstes verlenen aan mensen die niet in de mogelijkheid zijn u ze te vergelden,
s tijdverlies.

1 2 3 4 5 6 7

aarschijnlijk hebt u enkele persoonlijke vijanden die u niet eens kent.

1 2 3 4 5 6 7

anneer u ruzie maakt met iemand, zoudt u er speciaal moeten op letten zijn
ienswijze te verstaan.

1 2 3 4 5 6 7

U zoudt geen uitstaans moeten hebben met personen die u vijandig gezind zijn.

1   2   3   4   5   6   7

Wanneer iemand iets gezegd heeft om u te kwetsen, is het niet goed hem met
gelijke munt te betalen, zelfs als wat u van hem zegt de volledige waarheid is.

1   2   3   4   5   6   7

Een genoegen doen aan iemand die niet veel van u moet hebben, kan u een grote
voldoening schenken.

1   2   3   4   5   6   7

De meeste activiteiten zijn plezieriger, wanneer u er uw eigen bekwaamheden
kunt meten met die van anderen.

1   2   3   4   5   6   7

Het loont de moeite niet een compromis te maken en uw eigen voorkeur op te geven
juist maar om tot vrede te komen met een persoonlijke vijand.

1   2   3   4   5   6   7

U moet niet nederig zijn wanneer anderen daardoor uw bekwaamheden zouden kunnen
onderschatten.

1   2   3   4   5   6   7

Wanneer u betrokken bent in een persoonlijk geschil, moet u geen gunsten
verlenen aan personen die uw zijde niet willen kiezen.

1   2   3   4   5   6   7

Het is uiterst onaangenaam minder goed gekleed te zijn dan de andere mensen
waarmee u omgaat.

1   2   3   4   5   6   7

We zouden mensen van andere landen ertoe moeten brengen ons te komen bezoeken,
om ons hun standpunten uiteen te zetten.

1   2   3   4   5   6   7

U zoudt geen uitstaans moeten hebben met mensen welke u niet goedkeurt.

1   2   3   4   5   6   7

De volgende reeks vragen gaat over uw voorkeur en afkeur en uw gewoonten in het dagelijkse leven. Er bestaan geen goede en verkeerde antwoorden op deze vragen - het ene antwoord is het andere waard.

RICHTLIJNEN : Omring voor iedere vraag ofwel 1, 2 of 3, naargelang het antwoord dat u best ligt.

Indien uw antwoord "ja" is, omring dan nummer 1

Indien u niet kan beslissen, omring dan nummer 2

Indien uw antwoord "nee" is, omring dan nummer 3

———————————

Wedt u graag met heel kleine inzet alleen voor de spanning die u in weddingschappen vindt?

1   2   3

Zoudt u graag een stuntpiloot zijn in een luchtmeeting?

1   2   3

Zoudt u willen duiken van een hoge wipplank?

1   2   3

Speelt u graag wanneer er geld ingezet wordt?

1   2   3

Zoudt u graag meerijden met waaghalzen achter het stuur?

1   2   3

Slaat u dikwijls over van een gelukkige tot een droevige gemoedstemming, en omgekeerd?

1   2   3

Rijdt u nogal vlug met een wagen?

1   2   3

Zoudt u graag deelnemen aan een koers in een wagen met een "opgefokte" motor?

1   2   3

Wedt u graag voor geld op sportgebeurtenissen?

1   2   3

Voelt u zich dikwijls ongeduldig?

1   2   3

Investeert u graag geld in een veelbelovende uitvinding?

1   2   3

Zoudt u graag een testpiloot zijn?

1   2   3

Zoudt u graag met een motorboot in stroomversnellingen varen?

1   2   3

Wanneer u emotioneel overstuur bent, hebt u dan de neiging uw eetlust te
verliezen?

1   2   3

Zoudt u graag als een vliegende trapezist werken in een circus?

1   2   3

Zoudt u met een kleine boot blijven varen terwijl het stormt?

1   2   3

Zoudt u uw kans willen wagen door een job aan te nemen waarvan u niets afweet

1   2   3

Ergert het u, onderbroken te worden wanneer u zich concentreert?

1   2   3

Werkt u gewoonlijk snel?

1   2   3

Rijdt u graag snel met een wagen, wanneer er geen snelheidsbeperking is?

1   2   3

Met deze reeks punten wordt getracht te bepalen, op welke manier bepaalde belangrijke gebeurtenissen in onze maatschappij verschillende personen beïnvloeden. Elk punt bestaat uit twee standpunten; het ene met het getal 1 ervoor, en het andere met het getal 2 ervoor. Lees aandachtig beide standpunten voor ieder punt, en kies dan datgene (slechts één) dat best overeenstemt met uw_ persoonlijke overtuiging. Duidt uw keuze aan door het cijfer te omkringen dat het standpunt voorafgaat dat volgens u het meest correcte is.

Er bestaan geen juiste of onjuiste antwoorden op deze vragenlijst. Voor ieder punt kiezen een groot aantal personen het eerste standpunt, en een groot aantal het tweede.

1. Wanneer ik er moeite voor doe,, kan ik degenen die ik graag heb, tot mijn vrienden maken.

2. Sommige personen kunnen u niet verdragen, onverschillig wat u ook probeert.

----

1. Het ongeluk van de mensen hangt gewoonlijk af van de fouten die ze maken.

2. Soms voel ik dat ik niet genoeg controle heb over hetgeen er met mij gebeurt.

----

1. Op lange termijn krijgen de mensen het respect dat ze verdienen.

2. Ongelukkiglijk wordt de waarde van een individu dikwijls niet erkend, hoe hard hij zich ook inspant.

----

1. Sommige personen zijn geboren om te gehoorzamen, en andere om de bevelen te geven.

2. Op lange termijn zal de bekwaamste persoon uiteindelijk de bevelen geven.

----

1. Gewoonlijk kon ik zeggen of ik een schoolexamen goed of slecht gemaakt had, van zodra ik het beëindigd had.

2. Zelden kon ik voorspellen of ik goed of slecht gewerkt had voor een examen.

----

1. Indien iemand de juiste leraar heeft kan hij goede resultaten op school behalen, anders heeft hij problemen.

2. De punten die een persoon op school behaalt hangen van hem af.

----

1. Dikwijls kan ik niet verstaan, hoe het mogelijk is dat de mensen doen wat ik van hen verlang.

2. De mensen ertoe brengen te doen wat u wilt vraagt veel inspanning en geduld.

----

1. Een goede betrekking verkrijgen hangt gedeeltelijk af van het feit op de juiste plaats te zijn op het geschikte ogenblik.

2. Wanneer u bekwaamheid bezit, kan u altijd een betrekking krijgen.

----

1. Mensen voelen zich eenzaam, omdat ze niet weten hoe ze vriendelijk moeten zijn.

2. Vrienden maken hangt er in grote mate van af het geluk te hebben de juiste personen te ontmoeten.

FINLAND

Nimi _____

PERSOONALLISUUS/ASENNEKAAVA

Alla olevat kohdat muodostavat tutkimuksen siita, mita ihmiset ajattelevat muutamista sosiaalisista kysymyksista. Paras vastaus kuhunkin vaitteeseen on Teidan henkilokohtainen mielipiteenne. Monia eri nakokulmia on sisallytetty mukaan; saatatte havaita olevanne erittain paljon yhta mielta joidenkin vaitteiden suhteen ja yhta paljon eri mielta toisten kanssa; toisista ehka olette epavarma. Olettepa yhta - tai eri mielta minka tahansa vaitteen suhteen, voitte olla varma, etta nain on monien muidenkin ihmisten laita.

Ympyroikaa kynallanne se numero, joka mielestanne parhaiten ilmaisee, missa maarin olette yhta- tai eri mielta. Olkaa hyva ja merkitkaa vastanlesenne jokaiseen kontaan kayttaen seuraavaa asteikkoa:

7. erittain paljon samaa mielta   3. hiukan eri mielta

6. melko paljon samaa mielta   2. melko paljon eri mielta

5. hiukan samaa mielta   1. erittain paljon eri mielta

Jos todellakin olette taysin neutraali ko. kohdan suhteen, tai jos olette taysin epavarma siita tai ellette ymmarra sita, merkitkaa 4.

Kun joku on ollut epamiellyttava Teita kohteen, Teidan pitaisi yrittaa ymartaa, mika hanta vaivaa, niin etta voisitte olla avuksi.

1 2 3 4 5 6 7

Jopa ne ihmiset, jotka Teista vaikuttavat ystavallisilta, saattavat olla epaluotettavia, koska he ovat paaasiassa kiinnostuneita omista eduistaan.

1 2 3 4 5 6 7

Meidan tulisi aina auttaa avun tarpeessa olevia, vaikka he olisivatkin meita kohtaan epaystavallistia.

1 2 3 4 5 6 7

Joidenkin ihmisten asenne Teitä kohtaan on kertakaikkiaan kielteinen alunperin.

1 2 3 4 5 6 7

On ihmisiä, joihin ei kertakaikkiaan voi luottaa.

1 2 3 4 5 6 7

Riidellessamme toisten ihmisten kanssa, meidän pitäisi yrittämällä yrittaa myontaa, kun olemme vaarassa.

1 2 3 4 5 6 7

Jopa ystävällisiltä vaikuttavat kansat voivat olla epaluotettavia, koska ne ovat pääasiassa kiinnostuneita omista eduistaan.

1 2 3 4 5 6 7

Meidän pitäisi aina tuntea olevamme vastuullisia autamaan itseamme vahaonnisempia.

1 2 3 4 5 6 7

Useimmat ihmiset eivät ole aina suoria ja rehellisia, kun heidän omat etunsa ovat kysymyksessä.

1 2 3 4 5 6 7

Ei ole mitaan sen tyydytysta tuottavampaa, kuin tehda jotain, joka miellyttaa toista henkiloa.

1 2 3 4 5 6 7

Haurastyttavan monet ihmiset ovat julmia ja pahansuopia.

1 2 3 4 5 6 7

On ajanhukkaa tehda palveluksia ihmisille, joilla ei ole tilaisuutta vastapalveluksiin.

1 2 3 4 5 6 7

Teilla on todennakoisesti joitakin henkilokohtaisia vihamichia, joista ette edes tieda.

1 2 3 4 5 6 7

Kun riitelette jonkun kanssa, Teidan pitaisi koettamalla koettaa ymmartaa hanen nakokulmansa.

1 2 3 4 5 6 7

"itäisi pysyä" kokonaan erossa vihamielisistä" ihmisistä."

1 2 3 4 5 6 7

Kun joku on sanonut jotain loukatakseen Teitä", ei ole hyväksi maksaa

amalla mitalla, vaikka se mitä" hänestä" sanotte olisikin aivan totta.

1 2 3 4 5 6 7

'oi olla varsin tyydytystä tuottavaa olla mieliksi henkilölle", joka ei

•idä teistä."

1 2 3 4 5 6 7

'seimmat toimet ovat hauskempia, silloin kun voi verrata omia kykyjään""

oisten kykyihin.

1 2 3 4 5 6 7

i maksa vaivaa sovitella ja luopua omasta mieltymyksestään"", jotta

aasisi" sovintoon henkilökohtaisen vihamiehensä" kanssa.

1 2 3 4 5 6 7

eidän" ei pitäisi" olla vaatimaton, jos se saa ihmiset aliarvioimaan kykyjänne."

1 2 3 4 5 6 7

os olette nenkilökohtaisessa riidassa, Teidän" ei pitäisi" olla suosiolli-

en ihmisille, jotka eivät" asetu teidän" puolellenne.

1 2 3 4 5 6 7

n ólen harmillista olla huonommin puettu kuin useimmat, joiden kanssa

eurustelee.

1 2 3 4 5 6 7

eidän" pitäisi" yrittää"" saada ulkomaalaisia vierailemaan meilla ja

elittämään" omia" näkökantojaan.

1 2 3 4 5 6 7

'täisi pysyä" erossa ihmisistä", joita ei hyväksy."

1 2 3 4 5 6 7

eidän" pitäisi" kertoa toisille omista puutteistamme ja virheistämme" ihan suoraan.

1 2 3 4 5 6 7

Uhkausten käyttö on tehokkain tapa saada vastahakoiset ihmiset teke-
mään, mitä haluaa heidän tekevän.

1 2 3 4 5 6 7

On hyvä tietaa lahimmaistensa pulmat ja huolet, niin että voi

olla avuksi.

1 2 3 4 5 6 7

Satunnaisia hairahduksia lukuunottamatta useimmat ihmiset ovat

malko lailla luottamuksenarvoisia.

1 2 3 4 5 6 7

Seuraava kysymyssarja koskettelee tapojanne, mieltymyksianne ja
epamieltymyksianne jokapaivaisessa elamassa. Naihin kysymyksiin ei ole
mitsan oikeata tai vaaraa vastausta; yksi vastaus on yhta hyva kuin
toinenkin.

OHJEET: Ympyroikaa kynallanne kussakin kysymyksessa 1, 2 tai 3
         parhaiten soveltuvana vastauksena.

         Jos vastauksenne on Kylla, ympyroikaa no. 1
         Ellette osaa paattaa, ympyroikaa no. 2
         Jos vastauksenne on Ei, ympyroikaa no. 3.

Lyotteko mielellanne vetoa hyvin pienin panoksin vain siita nautinnosta,

jonka uhkapeli Teille tuottaa?

1 2 3

Haluaisitteko esittaa taitolentoa ilmailusirkuksessa?

1 2 3

Haluaisitteko sukeltaa korkealta ponnahduslaudalta?

1 2 3

Pelaatteko mielellanne, kun panoksena on raha?

1 2 3

Tahtoisitteko ajaa autohurjastelijoiden kyydissa?

1 2 3

Vaihtuuko mielialanne usein onnellisuudesta surullisuuteen?

1 2 3

Ajatteko autoa melko kovaa?

1 2 3

Haluaisitteko ajaa kuuman sarjan kilpa-autoa kilpaajoissa?

1 2 3

Lyotteko mielellänne vetoa urheilutapahtumista?

1 2 3

Tunnetteko itsenne usein kärsimättömäksi?

1 2 3

Sijoitatteko mielellänne rahaa lupaavaan keksintöön?

1 2 3

Haluaisitteko olla koelentaja?

1 2 3

Haluaisitteko laskea koskia moottorivencellä?

1 2 3

Onko Teillä taipumus menettaa ruokahalunne kiihdyksissä ollessanne?

1 2 3

Haluaisitteko työskennellä trapetsitaiturina sirkuksessa?

1 2 3

Haluaisitteko ajaa mysskyssä pienellä veneellä?

1 2 3

Ottaisitteko riskin hyväksymaua tyopaikan, josta ette tieda mitaan?

1 2 3

Ärsyttaako Teitä, jos Teitä häiritään keskittyessanne johonkin?

1 2 3

Teetteko työnne tavallisesti nopeasti?

1 2 3

Ajatteko mielellänne autoa melko lujaa, kun ei ole nopeusrajoitusta?

1 2 3

Haluaisitteko menna ensimmaisella rakettilennolla kuuhun?[2]

1 2 3

Tämä kysymysarja pyrkii selvittämään tapaa, jolla yhteiskuntamme tietyt
tärkeät tapahtumat vaikuttavat eri ihmisiin. Jokainen kohta koostuu
väiteparista, josta toinen on numeroitu ykkösellä, toinen kakkosella. Lu-
kekaa jokaisen kohdan väittämät huolellisesti ja valitkaa niistä se
(ja vain toinen), jonka uskotte varmemmin olevan oikein Teidän millestanne).
Ilmaiskaa valintanne ympyroimalla mielestanne oikean väittäman numero.
Tässä kyselykaavakkeessa ei ole oikeita tai vääriä vastauksia.
Jokaisessa kohdassa on paljon niitä, jotka valitsevat ykkösen ja toi-
saalta paljon kakkosen valitsijoita.

___

Olen enemman sitämmielta etta

1. Jos yritan, saan ystävikseni haluamani ihmiset.
2. Kuinka kovasti yrittaakin, ihmiset eivat yksinkertaisesti
   pida kaikista.

1. Ihmisten epäonnistumiset johtuvat tavallisesti heidän itsensatekemistaan
   virheista.
2. Joskus minusta tuntuu, etten itre voi tarpeeksi vaikuttaa suhen,
   mitaminminulle tapahtuu.

1. Ajan mittaan ihmiset saavat ansaitsemansa kunnioituksen tässa· maailmassa
2. Valitettavasti yksilon ansiokkuus jaa usein maailmalta huomaamatta,
   kuinka kovasti han yrittaneekin.

1. Toiset ovat syntyneet tottelemaan, toiset maaraamaan.
2. Ajan mittaan kyvykkäampi paattyy maaraamaan.

1. Tiesin tavallisesti koulussa heti kokeen paatyttya, oliko se mennyt
   hyvin vai huonosti.
2. Minusta tuntui usein, etten voinut ennustaa, minka numeron saisin kokees

1. Jos saa oikean opettajan, menestyy koulussa, muutoin joutuu vaikeuksiin.
2. Koulun antamat arvosanat riippuvat henkilosta itsestaan.

1. En voi usein ymmartaa, kuinka on mahdollista saada ihmiset tekemaan,
   mita haluan heidan tekevan.
2. Kysyy tyota ja karsivallisyytta saada muut ihmiset tekemaan,
   mita haluaa heidan tekevan.

1. Hyvan tyopaikan saaminen riippuu osaksi siita, etta on oikealla paikalla
   oikeaan aikaan.
2. Jos on kyvykas, saa aina tyopaikan.

1. Ihmiset ovat yksinäisiä, koska he eivät osaa olla ystävällisiä.

2. Ystävien saaminen perustuu suurimmaksi osaksi siihen, että
   on tarpeeksi onnea tavata oikeita ihmisiä.

---

[1]Item No. 5 from the English versión of the PAS was not included in the
Finnish translátion. This was due to the special nature of the diplomatic
ralationships between Finland and the USSR and due to the fact that the researchers
were citizens of the United States. We felt that these circumstances might well
bias responses to that item. A scale score = 4 was entered for each Finnish subject

[2]This was an extra item added to the Finnish version of the PAS for research
purposes. It was not included in calculating the dimensional scores on the PAS
for the Finnish subjects.

FRANCE

Les propositions que vous trouverez ci-dessous sont représentatives
d'un certain nombre d'opinions couramment formulées à l'égard de
différentes questions concernant la vie en société. L'expression de
votre stricte opinion personnelle est la meilleure réponse à donner
à chacune de ces propositions. De nombreux points de vue différents
sont présentés. Vous pouvez vous trouver en profond accord avec
certains, en désaccord tout aussi profond avec d'autres, ou encore en
position d'incertitude totale. Quelle que soit votre réaction vis à
vis d'une proposition particulière quelconque, vous pouvez être sûr
qu'un grand nombre de personnes ont éprouvé la même.

Pour chaque proposition, veuillez encercler à l'aide de votre crayon
le chiffre qui reflète le mieux jusqu'à quel point vous approuvez la
proposition en question. Servez vous du plan suivant et prenez garde
de n'omettre aucune proposition.

        7: Je suis tout à fait d'accord
        6: Je suis à peu près d'accord
        5: Je suis à peine d'accord

        3: Je ne suis pas tellement d'accord
        2: Je ne suis pas d'accord
        1: Je ne suis pas du tout d'accord

Si vous éprouvez une réaction totalement neutre vis à vis d'une
proposition, ou si vous vous sentez incertain à son égard, ou si
encore vous ne comprenez pas ce qu'elle signifie, marquez là du
chiffre 4.

Lorsque quelqu'un se montre désagréable à votre égard, vous devriez
éssayer de comprendre son problème de façon à pouvoir l'aider.

        1   2   3   4   5   6   7

Même les gens qui semblent amicaux à votre égard peuvent ne pas être
dignes de confiance car ils poursuivent surtout leurs interêts.

        1   2   3   4   5   6   7

Nous devrions toujours aider ceux qui ont besoin d'aide, même s'ils
se montrent hostiles à notre égard.

        1   2   3   4   5   6   7

Il y a des gens qui m'en veulent personnellement, tout bonnement.

        1   2   3   4   5   6   7

Vous ne deviendrez pas l'ami des gens qui vous sont hostiles au premier abord.

1   2   3   4   5   6   7

Il y a des gens a qui il est impossible de faire confiance.

1   2   3   4   5   6   7

Quand nous nous disputons avec autrui nous devrions nous faire une règle de reconnaître nos torts.

1   2   3   4   5   6   7

Il est difficile de se fier même aux pays amis, car ils sont guidés surtout par leurs propres interêts.

1   2   3   4   5   6   7

Nous devrions toujours nous sentir tenus d'aider ceux qui ont eu moins de chance que nous dans la vie.

I   2   3   4   5   6   7

La plupart des gens ne sont pas toujours francs et honnêtes lorsque leurs interêts sont en jeu.

1   2   3   4   5   6   7

Il n'y pas de satisfaction personnelle plus grande que celle de faire plaisir à autrui.

1   2   3   4   5   6   7

Un nombre surprenant de gens est cruel et aigri.

1   2   3   4   5   6   7

C'est perdre son temps que de rendre service à des gens qui ne sont pas en mesure de vous rendre la pareille.

1   2   3   4   5   6   7

Vous avez probablement des ennemis personnels que vous ne connaissez même pas.

1   2   3   4   5   6   7

Quand vous vous disputez avec quelqu'un vous devriez faire tout votre possible pour comprendre son point de vue.

1   2   3   4   5   6   7

Vous devriez vous garder d'avoir à faire aux gens qui vous sont hostil

1   2   3   4   5   6   7

Lorsque quelqu'un a prononcé des paroles destinées à vous blesser il n'est pas bon de lui "renvoyer la pierre", même si ce que vous vous prépariez à lui dire est parfaitement exact.

1   2   3   4   5   6   7

Faire plaisir à quelqu'un qui ne vous aime pas peut vous apporter beaucoup de satisfaction.

1   2   3   4   5   6   7

La plupart des activités sont plus amusantes si vous pouvez comparer vos propres capacités avec celles des autres.

1   2   3   4   5   6   7

On ne gagne rien à faire des concessions et à renoncer à ses préférenc dans le but de faire la paix avec un ennemi personnel.

1   2   3   4   5   6   7

Vous ne devriez pas vous montrer modeste si cela doit amener les gens à sous-estimer vos capacités.

1   2   3   4   5   6   7

Au cours d'une dispute personnelle, vous ne devriez jamais accorder un traitement de faveur à quelqu'un qui ne se rangera pas de votre coté.

1   2   3   4   5   6   7

Il est extrêmement désagréable d'être habillé plus pauvrement que la plupart des gens avec qui on est en relations.

1   2   3   4   5   6   7

Nous devrions encourager les étrangers à venir chez nous pour qu'ils nous exposent leurs opinions.

1   2   3   4   5   6   7

us devriez vous garder d'avoir affaire aux gens qui vous déplaisent.

1   2   3   4   5   6   7

us devrions être parfaitement honnêtes lorsque nous parlons de nos
opres érreurs et défauts.

1   2   3   4   5   6   7

rsque les gens refusent d'y "mettre du leur", la menace est la meilleure
son de les rendre un peu plus coopératifs.

1   2   3   4   5   6   7

est bon d'être au courant des problèmes et soucis des gens autour de
i, de façon à pouvoir les aider.

1   2   3   4   5   6   7

dépit de quelques exceptions, les gens sont à peu prés dignes de
fiance.

1   2   3   4   5   6   7

Les questions formant la série suivante concernent vos petites sympathie
et antipathies, vos inclinations, vos préférences et habitudes de la vie
de tous les jours. Il n'y a pas de réponse bonne ou de réponse mauvaise
à ces questions; une réponse en vaut une autre. Comme chacun sait: "Les
goûts et les couleurs ne se discutent pas".

INSTRUCTIONS: Pour chaque question, veuillez encercler à l'aide de votre
                crayon le chiffre qui, en accord avec le plan suivant,
                exprime le mieux votre réaction.

                Si votre réponse est Oui, encerclez le chiffre 1.
                Si vous êtes absolument indécis, encerclez le chiffre 2.
                Si votre réponse est Non, encerclez le chiffre 3.

Aimez-vous miser petit, uniquement pour le plaisir de jouer?

                         1   2   3

Aimeriez-vous faire de l'acrobatie aérienne dans un cirque d'aviation?

                         1   2   3

Aimeriez-vous plonger de très haut?

                         1   2   3

Aimez-vous jouer pour de l'argent?

                         1   2   3

Aimez-vous faire de la vitesse avec des fous du volant?

                         1   2   3

Passez-vous souvent de la gaieté à la tristesse?

                         1   2   3

Conduisez-vous vite?

                         1   2   3

Aimeriez-vous participer à une course automobile Formule I?

                         1   2   3

Aimez-vous jouer de l'argent dans des paris sportifs?

                    1   2   3

Etes-vous souvent impatient?

                    1   2   3

Aimez-vous investir de l'argent dans des inventions prometteuses?

                    1   2   3

Aimeriez-vous être pilote d'éssai?

                    1   2   3

Aimeriez-vous déscendre des rapides dans un canot automobile?

                    1   2   3

Sous le coup d'une émotion, avez-vous tendance à perdre l'appétit?

                    1   2   3

Aimeriez-vous faire du trapèze volant dans un cirque?

                    1   2   3

Aimeriez-vous affronter une tempête dans un petit bateau?

                    1   2   3

Seriez-vous prêt à prendre le risque d'accepter une situation au sujet
de laquelle vous ne connaissez rien?

                    1   2   3

Lorsque vous éssayez de vous concentrer, est-ce qu'une interruption
vous irrite?

                    1   2   3

Est-ce que vous travaillez vite?

                    1   2   3

Est-ce que vous aimez conduire vite en l'absence de toute limitation de
vitesse?

                    1   2   3

Cette série de propositions s'éfforce de révéler les différentes
manières dont les gens réagissent en face de certaines situations.
Chaque article se compose de deux propositions, la première portant
le numéro 1 et la seconde portant le numéro 2. Lisez chaque article
attentivement et choisissez celle des deux propositions qui, à
votre avis, reflète le mieux l'état des choses. Veuillez encercler
cette proposition qui vous paraît être la plus vraie; prenez garde
de n'encercler qu'une proposition pour chaque article. Ici encore,
il n'y a pas de réponses justes ou de réponses fausses. Pour chaque
article, un grand nombre de gens choisit la proposition 1 et un tout
aussi grand nombre choisit la proposition 2.

Il me semble plutôt que:

1. en faisant un éffort, je peux obtenir l'amitié des personnes
   qui m'attirent.
2. quoique vous fassiez, certaines personnes ne vous aimeront
   jamais.

1. généralement les malheurs des gens sont dûs à leurs propres
   érreurs.
2. parfois j'ai l'impression de ne pas avoir suffisamment de
   contrôle sur ce qui m'arrive.

1. à la longue, les gens reçoivent le respect qui leur est dû
   en ce monde.
2. malheureusement, la valeur d'un individu n'est pas souvent
   reconnue, en dépit de tous ses efforts.

1. certains sont nés pour recevoir des ordres, d'autres pour
   en donner.
2. à la longue, c'est celui qui est le plus compétent qui
   finit par donner les ordres.

1. en général, je pouvais dire si j'avais bien ou mal fait à
   un examen aussitôt après l'avoir passé.
2. souvent, un examen fini, j'avais l'impression d'être dans
   l'incapacité de prédire la note que j'allais avoir, même
   approximativement.

1. si l'on tombe sur de bons professeurs, on a des chances de
   réussir dans ses études; dans le cas contraire, les ennuis
   de toutes sortes commencent.
2. les notes que l'on obtient en classe dépendent surtout de soi.

1. souvent, je n'arrive pas à croire qu'il soit possible de
   faire faire aux gens ce que je voudrais qu'ils fassent.
2. il faut beaucoup de travail et de patience pour faire faire
   aux gens ce que l'on veut qu'ils fassent.

1. pour une bonne part, trouver un emploi c'est l'affaire d'être
   au bon endroit au bon moment.
2. si vous êtes qualifié, vous trouverez toujours un emploi.

1. les gens sont seuls parce qu'ils ne savent pas se faire des
   amis.
2. se faire des amis, c'est surtout avoir la chance de rencontrer
   les personnes adéquates.

Καταγραφή Προσωπικότητος /'Απόψεων

Τά κατωτέρω εἶναι μία μελέτη ἐπί τοῦ τί σκέπτονται οἱ ἄνθρωποι σχετικά
μέ ὡρισμένα κοινωνικά θέματα. Ἡ καλυτέρα ἀπάντησις σέ κάθε πρόταση εἶναι
ἡ προσωπική σου γνώμη. Ὑπάρχουν πολλές διαφορετικές ἀπόψεις. Θά διαπιστώσης
ἴσως ὅτι συμφωνεῖς ἀπολύτως μέ μερικές ἀπό τίς προτάσεις, ἤ ὅτι διαφωνεῖς
ἐξ ἴσου ἀπόλυτα μέ ἄλλες, ἤ ἴσως ὅτι δέν εἶσαι βέβαιος γιά ἄλλες. Ἀνεξαρτή-
τως τοῦ ἐάν συμφωνῆς ἤ διαφωνεῖς μέ ὁποιαδήποτε πρόταση, νά εἶσαι βέβαιος
ὅτι πολλοί ἄλλοι ἄνθρωποι αἰσθάνονται τό ἴδιο μέ σένα.

Γιά κάθε πρόταση σημείωσε μέ ἕνα κύκλο μέ τό μολύβι τόν ἀριθμό, ὁ ὁποῖος
ἀντιπροσωπεύει κατά τόν καλύτερο τρόπο τήν ἀντίδρ.ωσή σου, ὅσον ἀφορᾶ τό
κατά πόσον συμφωνεῖς ἤ διαφωνεῖς μέ τήν πρόταση. Σημείωσε ὅλες τίς προτάσεις κατά τόν ἀκόλουθο τρόπο:

7: Συμφωνῶ πάρα πολύ	3: Διαφωνῶ ἐν μέρει
6: Συμφωνῶ ἀρκετά	2: Διαφωνῶ ἀρκετά
5: Συμφωνῶ ἐν μέρει	1: Διαφωνῶ πάρα πολύ

Ἐάν εἶσαι πράγματι ἀπολύτως οὐδέτερος ἐπί ἑνός στοιχείου ἤ δέν εἶσαι
καθόλου βέβαιος γιά τό πῶς αἰσθάνεσαι, ἤ ἐάν δέν τό καταλαβαίνεις, σημείωσε
τόν ἀριθμό 4.

Ὅταν κάποιος σοῦ ἔχει συμπεριφερθῆ ἄσχημα, πρέπει νά προσπαθήσης νά
καταλάβης τί εἶναι αὐτό πού τόν ἐνοχλεῖ, γιά νά μπορέσης νά τόν βοηθήσης.

1 2 3 4 5 6 7

Ἀκόμη καί ἐάν οἱ ἄνθρωποι φαίνονται φιλικοί μαζί σου δέν μπορεῖς νά βασί
ζεσαι σέ αὐτούς διότι ἐνδιαφέρονται κυρίως γιά τό συμφέρον τους.

1 2 3 4 5 6 7

Πρέπει πάντοτε νά βοηθοῦμε αὐτούς πού ἔχουν ἀνάγκη, ἀκόμη καί ἐάν δέν
εἶναι φιλικοί μαζί μας.

1 2 3 4 5 6 7

Μερικοί ἄνθρωποι ἁπλῶς ἐπιζητοῦν τό κακό σου.

1 2 3 4 5 6 7

Εῖναι ἀδύνατον νά κάνης φίλους ἀνθρώπους πού εῖναι ἀπό τήν ἀρχή ἐχθρικοί
ἀπέναντί σου.

1 2 3 4 5 6 7

'Υπάρχουν μερικοί ἄνθρωποι τούς ὁποίους δέν μπορεῖ κανείς νά ἐμπιστεύεται.

1 2 3 4 5 6 7

Σέ περιπτώσεις φιλονικείας μέ ἄλλους πρέπει ὅταν κάνουμε λάθος νά προσπα-
θοῦμε νά τό παραδεχόμεθα.

1 2 3 4 5 6 7

Δέν μποροῦμε νά ἐμπιστευόμεθα ἀκόμη καί τά κράτη, τά ὁποῖα φαίνονται φιλικά
πρός ἐμᾶς, διότι ἐνδιαφέρονται κυρίως γιά τά ἰδικά τους συμφέροντα.

1 2 3 4 5 6 7

Πρέπει πάντοτε νά βοηθοῦμεν ἐκείνους οἱ ὁποῖοι εῖναι ἀτυχέστεροι ἀπό μᾶς.

1 2 3 4 5 6 7

Οἱ περισσότεροι ἄνθρωποι δέν εῖναι πάντοτε εὐθεῖς καί εἰλικρινεῖς, ὅταν
πρόκειται γιά τό δικό τους συμφέρον.

1 2 3 4 5 6 7

Δέν ὑπάρχει τίποτε περισσότερον ἱκανοποιητικό ἀπό τοῦ νά κάνη κανείς κάτι
πού εὐχαριστεῖ ἕναν ἄλλον.

1 2 3 4 5 6 7

Ἕνας μεγάλος ἀριθμός ἀνθρώπων εῖναι σκληροί καί κακοί.

1 2 3 4 5 6 7

Τό νά κάνης χατήρια σέ ἀνθρώπους πού δέν εῖναι σέ θέσι νά τά ἀνταποδώσουν
εῖναι χαμένος καιρός.

1 2 3 4 5 6 7

Εῖναι πολύ πιθανόν νά ἔχης μερικούς προσωπικούς ἐχθρούς χωρίς νά γνωρίζης
τίποτα σχετικά.

1 2 3 4 5 6 7

'Οταν φιλονικῆς μέ κάποιον πρέπει νά ποοσπαθῆς νά καταλάβης τήν δική του
διαφορετική ἄποψη: 1 2 3 4 5 6 7

Δέν πρέπει νά ἔχης καμμία σχέση μέ ἀνθρώπους πού σοῦ φέρονται ἐχθρικά.

1 2 3 4 5 6 7

'Οταν ἔχει πεῖ κανείς κάτι γιά νά σέ πληγώση, δέν εῖναι καλό νά τοῦ τό
ἀνταποδώσης ἀκόμη καί ἄν αὐτό πού θά πῆς γιά ἐκεῖνον εῖναι ἐντελῶς ἀληθινό.

1 2 3 4 5 6 7

Τό νά κάνης κάτι γιά νά εύχαριστήσης κάποιον πού δέν σέ συμπαθεῖ εἶναι δυνατόν νά σοῦ δώση μεγάλη εὐχαρίστηση.

1 2 3 4 5 6 7

Οἱ περισσότερες ἀσχολίες γίνονται πιό εὐχάριστες ὅταν μπορᾶς νά συγκρίνης τίς δικές σου ἱκανότητες μέ τῶν ἄλλων.

1 2 3 4 5 6 7

Δέν ἀξίζει νά κάνης παραχωρήσεις καί νά ἐγκαταλείπης τίς δικές σου προτιμήσεις γιά νά συμφιλιωθῆς μέ ἕνα προσωπικό ἐχθρό.

1 2 3 4 5 6 7

Δέν πρέπει νά εἶσαι μετριόφρων ἐάν πρόκειται νά ὑποτιμήσουν τίς ἱκανότητές σου οἱ ἄλλοι.

1 2 3 4 5 6 7

Ὅταν ἔχης μία προσωπική φιλονικεία, δέν πρέπει νά κάνης χατήρια σέ ἀνθρώπους πού δέν θά πάρουν τό μέρος σου.

1 2 3 4 5 6 7

Εἶναι φοβερά ἐνοχλητικό νά εἶσαι χειρότερα ντυμένος ἀπό τούς ἀνθρώπους μέ τούς ὁποίους ἔχεις σχέσεις.

1 2 3 4 5 6 7

Πρέπει νά ἐπιδιώκωμε νά μᾶς ἐπισκέπτωνται ἄνθρωποι ἀπό ἄλλες χῶρες καί νά μᾶς γνωρίζουν τίς ἀπόψεις τους.

1 2 3 4 5 6 7

Δέν πρέπει νά ἔχης σχέσεις μέ ἀνθρώπους τούς ὁποίους δέν ἐπιδοκιμάζεις.

1 2 3 4 5 6 7

Πρέπει νά εἴμεθα πολύ εἰλικρινεῖς ὅταν λέμε στούς ἄλλους τά ἐλαττώματα καί τά λάθη μας.

1 2 3 4 5 6 7

Ὅταν οἱ ἄνθρωποι δέν εἶναι συνεργάσιμοι ὁ πλέον ἀποτελεσματικός τρόπος γιά νά τούς κάνης νά κάνουν αὐτό πού θέλεις εἶναι ἡ χρῆσις ἀπειλῶν.

1 2 3 4 5 6 7

Εἶναι καλό νά γνωρίζης τά προβλήματα καί τίς στενοχώριες τῶν ἀνθρώπων γύρω σου, ὥστε νά μπορῆς νά τούς βοηθῆς.

1 2 3 4 5 6 7

Οἱ περισσότεροι ἄνθρωποι εἶναι τίς πιό πολλές φορές ἄξιοι ἐμπιστοσύνης.

1 2 3 4 5 6 7

Ἡ ἐπομένη σειρά ἐρωτήσεων ἀφορᾶ προτιμήσεις καὶ συνήθειες τῆς καθημερινῆς
ζωῆς· τὶ σοῦ ἀρέσει καὶ τὶ δὲν σοῦ ἀρέσει. Σὲ αὐτὲς τὶς ἐρωτήσεις δὲν ὑπάρχουν
σωστές ἤ λανθασμένες ἀπαντήσεις· μιά ἀπάντησις μπορεῖ νά εἶναι ἐξ ἴσου καλή
ὅσο καὶ μιά ἄλλη.

ΟΔΗΓΙΑΙ: Γιά κάθε ἐρώτησι, βάλε σὲ κύκλο μὲ τὸ μολύβι τὸν ἀριθμό 1, 2 ἤ
3 γιά τήν ἀπάντησι πού σοῦ πηγαίνει καλύτερα.

'Εάν ἡ ἀπάντησί σου εἶναι ΝΑΙ, βάλε σὲ κύκλο τὸν ἀριθμό 1.

'Εάν δὲν μπορεῖς νά ἀποφασίσης, βάλε σὲ κύκλο τὸν ἀριθμό 2.

'Εάν ἡ ἀπάντησί σου εἶναι ΟΧΙ βάλε σὲ κύκλο τὸν ἀριθμό 3.

Σοῦ ἀρέσει νά βάζης στοιχήματα γιά πολύ μικρά ποσά μόνον καὶ μόνον γιά
τήν εὐχαρίστησι τοῦ στοιχήματος;

                          1   2   3

Θά σοῦ ἄρεσε νά κάνης ἀκροβασίες σὲ μιά ἀεροπορική μονάδα ἀκροβατικῶν
πτήσεων;

                          1   2   3

Θά σοῦ ἄρεσε νά βουτήξης στό νερό ἀπό τήν ψηλή σανίδα τοῦ κολυμβητηρίου;

                          1   2   3

Σοῦ ἀρέσει νά στοιχηματίζης μὲ χρήματα σὲ παιγνίδια πού παίζεις;

                          1   2   3

Θά σοῦ ἄρεσε νά βρίσκεσαι στό ἴδιο αὐτοκίνητο μὲ ἕνα ριψοκίνδυνο ὁδηγό;

                          1   2   3

Ἔχεις συχνά ψυχικὲς μεταπτώσεις;

                          1   2   3

'Οδηγεῖς τό αὐτοκίνητό σου μὲ μεγάλη ταχύτητα;

                          1   2   3

Θά ἤθελες νά ἐλάμβανες μέρος σὲ ράλλυ;

                          1   2   3

Σοῦ ἀρέσει νά βάζης στοιχήματα σὲ ἀθλητικά παιγνίδια;

                          1   2   3

Αἰσθάνεσαι συχνά ἀνυπομονησία;

                          1   2   3

Σοῦ ἀρέσει νά βάλης χρήματα σὲ μιά ἐφεύρεση πού ὑπόσχεται πολλά γιά τό μέλλον;

                          1   2   3

Θά σοῦ ἄρεσε νά δοκιμασθῆς ὡς πιλότος νέων ἀεροπλάνων;

1 2 3

Θά qοῦ ἄρεσε νά πλεύσης εἰς ἔνα καταρρακτῶδες ποτάμι μέ μία βάρκα μέ μηχανή

1 2 3

Χάνεις συνῆθως τήν ὄρεξή σου ὄταν εἶσαι στενοχωρημένος;

1 2 3

Θά σοῦ ἄρεσε νά ἐργαζόσουν σέ τσῖρκο σάν ἀκροβάτης ἐναερίων ἀλμάτων;

1 2 3

Θά σοῦ ἄρεσε νά ταξιδέψης σέ τρικυμία μέσα σέ μία μικρή βάρκα;

1 2 3

Θά δεχόσουν μία ἐργασία χωρίς νά γνωρίζης τίποτα γι'αὐτήν;

1 2 3

Ἐκνευρίζεσαι ἐάν σέ διακόψουν ὄταν συγκεντρώνεσαι;

1 2 3

Δουλεύεις γρήγορα συνῆθως;

1 2 3

Σοῦ ἀρέσει νά ὁδηγῆς γρήγορα ὄταν δέν ὑπάρχει ὄριο ταχύτητος;

1 2 3

Ἡ ἐπομένη σειρά προτάσεων σκοπόν ἔχει νά ἀνακαλύψη τόν τρόπο κατά τόν ὁποῖον ὡρισμένα σημαντικά γεγονότα στήν κοινωνία μας ἐπηρεάζουν διαφόρους ἀνθρώπους. Κάθε μέρος ἀποτελεῖται ἀπό δύο προτάσεις, ἡ μία ἐκ τῶν ὁποίων ἔχει μπροστά της τόν ἀριθμόν 1 καί ἡ ἄλλη τόν ἀριθμό 2. Γιά κάθε περίπτωσι διάβασε καί τίς δύο προτάσεις προσεκτικά καί διάλεξε τήν μία ἐκ τῶν δύο (καί μόνον μία), ἡ ὁποία πιστεύεις ὅτι ἀντιπροσωπεύει πιό πολύ τήν δική σου περίπτωσι. Κάνε τήν ἐκλογή σου κυκλώνοντας μέ τό μολύβι τόν ἀριθμό τῆς προτάσεως πού πιστεύεις ὅτι εἶναι ἡ πλέον ἁρμόζουσα. Δέν ὑπάρχουν σωστές ἤ λανθασμένες ἀπαντήσεις σέ αὐτό τό ἐρωτηματολόγιον. Γιά τήν κάθε περίπτωσι ὑπάρχει ἔνας μεγάλος ἀριθμός ἀνθρώπων πού διαλέγει τό 1 καί ἔνας ἐπίσης μεγάλος ἀριθμός πού διαλέγει τό 2.

Προσωπικά, πιστεύω πιό πολύ ὅτι:

1. Ἐάν προσπαθήσω, μπορῶ νά κάνω φίλους μου τούς ἀνθρώπους πού μοῦ ἀρέσουν.
2. Ὅσο καί νά προσπαθῆς, μερικοί ἄνθρωποι ἀπλῶς δέν σέ συμπαθοῦν.

1. Οἱ δυστυχίες τῶν ἀνθρώπων εἶναι συνήθως ἀποτέλεσμα ἰδικῶν των λαθῶν.
2. Μερικές φορές αἰσθάνομαι ὅτι δέν ἔχω ἀρκετό ἔλεγχο σέ ὅτι μοῦ συμβαίνει.

1. Ἐν καιρῷ οἱ ἄνθρωποι δρέπουν τόν σεβασμό πού τούς ἀνήκει σέ αὐτό τόν κόσμο.
2. Δυστυχῶς, ἡ ἀξία ἑνός ἀνθρώπου συχνά περνάει χωρίς ἀναγνώρισι ὅσο καί ἐάν αὐτός.προσπαθῆ.

1. Μερικοί ἔχουν γεννηθῆ γιά νά παίρνουν διαταγές καί ἄλλοι γιά νά τίς δίνουν.
2. Τελικά, ὁ ἄνθρωπος μέ τίς μεγαλύτερες ἱκανότητες καταλήγει νά δίνη τίς διαταγές.

1. Ἠμποροῦσα νά ξέρω συνήθως ἐάν εἶχα γράψη καλά ἤ ὄχι στίς ἐξετάσεις στό σχολεῖο μόλις τελείωνε τό διαγώνισμα.
2. Συνήθως αἰσθανόμουνα ὅτι δέν μποροῦσα νά προβλέψω τί βαθμό θά ἔπαιρνα σέ ἕνα διαγώνισμα.

1. Ἐάν ἔχη κανείς τόν κατάλληλο δάσκαλο, μπορεῖ νά πάη καλά στό σχολεῖο, ἀλλοιῶς ὄχι.
2. Τό τί βαθμούς παίρνει κανείς στό σχολεῖο ἐξαρτᾶται ἀπό τόν ἴδιο.

1. Μοῦ εἶναι συχνά ἀδύνατον νά καταλάβω πῶς εἶναι δυνατόν νά καταφέρω τούς ἄλλους νά κάνουν αὐτό πού θέλω.
2. Χρειάζεται ὑπομονή καί πολλή δουλειά γιά νά καταφέρη κανείς τούς ἄλλους νά κάνουν αὐτό πού θέλει.

1. Τό νά ἀποκτήση κανείς μιά καλή ἐργασία ἐξαρτᾶται ἐν μέρει ἀπό τό γεγονός νά βρίσκεται στήν σωστή θέση, τήν σωστή στιγμή.
2. Ἐάν ἔχης ἱκανότητα, μπορεῖς πάντοτε νά βρῆς ἐργασία.

1. Οἱ ἄνθρωποι αἰσθάνονται μόνοι διότι δέν γνωρίζουν πῶς νά εἶναι φιλικοί πρός τούς ἄλλους.
2. Τό νά κάνη κανείς φίλους ἐξαρτᾶται κατά μέγα μέρος ἀπό τήν τύχη του νά συναντᾶ τούς κατάλληλους ἀνθρώπους.

JAPAN

参加者アンケート

下段の質問は，人間関係に関する事柄で，人々がどう考えるかという調査です。最上の答は
あなたの個人的な意見です。いろいろちがった観点が含されています。あなたはきっと，いく
つかの質問には，強く共感するでしょうし，他の質問には強い反感を覚えるでしょう。そして，
ある質問に対しては，はっきりしないでしょう。各質問内容に対し賛成にしろ，反対にしろ，
他の多くの人々もあなたと同じ様に感ずることだけは確かです。各々の質問に対して，次の基
準に従って，鉛筆で印をつけて下さい。

7. とても強く共感　　　　3. すこし反対

6. まあ共感　　　　　　　2. まあ反対

5. すこし共感　　　　　　1. 強く反対

もしあなたが，完全に中立的な意見であるか，それとも，どちらともきめかねるようなら，ま
た，どれにしたらよいかわからなければ，4に印をつけて下さい。

1. だれかがとてもいじわるなとき，何が彼をわずらわせているか，あなたは彼の助けになる
   ために，理解しようとするべきだ。

   　　　　　　　　1　2　3　4　5　6　7

2. 人々は，自分自身の利益にこだわっているから，たとえ彼らがあなたに好意的にみえても，
   あなたはそれを，信用できないかもしれない。

   　　　　　　　　1　2　3　4　5　6　7

3. 人々が好意的でなくても，常に助けの必要な人を助けるべきである。

   　　　　　　　　1　2　3　4　5　6　7

4. ある人は，ただ単なる悪意から，あなたに対していやなことをする。

   　　　　　　　　1　2　3　4　5　6　7

5. はじめからあなたを憎んでいる人を，友達にはできない。

   　　　　　　　　1　2　3　4　5　6　7

6. 信用のできない人は，いるものである。

   　　　　　　　　1　2　3　4　5　6　7

7. けんかの際でも．あなたが悪いときには．その点を認めるべきである。

           1 2 3 4 5 6 7

8. 好意的にみえる国家であっても．それ自身の利益にこだわっているから．信用できないかもしれない。

           1 2 3 4 5 6 7

9. あなたは．自分より不幸な人々を．助けるという責任を感ずるべきである。

           1 2 3 4 5 6 7

10. ほとんどの人々は．彼ら自身の利益がからんでいるときには．必ずしも率直で．正直であるわけではない。

           1 2 3 4 5 6 7

11. 他人を喜ばせるぐらい．満足を与えられることはない。

           1 2 3 4 5 6 7

12. 驚くべき多数の人が．残酷で意地悪である。

           1 2 3 4 5 6 7

13. 返札の期待できない地位にいる人に．なにかをしてやることは時間の浪費である。

           1 2 3 4 5 6 7

14. あなたは，気がついていないで．あなたの個人的な敵をもっているかもしれない。

           1 2 3 4 5 6 7

15. 誰かと言い争ったとき．その人の考えを理解するように．特別の努力をすべきである。

           1 2 3 4 5 6 7

16. 反感を示す人に対しては．はじめから何も関係すべきではない。

           1 2 3 4 5 6 7

17. 誰かがあなたを傷つけるようなことを言ったとき，たとえあなたが完全に正しくても．その人にしかえしをするのはよくない。

           1 2 3 4 5 6 7

18. あなたをきらっている人を．喜ばせる成は．大きな満足である。

           1 2 3 4 5 6 7

19. あなたの能力を他の人と競いあえるときは．仕事がよけい楽しくなる。

           1 2 3 4 5 6 7

20. 個人的な敵とおだやかにやっていくために．妥協したりあなたのやりたいことを．途中であきらめたりするのは意味がない。

           1 2 3 4 5 6 7

21. 他人が，あなたの能力を過小評価するようなら，控え目にしているべきではない。

        1 2 3 4 5 6 7

22. 個人的ないざこざがあるとき，味方でない人に好意を示すべきではない。

        1 2 3 4 5 6 7

23. 付き合っている人々より，貧弱な洋服をきていることは，とてもいやなことである。

        1 2 3 4 5 6 7

24. 外国人に訪問してもらい，彼らの観点を説明してもらうようにすべきである。

        1 2 3 4 5 6 7

25. あなたが受けいれられない人々に，何ら関係を持つべきではない。

        1 2 3 4 5 6 7

26. 自分の短所やまちがいを他人に話すときは，完全に気楽になるべきである。

        1 2 3 4 5 6 7

27. 人々が非協力的であるとき，あなたの思っていることをやらせるには，おどかしが一番効果的である。

        1 2 3 4 5 6 7

28. まわりにいる人々の問題や悩みを知るのは，あなたが，彼らの助けになるためにはよい考えである。

        1 2 3 4 5 6 7

29. 時々のまちがいにもかかわらず，人々はたよりになるものである。

        1 2 3 4 5 6 7

次の質問は，あなたの日常の好みに関してです。正解，不正解はありません。一つの答は，他の答と同じように，立派なものです。

    指示：次の基準に従って，鉛筆で印をつけて下さい。

        「そう思う」のでしたら   No. 1

        決めかねるのでしたら   No. 2

        「ちがうと思う」のでしたら   No. 3

30. 少しのお金で，単なる楽しみだけのために，かけをしたいですか。

        1   2   3

31. 空中サーカスで，曲芸飛行をしたいですか。

        1   2   3

32. プールで、高とびこみをしたいですか。

                    1   2   3

33. 金がかかっているとき、ゲームをしたいですか。

                    1   2   3

34. ショーのための危険な運転をする人と一緒に、ドライブをしたいですか。

                    1   2   3

35. 時々、幸福から不幸に気分が変わりますか。

                    1   2   3

36. 車を比較的速く運転しますか。

                    1   2   3

37. カーレースで、競技用の自動車を運転したいですか。

                    1   2   3

38. 運動競技に、お金をかけたいですか。

                    1   2   3

39. 自分で、いつもいらいらしやすいと感じますか。

                    1   2   3

40. 将来が期待される発明に、投資したいですか。

                    1   2   3

41. テストパイロットに、なりたいですか。

                    1   2   3

42. 波が高くて危険なときに、モーターボートで走りたいですか？

                    1   2   3

43. 感情的に動揺しているとき、食欲をなくしがちですか。

                    1   2   3

44. サーカスで、空中ブランコの仕事がしたいですか、

                    1   2   3

45. 小さなボートで、嵐の中にとどまって、こいでいたいですか。

                    1   2   3

46. なにも知らない仕事の機会があるとき、よろこんでそれを受けますか。

                    1   2   3

47. 集中しているときに，じゃまされるといら出ちますか。

              1   2   3

48. 仕事をするのが，一般にはやいですか。

              1   2   3

49. 速度制限がないとき，速めに車を運転したいですか。

              1   2   3

　次の質問は，人々に影響を及ぼす，社会的な重要な出来事に関してのやり方を，見つけ出そうとする為のものです。

　質問は対になっています。それには，各々1，2の番号がついています。その二つのうち，たった一つだけあなたがより共感できる方に，しるしをつけて下さい。正解，不正解はありません。多数の人が，1を選んだり2を選んだりします。

　次の二つのうち，あたたがより強く共感する方を選んで下さい。

1. 努力をすれば，私が友達にしたいと思っている人を，得ることが出来る。
2. どんなに努力をしても，ただ単にあなたを好きにたらない人もいる。

1. 人々の不運は，普通彼らが，まちがいをおかした結果である。
2. 時々，私に起こることに対して，私自身で何も出来ないような気がする。

1. 長期的には，彼らが受ける価値のある尊敬をこの世で得る。
2. 不運にして個人の価値は，彼らがいかに努力してみても，認められないことが多くある。

1. ある人は命令する人に生まれつき，ある人は命令をうけるように生まれついている。
2. 長期的には，能力のある人が命令する人になる。

1. 試験が終わったと同時に，うまくやれたかどうかわかる。
2. どんな結果か，試験が終わった時にはわからない。

1. もしも正しい先生につけば，彼は学校でよくやれるようになる。さもなければ，問題を持つだろう。
2. 学校での評価は，彼の努力しだいである。

1. どうやったら、彼らに私の思うことを、やらせることができるかわからない。

2. 人々に、あなたの望むことをやらせるには、忍耐と努力がいる。

1. よい仕事を得るということは、ひとつには運が左右する。

2. もしも能力があるなら、あなたはいつでも仕事を得られる。

1. 人々は、どうやったら親しくなれるか知らないから孤独である。

2. 友達になれるかどうかは、いい人にめぐりあえるという事しだいである。

SPAIN

<u>CUESTIONARIO DE ACTITUDES PERSONALES</u>

Las preguntas corresponden a lo que Vd. piensa acerca de algunas cuestiones sociales. La mejor respuesta a cada pregunta será su opinión personal. Puede estar de acuerdo totalmente con alguna de las proposiciones, en desacuerdo con otras y quizás incierto acerca de otras. Tanto si está de acuerdo o en desacuerdo puede estar seguro que mucha gente siente de la misma forma que Vd.

En cada pregunta rodee con lápiz el número que exprese mejor su reacción. Marque cada pregunta usando el esquema siguiente:

<u>de acuerdo</u>   <u>en desacuerdo</u>

7. muchisimo   3. poco
6. algo   2. algo
5. poco   1. muchisimo

4. completamente neutral
   completamente incierto
   no entiendo la pregunta

Cuando alguien ha sido malo con Vd. debe intentar entender lo que le pasa, de tal forma que pueda serle útil a él.

1 2 3 4 5 6 7

Incluso la gente que es amable con Vd. no es de fiar porque están principalmente preocupados con sus propios intereses.

1 2 3 4 5 6 7

Debemos siempre ayudar a los que necesitan ayuda, incluso si ellos son poco amables con nosotros.

1 2 3 4 5 6 7

Siento que tengo enemigos.

1 2 3 4 5 6 7

Vd. no puede hacer amigos con gente que le es hostil.

1 2 3 4 5 6 7

Hay gente con la que uno no se puede fiar.

1 2 3 4 5 6 7

En argumentos con otros debemos aceptar nuestras equivocaciones.

1 2 3 4 5 6 7

Incluso las naciones que aparecen amables pueden ser indignas
de confianza por estar principalmente preocupadas con sus
propios intereses.

1 2 3 4 5 6 7

Debemos sentirnos responsables y ayudar a los otros menos afor-
tunados que nosotros.

1 2 3 4 5 6 7

La mayor parte de la gente no es siempre honesta y franca
cuando están envueltos en la cuestión de sus propios intereses.

1 2 3 4 5 6 7

No hay nada más satisfactorio que hacer algo que agrade a
otra persona.

1 2 3 4 5 6 7

Un sorprendente número de gente es cruel y maligna.

1 2 3 4 5 6 7

Hacer favores que no pueden ser devueltos es una pérdida de
tiempo.

1 2 3 4 5 6 7

Es muy probable que Vd. tiene enemigos personales que ni
siquiera conoce.

1 2 3 4 5 6 7

Cuando discute con alguien debe hacer un especial esfuerzo
para entender el punto de vista de su interlocutor.

1 2 3 4 5 6 7

No debe tratar con gente que le es hostil.

1 2 3 4 5 6 7

Cuando alguien le ha dicho algo que le hiere, no es bueno
contestar, aunque las cosas que pueda Vd. decir sean perfec-
tamente verdaderas.

1 2 3 4 5 6 7

Hacer algo para agradar una persona a quien Vd. no gusta
puede darle a Vd. mucha satisfacción.

    1 2 3 4 5 6 7

La mayor parte de las actividades son mas divertidas cuando
Vd. puede comparar sus propias habilidades con las de los
otros.

    1 2 3 4 5 6 7

No vale la pena hacer "compromisos" y abdicar sus propias
preferencias para hacer paz con su enemigo.

    1 2 3 4 5 6 7

No debe ser modesto si ello le lleva a ser subestimado en
sus habilidades.

    1 2 3 4 5 6 7

Cuando está envuelto en disputas personales no debe hacer
favores a sus adversarios.

    1 2 3 4 5 6 7

Es extremadamente preocupante andar más pobremente vestido
que la mayor parte de la gente con la que esta tratando.

    1 2 3 4 5 6 7

Debemos intentar llevar gente de otros países para visitarnos
y explicarnos sus puntos de vista.

    1 2 3 4 5 6 7

No debemos hacer nada con la gente con la que no estamos
de acuerdo.

    1 2 3 4 5 6 7

Debemos ser completamente francos acerca de nuestros defectos
y equivocaciones.

    1 2 3 4 5 6 7

Cuando la gente no es cooperativa, la forma más efectiva de
obtener lo que quiere es usar amenazas.

    1 2 3 4 5 6 7

Es bueno conocer los problemas y las preocupaciones de la
gente que le rodea, de tal forma que pueda serles útil.

    1 2 3 4 5 6 7

A pesar de las faltas ocasionales, la mayor parte de la gente
merece confianza.

1 2 3 4 5 6 7

La siguiente serie de cuestiones son acerca de sus gustos,
preferencias y hábitos de cada dia. No hay respuestas correctas
o incorrectas. Una respuesta puede ser tan buena como la otra.

Rodee con su lápiz el número 1, 2 o 3 según la respuesta
elegida.

Si su respuesta es SI, rodee el numero 1
Si no puede decidir, rodee el numero 2
Si su respuesta es NO, rodee el numero 3

¿Le gusta apostar pequeñas apuestas justamente por la satisfacción
que Vd. obtiene del juego?

1 2 3

¿Le gustaría actuar en un circo aéreo?

1 2 3

¿Le gustaría bucear saltando desde un alto trampolín?

1 2 3

¿Le gusta jugar cuando hay dinero comprometido?

1 2 3

¿Le gustaría ser pasajero en coche de un conductor temerario?

1 2 3

¿Pasa fácilmente de la felicidad a la tristeza?

1 2 3

¿Conduce el automóvil rapidamente?

1 2 3

¿Le gustaría conducir un coche de carreras?

1 2 3

¿Le gusta jugar dinero en juegos atléticos?

1 2 3

¿Se siente Vd. a menudo impaciente?

1 2 3

¿Le gusta invertir dinero en un invento que promete?

1 2 3

¿Le gustaría ser un piloto de prueba?

1 2 3

¿Le gustaría conducir un autobote en un río veloz?

1 2 3

Cuando Vd. está emocionalmente preocupado, ¿tiende a perder su apetito?

1 2 3

¿Le gustaría trabajar como acróbata trapecista en un circo?

1 2 3

¿Le gustaría en tiempo de tormenta slair en un pequeño bote?

1 2 3

¿Le gustaría aceptar un cargo del que Vd. no conoce nada?

1 2 3

¿Le irrita ser interrumpido cuando está concentrando?

1 2 3

¿Trabaja Vd. de costumbre con rapidez?

1 2 3

¿Le gusta conducir el coche más bien rápido cuando no hay limitación de velocidad?

1 2 3

Esta serie de preguntas intenta descubrir cómo ciertos importantes acontecimientos en nuestra sociedad afectan a los diferentes tipos humanos. Cada apartado tiene dos proposiciones, una con el número uno y otra con el número dos. Lea cuidadosamente las dos proposiciones y escoja solamente la que le parezca más adecuada marcándola con un redondel. NO HAY contestaciones correctas e incorrectas. En cada pregunta muchos escogen la 1^a y otros la 2^a.

1. Si hago un esfuerzo puedo hacer que la gente que me gusta sean mis amigos.

2. No importa lo que Vd. haga para ser aceptado por cierto tipo de gente.

1. Las desgracias de la gente nacen normalmente de las equivocaciones que hacen.

2. Algunas veces siento que no tengo suficiente control en lo que me sucede.

1. A lo largo, en este mundo, la gente tiene el respeto que merece.

2. Desafortunadamente la valía de un individuo pasa a menudo irreconocida no importa el esfuerzo que haga.

1. Hay gente que ha nacido para recibir órdenes y otros que han nacido para darlas.

2. A lo largo el que tiene más habilidad acaba por dar órdenes.

1. Normalmente puedo predecir el resultado bueno o malo de un examen despues de hacerlo.

2. A menudo siento que no puedo predecir la nota del examen.

1. Si uno tiene un buen profesor el estudiante va bien en clase, de lo contrario tiene dificultades.

2. Las notas que la persona obtiene en la escuela dependen de él.

1. A menudo no se como hacer que la gente haga lo que yo quiero.

2. Hacer que la gente haga lo que yo quiero requiere duro trabajo y paciencia.

1. Tener un buen empleo depende en parte del sitio y tiempo oportuno.

2. Con habilidad seimpre se puede obtener un empleo.

1. La gente es solitaria porque no sabe ser amable.

2. Hacer buenos amigos es en gran parte una cuestión de suerte.

THAILAND

บุคคลิก/ความคิดเห็น

ชื่อ ....

    ประโยคต่อไปนี้ตั้งขึ้นเพื่อศึกษาทัศนคติของคนเราเกี่ยวกับปัญหาทางสังคมหลายประการด้วยกัน ในการตอบประโยคเหล่านี้ โปรดใช้ความคิดเห็นของตัวท่านเองเป็นหลัก ประโยคเหล่านี้ครอบคลุมความ คิดเห็นต่าง ๆ หลาย ๆ ประการด้วยกัน ท่านอาจจะเห็นด้วยอย่างมากกับคำตอบบางข้อ แต่ท่านอาจจะ ฉัดแย้งอย่างมากกับคำตอบบางข้อ หรือในบางกรณีท่านอาจจะไม่แน่ใจว่าคำตอบไหนดีที่สุด ไม่ว่าท่านจะ เห็นด้วยหรือไม่เห็นด้วยกับคำตอบใดก็ตามโปรดอย่าได้กังวลเพราะคนอื่น ๆ ก็คงจะรู้สึกเช่นเดียวกับท่าน

    ในการตอบคำถามทุกข้อ โปรดเขียนวงกลมล้อมรอบตัวเลขซึ่งแทนคำตอบที่ท่านเห็นด้วย โปรด ตอบทุกข้อโดยใช้ระหัสตัวเลขดังต่อไปนี้

7 - ข้าพเจ้าเห็นด้วยอย่างมาก   3 - ข้าพเจ้ามีความเห็นขัดแย้งบางเล็กน้อย

6 - ข้าพเจ้าเห็นด้วยเป็นส่วนใหญ่   2 - ข้าพเจ้าไม่เห็นด้วยเป็นส่วนใหญ่

5 - ข้าพเจ้าเห็นด้วยเพียงเล็กน้อย   1 - ข้าพเจ้าไม่เห็นด้วยเลย

    ถ้าท่านมีความคิดเห็นเป็นกลาง หรือไม่แน่ใจว่าจะเลือกคำตอบข้อไหน หรือท่านไม่เข้าใจคำตอบ

<u>โปรดวงกลมเลข 4</u>

1.   เมื่ออยู่ใกล้ประพฤติตัวหยาบคายกับท่าน เพื่อที่ท่านจะช่วยเหลือเขาได้ ท่านควรที่จะศึกษาให้เข้าใจ ถึงสาเหตุที่ทำให้เขาประพฤติตัวเช่นนั้น

          1   2   3   4   5   6   7

2.   แม้บุคคลบางคนจะแสดงตัวเป็นมิตรกับท่าน ท่านก็ไม่ควรจะวางใจนัก เพราะบุคคลบางคนอาจแสดง ตัวเช่นนั้น เพื่อหวังผลประโยชน์ส่วนตัวของเขาเป็นใหญ่

          1   2   3   4   5   6   7

3.   เราควรช่วยเหลือบุคคลที่ต้องการความช่วยเหลือ ถึงแม้ว่าเขาจะไม่แสดงตัวเป็นมิตรต่อเรา

          1   2   3   4   5   6   7

4.

          1   2   3   4   5   6   7

5. ท่านไม่สามารถที่จะทำตัวเป็นมิตรกับบุคคลที่แสดงตัวเป็นศัตรูต่อท่านตั้งแต่พบกันเป็นโอกาสแรก

      1   2   3   4   5   6   7

6. บุคคลบางประเภทไว้ใจไม่ได้เลย

      1   2   3   4   5   6   7

7. ในกรณีที่มีการถกเถียงกัน เราควรถือหลักว่า เราจะยอมรับผิดเมื่อเรารู้ว่าเราเป็นฝ่ายผิด

      1   2   3   4   5   6   7

8. แม้ประเทศบางประเทศจะแสดงความเป็นมิตรต่อเรา เราก็ไม่ควรวางใจนัก เพราะประเทศ
   เหล่านั้นอาจกระทำตัวเป็นมิตร เพื่อหวังผลประโยชน์ของเขาเป็นส่วนใหญ่

      1   2   3   4   5   6   7

9. เราควรจะถือหลักว่า เราจะช่วยเหลือคนที่ตกอยู่ในสถานการณ์ที่ด้อยกว่าเรา

      1   2   3   4   5   6   7

10. บุคคลส่วนใหญ่จะไม่ตรงไปตรงมาและถือความสัตย์ ถ้าหากการกระทำดังกล่าวจะมีผลกระทบกระเทือน
    ผลประโยชน์ส่วนตัวของเขา

       1   2   3   4   5   6   7

11. ไม่มีสิ่งใดที่น่าซึ้งพอใจไปมากกว่าที่ท่านได้ทำสิ่งที่ทำให้คนอื่นพอใจได้

       1   2   3   4   5   6   7

12. คนที่โหดร้ายและชอบเหยียดหยามคน มีจำนวนมากกว่าที่ท่านจะคาดถึง

       1   2   3   4   5   6   7

13. การช่วยเหลือคนที่ไม่สามารถตอบแทนเราได้ เป็นการเสียเวลา

       1   2   3   4   5   6   7

14. มันเป็นไปได้ที่ท่านจะมีศัตรูหลายคนที่ท่านคาดไม่ถึง

       1   2   3   4   5   6   7

15. เมื่อท่านมีการถกเถียงกับคนอื่น ท่านควรจะใช้ความพยายามเป็นพิเศษให้เข้าใจความคิดเห็นของเขา

       1   2   3   4   5   6   7

16. ท่านไม่ควรจะยุ่งเกี่ยวกับคนที่เป็นศัตรูมุ่งร้ายต่อท่าน

    1   2   3   4   5   6   7

17. เมื่อมีคนมาฟ้องให้ท่านเจ็บใจ ท่านไม่ควรไปโต้ตอบเขา ถึงแม้ว่าสิ่งที่ท่านจะพูดเกี่ยวกับเขานั้นเป็นความจริง

    1   2   3   4   5   6   7

18. ท่านอาจได้รับความพึงพอใจ จากการที่ท่านสามารถทำบางสิ่งบางอย่างที่ทำให้คนที่ไม่ชอบท่านเลย เกิดความสบายใจได้

    1   2   3   4   5   6   7

19. กิจกรรมส่วนมากจะมีความน่าสนใจมากขึ้น ถ้ามีการแข่งขันระหว่างผลงานของท่านและของคู่แข่งขัน

    1   2   3   4   5   6   7

20. มันไม่คุ้มที่ท่านจะต้องประณีประนอมหรือยอมอ่อนให้ศัตรูของท่าน เพื่อแลกกับความสงบราบรื่น

    1   2   3   4   5   6   7

21. ท่านไม่ควรถ่อมตัวของท่าน ถ้าการกระทำเช่นนั้นจะทำให้คนอื่นไม่ทราบถึงความสามารถอันแท้จริงของท่าน

    1   2   3   4   5   6   7

22. ขณะที่ท่านอยู่ในระหว่างมีการโต้เถียงกัน ท่านไม่ควรช่วยเหลือคนที่ท่านทราบว่าจะไม่ยอมมาเป็นพวกของท่าน

    1   2   3   4   5   6   7

23. ท่านจะรู้สึกไม่สบายใจเป็นอันมาก ถ้าท่านแต่งตัวด้อยกว่าคนอื่นที่ท่านสังคมด้วย

    1   2   3   4   5   6   7

24. เราควรพยายามชักชวนกนต่างชาติให้มาเยี่ยมเยียนประเทศของเรา และแสดงทัศนคติของเขา

    1   2   3   4   5   6   7

25. เราไม่ควรยุ่งเกี่ยวกับคนที่เราไม่ชอบ

    1   2   3   4   5   6   7

26.   ในการเล่าถึงความผิดหรือข้อบกพร่องของเรา เราควรพูดถึงมันอย่างเปิดเผยตรงไปตรงมา

                1   2   3   4   5   6   7

27   ถ้าบุคคลใกล้ไม่ยอมร่วมมือกับเรา วิธีที่ดีที่สุดที่จะชักชวนเขาให้มาร่วมมือกับเราก็คือการขู่

                1   2   3   4   5   6   7

28.   เราควรรู้ถึงปัญหาต่าง ๆ ของคนรอบ ๆ เรา เพื่อที่เราจะได้ช่วยเหลือเขาเหล่านั้น

                1   2   3   4   5   6   7

29.   โดยปรกติแล้วเราไว้ใจคนส่วนใหญ่ได้ ถึงแม้ว่าบางครั้งบางคราวเขาอาจจะประพฤติตัวไม่เป็นที่
      น่าไว้ใจบ้าง

                1   2   3   4   5   6   7

คำถามชุดต่อไปนี้เกี่ยวกับ สิ่งที่ท่านชอบ หรือไม่ชอบ นิสัย ความนิยมในชีวิตประจำวันของท่าน
คำตอบสำหรับคำถามเหล่านี้ ไม่มีการผิดการถูก

      วิธีตอบ โปรดเขียนวงกลมล้อมรอบตัวเลข ข้อ 1 2 หรือ 3 ซึ่งเป็นคำตอบที่ท่านเห็นสมควรที่สุด

                ถ้าท่านเห็นด้วย โปรดวงกลมเลข 1
                ถ้าท่านไม่แน่ใจ โปรดวงกลมเลข 2
                ถ้าท่านไม่เห็นด้วย โปรดวงกลมเลข 3

30.   ท่านชอบเสี่ยงเงิน เนื่อการพนันเล็ก ๆ น้อย ๆ เพราะต้องการความสนุกสนานจากการพนันนั้นหรือเปล่า

                        1   2   3

31.   ท่านอยากเป็นนักขับเครื่องบินผาดโผนไหม

                        1   2   3

32.   ท่านชอบกระโดดน้ำจากที่สูง ๆ ไหม

                        1   2   3

33.   ท่านชอบร่วมในการจะเล่นก็มีการพนันเอาเงินกันหรือไม่

                        1   2   3

34.   ท่านอยากนั่งรถกับนักขับรถผาดโผนไหม

                        1   2   3

35. ท่านเป็นคนที่มีจิตใจวอกแวก กลับไปกลับมาระหว่าง ความทุกข์ ความสุข หรือเปล่า

                      1   2   3

36. ท่านเป็นคนขับรถค่อนข้างเร็วหรือไม่

                      1   2   3

37. ท่านอยากเป็นนักขับรถแข่ง ในการแข่งรถไหม

                      1   2   3

38. ท่านชอบวางเงินพนันในการแข่งกรีฑาไหม

                      1   2   3

39. ท่านเป็นคนใจร้อนบ่อย ๆ ไหม

                      1   2   3

40. ท่านอยากลงทุนในสิ่งประดิษฐ์ใหม่ ๆ ที่มีหวังจะประสบผลสำเร็จไหม

                      1   2   3

41. ท่านอยากเป็นนักขับเครื่องบินทดลองหรือไม่

                      1   2   3

42. ท่านชอบร้องแก่งไหม

                      1   2   3

43. เวลาท่านเสียอกเสียใจ ท่านรู้สึกเบื่ออาหารไหม

                      1   2   3

44. ท่านอยากเป็นนักกายกรรมห้อยโหน ในละครสัตว์ไหม

                      1   2   3

45. ถ้าขณะที่ท่านนั่งเรือเล็ก ๆ อยู่นั้น เกิดมีพายุขึ้น ท่านกล้าที่จะนั่งต่อไปไหม

                      1   2   3

46. ท่านกล้าเสี่ยงที่จะรับงาน โดยไม่ทราบว่างานนั้นเกี่ยวข้องกับงานอะไรหรือไม่

                      1   2   3

47. ท่านโกรธเคืองไหม ถ้ามีคนมารบกวนท่านในขณะที่ท่านกำลังใช้สมาธิ

                    1   2   3

48. โดยปรกติท่านเป็นคนทำงานเร็วหรือเปล่า

                    1   2   3

49. บนถนนที่ทางการมิได้กำหนดความเร็วไว้ท่านชอบรถเร็วไ

                    1   2   3

            ประโยคชุดนี้มุ่งที่จะหาคำตอบว่า   เหตุการณ์สำคัญๆในสังคมเรามีผลต่อบุคคลกลุ่มต่างๆ
อย่างไร   ในแต่ละชุดจะมีประโยคคู่หนึ่ง ซึ่งประโยคแรกนำหน้าด้วยเลข 1 ประโยคที่สอง
นำหน้าด้วยเลข 2
            จงอ่านประโยคแต่ละคู่อย่างละเอียดแล้วเลือกประโยคเพียงประโยคเดียว ซึ่งท่าน
เชื่อว่าเป็นประโยคที่ถูกต้องที่สุดตามความเห็นของท่าน   โดยวงกลมตัวเลขข้างหน้าประโยค
ที่ท่านเห็นว่าถูกต้อง
            ประโยคเหล่านี้เป็นเพียงความเห็น   ไม่มีคำตอบใดที่เป็นคำตอบที่ถูกหรือผิด ˙ คนเป็น
จำนวนมากอาจเลือก 1 และอีกเป็นจำนวนมากอาจเลือก 2
<u>ข้าพเจ้าเชื่ออย่างยิ่งว่า</u>
        1) ถ้าข้าพเจ้าพยายาม ข้าพเจ้าเป็นมิตรได้กับบุคคลที่ข้าพเจ้าชอบ
        2) ไม่ว่าท่วนจะใช้ความพยายามในการผูกมิตรกับคนบางคนเท่าไกก็ตาม   เขาก็จะไม่ชอบ
            ท่านอยู่ดี
        1) โดยปรกติแล้วความล้มเหลวในชีวิตมนุษย์เกิดจากการกระทำที่ผิดพลาดของเราเอง
        2) บางครั้งข้าพเจ้ารู้สึกว่าข้าพเจ้าไม่สามารถกำหนดชะตากรรมที่เกิดขึ้นกับตัวข้าพเจ้า
            ได้เพียงพอ
        1) ในที่สุด คนเราก็จะได้รับความเคารพนับถือตามสมควรแก่ความประพฤติของเขา
        2) มันเป็นสิ่งที่น่าเสียดายว่า คุณค่าของบุคคลมักจะถูกผู้อื่นมองข้ามไป ถึงแม้ว่าเขาจะ
            พยายามหาความดีเท่าใดก็ตาม
        1) คนบางคนเกิดมาเพื่อรับคำสั่ง และบางคนเกิดมาเพื่อออกคำสั่ง
        2) ในที่สุด ผู้ที่มีความสามารถเหนือกว่าผู้อื่นจะเป็นผู้ที่ออกคำสั่ง

1) ข้าพเจ้าสามารถบอกได้ว่า ข้าพเจ้าสอบได้ดีหรือไม่ดีเพียงใรหลังจากที่ข้าพเจ้าสอบเสร็จใหม่ๆ

2) หลายครั้งทีเดียว ที่ข้าพเจ้ารู้สึกว่าข้าพเจ้าไม่สามารถประมาณว่าข้าพเจ้าสอบได้ดีเพียงใร

1) ถ้าใครได้ครูที่ดีเขาก็อาจจะเรียนได้ดี   แต่ถ้าใครได้ครูที่ไม่ดีเขาก็อาจมีปัญหา

2) ผลการเรียนของใครก็ตามขึ้นอยู่กับความสามารถของเขา

1) บ่อยครั้งทีเดียว ที่ข้าพเจ้าไม่เข้าใจว่าข้าพเจ้าสามารถทำให้คนอื่นทำสิ่งที่ข้าพเจ้า
   ต้องการให้เขาทำอย่างไร

2) การที่ท่านจะให้ผู้อื่นกระทำในสิ่งที่ท่านต้องการนั้น ท่านจะต้องอดทนและใช้ความพยายามมาก

1) การได้งานที่ดีนั้นขึ้นอยู่กับจังหวะ

2) ถ้าท่านมีความสามารถท่านจะหางานทำได้เสมอ

1) คนที่ว้าเหว่นั้นเป็นเพราะเขาไม่สามารถปฏิบัติตัวให้เป็นมิตรกับคนอื่นได้

2) การผูกมิตรกับคนอื่นขึ้นอยู่กับว่า เราโชคดีพบคนที่เราสามารถผูกมิตรกับเขาได้เสียเป็น
   ส่วนใหญ่

Appendix B

Instructions, Record and Offer Sheets
for Buyers, Sellers

1. English (England)
   a. Instructions
   b. Buyer, Seller Record Sheet
   c. Offer Sheet

2. English (U. S. A.)
   a. Instructions
   b. Buyer, Seller Record Sheet
   c. Offer Sheet

3. Flemish (Belgium)
   a. Instructions
   b. Buyer, Seller, Profit Sheet
   c. Offer Sheet

4. Finnish (Finland)
   a. Instructions
   b. Buyer, Seller Profit Sheet
   c. Offer Sheet

5. French (France)
   a. Instructions
   b. Buyer Seller Profit Sheet
   c. Offer Sheet

6. Japanese (Japan)
   a. Instructions
   b. Buyer, Seller Profit Sheet
   c. Offer Sheet

7. Spanish (Spain)
   a. Instructions
   b. Buyer, Seller Record Sheet
   c. Offer Sheet

8. Thai (Thailand)
   a. Instructions
   b Buyer, Seller Record Sheet
   c. Offer Sheet

ENGLAND

Instructions to the Buyer

Funds have been provided for the conduct of research regarding economic decisions. If you follow instructions carefully and make appropriate decisions, you may earn an appreciable amount of money. You cannot lose your own money, but a poor choice will result in little or not profit to you. *You will keep all the money that you earn.*

You have been paired, at random, with one other person. You will not be told with whom you have been paired, nor will you be permitted to speak to this person or any person participating in this research, as the decision making process must be carried out in silence. You and your anonymous counterpart will engage in a negotiation process to be carried out by means of written bids. Imagine that you and he must exchange some fictitious commodity. You have been selected (at random) to act as the *buyer* of this commodity and he has been selected (at random) to act as the seller. The task for the two of you is to negotiate, by means of written price-quantity offers, a single agreement on the *price* of the commodity to be exchanged between you, and the *quantity* to be exchanged at this price.

A table labeled *Buyer's Payoff Table* has been furnished you. The figures in the body of this table represent the profit that we will pay you, depending on the price and quantity you and the seller agree upon. Prices are listed down the left-hand side, quantities across the top. Thus, if you and the seller agree upon a price of 120 and a quantity of 19, we will pay you £ 4/12/6. At a price of 200 and a quantity of 6, we will pay you £ 1/5/5. You will not be told the amount of money we are paying the seller at these prices and quantities. In general, however, price-quantity agreements giving you a high profit will result in a low profit to him, while agreements giving you a low profit will result in a high profit to him.

The negotiation will begin by the seller making a price-quantity offer. He may choose any price along the left-hand margin, and any quantity across the top of his payoff table. He will write his price-quantity offer on a yellow sheet labeled *Price-Quantity Offers*. This yellow sheet will then be brought to you. You must either accept the seller's offer, in which case you should write "accept" on the yellow sheet, or make a new price-quantity offer of your own in the appropriate columns (Buyer's Price Offer, Buyer's Quantity Offer) on the yellow sheet. Your offer must also be written on the sheet labeled *Buyer's Record Sheet*. The yellow sheet will then be taken to the seller, who must accept your offer, or make another offer himself.

Each time you make a new offer you must write your offer on the Buyer's Record Sheet as well as on the Price-Quantity Sheet. You may make the same offer as many times as you wish, or vary your offer each time. When you have decided on your next offer, raise your hand and the yellow sheet will be taken to the seller. The sheet will be returned to you as soon as he has decided on a new offer, or has accepted your offer. He may accept only your last offer, and you may accept only his latest offer. In other words, neither of you may go back and accept a previous offer. You may *not* write messages to the seller, or communicate with him in any way except through the written price quantity offers.

The process of exchanging offers thus continues until one of you writes "accept" on the record sheet. Note that only one agreement is to be made between the two of you, and only *one* payoff will be made. As soon as you two reach agreement on a price and quantity, your part in this research has ended. Normally, you and the seller should reach agreement within one hour's bargaining time, although an additional 30 minutes will be given if necessary. If, at the end of this period of 1½ hours, the two of you have not reached an agreement, the bargaining session will end and *both you and the seller will be paid nothing (zero profit) for the session.* If you do reach agreement you will be paid an amount equal to the profit shown in your payoff table.

If you have any questions about the negotiation process or the payoff table, please ask them now. Do *not*, however, inquire about or suggest appropriate bargaining strategies. *There is no "correct solution."* We are interested in your own approach to this negotiation problem.

Instruction to the Seller

Funds have been provided for the conduct of research regarding economic decisions. If you follow instructions carefully and make appropriate decisions, you may earn an appreciable amount of money. You cannot lose your own money, but a poor choice will result in little or no profit to you. *You will keep all the money that you earn.*

You have been paired, at random, with one other person. You will not be told with whom you have been paired, nor will you be permitted to speak to this person or any person participating in this research, as the decision making process must be carried out in silence. You and your anonymous counterpart will engage in a negotiation process to be carried out by means of written bids. Imagine that you and he must exchange some fictitious commodity. You have been selected (at random) to act as the *seller* of this commodity and he has been selected (at random) to act as the buyer. The task for the two of you is to negotiate, by means of written price-quantity offers, a *single* agreement on the *price* of the commodity to be exchanged between you, and the *quantity* to be exchanged at this price.

A table labeled *Seller's Payoff Table* has been furnished you. The figures in the body of this table represent the profit that we will pay you, depending on the price and quantity you and the buyer agree upon. Prices are listed down the left-hand side, quantities across the top. Thus, if you and the buyer agree upon a price of 205 and a quantity of 14, we will pay you £ 4/12/6. At a price of 115 and a quantity of 1, we will pay you £ 1/5/5. You will not be told the amount of money we are paying the buyer at these prices and quantities. In general, however, price-quantity agreements giving you a high profit will result in a low profit to him, while agreements giving you a low profit will result in a high profit to him.

The negotiation process will begin by you, the seller, making a price quantity offer to the buyer. You may choose any price along the left margin, and any quantity across the top. You must write your price-quantity offer in two places. First, record your offer on the sheet labeled *Seller's Record Sheet*, writing your price offer in the first column and your quantity offer in the second column. Then record this offer on the first row of the yellow sheet labeled *Price-Quantity Offers*. This yellow sheet will be taken to the buyer, who must either accept your offer, or make a counter offer of a new price and quantity. If he accepts your offer, he will write "accept" on the yellow sheet; otherwise, he will write his offer in the appropriate columns on the yellow offer sheet, and this sheet will be returned to you. You must then either accept his offer, in which case you will write accept on the yellow sheet, or make a new price-quantity offer of your own.

Each time you make a new offer you must write your offer on the Seller's Record Sheet as well as on the Price-Quantity Sheet. You may make the same offer as many times as you wish, or vary your offer each time. When you have decided on your next offer, raise your hand and the yellow sheet will be taken to the buyer. The sheet will be returned to you as soon as he has decided on a new offer, or has accepted your offer. He may accept only your last offer, and you may accept only his latest offer. You may *not* write messages to the buyer, or communicate with him in any other way except through the written price quantity offers.

The process of exchanging offers thus continues until one of you writes "accept" on the record sheet. Note that only *one* agreement is to be made between the two of you, and only *one* payoff will be made. As soon as you two reach agreement on a price and quantity, your part in this research has ended. Normally, you and the buyer should reach agreement within one hour's bargaining time, although an additional 30 minutes will be given if necessary. If, at the end of this period of 1½ hours, the two of you have not reached an agreement, the bargaining session will end and *both you and the buyer will be paid nothing (zero profit) for the session*. If you do reach agreement, you will be paid an amount equal to the profit shown in your payoff table.

If you have any questions about the negotiation process or the payoff table, please ask them now. Do *not*, however, inquire about or suggest appropriate bargaining strategies. *There is no "correct solution."* We are interested in your own approach to this negotiation problem.

Price Quantity Offers

Number	Seller's Offers			Buyer's Offers	
	Price	Quantity		Price	Quantity
1					
2					
3					
4					
5					
6					
7					
8					
9					
10					
11					
12					
13					
14					
15					
16					
17					
18					
19					
20					
21					
22					
23					
24					
25					

Buyer's Record Sheet

	Seller's Offers				Buyer's Offers		
Number	Price	Quantity	My Profit		Price	Quantity	My Profit
1							
2							
3							
4							
5							
6							
7							
8							
9							
10							
11							
12							
13							
14							
15							
16							
17							
18							
19							
20							
21							
22							
23							
24							
25							

Seller's Record Sheet

Number	My Offers				Buyer's Offers		
	Price	Quantity	My Profit		Price	Quantity	My Profit
1							
2							
3							
4							
5							
6							
7							
8							
9							
10							
11							
12							
13							
14							
15							
16							
17							
18							
19							
20							
21							
22							
23							
24							
25							

UNITED STATES

Instructions to the Buyer

Funds have been provided for the conduct of research regarding economic decisions. If you follow instructions carefully and make appropriate decisions, you may earn an appreciable amount of money. You cannot lose you own money, but a poor choice will result in little or no profit to you. *You will keep all the money that you earn.*

You have been paired, at random, with one other person. You will not be told with whom you have been paired, nor will you be permitted to speak to this person or any person participating in this research, as the decision making process must be carried out in silence. You and your anonymous counterpart will engage in a negotiation process to be carried out by means of written bids. Imagine that you and he must exchange some fictitious commodity. You have been selected (at random) to act as the *buyer* of this commodity and he has been selected (at random) to act as the seller. The task for the two of you is to negotiate, by means of written price-quantity offers, a single agreement on the *price* of the commodity to be exchanged between you, and the *quantity* to be exchanged at this price.

A table labeled *Buyer's Payoff Table* has been furnished you. The figures in the body of this table represent the profit that we will pay you, depending on the price and quantity you and the seller agree upon. Prices are listed down in the left-hand side, quantities across the top. Thus, if you and the seller agree upon a price of 120 and a quantity of 19, we will pay you $11.10. At a price of 200 and a quantity of 6, we will pay you $3.05. You will not be told the amount of money we are paying the seller at these prices and quantities. In general, however, price-quantity agreements giving you a high profit will result in a low profit to him, while agreements giving you a low profit will result in a high profit to him.

The negotiation will begin by the seller making a price-quantity offer. He may choose any price along the left-hand margin, and any quantity across the top of his payoff table. He will write his price-quantity offer on a yellow sheet labeled *Price-Quantity Offers*. This yellow sheet will then be brought to you. You must either accept the seller's offer, in which case you should write "accept" on the yellow sheet, or make a new price-quantity offer of your own in the appropriate columns (Buyer's Price Offer, Buyer's Quantity Offer) on the yellow sheet. Your offer must also be written on the sheet labeled *Buyer's Record Sheet*. The yellow sheet will then be taken to the seller, who must accept your offer, or make another offer himself.

Each time you make a new offer you must write your offer on the Buyer's Record Sheet as well as on the Price-Quantity Sheet. You may make the same offer as many times as you wish, or vary your offer each time. When you have decided on your next offer, raise your hand and the yellow sheet will be taken to the seller. The sheet will be returned to you as soon as he has decided on a new offer, or has accepted your offer. He may accept only your last offer, and you may accept only his latest offer. In other words, neither of you may go back and accept a previous offer. You may *not* write messages to the seller, or communicate with him in any other way except through the written price-quantity offers.

The process of exchanging offers thus continues until one of you writes "accept" on the record sheet. Note that only *one* agreement is to be made between the two of you, and only *one* payoff will be made. As soon as you two reach agreement on a price and quantity, your part in this research has ended. Normally, you and the seller should reach agreement within one hour's bargaining time, although an additional 30 minutes will be given if necessary. If, at the end of this period of 1½ hours, the two of you have not reached an agreement, the bargaining session will end and *both you and the seller will be paid nothing (zero profit) for the session.* If you do reach agreement you will be paid an amount equal to the profit shown in your payoff table.

If you have any questions about the negotiation process or the payoff table, please ask them now. Do *not*, however, inquire about or suggest appropriate bargaining strategies. *There is no "correct solution."* We are interested in your own approach to this negotiation problem.

Instructions to the Seller

Funds have been provided for the conduct of research regarding economic decisions. If you follow instructions carefully and make appropriate decisions, you may earn an appreciable amount of money. You cannot lose your own money, but a poor choice will result in little or no profit to you. *You will keep all the money that you earn.*

You have been paired, at random, with one other person. You will not be told with whom you have been paired, nor will you be permitted to speak to this person or any person participating in this research, as the decision making process must be carried out in silence. You and your anonymous counterpart will engage in a negotiation process to be carried out by means of written bids. Imagine that you and he must exchange some fictitious commodity. You have been selected (at random) to act as the *seller* of this commodity and he has been selected (at random) to act as the buyer. The task for the two of you is to negotiate, by means of written price-quantity offers, a *single* agreement on the price of the commodity to be exchanged between you, and the *quantity* to be exchanged at this price.

A table labeled *Seller's Payoff Table* has been furnished you. The figures in the body of this table represent the profit that we will pay you, depending on the price and quantity you and the buyer agree upon. Prices are listed down the left-hand side, quantities across the top. Thus, if you and the buyer agree upon a price of 205 and a quantity of 14, we will pay you $11.10. At a price of 115 and a quantity of 1, we will pay you $3.05. You will not be told the amount of money we are paying the buyer at these prices and quantities. In general, however, price-quantity agreements giving you a high profit will result in a low profit to him, while agreements giving you a low profit will result in a high profit to him.

The negotiation process will begin by you, the seller, making a price quantity offer to the buyer. You may choose any price along the left margin, and any quantity across the top. You must write your price-quantity offer in two places. First, record your offer on the sheet labeled *Seller's Record Sheet*, writing your price offer in the first column and your quantity offer in the second column. Then record this offer on the first row of the yellow sheet labeled *Price-Quantity Offers*. This yellow sheet will be taken to the buyer, who must either accept your offer, or make a counter offer of a new price and quantity. If he accepts your offer he will write "accept" on the yellow sheet; otherwise, he will write his offer in the appropriate columns on the yellow offer sheet, and this sheet will be returned to you. You must then either accept his offer, in which case you will write accept on the yellow sheet, or make a new price-quantity offer of your own.

Each time you make a new offer you must write your offer on the Seller's Record Sheet as well as on the Price-Quantity Sheet. You may make the same offer as many times as you wish, or vary your offer each time. When you have decided on your next offer, raise your hand and the yellow sheet will be taken to the buyer. The sheet will be returned to you as soon as he has decided on a new offer, or has accepted your offer. He may accept only your last offer, and you may accept only his latest offer. In other words, neither of you may go back and accept a previous offer. You may *not* write messages to the buyer, or communicate with him in any other way except through the written price quantity offers.

The process of exchanging offers thus continues until one of you writes "accept" on the record sheet. Note than only *one* agreement is to be made between the two of you, and only *one* payoff will be made. As soon as you two reach agreement on a price and quantity, your part in this research has ended. Normally, you and the buyer should reach agreement within one hour's bargaining time, although an additional 30 minutes will be given if necessary. If, at the end of this period of 1½ hours, the two of you have not reached an agreement, the bargaining session will end and *both you and the buyer will be paid nothing (zero profit) for the session.* If you do reach agreement, you will be paid an amount equal to the profit shown in your payoff table.

If you have any questions about the negotiation process or the payoff table, please ask them now. Do *not*, however, inquire about or suggest appropriate bargaining strategies. *There is no "correct solution."* We are interested in your own approach to this negotiation problem.

Price Quantity Offers

	Seller's Offers			Buyer's Offers	
Number	Price	Quantity		Price	Quantity
1					
2					
3					
4					
5					
6					
7					
8					
9					
10					
11					
12					
13					
14					
15					
16					
17					
18					
19					
20					
21					
22					
23					
24					
25					

Buyer's Record Sheet

Number	Seller's Offers				Buyer's Offers		
	Price	Quantity	My Profit		Price	Quantity	My Profit
1							
2							
3							
4							
5							
6							
7							
8							
9							
10							
11							
12							
13							
14							
15							
16							
17							
18							
19							
20							
21							
22							
23							
24							
25							

Seller's Record Sheet

	My Offers				Buyer's Offers		
Number	Price	Quantity	My Profit		Price	Quantity	My Profit
1							
2							
3							
4							
5							
6							
7							
8							
9							
10							
11							
12							
13							
14							
15							
16							
17							
18							
19							
20							
21							
22							
23							
24							
25							

BELGIUM (FLEMISH)

Spelregels: Instructions to the Buyer

Fondsen werden ter beschikking gesteld om vorsingswerk te doen aangaande econo-
mische beslissingen. U kunt een te waarderen bedrag verdienen indien u de richtlijnen nauwkeurig volgt en de gepaste beslissingen neemt. U kunt uw eigen geld
niet verliezen, doch door een gebrekkige keuze zal u geen of weinig winst maken.
U mag al het geld behouden dat u verdient in dit beslissingsspel.

U bent door loting samengevoegd met een andere persoon. Er zal u niet gezegd
worden met wie, u zult ook geen toelating krijgen met hem te spreken, noch met
enig ander persoon tijdens deze proef, aangezien het beslissingsproces, stilzwijgend moet gevoerd worden. Uzelf en uw anonieme tegenspeler zullen een onderhandelingsproces voeren aan de hand van geschreven voorstellen. Beeld u
in dat u met hem een fictief goed moet uitwisselen. U bent door loting aangewezen als de koper en hij werd op dezelfde wijze aangewezen als verkoper.
De taak voor u beiden is, door middel van schriftelijke voorstellen inzake prijs
en hoeveelheid van het goed, in de onderhandeling te komen tot één enkel akkoord
aangaande de prijs van het tussen u beiden te ruilen goed, en aangaande de te
ruilen hoeveelheid voor deze prijs.

Een "Kopers Winsttabel" werd u gegeven. De cijfers in de tabel tonen u de
winsten die we u zullen werkelijk uitbetalen (in belgische franken), afhangend
van de prijs en de hoeveelheid, waarover u en de verkoper uiteindelijk tot een
akkoord komt. De prijzen zijn aangeduid in de eerste kolom van links, de
hoeveelheden in de bovenste horizontale rij.

Bijvoorbeeld : indien u en de verkoper een akkoord bereikt over een prijs van
265 en een hoeveelheid 14, dan zal uw winst 555 BF bedragen. Aan een prijs van
115 en een hoeveelheid van 1, zullen we u 153 BF uitbetalen. Er zal u niet
meegedeeld worden hoeveel de verkoper aan deze prijzen en hoeveelheden verdient.
Algemeen gesproken echter, zullen akkoorden over prijs en hoeveelheid welke
u een hoge winst geven, hem een lage winst laten, terwijl akkoorden die op een
lage winst voor u zullen uitlopen, hem een hoge winst zullen opleveren.

Het onderhandelingsproces zal aangevangen worden met een prijs/hoeveelheid aanb
vanwege de verkoper. Hij mag om het even welke prijs kiezen uit de eerste lin
kolom, en om het even welke hoeveelheid uit de bovenste rij van zijn Winsttabel
Hij zal zijn aanbod neerschrijven op een geel blad, het "Prijs/Hoeveelheid Voor
stellen"-blad genoemd. Dit blad zal dan aan u overgemaakt worden. U moet ofwel

het voorstel van de verkoper aannemen, en in dit geval noteert u "aangenomen"
op het gele blad, ofwel een tegenvoorstel doen voor prijs en hoeveelheid, hetwelk u dan in de gepaste kolommen van het gele blad noteert (Prijs-aanbod van
de koper, Hoeveelheid-aanbod van de koper). Uw bod moet ook ingeschreven worden in het "Kopers Notitieblad". Het gele blad zal dan naar de verkoper teruggebracht worden, die ofwel uw voorstel aanvaardt, ofwel een nieuw voorstel
moet maken.

Telkens u een nieuw voorstel maakt, moet u dit inschrijven op het "Kopers
Notitieblad", alsmede op het gele Prijs/Hoeveelheid blad. U mag hetzelfde
voorstel herhalen zoveel keren als u wil, of telkens het voorstel wijzigen.
Wanneer u een beslissing getroffen heeft aangaande uw nieuw voorstel, steek dan
uw hand op, en het gele blad zal naar de verkoper gebracht worden. Het zal
u teruggeven worden van zodra hij tot een tegenbod besloten heeft, of uw offerte
heeft aanvaard.

Hij mag alleen uw laatste voorstel aannemen, en u slechts zijn laatste aanbod.
Met andere woorden, niemand van u beiden mag teruggrijpen naar een voorgaand
voorstel of tegenvoorstel. U mag geen berichten naar de verkoper sturen, noch
in contact komen met hem op een andere wijze dan de geschreven prijs/hoeveelheid-voorstellen.

Het uitwisselingsproces van offertes zal dus duren tot één van u beiden "aangenomen" op het notitieblad schrijft. Noteer dat slechts één akkoord tussen u
beiden moet gemaakt worden en dat slechts één uitbetaling zal gedaan worden.

Van zodra u een akkoord over prijs en hoeveelheid bereikt heeft, is uw aandeel
in dit opzoekingswerk ten einde.
Normalerwijze zou   u beiden tot een akkoord moeten kunnen komen binnen het
uur. 30 minuten zullen echter toegevoegd worden indien nodig. Indien u beiden
geen akkoord bereikt heeft op het einde van dit anderhalf uur, zal de onderhandelingszitting afgelopen zijn en zal geen van u beiden voor deze zitting iets
ontvangen (winst : null).

Indien u een akkoord bereikt zult u een bedrag ontvangen gelijk aan de winst
vermeld in uw winst-tabel.

Indien u vragen heeft over het onderhandelingsproces of de winsttabellen,
vraag ze nu. Stel echter geen vragen aangaande gepaste onderhandelingsstrategieën
en stel er ook geen voor. Er bestaat geen "correcte oplossing". Het is uw
persoonlijke benadering van dit probleem die ons interesseert.

Spelregels: Instructions to the Seller

Er werden fondsen ter beschikking gesteld om vorsingswerk te doen omtrent eco-
nomische beslissingen. U kunt een te waarderen bedrag verdienen, indien u de
richtlijnen van het spel nauwkeurig volgt en de gepaste beslissingen neemt.
Uw eigen geld kunt u niet verliezen, doch door een gebrekkige keuze zal u geen
of weinig winst maken. U mag al het geld dat u verdient in dit beslissingsspel
ook werkelijk behouden.

Door het lot werd u samengevoegd met een andere persoon. Er wordt u niet gezegd
met wie u speelt en u zult ook geen toelating krijgen met hem te spreken, noch
met enig andere persoon tijdens deze proef, aangezien het belissingsproces
stilzwijgend moet gevoerd worden. Uzelf en uw onbekende tegenspeler zullen
een onderhandelingsproces voeren aan de hand van geschreven voorstellen.
Beeld U zich in dat u met hem een fictief goed moet uitwisselen. Het lot heeft
u als verkoper aangeduid en hij werd als koper aangewezen. Uw taak bestaat
erin door middel van schriftelijke voorstellen inzake prijs en hoeveelheid
van het goed, in de onderhandeling te komen tot één enkel akkoord inzake de
prijs van het tussen u beiden te ruilen goed en aangaande de te ruilen hoeveelheid voor deze prijs.

Een "Verkopers-winsttabel" werd u gegeven. De cijfers in de tabel tonen u de
winsten die we u werkelijk zullen uitbetalen in belgische franken, afhangend
van de prijs en de hoeveelheid waarover u en de koper uiteindelijk tot een
akkoord komt. De prijzen zijn aangeduid in de eerste kolom van links, de
hoeveelheden in de bovenste horizontale rij. Bijvoorbeeld : indien u en de
koper een akkoord bereikt over een prijs van 200 en een hoeveelheid van 7,
dan zal de winst 555 BF bedragen. Aan een prijs van 155 en een hoeveelheid
van 1, zullen we u 153 BF uitbetalen. Er zal u niet worden meegedeeld hoeveel
de koper aan deze prijzen en hoeveelheden verdient. Over 't algemeen zullen
echter de akkoorden over prijs en hoeveelheid welke u een hoge winst geven,
hem een lage winst laten, terwijl akkoorden die voor u op een lage winst uitlopen, hem hoge winst opleveren.
Het onderhandelingsproces zal inzetten met een prijs/hoeveelheid-offerte vanwege
uzelf als verkoper aan de koper. U mag om het even welke prijs kiezen uit
de eerste linker kolom en om het even welke hoeveelheid uit de bovenste rij
van uw winsttabel. U moet uw offertes op twee plaatsen inschrijven :
eensdeels in de eerste kolom uw prijsofferte en in de tweede kolom uw hoeveel-
heidsaanbod op uw "Verkopersnotitieblad", en anderdeels ook in de eerste rij van

het gele formulier dat de naam draag van "Prijs-Hoeveelheid". Dit gele formulier
wordt aan de koper overgemaakt, die ofwel uw offerte aanvaardt ofwel een tegenvoorstel over prijs en aantal moet doen. Zo hij uw aanbod aanvaardt dan zal hij
op het gele formulier "aangenomen" neerschrijven, zoniet zal hij zijn offerte
in de betreffende kolom van het gele blad aanbrengen dat bij u terug zal worden
bezorgd. Dan kunt u zijn offerte aanvaarden door dit op het gele blad aan te
merken, of doet u een eigen tegenvoorstel inzake prijs en aantal.

Telkens u een nieuwe offerte doet, moet u deze neerschrijven zowel op uw
"Verkopersnotitieblad" als op het gele "Prijs/Hoeveelheidblad". U mag hetzelfde
voorstel herhalen zoveel maal als u wilt of telkens het aanbod wijzigen. Zo
u tot een nieuw voorstel hebt beslist, doe teken met de hand en het gele blad
zal naar de koper worden gebracht. Het zal u worden teruggegeven zodra hij
tot een tegenbod besloten heeft ofwel uw offerte heeft aanvaard.

Hij mag alleen uw laatste voorstel aannemen en u slechts zijn laatste aanbod.
Met andere woorden, niemand van u beiden mag teruggrijpen naar een voorgaand
voorstel of tegenvoorstel. U mag geen berichten naar de koper sturen, noch in
contact treden met hem op een andere wijze dan de geschreven prijs/hoeveelheid-
voorstellen.

Het uitwisselingsproces van offertes zal dus duren tot één van beiden "aangenomen"
op het notitieblad schrijft. Noteer dat slechts één akkoord tussen u beiden
moet gemaakt worden en dat slechts één uitbetaling zal gedaan worden.

Van zodra u een akkoord over prijs en hoeveelheid bereikt heeft, is uw aandeel
in dit opzoekingswerk ten einde.

Normalerwijze zou u beiden tot een akkoord moeten kunnen komen binnen het
uur. 30 minuten zullen echter toegevoegd worden indien nodig. Indien u beiden
geen akkoord bereikt heeft op het einde van dit anderhalf uur, zal de onderhandelingszitting afgelopen zijn en zal geen van u beiden voor deze zitting
iets ontvangen (winst : nul).

Indien u een akkoord bereikt zult u een bedrag ontvangen gelijk aan de winst
vermeld in uw winst-tabel.

Indien u vragen heeft over het onderhandelingsproces of de winsttabellen,
vraag ze nu. Stel echter geen vragen aangaande gepaste onderhandelingsstrategieën, en stel er ook geen voor. Er bestaat geen "correcte oplossing".
Het is uw persoonlijke benadering van dit probleem die ons interesseert.

PRIJS-HOEVEELMEID

Verkopers Voorstellen   Kopers Voorstellen

Nummer	Prijs	Hoeveelheid		Prijs	Hoeveelheid
1					
2					
3					
4					
5					
6					
7					
8					
9					
10					
11					
12					
13					
14					
15					
16					
17					
18					
19					
20					
21					
22					
23					
24					
25					

Verkopers Voorstellen   Kopers Voorstellen

Nummer	Prijs	Hoeveelheid	Mijn Winst	Prijs	Hoeveelheid	Mijn Winst
1						
2						
3						
4						
5						
6						
7						
8						
9						
10						
11						
12						
13						
14						
15						
16						
17						
18						
19						
20						
21						
22						
23						
24						
25						

Verkopers Voorstellen   Kopers Voorstellen

Nummer	Prijs	Hoeveelheid	Mijn Winst		Prijs	Hoeveelheid	Mijn Winst
1							
2							
3							
4							
5							
6							
7							
8							
9							
10							
11							
12							
13							
14							
15							
16							
17							
18							
19							
20							
21							
22							
23							
24							
25							

FINLAND

Objeet: Instructions to the Buyer

Tietty määrä rahaa on käytettävissä tutkimuksen suorittamiseen,
joka koskee taloudellisia ratkaisuja. Jos seuraatte ohjeita huolellisesti ja teette tarkoituksenmukaiset ratkaisut, saatatte ansaita
huomattavan summan rahaa. Ette voi mentää omaa rahaanne, mutta
huono valinta johtaa teidän kannaltanne vähäiseen tai olemattomaan
voittoon. Saatte pitää kaiken ansaitsemanne rahan.

Teidät on valittu erään toisen henkilön pariksi satunnaisotannalla.
Teille ei sanota, kenen pariksi olette joutunut, eikä teidän sallita
puhua tälle henkilölle tai kenellekään tähän tutkimukseen osallistuvalle, koska päätöksentekoprosessi pitää suorittaa hiljaisuudessa.
Te ja teidän tuntematon toverinne ryhdeytte neuvotteluihin, jotka
suoritetaan kirjallisten tarjousten muodossa. Kuvitelkaa että
teidän ja hänen täytyy käydä kauppaa jostain kuvitellusta hyödykkeestä.
Teidät on valittu (satunnaisotannalla) toimimaan tämän hyödykkeen
ostajana ja hänet on valittu (satunnaisotannalla) toiminaan myyjänä.
Teidän kahden tehtävänä on päästä sopimukseen kirjallisten hinta- ja
määrätarjousten avulla hyödykkeen hinnasta, josta käytte kauppaa,
ja määrästä, joka myydään tähän hintaan.

Teille on annettu taulukko nimeltään Ostajan voittotaulukko. Tässä
taulukossa olevat luvut merkitsevät voittoa (penniä)   jonka me
maksamme teille riippuen teidän ja myyjän sopimasta hinnasta ja
määrästä. Hinnat on luetteloitu vasemmalla puolella, määrät poikittain yläosassa. Täten jos Te ja myyjä sovitte hinnasta 120 ja
määrästä 19, me maksamme teille 4662 penniä. Hinnasta 200 ja
ja määrästä 6 maksamme 1281 penniä. Teille ei kerrota, kuinka
paljon maksamme myyjälle näistä hinnoista ja määristä. Kuitenkin
yleisesti puhuen hinta- ja määräsopimukset, jotka tuottavat teille
suurta voittoa, tuottavat hänelle pientä, kun taas Teille pientä
voittoa tuottavat sopimukset tuottavat hänelle suurta.

Myyjä alkaa neuvotteluprosessin tekemällä hinta- ja määrätarjouksen.
Hän saa valita minkä tahansa hinnan vasemmasta marginaalista ja
minkä tahansa määrän yläosan poikittaisrivistä. Hän kirjoittaa hinta-
ja määrätarjouksensa keltaiselle lomakkeelle nimeltä Hinta- ja määrä-
tarjoukset. Tämä keltainen lomake tuodaan sitten teille. Teidän täytyy joko hyväksyä myyjän tarjous, missä tapauksessa teidän pitää
kirjoittaa "Hyväksyn" keltaiselle lomakkeelle tai tehdä uusi oma hinta-
ja määrätarjouksenne keltaisen lomakkeen asianmukaiseen sarakkeeseen
(Ostajan hintatarjous, Ostajan määrätarjous). Tarjouksenne teidän
pitää myös merkitä Ostajan pöytäkirja-nimiseen lomakkeeseen. Keltainen lomake viedään sitten myyjälle, jonka täytyy hyväksyä teidän
tarjouksenne tai tehdä itse uusi tarjous.

Joka kerta kun teette uuden tarjouksen, teidän täytyy merkitä se
Ostajan pöytäkirjaan sekä Hinta- ja määrälomakkeeseen. Voitte tehdä
saman tarjouksen niin monta kertaa kuin haluatte, tai vaihdella tar-
joustanne joka kerta. Kun olette tehneet päätöksenne seuraavan tarjouksenne suhteen, nostakaa kätenne pystyyn ja keltainen lomake viedään myyjälle. Lomake palautetaan teille niin pian kuin hän on
päättänyt uudesta tarjouksesta tai hyväksynyt teidän tarjouksenne.
Hän saa hyväksyä vain teidän viimeisen tarjouksenne ja te saatte
hyväksyä vain hänen viimeisimmän tarjouksensa. Toisin sanoen kumpikaan teistä ei saa palata taaksepäin ja hyväksyä edellistä tarjousta.
Te ette saa kirjoittaa viestejä myyjälle tai olla yhteydessä häneen millään muulla lailla lukuunottamatta kirjoitettuja hinta- ja
määrätarjouksia.

Tarjoustenvaihtoprosessi jatkuu täten kunnes jompikumpi teistä kirjoittaa "Hyväksyn" pöytäkirjaan. Huomatkaa että teidän on päästävä
vain yhteen sopimukseen keskenänne ja että vain yhdestä maksetaan
voittoa. Niin pian kuin te kasi pääsette sopimukseen hinnasta ja
määrästä, teidän osanne tässä tutkimuksessa on päättynyt. Normaalisti
teidän ja myyjän tulisi päästä sopimukseen yhden neuvottelutunnin
aikana, vaikka tosin ylimääräiset 30 minuttia annetaan tarvittaessa.

Mikäli te kaksi ette ole tämän 11/2 -tuntisen kuluessa päässeet
sopimukseen, neuvottelutuokio loppuu, eikä Teille eikä myyjälle
makseta mitään (nollavoitto) istunnosta. Jos sen sijaan pääsette
sopimukseen, teille maksetaan voittotaulukon mukainen summa.

Jos teillä on kysymyksiä neuvotteluprosessin tai voittotaulukon
suhteen, olkaa hyvä ja kysykää nyt. Älkää kuitenkaan tiedustelko
sopivista neuvottelustrategioista tai ehdottako niitä. Ei ole
mitään oikeata ratkaisua. Olemme kiinnostuneita Teidän omasta
lähestymistavastanne tähän neuvotteluongelmaan.

Ohjeet: Instructions to the Seller

Tietty määrä rahaa on käytettävissä tutkimuksen suorittamiseen,
joka koskee taloudellisia ratkaisuja. Jos seuraatte ohjeita
huolellisesti ja teette tarkoituksenmukaiset ratkaisut, saatatte
ansaita huomattavan summan rahaa. Ette voi menettää omaa rahaanne, mutta huono valinta johtaa teidän kannaltanne vähäiseen
tai olemattomaan voittoon. Saatte pitää kaiken ansaitsemanne
rahan.

Teidät on valittu erään toisen henkilön pariksi satunnaisotannalla.
Teille ei sanota, kenen pariksi olette joutunut, eikä teidän sallita puhua tälle henkilölle tai kenellekään tähän tutkimukseen
osallistuvalle, koska päätöksentekoprosessi pitää suorittaa hiljaisuudessa. Te ja teidän tuntematon toverinne ryhdytte neuvotteluihin, jotka suoritetaan kirjallisten tarjousten muodossa.
Kuvitelkaa että teidän ja hänen täytyy käydä kauppa jostain
kuvitellusta hyödykkeestä. Teidät on (satunnaisotannalla) valittu
toimimaan tämän hyödykkeen myyjänä ja hänet on (satunnaisotannalla)
valittu toimimaan ostajana. Teidän kahden tehtävänä on päästä
sopimukseen kirjallisten hinta- ja määrätarjousten avulla hyödykkeen hinnasta, josta käytte kauppaa keskenänne ja määrästä,
joka myydään tähän hintaan.

Teille on annettu taulukko nimeltään Myyjän voittotaulukko.
Tässä taulukossa olevat luvut merkitsevät voittoa (penniä)

jonka me maksamme riippuen teidän ja ostajan sopimasta hinnasta
ja määrästä. Hinnat on luetteloitu vasemmalla puolella alakkain,
määrät poikittain yläosassa. Täten, jos Te ja ostaja sovitte
hinnasta 205 ja määrästä 14, me maksamme teille 4662 penniä.
Hinnasta 115 ja määrästä 1 maksamme 1281 penniä. Teille ei
sanota, kuinka paljon maksamme ostajalle näistä hinnoista ja
määristä. Kuitenkin yleisesti puhuen hinta- ja määräsopimukset,
jotka tuottavat teille suurta voittoa, tuottavat hänelle pientä
voittoa; kun taas teille pientä voittoa tuottavat sopimukset
tuottavat hänelle suurta.

Te myyjänä aloitatte neuvotteluprosessin tekemällä hinta- ja määrätarjouksen ostajalle. Saatte valita minkä tahansa hinnan
vasemmasta marginaalista ja minkä tahansa määrän yläosan poikittaisrivistä. Kirjoittakaa hinta- ja määrätarjouksenne kah-
teen paikkaan. Ensiksi, merkitkää muistiin tarjouksenne lomakkeelle nimeltä Myyjän pöytäkirja kirjoittamalla hintatarjouk-
senne ensimmäiseen sarakkeeseen ja määrätarjouksenne toiseen.
Merkitkää sitten tämä tarjous keltaisen Hinta- ja Määrätarjous-
lomakkeen ensimmäiselle riville. Tämä keltainen lomake viedään ostajalle, jonka täytyy joko hyväksyä tarjous tai tehdä
vastaehdotus uudesta hinnasta ja määrästä. Jos hän hyväksyy
Teidän tarjouksenne, hän kirjoittaa "Hyväksyn" keltaiselle lomakkeelle; muussa tapauksessa hän kirjoittaa tarjouksensa keltaisen tarjouslomakkeen asianmukaiseen sarakkeeseen ja tämä
lomake palautetaan Teille. Teidän täytyy silloin joko hyväksyä
hänen tarjouksensa, missä tapauksessa kirjoitatte "Hyväksyn"
keltaiselle lomakkeelle, tai tehdä oma uusi hinta- ja määrätarjouksenne.

Joka kerta tehdessänne uuden tarjouksen teidän täytyy merkitä se
Myyjän pöytäkirjaan samoin kuin Hinta- ja Määrälomakkeeseen.

Voitte tehdä saman tarjouksen niin monta kertaa kuin haluatte, tai
muuttaa tarjousta joka kerta. Kun olette päättänyt seuraavasta

tarjouksestanne, nostakaa kätenne ja keltainen lomake viedään ostajalle. Lomake palautetaan Teille niin pian kuin hän on tehnyt
päätöksensä uuden tarjouksen suhteen tai hyväksynyt teidän tarjouksenne. Hän saa hyväksyä vain teidän viimeisen tarjouksenne,
ja Te saatte hyväksyä vain hänen viimeisimmän tarjouksensa. Toisin sanoen kumpikaan teistä ei saa mennä taaksepäin ja hyväksyä
edeltävää tarjousta. Te ette saa kirjoittaa viestejä ostajalle
tai olla yhteydessä häneen millään muulla lailla lukuunottamatta
kirjoitettuja hinta- ja määrätarjouksia.

Tarjoustenvaihtoprosessi jatkuu täten kunnes jompi kumpi teistä
kirjoittaa "Hyväksyn" pöytäkirjaan. Huomatkaa että teidän on
päästävä vain yhteen ainoaan sopimukseen keskenänne, ja vain
yhdestä maksetaan voittoa. Niin pian kuin te kaksi pääsette sopimukseen hinnasta ja määrästä, teidän osanne tässä tutkimuksessa
on päättynyt. Normaalisti Teidän ja ostajan tulisi päästä sopimukseen yhden neuvottelutunnin aikana, vaikka tosin ylimääräiset
30 minuuttia annetaan tarvittaessa. Mikäli te kaksi ette ole tämän 11/2 -tuntisen kuluessa päässet sopimukseen, neuvottelutuokio
loppuu eikä Teille eikä ostajalle makseta mitään (nollavoitto)
istunnosta. Jos sen sijaan pääsette sopimukseen teille maksetaan
voittotaulukon mukainen summa.

Jos teillä on kysymyksiä neuvotteluprosessin tai voittotaulukon
suhteen, olkaa hyvä ja kysykää nyt. Älkää kuitenkaan tiedustelko
sopivista neuvottelumenetelmistä tai ehdottako niitä. Ei ole
mitään oikeata ratkaisua. Olemme kiinnostuneita Teidän omasta
lähestymistavastanne tähän neuvotteluongelmaan.

Ostajan pöytäkirja

Nimi _____

Myyjän tarjoukset   Minun tarjoukseni

Numero	Hinta	Määrä	Minun voittoni	Hinta	Määrä	Minun voittoni
1						
2						
3						
4						
5						
6						
7						
8						
9						
10						
11						
12						
13						
14						
15						
16						
17						
18						
19						
20						
21						
22						
23						
24						
25						

<u>Myyjan poytakirja</u>

Nimi _____

Minun tarjoukseni   <u>Ostajan tarjoukset</u>

Numero	Hinta	Maara	Minun voittoni	Hinta	Maara	Minun voittoni
1						
2						
3						
4						
5						
6						
7						
8						
9						
10						
11						
12						
13						
14						
15						
16						
17						
18						
19						
20						
21						
22						
23						
24						
25						

Hinta - ja määrätarjoukset

Myyjän tarjoukset   Ostajan tarjoukset

Numero	Hinta	Määrä		Hinta	Määrä
1					
2					
3					
4					
5					
6					
7					
8					
9					
10					
11					
12					
13					
14					
15					
16					
17					
18					
19					
20					
21					
22					
23					
24					
25					

FRANCE

Instructions to the Buyer

Des fonds ont été pourvus pour la recherche des processus de
décision à caractère économique. Si vous suivez soigneusement les
instructions ci-dessous, et si vous prenez les décisions appropriées,
vous pourrez gagner une somme d'argent appréciable. En aucun cas vous
ne perdrez votre argent, mais un mauvais choix se traduira pour vous
par un maigre profit ou pas de profit du tout. Vous pourrez garder
tout votre gain.

        Vous avez été groupés, au hasard, avec une autre personne. On
ne vous dira pas qui est cette personne, et il ne vous sera permis de
parler ni à elle, ni à n'importe quelle autre personne participant à
cette expérience, car les décisions doivent être prises et exécutées
en silence. Vous serez engagés, votre partenaire anonyme et vous, dans
un processus de négociation; ces négociations se feront par offres
écrites. Imaginez que vous deviez échanger entre vous une certaine
marchandise. Vous avez été choisi, (au hasard), pour assumer les
fonctions d'Acheteur de cette marchandise, et il a été choisi, (toujours
au hasard), pour assumer celles de Vendeur. Votre tâche commune est
de parvenir à l'aide d'offres écrites prix-quantités, à un accord
mutuel sur le prix de cette marchandise et sur la quantité à échanger
à ce prix-là.

        Un tableau intitulé "tableau des revenus de l'Acheteur" vous a
été remis. Les nombres imprimés dans ce tableau représentent les revenus,
(in centimes),   que vous recevrez, selon le prix et la quantité sur
lesquels vous vous serez mis d'accord avec le Vendeur. Les prix
possibles sont inscrits dans la première colonne, à l'extrême gauche
du tableau, et les quantités possibles dans la première rangée, en
tête du tableau. Donc, si le Vendeur et vous tombez d'accord sur un
prix de 120 pour une quantité de 19, votre revenu sera de 5550 centimes.
Pour un prix de 200 et une quantité de 6, votre revenu sera de 1525 centimes.
Nous ne vous dirons pas quels sont les revenus du Vendeur pour les
différentes combinaisons prix-quantités; mais, en général, les
combinaisons qui, si elles sont acceptées, se traduisent par un bénéfice
important pour vous se soldent par un maigre profit pour lui, tandis que
celles qui se soldent par un maigre profit pour vous se traduisent par
un bénéfice important pour lui.

        Les négociations commenceront par une offre prix-quantité faite
par le vendeur. Il peut choisir n'importe quel prix inscrit dans la colonne
d'extrême gauche de son tableau de revenus, et n'importe quelle quantité
inscrite dans la rangée du haut de ce même tableau. Il écrira son offre

prix-quantité sur une feuille jaune intitulée "Offres Prix-Quantités".
Cette feuille jaune vous sera alors apportée. Vous devrez soit accepter
l'offre du Vendeur, auquel cas vous écrirez "accepté" sur la feuille jaune,
soit lui faire votre propre offre prix-quantité que vous inscrirez dans
les colonnes appropriées (Prix offert par l'Acheteur, Quantité offerte par
l'Acheteur) sur cette même feuille jaune. Votre offre doit aussi être enregistrée
sur la feuille intitulée "Feuille de Memo de l'Acheteur". La feuille jaune
sera ensuite retournée au Vendeur qui devra soit accepter votre offre,
soit vous en faire une nouvelle.

Chaque fois que vous faites une offre nouvelle vous devez l'enregistrer
et sur la "Feuille de Memo de l'Acheteur", et sur la feuille jaune "Offres
Prix-Quantités". Vous pouvez faire la même offre autant de fois que vous le
désirez, ou faire chaque fois une offre différente. Quand vous avez décidé
de l'offre que vous allez faire et l'avez enregistrée, veuillez lever la main;
la feuille jaune sera alors apportée au Vendeur. Elle vous sera retournée
dès qu'il aura décidé de vous faire une offre nouvelle ou aura accepté la
vôtre. Il ne pourra accepter que votre offre dernière en date de même que
vous ne pourrez accepter que son offre dernière en date. En d'autres termes,
ni lui ni vous n'avez le droit de revenir en arrière et d'accepter une offre
précédente. Vous ne devez pas écrire de messages au Vendeur ou communiquer
avec lui d'une manière quelconque, si ce n'est par les offres écrites
prix-quantités.

Ces échanges d'offres continueront jusqu'à ce que l'un d'entre vous écrive
"accepté" sur la feuille jaune prix-quantités. Notez qu'un seul accord peut
être conclu entre vous deux. Conséquemment, chacun de vous ne recevra qu'un
seul gain. Dès que vous serez tombés d'accord sur un prix et une quantité,
votre rôle dans cette expérience sera terminé. Normalement, vous ne devriez
pas avoir besoin de plus d'une heure de négociation pour tomber d'accord;
toutefois une demi-heure supplémentaire vous sera accordée si cela est nécessaire.
Si, à la fin de cette période d'une heure et demi, le Vendeur et vous même
n'êtes pas arrivés à un accord, la session de négociation prendra fin,
et vous aussi bien que lui ne recevrez aucun gain (revenu nul) pour
cette session. Si, par contre, vous arrivez à un accord, il vous
sera versé une somme d'argent égale à celle inscrite sur votre
tableau de revenus.

Si vous avez des questions à poser concernant le processus de
négociation ou les tableaux de revenus, nous vous prions de les poser
maintenant. Toutefois, n'émettez pas de questions ou de suggestions
concernant les bonnes ou les mauvaises stratégies de négociation. Il
n'y a pas de solution correcte. Ce qui nous intéresse, c'est la
manière dont vous approchez le problème.

Instructions to the Seller

Des fonds ont été pourvus pour la recherche des processus de décision
à caractère économique. Si vous suivez soigneusement les instructions ci-dessous,
et si vous prenez les décisions appropriées, vous pouvez gagner une somme d'argent
appréciable. En aucun cas vous ne perdrez votre argent, mais un mauvais choix
se traduira par un maigre profit ou pas de profit du tout. Vous pourrez garder
tout votre gain.

Vous avez été groupés, au hasard, avec une autre personne. On ne vous
dira pas qui est cette personne, et il ne vous sera permis de parler ni à elle,
ni à n'importe quelle autre personne participant à cette expérience, car les
décisions doivent être prises et exécutées en silence. Vous serez engagés,
votre partenaire anonyme et vous, dans un processus de négociation; ces
négociations se feront par offres écrites. Imaginez que vous deviez échanger
entre vous une certaine marchandise. Vous avez été choisi, (au hasard), pour
assumer les fonctions de Vendeur de cette marchandise, et il a été choisi,
(toujours au hasard), pour assumer celle d'Acheteur. Votre tâche commune est
de parvenir à l'aide d'offres écrites prix-quantités, à un accord mutuel sur
le prix de cette marchandise et sur la quantité à échanger à ce prix là.

Un tableau intitulé "Tableau des Revenus du Vendeur" vous a été remis.
Les nombres imprimés dans ce tableau représentent les revenus, (in centimes),
que vous recevrez, selon le prix et la quantité sur lesquels vous vous serez
mis d'accord avec l'Acheteur. Les prix possibles sont inscrits dans la première
colonne, à l'extrême gauche du tableau, et les quantités possibles dans la
première rangée, en tête du tableau. Donc, si l'Acheteur et vous tombez d'accord
sur un prix de 205 pour une quantité de 14, votre revenu sera de 5550 centimes.
Pour un prix de 115 et une quantité de 1, votre revenu sera de 1525 centimes.
ne vous dirons pas quels sont les revenus de l'Acheteur pour les différentes
combinaisons prix-quantités; mais, en général, les combinaisons qui, si elles
sont acceptées, se traduisent par un bénéfice important pour vous se soldent
par un maigre profit pour lui, tandis que celles qui se soldent par un maigre
profit pour vous se traduisent par un bénéfice important pour lui.

Vous, le Vendeur, déclencherez le processus de négociation en faisant une
offre prix-quantité à l'Acheteur. Vous pouvez choisir n'importe quel prix
inscrit dans la colonne d'extrême gauche et n'importe quelle quantité inscrite
dans la rangée du haut. Vous devez enregistrer votre offre prix-quantité en
deux endroits. Premièrement, enregistrez votre offre sur la feuille intitulée
"Feuille de Mémo du Vendeur" en inscrivant le prix que vous proposez dans
la première colonne et la quantité que vous proposez dans la deuxième colonne.
Puis, enregistrez cette offre sur la première ligne de la feuille jaune intitulée
"Offres Prix-Quantités". Cette feuille jaune sera apportée à l'Acheteur qui
devra soit accepter votre offre, soit vous en faire une autre différente quant
au prix, à la quantité, ou aux deux ensemble. Si il accepte votre offre il

écrira "accepté" sur la feuille jaune; dans le cas contraire, il écrira son offre propre sur la feuille jaune en utilisant les colonnes appropriées, et cette feuille vous sera retournée. Vous devrez alors soit accepter son offre, auquel cas vous écrirez "accepté" sur la feuille jaune, soit faire une nouvelle offre prix-quantité.

Chaque fois que vous faites une offre nouvelle vous devez l'enregistrer et sur la "Feuille de Memo du Vendeur", et sur la feuille jaune "Offres Prix-Quantités". Vous pouvez faire la même offre autant de fois que vous le désirez, ou faire chaque fois une offre différente. Quand vous avez décidé de l'offre que vous allez faire et l'avez enregistrée, veuillez lever la main; la feuille jaune sera alors apportée à l'Acheteur. Elle vous sera retournée dès qu'il aura décidé de vous faire une offre nouvelle ou aura accepté la vôtre. Il ne pourra accepter que votre offre dernière en date de même que vous ne pourrez accepter que son offre dernière en date. En d'autres termes, ni lui ni vous n'avez le droit de revenir en arrière et d'accepter une offre précédente. Vous ne devez pas écrire de messages à l'Acheteur ou communiquer avec lui d'une manière quelconque, si ce n'est par les offres écrites prix-quantités.

Ces échanges d'offres continueront jusqu'à ce que l'un d'entre vous écrive "accepté" sur la feuille jaune prix-quantités. Notez qu'un seul accord peut être conclu entre vous deux. Conséquemment, chacun de vous ne recevra qu'un seul gain. Dès que vous serez tombés d'accord sur un prix et une quantité, votre rôle dans cette expérience sera terminé. Normalement, vous ne devriez pas avoir besoin de plus d'une heure de négociation pour tomber d'accord; toutefois une demi-heure supplémentaire vous sera accordée si cela est nécessaire. Si, à la fin de cette période d'une heure et demi, l'Acheteur et vous même n'êtes pas arrivés à un accord, la session de négociation prendra fin, et vous aussi bien que lui ne recevrez aucun gain (revenu nul) pour cette session. Si, par contre, vous arrivez à un accord, il vous sera versé une somme d'argent égale à celle inscrite sur votre tableau de revenus.

Si vous avez des questions à poser concernant le processus de négociation ou les tableaux de revenus, nous vous prions de les poser maintenant. Toutefois, n'émettez pas de questions ou de suggestions concernant les bonnes ou les mauvaises stratégies de négociation. Il n'y a pas de solution correcte. Ce qui nous intéresse, c'est la manière dont vous approchez le problème.

Feuille de Memo de l'Acheteur

Offres du Vendeur   Offres de l'Acheteur

Numero	Prix	Quantité	Mon Revenu	Son Revenu	Prix	Quantité	Mon Revenu	Son Revenu
1								
2								
3								
4								
5								
6								
7								
8								
9								
10								
11								
12								
13								
14								
15								
16								
17								
18								
19								
20								
21								
22								
23								
24								
25								

Feuille de Memo du Vendeau

Nos Offres   Offres de l'Acheteur

Numero	Prix	Quantité	Mon Revenu	Prix	Quantité	Mon Revenu
1						
2						
3						
4						
5						
6						
7						
8						
9						
10						
11						
12						
13						
14						
15						
16						
17						
18						
19						
20						
21						
22						
23						
24						
25						

OFFRES PRIX QUANTITES

Offres du Vendeur   Offres de l'Acheteur

Numero	Prix	Quantite		Prix	Quantite
1					
2					
3					
4					
5					
6					
7					
8					
9					
10					
11					
12					
13					
14					
15					
16					
17					
18					
19					
20					
21					
22					
23					
24					
25					

JAPAN

買い手への説明

Instructions to the Buyer

　この経済的意思決定に関する調査のために、資金が用意されています。この実験に参加されてもしあなたが注意深く指示通り、適切な決定を行なうなら、一定金額のお金を得ることが出来ます。あなた自身のお金を失うことはありません。しかし、不適当な選択は、あなたにとってほとんど、あるいは全くの無利益に終ります。あなたが得たお金は全部あなたの所有になります。

　あなたは無差別に、誰か他の人と組にされています。誰と組んでいるかは教えられていません。それに、この実験に参加している人の誰にも話しかける事も許されていません。それは丁度、意志決定は沈黙のうちになされなければならないのと同じです。あなたとあなたの相手はwritten bid（書式入札）によって、交渉を行ないます。あなたと相手が、仮想の品物を交換することを考えて下さい。あなたは無差別に、品物の買手としてえらばれ、同様に、あなたの相手は売手として選ばれています。あなたがたの仕事は、書面での価格改善の申し出によって、あなたがたの間で交換される品物の価格と、その価格での改善について、一つの同意に達するために交渉をすることです。

　買手のための支払い表は、あなたに用意されています。表の中の数字は、買手と売手の間で同意に達した価格と改善に応じて私達があなたに支払う利益をあらわしています。価格は左側に上から下へ、改善は上側に左から右へ書かれています。ですからあなたと売手が価格１２０、改善１９で同意するのでしたら、私達はあなたに￥３４１９支払います。価格１２０、改善６でしたら、￥２４１８支払います。あなたにはその価格と改善について、私達が売手に支払う金額は伝えられません。けれども一般的に言って、あなたに高い利益をもたらす価格と改善での同意は、相手に少ない利益を与え、反対にあなたの少ない利益での同意は、相手に高い利益をもたらすことになります。

　交渉は、価格・改善を申し出る売手から始められます。売手は左側の列の価格のうち、どれかを選びます。それから支払い表の中から一番高い利益の改善を選びます。その価格・改善の申し出は価格・改善申し出と書かれた黄色い用紙に書きこまれます。この用紙はあなたのところへ来ます。あなたは売手の申し出を受けいれるか、さもなければ新たな、あなた自身の価格・改善の申し出を、買い手の価格・改善申し出と示されたところに書きこみます。売手の申し出を受けいれるときには「受話」と書きこんで下さい。あなたの申し出は「買い手記録」と書かれた用紙にも記入しておかなければなりません。黄色い用紙は、また、売手のところへ持っていかれます。売手は、あなたの申し出を受けいれるか、新たな申し出をするかを決めなければなりません。

　新たな申し出をするたびに．あなたはあなたの申し出を買手記録の用紙と価格・改訂申し出の用紙に書きこさなければなりません。同じ申し出を何度でも繰り返すことは出来ます。又は勿論毎回違った申し出をしてもいい訳です。とにかく申し出を決定すれば手をあげて合図いをなして下さい。その用紙は，売手が新しい申し出を決めたか，またはあなたの申し出を受けいれたかしたときに，あなたのところに渡されます。売手はあなたの最新の申し出のみをうけいれることが出来ます。あなたは売手の最新の申し出のみを受けいれることが出来ます。すなわち，あなたたちのどちらも以前の申し出にさかのぼって受けいれることは出来ません。あなた達は一切の伝言をしてはいけませんし，書面での価格・改訂申し出以外の方法で連絡しあってもいけません。

　申し出の交換は．あなたがたのどちらかが「受信」と記録用紙に書くまで続けられます。たった一度の同意がなされるという事と．たった一度の支払いがなされるという事に気をつけて下さい。あなたがた二人が，価格と改訂について同意にましたとき．この実験での役目は終わります。ふつう一時間以内で．交渉は同意に達するはずですが．必要ならば．三十分の追加時間が許されています。もしこの一時間半以内にあなたがた二人が同意に達しない場合は．売買取引は終わり．二人とも何も支払われません（利益なし）。同意にましたのでしたら．あなたの支払い表に示された額と同じだけの金額が支払われます。

　もしこの交渉過程について．質問がありましたら今聞いて下さい。しかし．取引の戦略に関するせんさくや提案はしてはいけません。「正解」はありません。私達はあなた自身の取引交渉に対してのアプローチを知りたいのです。

売 り 手 へ の 説 明

Instructions to the Seller

　この性質的な意思決定に関する調査の為に資金が用意されています。この実験に参加されてもし．あなたが注意深く指示通り適切な決定を行うなら．一定金額のお金を得ることが出来ます。あなた自身のお金を失う事はありません。しかし．不適当な選択は．あなたにとってほとんどあるいは全くの浜利益に終ります。あなたが得たお金は全部あなたのものになります。

　あなたは．誰かと無差別に一組にされています。誰と組んでいるかは．教えられていません。それにこの実験に参加している人の誰にも話しかける事を許されていません。それは丁度意思決定が沈黙のうちになされなければならないのと同じです。あなたとあなたの相手は書式入札によって．交渉を行います。あなたと相手が．仮想の品物を交換する事を考えて下さい。あな

たは，無差別に品物の売手としてえらばれ，同様に，あなたの相手は，買手として選ばれています。あなたがたの仕事は書面での価格改善の申し出でによって，あなたがたの間で交換される品物の価格と，その価格での数量について，一つの同意に達する為の交渉をする事です。

　<u>売手の為の支払い表</u>は，あなた方の為に用意されています。表の中の数字は，買手と売手の間で同意に達した価格と数量に応じて，私達があなたに支払う利益をあらわしています。価格は，左から右へ書かれています。ですから，あなたと買手が価格２０５，数量１４で同意するのでしたら私達は，あなたに¥る４１９支払います。価格１１５，数量１でしたら¥９３９払います。私達が，買手に支払う金額は伝えられません。けれども一般的に言って，あなたに高い利益をもたらす価格と数量での同意は，相手に少ない利益を与え反対にあなたの少ない利益での同意は，相手に高い利益を与える事になります。

　交渉は，価格・数量を売手が申し出ることから始められています。あなたは，左側の列の価格のうちどれかをえらびます。それから，支払い表の中から，一番高い利益の数量をえらびます。あなたは，二ヶ所に価格改善の申し出を書きこまなければなりません。最初に，あなたの申し出を売手記録用紙に書きこんで下さい。（最初の列に価格，２番目の列に数量）。そして，次にこの申し出を，価格・数量申し出と書かれた黄色い用紙に記入して下さい。この黄色い用紙は，買手の所にはこばれ，彼によってあなたの申し出が受理されるか，あるいは，新たな申し出がなされるか決められます。もし，彼が受理すれば，彼は"受理"と黄色い用紙に書きこむことになります。さもなければ，彼の申し出が黄色い用紙の２列めの行に書きこまれ，あなたの所にもちはこばれます。あなたは，彼の申し出を受理するか（その時は受理と書きこむ），あるいは，新たな数量・価格の申し出をしなければいけません。

　新たな申し出をするたびに，あなたはあなたの申し出を<u>売手記録用紙</u>と<u>価格改善申し出</u>の用紙に書きこまなければなりません。同じ価格・数量の申し出を何度でも繰り返すことは出来ます。又は，勿論前回違った申し出をしてもいい訳です。とにかく申し出を決定する度毎をあげて下さい。そして黄色い紙を渡して下さい。その用紙は，買手が新たな申し出を決めた時，あるいは，あなたの申し出を受理した時に，あなたの所にもどされます。買手は，あなたの最新の申し出のみをうけることが出来ます。あなたも，買手の最新の申し出のみを受けることが出来ます。即ち，あとにさかのぼって，前の申し出に同意する事はゆるされません。あなた方は，一切の伝言をしてはいけません。書面での申し出以外の方法で連絡しあってもいけません。

　申し出の交換は，あなたがたのどちらかが「受理」と記録用紙に書くまで続けられます。たった一度の同意がなされるという事と，たった一度だけの支払いがなされるという事に，気をつけて下さい。あなた方二人が，価格と数量についての同意に達した時，あなたの役割は，紙

〜さ〜す 普通一時間以内で交渉は同意に達するはずですが必要たら30分の追加時間が許されます。もしも、一時間半以内に同意に達しない時は、売買取引きは終り、二人ともたにも支払らわれません（利益なし）。同意に達したのでしたら、あなたの支払い表に示された額と同じ額だけが、あなたに支払われます。

　もしも交渉過程について、質問がありましたら今聞いて下さい。しかし、取引きの戦略、かけ引きに関する質問は、許されません。「正解」はありません。私共は、あなた自身の値引交渉に際してのアプローチを知りたいのです。

Buyer's Record Sheet
51

	先手の申し出 Seller's Offers				買手（私）の申し出 My Offers		
番 号 Number	価 格 Price	数 量 Quantity	私 の 利 益 My Profit	価 格 Price	数 量 Qauntity	私 の 利 益 My Profit	
1							
2							
3							
4							
5							
6							
7							
8							
9							
10							
11							
12							
13							
14							
15							
16							
17							
18							
19							
20							
21							
22							
23							
24							

売手の記録用紙
Seller's Record Sheet

売手(私)の申し出　　　　　　　　　買手の申し出
My Offers　　　　　　　　　　　　　Buyer's Offers

番号	価格	数量	私の利益	価格	数量	私の利益
Number	Price	Quantity	My Profit	Price	Qauntity	My Profit
1						
2						
3						
4						
5						
6						
7						
8						
9						
10						
11						
12						
13						
14						
15						
16						
17						
18						
19						
20						
21						
22						
23						
24						

価格数量の申し出

Price-Quantity Offers

売手の申し出
Seller's Offers

買手の申し出
Buyer's Offers

番 号 Number	価 格 Price	数 量 Quantity		価 格 Price	数 量 Quantity	
1						
2						
3						
4						
5						
6						
7						
8						
9						
10						
11						
12						
13						

SPAIN

Instrucciones

Instructions to the Buyer

Se ha subvencionado una investigación sobre decisiones de tipo
económico. Si Vd. sigue las instrucciones cuidadosamente y ha-
ce las oportunas decisiones, puede ganar una no despreciable
cantidad de dinero. No puede perder su propio dinero, pero una
elección desafortunada le proporcionará pocos o ningún beneficio.
Puede quedarse con todo el dinero que gane.

Vd. ha sido aparejado, al azar, con otra persona. No sabrá con
quien ni le será permitido hablar con nadie que participe en este juego ya que el proceso de decisión se tiene que llevar a cabo
en silencio. Vd. y su anónimo compañero negociarán por medio de
ofertas escritas. Imagínese que debe negociar algo con él. Vd. ha
sido seleccionado al azar para actuar como comprador y el ha sido seleccionado también al azar, para actuar como vendedor. La
tarea para Vds., dos es la de acordar el precio de lo que hay que
cambiar y la cantidad a cambiar a este precio. Hay que acordar un
sólo precio y una sola cantidad.

Le han sido entregada la Tabla de Pagos al Comprador. Las cantidades en la Tabla de Pagos al Comprador representan (en pesetas)
el dinero que le pagaremos en función del precio y la cantidad
acordada con el vendedor. Los precios están colocados verticalmente a la izquierda, las cantidades, horizontalmente, en la parte
superior. Si Vd. y el vendedor acuerdan un precio de 120 y una cantidad de 19, le pagaremos 177 pesetas. A un precio de 200 y una cantidad de 6 le pagaremos 214 pesetas. Vd. no sabrá el beneficio que
el vendedor esté haciendo con estos precios y cantidades. En general, sin embargo, los acuerdos cantidad-precio que le den a Vd. un
gran beneficio le resultarán poco provechosos para el otro, mientras que las transacciones que le den poco provecho a Vd. le resultarán muy provechosas a él.

El vendedor empezará las negociaciones haciendo una oferta en precio y cantidad escogiendo cualquier precio a lo largo del margen
izquierdo y cualquier cantidad de la parte superior. El escribirá
su oferta en precio-cantidad en una hoja amarilla llamada Ofertas
Precio Cantidad. Más tarde le traerán esta hoja amarilla. Si Vd.
acepta la oferta ponga "acepto". Si no la acepta haga nueva oferta precio-cantidad en las columnas ad-hoc de la hoja amarilla (O-
ferta de Precio del Comprador. Oferta de Cantidad del Comprador).
Su oferta también debe ser escrita en una Hoja Regitro del Comprador La hoja amarilla será llevada al vendedor que debe aceptar su oferta, o hacerle una contraoferta.

El proceso de intercambio de ofertas continúa hasta que uno de
Vds. escriba "acepto". No olvide que solo se tiene que "aceptar"
una vez durante el juego. Tan pronto como lleguen a un acuerdo sobre el precio y la cantidad, su misión ha terminado. Normalmente,
Vd. y el comprador tienen que alcanzar un acuerdo dentro de la hora de negociación. Con todo se pueden conceder 30 minutos extra
si es necesario. Si después de una hora y media no han llegado a
ningún acuerdo, ninguno de Vds. recibirá cantidad alguna en concepto de beneficios. Si por el contrario llegan a un acuerdo recibirán en metálico una cantidad igual a los beneficios señalados
en sus respectivas hojas de pagos.

Si tiene algunas preguntas sobre el proceso de negociación o de
la tabla de pagos, por favor consúltenos ahora mismo. No hay una
solución correcta. Estamos interesados en conocer la forma en que
Vd. enfoca este problema de negociación.

Instrucciones

Instructions to the Seller

...na subvencionado una investigación sobre decisiones de tipo dinámico. Si Vd. sigue las instrucciones cuidadosamente y ha-... las oportunas decisiones, puede ganar una no despreciable entidad de dinero. No puede perder su propio dinero pero una elección desafortunada le proporcionará pocos o ningún beneficio. Puede quedarse con todo el dinero que gane.

Vd. ha sido aparejado, al azar, con otra persona. No sabrá con quién ni le será permitido hablar con nadie que participe en este juego ya que el proceso de decisión se tiene que llevar a cabo en silencio. Vd. y su anónimo compañero negocian por medio de ofertas escritas. Imagínese que debe negociar algo con él. Vd. ha sido seleccionado al azar para actuar como vendedor, y él ha sido seleccionado, al azar, para actuar como comprador La tarea para Vds. dos es la de acordar el precio de lo que hay que cambiar y la cantidad a cambiar a este precio. Hay que acordar un solo precio y, una sola cantidad.

Le ha sido entregada la Tabla de Pagos al Vendedor. Las cantidades en la Tabla de Pagos al Vendedor representan (en pesetas) el dinero que le pagaremos en función del precio y la cantidad acordada con el comprador. Los precios están colocados verticalmente a la izquierda, las cantidades, horizontalmente, en la parte superior. Si Vd. y el comprador acuerdan un precio de 205 y una cantidad de 14 le pagaremos 177 pesetas. A un precio de 115 y cantidad 1 le pagaremos 214 pesetas. Vd. no sabrá el beneficio que el comprador está haciendo con estos precios y cantidades. En general, sin embargo, los acuerdos cantidad-precio que le den a Vd. un gran beneficio le resultarán poco provechosos para el otro, mientras que las transacciones que le den poco provecho a Vd., le resultarán muy provechosas a él.

Vd. empezará el proceso de negociación haciendo una oferta de precio y cantidad al comprador. Puede escoger cualquier precio a lo largo del margen izquierdo y cualquier cantidad de la parte superior. Debe escribir su oferta precio-cantidad en dos lugares. Primero, anote su oferta en la Hoja Registro del Vendedor, escribiendo su oferta de precio en la primera columna y su oferta de cantidad en la segunda columna. Después ponga su oferta en la primera columna de su hoja amarilla llamada Ofertas Precio-Cantidad. Esta hoja amarilla le será entregada al comprador quien puede aceptar o hacer una contra oferta a un nuevo precio y cantidad. Si acepta su oferta escribirá "acepto" en la hoja amarilla; de lo contrario, escribirá su contraoferta en la columna apropiada de la hoja amarilla de oferta. Esta hoja le será devuelta. Si Vd. acepta la oferta escriba acepto en la hoja amarilla, de lo contrario haga una nueva oferta de precio y cantidad.

El proceso de intercambio de ofertas continúa hasta que uno de Vds. escriba "acepto". No olvide que solo se tiene que "aceptar" una vez durante todo el juego. Tan pronto como lleguen a un acuerdo sobre el precio y la cantidad, su misión ha terminado. Normalmente, Vd. y el comprador tienen que alcanzar un acuerdo dentro de la hora de negociación. Con todo se pueden conceder 30 minutos extra si es necesario. Si después de una hora y media no han llegado a ningún acuerdo, ninguno de Vds. percibirá cantidad alguna en concepto de beneficios. Si por el contrario llegan a un acuerdo recibirán en metálico una cantidad igual a los beneficios señalados en sus respectivas hojas de pagos.

Si tiene Vd. algunas preguntas sobre el proceso de negociación o de la tabla de pagos, por favor consúltenos ahora mismo. No hay una solución correcta. Estamos interesados en conocer la forma en que Vd. enfoca este problema de negociación.

Registro del Comprador

<u>Ofertas del vendedor</u>   <u>Ofertas del comprador</u>

Número	Precio	Cantidad	Mi beneficio	Precio	Cantidad	Mi beneficio
1						
2						
3						
4						
5						
6						
7						
8						
9						
10						
11						
12						
13						
14						
15						
16						
17						
18						
19						
20						
21						
22						
23						
24						
25						

Registro del Vendedor

Mis ofertas   Ofertas del comprador

Número	Precio	Cantidad	Mi beneficio	Precio	Cantidad	Mi beneficio
1						
2						
3						
4						
5						
6						
7						
8						
9						
10						
11						
12						
13						
14						
15						
16						
17						
18						
19						
20						
21						
22						
23						
24						
25						

Ofertas Precio – Cantidad

	Ofertas de venta			Ofertas de Compra	
Número	Precio	Cantidad		Precio	Cantidad
1					
2					
3					
4					
5					
6					
7					
8					
9					
10					
11					
12					
13					
14					
15					
16					
17					
18					
19					
20					
21					
22					
23					
24					
25					

THAILAND

กติกาผู้ซื้อ: Instructions to the Buyer

ได้มีการอนุมัติให้ใช้เงินก่อนหน้านึ่งสำหรับการค้นคว้า เรื่องการตัดสินปัญหาทางเศรษกิจ ถ้าท่าน
ปฏิบัติตามกติกาด้วยความระมัดระวัง และเลือกวิธีทางที่ถูกต้องแล้ว ท่านอาจจะได้รับเงินจำนวนมากพอ
สมควร ท่านจะไม่สูญเสียเงินของท่านเองเลยแต่ถ้าหากท่านเลือกวิธีทางที่ไม่ดีนัก ท่านจะได้รับเงินจำนวน
น้อย หรืออาจไม่ได้รับเลย เงินที่ท่านได้จากการจะเริ่นครั้งนี้จะเป็นของท่านเองทั้งหมด

เราได้จับคู่ของท่านโดยสุ่มมาจากคนกลุ่มหนึ่ง โดยที่ท่านจะไม่ทราบว่าคู่แข่งของท่านคือใคร เนื่อง
จากการตัดสินเกี่ยวกับปัญหานี้จะดำเนินไปอย่างเงียบเงียบ เราจะไม่อนุญาติให้ท่านพูดกับบุคคลอื่นนั้นหรือผู้ใด
ก็ตามที่อยู่ในวงการศึกษาค้นคว้านี้ ท่านและคู่แข่งขันของท่านจะทำงานร่วมกันในการติดต่ออย่างหนึ่ง ซึ่งจะ
ทำการประมูลด้วยข้อเขียน สมมติว่าท่านจะทำการซื้อรายสินค้าอย่างหนึ่ง เราจัดให้ท่านเป็นผู้ซื้อสินค้านี้
และคู่แข่งขันเป็นผู้ขาย หน้าที่ของท่านทั้งสองคือทำการซื้อขายตกลงกันโดยท่านเขียนราคาและจำนวนที่ท่านจะซื้อ
ขายตกลงกัน

เราได้จัดหา "ตารางผู้ซื้อตอบแทน" ให้ท่าน ตัวเจขบนตารางนี้แสดงให้เห็นถึงกำไรที่เราจะจ่าย
ให้ท่านซึ่งขึ้นอยู่กับราคา และปริมาณที่ท่านและคนขายตกลงกัน ตัวเจขราคาอยู่ทางด้านซ้ายมือ ปริมาณอยู่
ด้านบน ดังนั้น ถ้าท่านและผู้ขายตกลงกันในราคา 120 และจำนวน 19 เราจะจ่ายให้ท่าน 247 บาท ถ้า
ท่านตกลงที่ราคา 200 และจำนวน 6 เราจะจ่ายให้ท่าน 68 บาท เราจะไม่บอกให้ท่านทราบถึงจำนวนเงิน
ที่เราจะจ่ายให้ผู้ขายตามราคาและปริมาณดังกล่าวนี้ แต่โดยทั่วไปแล้วถ้าท่านได้กำไรสูงจากการซื้อในราคา
และปริมาณจำนวนหนึ่ง ผู้ขายฝ่ายตรงข้ามก็จะได้รับกำไรน้อย ในทางตรงข้าม การตกลงราคาและปริมาณ
ที่ให้กำไรน้อยแก่ท่านจะมีเจกำไรสูงแก่คู่ของท่าน

วิธีการดำเนินงานการตกลง จะเริ่มโดยผู้ขายจะเสนอราคาและปริมาณขาย เราจะเลือกราคาหนึ่ง
ราคาใดจากตัวเจขทางซ้ายมือของตาราง และปริมาณทางด้านบนของตารางของผู้ขายของเราก็ได้ เราจะ
เขียนราคาและปริมาณเสนอ ลงบนกระดาษแผ่นเหลืองที่มีป้ายเขียนว่า "ข้อเสนอราคาและปริมาณ" จะมีผู้นำ
กระดาษแผ่นนี้มาให้ท่าน ท่านอาจจะรับข้อเสนอของเราหรืออาจยื่นข้อเสนอใหม่ ถ้าท่านรับข้อเสนอของเรา
ท่านจะเขียนคำว่า "รับข้อเสนอ" ลงบนกระดาษแผ่นเหลืองนี้ ถ้าท่านจะเสนอข้อเสนอใหม่ก็ให้เขียนข้อเสนอ
ใหม่ในช่องที่ถูกต้อง (ข้อเสนอราคาของผู้ซื้อ, ข้อเสนอจำนวนของผู้ซื้อ) ท่านต้องเขียนข้อเสนอของท่านลงบน
กระดาษนี้มีกรอบของผู้ซื้อด้วย เราจะนำกระดาษแผ่นเหลืองไปให้ผู้ขาย เราอาจจะรับข้อเสนอของท่านหรืออาจ
ยื่นข้อเสนอใหม่มาอีก.

ทุกครั้งที่ท่านเสนอราคาและปริมาณใหม่ ท่านจะต้องเขียนข้อเสนอนี้ลงในฟอร์มของผู้ซื้อ และฟอร์ม
ราคาและปริมาณ ท่านจะยื่นข้อเสนอข้อเดิมที่ครั้งก็ได้แล้วแต่ท่าน หรือท่านจะเปลี่ยนข้อเสนอใหม่ได้ทุกครั้ง
ก็ได้ เมื่อท่านได้ตัดสินใจเกี่ยวกับข้อเสนอครั้งก่อนไปให้หมายณถี่อื่น และเราจะนำกระดาษสีเหลืองนี้ไป
ให้ผู้ขาย เราจะนำกระดาษแผ่นนี้กลับมาถึงท่านทันทีที่เรายื่นข้อเสนอใหม่ หรือรับข้อเสนอของท่าน ในการ
ตกลงกันนั้นจะต้องใช้ข้อเสนอครั้งสุดท้ายเสมอ จะกลับไปใช้ข้อเสนอของคราวก่อน ๆ ที่แล้วมาในการตกลง

ครั้งหลังสุดไม่ได้   เราไม่อนุญาตให้ท่านเขียนข้อความใด ๆ หรือติดต่อกับผู้ขายโดยวิธีหนึ่งวิธีใด   ยกเว้นการ
เขียนเสนอราคาและปริมาณเท่านั้น

      การแลกเปลี่ยนข้อเสนอนี้จะทำเนินไปจนกระทั่งท่านหรือผู้ขายเขียนคำว่า "รับข้อเสนอ" ลงบนกระดาษ
บันทึก โปรดทราบด้วยว่าเราจะจ่ายเงินตามข้อตกลงรอบสุดท้ายที่ตอบรับเหมือนรอบเดียว คือจ่ายเมื่อท่านและ
ผู้ขายตกลงกันได้ในเรื่องราคาและปริมาณ

      โดยปรกติแล้วท่านและผู้ขายควรตกลงกันได้ภายในเวลาหนึ่งชั่วโมง แต่เราจะให้เวลาเกิน 30 นาที
ถ้าเห็นว่าจำเป็น ถ้าท่านและผู้ขายไม่สามารถตกลงกันได้ภายในเวลาหนึ่งชั่วโมงครึ่ง การต่อรองก็จะสิ้นสุดลง
และเราจะไม่จ่ายอะไรให้แก่ท่านและผู้ขายเลย

      ถ้าท่านมีปัญหาประการใดเกี่ยวกับการเล่นเกมส์นี้ โปรดถามเจ้าเกี่ยวนี้ กรุณาอย่าถามหรือขอคำแนะ
นำเกี่ยวกับวิธีการต่อรองกัน ไม่ว่าวิธีต่อรองที่ถูกหรือผิด เราเพียงสนใจศึกษาว่าท่านทั้งสองจะใช้วิธีการต่อ
รองกันอย่างไร.

กติกาผู้ขาย : Instructions to the Seller

      ได้มีการอนุญาตให้ใช้เงินก้อนหนึ่งสำหรับการค้นคว้าศึกษา เรื่องการตัดสินปัญหาทางเศรษฐกิจ ถ้าท่าน
ปฏิบัติตามกติกาด้วยความระมัดระวัง และเลือกวิธีทางที่ถูกต้องแล้ว ท่านอาจจะได้รับเงินมากพอสมควร
ท่านจะไม่สูญเสียเงินของท่านเลย แต่ถ้าหากท่านเลือกวิธีทางที่ไม่ดีนัก ท่านจะได้รับเงินจำนวนน้อย หรือ
ไม่ได้รับเลย เงินที่ท่านได้จากการจะเล่นครั้งนี้จะเป็นของท่านทั้งหมด

      เราได้จับคู่ของท่านโดยสุ่มมาจากคนกลุ่มหนึ่ง โดยที่ท่านจะไม่ทราบว่าคู่แข่งขันของท่านคือใคร เนื่อง
จากการตัดสินเกี่ยวกับปัญหานี้จะดำเนินไปอย่างเรียบร้อย เราจะไม่อนุญาตให้ท่านพูดกับบุคคลคนนั้นหรือผู้ใดก็
ตามที่อยู่ในวงการศึกษาค้นคว้าครั้งนี้ ท่านและคู่แข่งขันจะทำงานร่วมกันในการติดต่ออย่างหนึ่งซึ่งจะดำเนิน
โดยการประมูลด้วยข้อเขียน สมมติว่าท่านจะทำการซื้อขายสินค้าอย่างหนึ่ง เราจัดให้ท่านเป็นผู้ขายสินค้านี้
และคู่แข่งขันเป็นผู้ซื้อ หน้าที่ของท่านทั้งสองก็คือทำการซื้อขายตกลงกัน โดยท่านเขียนราคาและจำนวนที่ท่าน
จะซื้อขายตกลงกัน

      เราได้จัดหา "ตารางตอบแทนผู้ขาย" ให้ท่าน ตัวเลขบนตารางแสดงให้เห็นถึงกำไรที่เราจะจ่าย
ให้ท่านซึ่งขึ้นอยู่กับราคาและปริมาณที่ท่านและคนซื้อตกลงกันตัวเลขราคาอยู่ทางด้านซ้ายมือ ปริมาณอยู่ด้านบน
ดังนั้น ถ้าท่านและผู้ซื้อตกลงกันในราคา 205 และจำนวน 14 เราจะจ่ายท่าน 247 บาท ถ้าท่านตก
ลงที่ราคา 115 และจำนวน 1 เราจะจ่ายท่าน 68 บาท เราจะไม่บอกให้ท่านทราบถึงจำนวนเงินที่เรา
จะจ่ายให้ผู้ซื้อตามราคาและปริมาณดังกล่าวนี้ แต่โดยทั่วไปแล้วถ้าท่านได้กำไรสูงจากการรายในราคาและ
ปริมาณจำนวนหนึ่ง ผู้ซื้อฝ่ายตรงข้ามก็จะได้รับกำไรน้อย ในทางตรงกันข้าม การตกลงราคาและปริมาณที่
ให้กำไรน้อยแก่ท่าน จะมีผลให้กำไรสูงแก่คู่ของท่าน

วิธีการดำเนินงาน การตกลงจะเริ่มจากท่านซึ่งเป็นผู้ขายก่อน โดยท่านจะเป็นฝ่ายเสนอราคาและ
ปริมาณแก่ผู้ซื้อ ท่านจะเลือกราคาหนึ่งราคาใดจากตัวเลขทางซ้ายมือของตารางจ่ายก็ได้ และปริมาณทางด้านบน
ท่านต้องเขียนราคาและปริมาณที่ท่านเสนอลงในที่สองแห่ง ประการแรก ให้ท่านเขียนข้อเสนอของท่านลงบน
กระดาษมีป้ายเขียนว่า "กระดาษบันทึกของผู้ขาย" เขียนราคาที่ท่านเสนอลงในช่องแรก และปริมาณในช่อง
ที่สอง ต่อจากนี้ให้ท่านเขียนข้อเสนอราคาและปริมาณนี้ลงในช่องแรกของกระดาษสีเหลืองที่เขียนว่า "ข้อ
เสนอราคาและปริมาณ" เราจะนำกระดาษแผ่นนี้ไปให้ผู้ซื้อ เขาอาจจะรับข้อเสนอของท่านหรือยื่นข้อเสนอใหม่
ถ้าเขารับข้อเสนอของท่าน เขาจะเขียนคำว่า "รับข้อเสนอลงบนกระดาษสีเหลืองนี้ มิฉะนั้นแล้วเขาจะ
เขียนข้อเสนอใหม่ลงในช่องที่ถูกต้องบนกระดาษสีเหลืองนี้ และเราจะนำกระดาษแผ่นนี้กลับมาให้ท่าน ใน
กรณีนี้ท่านจะพิจารณาว่าท่านจะรับข้อเสนอใหม่ของเขาหรือไม่ ถ้าท่านตกลงท่านจะต้องเขียนคำว่า "รับข้อเสนอ"
ลงบนกระดาษสีเหลืองนี้ ถ้าท่านไม่ยอมรับท่านจะเขียนข้อเสนอใหม่ของท่านลงไป

ทุกครั้งที่ท่านเสนอราคาและปริมาณใหม่ ท่านจะต้องเขียนข้อเสนอนี้ลงในฟอร์มของผู้ขายและฟอร์ม
ราคาและปริมาณ ท่านจะยื่นข้อเสนอซ้อเดิมกี่ครั้งก็ได้แล้วแต่ท่าน หรือท่านจะเปลี่ยนข้อเสนอใหม่ทุกครั้งก็ได้
เมื่อท่านได้ตัดสินใจเกี่ยวกับข้อเสนอครั้งต่อไป ให้ท่านยกมือขึ้น และเราจะนำกระดาษสีเหลืองนี้ไปให้ผู้ซื้อ
เราจะนำกระดาษแผ่นนี้กลับมาให้ท่านทันทีที่เขายื่นข้อเสนอใหม่ หรือรับข้อเสนอของท่าน เขาต้องรับข้อเสนอ
ครั้งสุดท้ายของท่าน และท่านต้องรับข้อเสนอครั้งสุดท้ายของเขา จะตกลงกันโดยใช้ข้อเสนอครั้งที่แล้ว ๆ
มาไม่ได้

กล่าวอีกอย่างหนึ่งก็คือ ทั้งท่านและเขาต่างก็กลับไปรับข้อเสนอข้อเดิมที่ผ่านมาไม่ได้ เราไม่อนุญาติ
ให้ท่านเขียนข้อความถึงผู้ซื้อ หรือติดต่อกับเราโดยวิธีหนึ่งวิธีใด ยกเว้นการเขียนเสนอราคาและปริมาณ
เท่านั้น

การแลกเปลี่ยนข้อเสนอนี้จะดำเนินจนกระทั่ง ท่านและผู้ซื้อคนใดคนหนึ่งเขียนคำว่า "รับข้อเสนอ"
ลงบนกระดาษบันทึก โปรดทราบด้วยว่าเราจะจ่ายเงินตามข้อตกลงเพียงข้อเดียว คือเมื่อท่านและผู้ซื้อ
ตกลงกันในเรื่องราคาและปริมาณได้ และเกมส์นี้ก็สิ้นสุดลง

โดยปรกติแล้วท่านและผู้ซื้อควรจะตกลงกันได้ภายในเวลาหนึ่งชั่วโมง แต่เราจะให้เวลาเกิน
30 นาที ถ้าเห็นว่าจำเป็น ถ้าหากท่านและผู้ซื้อไม่สามารถตกลงกันได้ภายในเวลาหนึ่งชั่วโมงครึ่ง การ
ต่อรองก็จะสิ้นสุดลง และเราจะไม่จ่ายอะไรให้แก่ท่านและผู้ซื้อเลย

แต่ถ้าหากท่านและผู้ซื้อตกลงกันได้ เราจะจ่ายกำไรให้แก่ท่านตามจำนวนตารางจ่ายของท่าน

ถ้าท่านมีปัญหาประการใดเกี่ยวกับการเล่นครั้งนี้ โปรดถามเสียเดี๋ยวนี้ อย่างไรก็ตามโปรดอย่าถาม
หรือแนะนำเกี่ยวกับวิธีดำเนินการต่อรองกัน ไม่มีวิธีการที่ถูกต้อง เราสนใจในวิธีการที่ท่านทั้งสองจะใช้ตกลง
กัน

บันทึกผู้ซื้อ

ครั้งที่	ราคา	ปริมาณ	กำไรผู้ซื้อ		ราคา	ปริมาณ	กำไรผู้ซื้อ
1							
2							
3							
4							
5							
6							
7							
8							
9							
10							
11							
12							
13							
14							
15							
16							
17							
18							
19							
20							
21							
22							
23							
24							
25							

บันทึกของผู้ขาย

	ข้อเสนอของผู้ขาย			ข้อเสนอของผู้ซื้อ		
ครั้งที่	ราคา	ปริมาณ	กำไรผู้ขาย	ราคา	ปริมาณ	กำไรผู้ขาย
1						
2						
3						
4						
5						
6						
7						
8						
9						
10						
11						
12						
13						
14						
15						
16						
17						
18						
19						
20						
21						
22						
23						
24						
25						

ข้อเสนอ ราคา - ปริมาณ

	ข้อเสนอผู้ชาย		ข้อเสนอผู้ซื้อ	
ครั้งที่	ราคา	ปริมาณ	ราคา	ปริมาณ
1				
2				
3				
4				
5				
6				
7				
8				
9				
10				
11				
12				
13				
14				
15				
16				
17				
18				
19				
20				
21				
22				
23				
24				
25				

Appendix C

Payoff Tables for Buyers, Sellers

1. English (England, in pounds)
2. English (U. S. A., in dollars)
3. Flemish (Belgium, in francs)
4. Finnish (Finland, in marks)
5. French (France, in centimes)
6. Japanese (Japan, in yen)
7. Spanish (Spain, in pesos)
8. Thai (Thailand, in baht)

England (pounds)

BUYERS PAYOFF TABLE

Price	1	2	3	4	5	6	7	8	9	10	11	12	13	14	15	16	17	18	19	20
205	0/10/5	0/14/7	0/17/11	1/0/5	1/2/1	1/2/11	1/2/11	1/2/1	1/0/5	0/17/11	0/14/7	0/10/5	0/5/5	0	0	0	0	0	0	0
200	0/10/10	0/15/5	0/19/2	1/2/1	1/4/2	1/5/5	1/5/10	1/5/5	1/4/2	1/2/1	0/19/2	0/15/5	0/10/10	0/5/5	0	0	0	0	0	0
195	0/11/3	0/16/3	1/0/5	1/3/9	1/6/3	1/7/11	1/8/9	1/8/9	1/7/11	1/6/3	1/3/9	1/0/5	0/16/3	0/11/3	0/5/5	0	0	0	0	0
190	0/11/8	0/17/1	1/1/8	1/5/5	1/8/4	1/10/5	1/11/8	1/12/1	1/11/8	1/10/5	1/8/4	1/5/5	1/1/8	0/17/1	0/11/8	0/5/5	0	0	0	0
185	0/12/1	0/17/11	1/2/11	1/7/1	1/10/5	1/12/11	1/14/7	1/15/5	1/15/5	1/14/7	1/12/11	1/10/5	1/7/1	1/2/11	0/17/11	0/12/1	0/5/5	0	0	0
180	0/12/6	0/18/9	1/4/2	1/8/9	1/12/6	1/15/5	1/17/6	1/18/9	1/19/2	1/18/9	1/17/6	1/15/5	1/12/6	1/8/9	1/4/2	0/18/9	0/12/6	0/5/5	0	0
175	0/12/11	0/19/7	1/5/5	1/10/5	1/14/7	1/17/11	2/0/5	2/2/1	2/2/11	2/2/11	2/2/1	2/0/5	1/17/11	1/14/7	1/10/5	1/5/5	0/19/7	0/12/11	0/5/5	0
170	0/13/4	1/0/5	1/6/8	1/12/1	1/16/8	2/0/5	2/3/4	2/5/5	2/6/8	2/7/1	2/6/8	2/5/5	2/3/4	2/0/5	1/16/8	1/12/1	1/6/8	1/0/5	0/13/4	0/5/5
165	0/13/9	1/1/3	1/7/11	1/13/9	1/18/9	2/2/11	2/6/3	2/8/9	2/10/5	2/11/3	2/11/3	2/10/5	2/8/9	2/6/3	2/2/11	1/18/9	1/13/9	1/7/11	1/1/3	0/13/9
160	0/14/2	1/2/1	1/9/2	1/15/5	2/0/10	2/5/5	2/9/2	2/12/1	2/14/2	2/15/5	2/15/10	2/15/5	2/14/2	2/12/1	2/9/2	2/5/5	2/0/10	1/15/5	1/9/2	1/2/1
155	0/14/7	1/2/11	1/10/5	1/17/1	2/2/11	2/7/11	2/12/1	2/15/5	2/17/11	2/19/7	3/0/5	3/0/5	2/19/7	2/17/11	2/15/5	2/12/1	2/7/11	2/2/11	1/17/1	1/10/5
150	0/15/0	1/3/9	1/11/8	1/18/9	2/5/0	2/10/5	2/15/0	2/18/9	3/1/8	3/3/9	3/5/0	3/5/5	3/5/0	3/3/9	3/1/8	2/18/9	2/15/0	2/10/5	2/5/0	1/18/9
145	0/15/5	1/4/7	1/12/11	2/0/5	2/7/1	2/12/11	2/17/11	3/2/1	3/5/5	3/7/11	3/9/7	3/10/5	3/10/5	3/9/7	3/7/11	3/5/5	3/2/1	2/17/11	2/12/11	2/7/1
140	0/15/10	1/5/5	1/14/2	2/2/1	2/9/2	2/15/5	3/0/10	3/5/5	3/9/2	3/12/1	3/14/2	3/15/5	3/15/10	3/15/5	3/14/2	3/12/1	3/9/2	3/5/5	3/0/10	2/15/5
135	0/16/3	1/6/3	1/15/5	2/3/9	2/11/3	2/17/11	3/3/9	3/8/9	3/12/11	3/16/3	3/18/9	4/0/5	4/1/3	4/1/3	4/0/5	3/18/9	3/16/3	3/12/11	3/8/9	3/3/9
130	0/16/8	1/7/1	1/16/8	2/5/5	2/13/4	3/0/5	3/6/8	3/12/1	3/16/8	4/0/5	4/3/4	4/5/5	4/6/8	4/7/1	4/6/8	4/5/5	4/3/4	4/0/5	3/16/8	3/12/1
125	0/17/1	1/7/11	1/17/11	2/7/1	2/15/5	3/2/11	3/9/7	3/15/5	4/0/5	4/4/7	4/7/11	4/10/5	4/12/1	4/12/11	4/12/11	4/12/1	4/10/5	4/7/11	4/4/7	4/0/5
120	0/17/6	1/8/9	1/19/2	2/8/9	2/17/6	3/5/5	3/12/6	3/18/9	4/4/2	4/8/9	4/12/6	4/15/5	4/17/6	4/18/9	4/19/2	4/18/9	4/17/6	4/15/5	4/12/6	4/8/9
115	0/17/11	1/9/7	2/0/5	2/10/5	2/19/7	3/7/11	3/15/5	4/2/1	4/7/11	4/12/11	4/17/1	5/0/5	5/2/11	5/4/7	5/5/5	5/5/5	5/4/7	5/2/11	5/0/5	4/17/1
110	0/18/4	1/10/5	2/1/8	2/12/1	3/1/8	3/10/5	3/18/4	4/5/5	4/11/8	4/17/1	5/1/8	5/5/5	5/8/4	5/10/5	5/11/8	5/12/1	5/11/8	5/10/5	5/8/4	5/5/5
105	0/18/9	1/11/3	2/2/11	2/13/9	3/3/9	3/12/11	4/1/3	4/8/9	4/15/5	5/1/3	5/6/3	5/10/5	5/13/9	5/16/3	5/17/11	5/18/9	5/18/9	5/17/11	5/16/3	5/13/9

SELLERS PAYOFF TABLE

Price	1	2	3	4	5	6	7	8	9	10	11	12	13	14	15	16	17	18	19	20
205	1/12/11	2/7/6	3/0/5	3/11/8	4/1/3	4/9/2	4/15/5	5/0/0	5/2/11	5/4/2	5/3/9	5/1/8	4/17/11	4/12/6	4/5/5	3/16/8	3/6/3	2/14/2	2/0/5	1/5/0
200	1/12/6	2/6/8	2/19/2	3/10/0	3/19/2	4/6/8	4/12/6	4/16/8	4/19/2	5/0/0	4/19/2	4/16/8	4/12/6	4/6/8	3/19/2	3/10/0	2/19/2	2/6/8	1/12/6	0/16/8
195	1/12/1	2/5/10	2/17/11	3/8/4	3/17/1	4/4/2	4/9/7	4/13/4	4/15/5	4/15/10	4/14/7	4/11/8	4/7/1	4/0/10	3/12/11	3/3/4	2/12/1	1/19/2	1/4/7	0/8/4
190	1/11/8	2/5/0	2/16/8	3/6/8	3/15/0	4/1/8	4/6/8	4/10/0	4/11/8	4/11/8	4/10/0	4/6/8	4/1/8	3/15/0	3/6/8	2/16/8	2/5/0	1/11/8	0/16/8	0
185	1/11/3	2/4/2	2/15/5	3/5/0	3/12/11	3/19/2	4/3/9	4/6/8	4/7/11	4/7/6	4/5/5	4/1/8	3/16/3	3/9/2	3/0/5	2/10/0	1/17/11	1/4/2	0/8/9	0
180	1/10/10	2/3/4	2/14/2	3/3/4	3/10/10	3/16/8	4/0/10	4/3/4	4/4/2	4/3/4	4/0/10	3/16/8	3/10/10	3/3/4	2/14/2	2/3/4	1/10/10	0/16/8	0/0/10	0
175	1/10/5	2/2/6	2/12/11	3/1/8	3/8/9	3/14/2	3/17/11	4/0/0	4/0/5	3/19/2	3/16/3	3/11/8	3/5/5	2/17/6	2/7/11	1/16/8	1/3/9	0/9/2	0	0
170	1/10/0	2/1/8	2/11/8	3/0/0	3/6/8	3/11/8	3/15/0	3/16/8	3/16/8	3/15/0	3/11/8	3/6/8	3/0/0	2/11/8	2/1/8	1/10/0	0/16/8	0/1/8	0	0
165	1/9/7	2/0/10	2/10/5	2/18/4	3/4/7	3/9/2	3/12/1	3/13/4	3/12/11	3/10/10	3/7/1	3/1/8	2/14/7	2/5/10	1/15/5	1/3/4	0/9/7	0	0	0
160	1/9/2	2/0/0	2/9/2	2/16/8	3/2/6	3/6/8	3/9/2	3/10/0	3/9/2	3/6/8	3/2/6	2/16/8	2/9/2	2/0/0	1/9/2	0/16/8	0/2/6	0	0	0
155	1/8/9	1/19/2	2/7/11	2/15/0	3/0/5	3/4/2	3/6/3	3/6/8	3/5/5	3/2/6	2/17/11	2/11/8	2/3/9	1/14/2	1/2/11	0/10/0	0	0	0	0
150	1/8/4	1/18/4	2/6/8	2/13/4	2/18/4	3/1/8	3/3/4	3/3/4	3/1/8	2/18/4	2/13/4	2/6/8	1/18/4	1/8/4	0/16/8	0/3/4	0	0	0	0
145	1/7/11	1/17/6	2/5/5	2/11/8	2/16/3	2/19/2	3/0/5	3/0/0	2/17/11	2/14/2	2/8/9	2/1/8	1/12/11	1/2/6	0/10/5	0	0	0	0	0
140	1/7/6	1/16/8	2/4/2	2/10/0	2/14/2	2/16/8	2/17/6	2/16/8	2/14/2	2/10/0	2/4/2	1/16/8	1/7/6	0/16/8	0/4/2	0	0	0	0	0
135	1/7/1	1/15/10	2/2/11	2/8/4	2/12/1	2/14/2	2/14/7	2/13/4	2/10/5	2/5/10	1/19/7	1/11/8	1/2/1	0/10/10	0	0	0	0	0	0
130	1/6/8	1/15/0	2/1/8	2/6/8	2/10/0	2/11/8	2/11/8	2/10/0	2/6/8	2/1/8	1/15/0	1/6/8	0/16/8	0/5/0	0	0	0	0	0	0
125	1/6/3	1/14/2	2/0/5	2/5/0	2/7/11	2/9/2	2/8/9	2/6/8	2/2/11	1/17/6	1/10/5	1/1/8	0/11/3	0	0	0	0	0	0	0
120	1/5/10	1/13/4	1/19/2	2/3/4	2/5/10	2/6/8	2/5/10	2/3/4	1/19/2	1/13/4	1/5/10	0/16/8	0/5/10	0	0	0	0	0	0	0
115	1/5/5	1/12/6	1/17/11	2/1/8	2/3/9	2/4/2	2/2/11	2/0/0	1/15/5	1/9/2	1/1/3	0/11/8	0/0/5	0	0	0	0	0	0	0
110	1/5/0	1/11/8	1/16/8	2/0/0	2/1/8	2/1/8	2/0/0	1/16/8	1/11/8	1/5/0	0/16/8	0/6/8	0	0	0	0	0	0	0	0
105	1/4/7	1/10/10	1/15/5	1/18/4	1/19/7	1/19/2	1/17/1	1/13/4	1/7/11	1/0/10	0/12/1	0/1/8	0	0	0	0	0	0	0	0

Buyers Payoff Table

Price	\multicolumn{20}{c}{Quantity}

Price	1	2	3	4	5	6	7	8	9	10	11	12	13	14	15	16	17	18	19	20
205	125	175	215	245	265	275	275	265	245	215	175	125	65	0	0	0	0	0	0	0
200	130	185	230	265	290	305	310	305	290	265	230	185	130	65	0	0	0	0	0	0
195	135	195	245	285	315	335	345	345	335	315	285	245	195	135	65	0	0	0	0	0
190	140	205	260	305	340	365	380	385	380	365	340	305	260	205	140	65	0	0	0	0
185	145	215	275	325	365	395	415	425	425	415	395	365	325	275	215	145	65	0	0	0
180	150	225	290	345	390	425	450	465	470	465	450	425	390	345	290	225	150	65	0	0
175	155	235	305	365	415	455	485	505	515	515	505	485	455	415	365	305	235	155	65	0
170	160	245	320	385	440	485	520	545	560	565	560	545	520	485	440	385	320	245	160	65
165	165	255	335	405	465	515	555	585	605	615	615	605	585	555	515	465	405	335	255	165
160	170	265	350	425	490	545	590	625	650	665	670	665	650	625	590	545	490	425	350	265
155	175	275	365	445	515	575	625	665	695	715	725	725	715	695	665	625	575	515	445	365
150	180	285	380	465	540	605	660	705	740	765	780	785	780	765	740	705	660	605	540	465
145	185	295	395	485	565	635	695	745	785	815	835	845	845	835	815	785	745	695	635	565
140	190	305	410	505	590	665	730	785	830	865	890	905	910	905	890	865	830	785	730	665
135	195	315	425	525	615	695	765	825	875	915	945	965	975	975	965	945	915	875	825	765
130	200	325	440	545	640	725	800	865	920	965	1000	1025	1040	1045	1040	1025	1000	965	920	865
125	205	335	455	565	665	755	835	905	965	1015	1055	1085	1105	1115	1115	1105	1085	1055	1015	965
120	210	345	470	585	690	785	870	945	1010	1065	1110	1145	1170	1185	1190	1185	1170	1145	1110	1065
115	215	355	485	605	715	815	905	985	1055	1115	1165	1205	1235	1255	1255	1265	1255	1235	1205	1165
110	220	365	500	625	740	845	940	1025	1100	1165	1220	1265	1300	1325	1340	1345	1340	1325	1300	1265
105	225	375	515	645	765	875	975	1065	1145	1215	1275	1325	1365	1395	1415	1425	1425	1415	1395	1365

Sellers Payoff Table

Price	\multicolumn{20}{c}{Quantity}

Price	1	2	3	4	5	6	7	8	9	10	11	12	13	14	15	16	17	18	19	20
205	395	570	725	860	975	1070	1145	1200	1235	1250	1245	1220	1175	1110	1025	920	795	650	485	300
200	390	560	710	840	950	1040	1110	1160	1190	1200	1190	1160	1110	1040	950	840	710	560	390	200
195	385	550	695	820	925	1010	1075	1120	1145	1150	1135	1100	1045	970	875	760	625	470	295	100
190	380	540	680	800	900	980	1040	1080	1100	1100	1090	1040	980	900	800	680	540	380	200	0
185	375	530	665	780	875	950	1005	1040	1055	1050	1025	980	915	830	725	600	455	290	105	0
180	370	520	650	760	850	920	970	1000	1010	1000	970	920	850	760	650	520	370	200	10	0
175	365	510	635	740	825	890	935	960	965	950	915	860	785	690	575	440	285	110	0	0
170	360	500	620	720	800	860	900	920	920	900	860	800	720	620	500	360	200	20	0	0
165	355	490	605	700	775	830	865	880	875	850	805	740	655	550	425	280	115	0	0	0
160	350	480	590	680	750	800	830	840	830	800	750	680	590	480	350	200	30	0	0	0
155	345	470	575	660	725	770	795	800	785	750	695	620	525	410	275	120	0	0	0	0
150	340	460	560	640	700	740	760	760	740	700	640	560	460	340	200	40	0	0	0	0
145	335	450	545	620	675	710	725	720	695	650	585	500	395	270	125	0	0	0	0	0
140	330	440	530	600	650	680	690	680	650	600	530	440	330	200	50	0	0	0	0	0
135	325	430	515	580	625	650	655	640	605	550	475	380	265	130	0	0	0	0	0	0
130	320	420	500	560	600	620	620	600	560	500	420	320	200	60	0	0	0	0	0	0
125	315	410	485	540	575	590	585	560	515	450	365	260	135	0	0	0	0	0	0	0
120	310	400	470	520	550	560	550	520	470	400	310	200	70	0	0	0	0	0	0	0
115	305	390	455	500	525	530	515	480	425	350	255	140	5	0	0	0	0	0	0	0
110	300	380	440	480	500	500	480	440	380	300	200	80	0	0	0	0	0	0	0	0
105	295	370	425	460	475	470	445	400	335	250	145	20	0	0	0	0	0	0	0	0

Belgium (francs)
Kopers Winst Tabel

Kwantiteit

Prijs	1	2	3	4	5	6	7	8	9	10	11	12	13	14	15	16	17	18	19	20
205	63	88	108	123	133	138	138	133	123	108	88	63	33	0	0	0	0	0	0	0
200	65	93	115	133	145	153	155	153	145	133	115	93	65	33	0	0	0	0	0	0
195	68	98	123	143	158	168	173	173	168	158	143	123	98	68	33	0	0	0	0	0
190	70	103	130	153	170	183	190	193	190	183	170	153	130	103	70	33	0	0	0	0
185	73	108	138	163	183	198	208	213	213	208	198	183	163	138	108	73	33	0	0	0
180	75	113	145	173	195	213	225	233	235	233	225	213	195	173	145	113	75	33	0	0
175	78	118	153	183	208	228	243	253	258	258	253	243	228	208	183	153	118	78	33	0
170	80	123	160	193	220	243	260	273	280	283	280	273	260	243	220	193	160	123	80	33
165	83	128	168	203	233	258	278	293	303	308	308	303	293	278	258	233	203	168	128	83
160	85	133	175	213	245	273	295	313	325	333	335	333	325	313	295	273	245	213	175	133
155	88	138	183	223	258	288	313	333	348	358	363	363	358	348	333	313	288	258	223	183
150	90	143	190	233	270	303	330	353	370	383	390	393	390	383	370	353	330	303	270	233
145	93	148	198	243	283	318	348	373	393	408	418	423	423	418	408	393	373	348	318	283
140	95	153	205	253	295	333	365	393	415	433	445	453	455	453	445	433	415	393	365	333
135	98	158	213	263	308	348	383	413	438	458	473	483	488	488	483	473	458	438	413	383
130	100	163	220	273	320	363	400	433	460	483	500	513	520	523	520	513	500	483	460	433
125	103	168	228	283	333	378	418	453	483	508	528	543	553	558	558	553	543	523	508	483
120	105	173	235	293	345	393	435	473	505	533	555	573	585	593	595	593	585	573	555	533
115	108	178	243	303	358	408	453	493	528	558	583	603	618	628	633	633	628	613	603	583
110	110	183	250	313	370	423	470	513	550	583	610	633	650	663	670	673	670	663	650	633
105	113	188	258	323	383	438	488	533	573	608	638	663	683	698	708	713	713	708	698	683

Verkopers Winst Tabel

Kwantiteit

Prijs	1	2	3	4	5	6	7	8	9	10	11	12	13	14	15	16	17	18	19	20
205	198	285	363	430	488	535	573	600	618	625	623	610	588	555	513	460	398	325	243	150
200	195	280	355	420	475	520	555	580	595	600	595	580	555	520	475	420	355	280	195	100
195	193	275	348	410	463	505	538	560	573	575	568	550	523	485	438	380	313	235	148	50
190	190	270	340	400	450	490	520	540	550	550	540	520	490	450	400	340	270	190	100	0
185	188	265	333	390	438	475	503	520	528	525	513	490	458	415	363	300	228	145	53	0
180	185	260	325	380	425	460	485	500	505	500	485	460	425	380	325	260	185	100	5	0
175	183	255	318	370	413	445	468	480	483	475	458	430	393	345	288	220	143	55	0	0
170	180	250	310	360	400	430	450	460	460	450	430	400	360	310	250	180	100	10	0	0
165	178	245	303	350	388	415	433	440	438	425	403	370	328	275	213	140	58	0	0	0
160	175	240	295	340	375	400	415	420	415	400	375	340	295	240	175	100	15	0	0	0
155	173	235	288	330	363	385	398	400	393	375	348	310	263	205	138	60	0	0	0	0
150	170	230	280	320	350	370	380	380	370	350	320	280	230	170	100	20	0	0	0	0
145	168	225	273	310	338	355	363	360	348	325	293	250	198	135	63	0	0	0	0	0
140	165	220	265	300	325	340	345	340	325	300	265	220	165	100	25	0	0	0	0	0
135	163	215	258	290	313	325	328	320	303	275	238	190	133	65	0	0	0	0	0	0
130	160	210	250	280	300	310	310	300	280	250	210	160	100	30	0	0	0	0	0	0
125	158	205	243	270	288	295	293	280	258	225	183	130	68	0	0	0	0	0	0	0
120	155	200	235	260	275	280	275	260	235	200	155	100	35	0	0	0	0	0	0	0
115	153	195	228	250	263	265	258	240	213	175	128	70	0	0	0	0	0	0	0	0
110	150	190	220	240	250	250	240	220	190	150	100	40	0	0	0	0	0	0	0	0
105	148	185	213	230	238	235	223	200	168	125	73	10	0	0	0	0	0	0	0	0

Finland (marks)
Ostajan Voittotaulukko

Maara

Hinta	1	2	3	4	5	6	7	8	9	10	11	12	13	14	15	16	17	18	19	20
205	525	735	903	1029	1113	1155	1155	1113	1029	903	735	525	273	0	0	0	0	0	0	0
200	546	777	966	1113	1218	1281	1302	1281	1218	1113	966	777	546	273	0	0	0	0	0	0
195	567	819	1029	1197	1323	1407	1449	1449	1407	1323	1197	1029	819	567	273	0	0	0	0	0
190	588	861	1092	1281	1428	1533	1596	1617	1596	1533	1428	1281	1092	861	588	273	0	0	0	0
185	609	903	1155	1365	1533	1659	1743	1785	1785	1743	1659	1533	1365	1155	903	609	273	0	0	0
180	630	945	1218	1449	1638	1785	1890	1953	1974	1953	1890	1785	1638	1449	1218	945	630	273	0	0
175	651	987	1281	1533	1743	1911	2037	2121	2163	2163	2121	2037	1911	1743	1533	1281	987	651	273	0
170	672	1029	1344	1617	1848	2037	2184	2289	2352	2373	2352	2289	2184	2037	1848	1617	1344	1029	672	273
165	693	1071	1407	1701	1953	2163	2331	2457	2541	2583	2583	2541	2457	2331	2163	1953	1701	1407	1071	693
160	714	1113	1470	1785	2058	2289	2478	2625	2730	2793	2814	2793	2730	2625	2478	2289	2058	1785	1470	1113
155	735	1155	1533	1869	2163	2415	2625	2793	2919	3003	3045	3045	3003	2919	2793	2625	2415	2163	1869	1533
150	756	1197	1596	1953	2268	2541	2772	2961	3108	3213	3276	3297	3276	3213	3108	2961	2772	2541	2268	1953
145	777	1239	1659	2037	2373	2667	2919	3129	3297	3423	3507	3549	3549	3507	3423	3297	3129	2919	2667	2373
140	798	1281	1722	2121	2478	2793	3066	3297	3486	3633	3738	3801	3822	3801	3738	3633	3486	3297	3066	2793
135	819	1323	1785	2205	2583	2919	3213	3465	3675	3843	3969	4053	4095	4095	4053	3969	3843	3675	3465	3213
130	840	1365	1848	2289	2688	3045	3360	3633	3864	4053	4200	4305	4368	4389	4368	4305	4200	4053	3864	3633
125	861	1407	1911	2373	2793	3171	3507	3801	4053	4263	4431	4557	4641	4683	4683	4641	4557	4431	4263	4053
120	882	1449	1974	2457	2898	3297	3654	3969	4242	4473	4662	4809	4914	4977	4998	4977	4914	4809	4662	4473
115	903	1491	2037	2541	3003	3423	3801	4137	4431	4683	4893	5061	5187	5271	5313	5313	5271	5187	5061	4893
110	924	1533	2100	2625	3108	3549	3948	4305	4620	4893	5124	5313	5460	5565	5628	5649	5628	5565	5460	5313
105	945	1575	2163	2709	3213	3675	4095	4473	4809	5103	5355	5565	5733	5859	5943	5985	5985	5943	5859	5733

Myyjan Voittotaulukko

Maara

Hinta	1	2	3	4	5	6	7	8	9	10	11	12	13	14	15	16	17	18	19	20
205	1659	2394	3045	3612	4095	4494	4809	5040	5187	5250	5229	5124	4935	4662	4305	3864	3339	2730	2037	1260
200	1638	2352	2982	3528	3990	4368	4662	4872	4998	5040	4998	4872	4662	4368	3990	3528	2982	2352	1638	840
195	1617	2310	2919	3444	3885	4242	4515	4704	4809	4830	4787	4620	4389	4074	3675	3192	2625	1974	1239	420
190	1596	2268	2856	3360	3780	4116	4368	4536	4620	4620	4536	4368	4116	3780	3360	2856	2268	1596	840	0
185	1575	2226	2793	3276	3675	3990	4221	4368	4431	4410	4305	4116	3843	3486	3045	2520	1911	1218	441	0
180	1554	2184	2730	3192	3570	3864	4074	4200	4242	4200	4074	3864	3570	3192	2730	2184	1554	840	42	0
175	1533	2142	2667	3108	3465	3738	3927	4032	4053	3990	3843	3612	3297	2898	2415	1848	1197	462	0	0
170	1512	2100	2604	3024	3360	3612	3780	3864	3864	3780	3612	3360	3024	2604	2100	1512	840	84	0	0
165	1491	2058	2541	2940	3255	3486	3633	3696	3675	3570	3381	3108	2751	2310	1785	1176	483	0	0	0
160	1470	2016	2478	2856	3150	3360	3486	3528	3486	3360	3150	2856	2478	2016	1470	840	126	0	0	0
155	1449	1974	2415	2772	3045	3234	3339	3360	3297	3150	2919	2604	2205	1722	1155	504	0	0	0	0
150	1428	1932	2352	2688	2940	3108	3192	3192	3108	2940	2688	2352	1932	1428	840	168	0	0	0	0
145	1407	1890	2289	2604	2835	2982	3045	3024	2919	2730	2457	2100	1659	1134	525	0	0	0	0	0
140	1386	1848	2226	2520	2730	2856	2898	2856	2730	2520	2226	1848	1386	840	210	0	0	0	0	0
135	1365	1806	2163	2436	2625	2730	2751	2688	2541	2310	1995	1596	1113	546	0	0	0	0	0	0
130	1344	1764	2100	2352	2520	2604	2604	2520	2352	2100	1764	1344	840	252	0	0	0	0	0	0
125	1323	1722	2037	2268	2415	2478	2457	2352	2163	1890	1533	1092	567	0	0	0	0	0	0	0
120	1302	1680	1974	2184	2310	2352	2310	2184	1974	1680	1302	840	294	0	0	0	0	0	0	0
115	1281	1638	1911	2100	2205	2226	2163	2016	1785	1470	1071	588	21	0	0	0	0	0	0	0
110	1260	1596	1848	2016	2100	2100	2016	1848	1596	1260	840	336	0	0	0	0	0	0	0	0
105	1239	1554	1785	1932	1995	1974	1869	1680	1407	1050	609	84	0	0	0	0	0	0	0	0

France (centimes)
Buyers Payoff Table

Quantity

Price	1	2	3	4	5	6	7	8	9	10	11	12	13	14	15	16	17	18	19	20
205	625	875	1075	1225	1325	1375	1375	1325	1225	1075	875	625	325	0	0	0	0	0	0	0
200	650	925	1150	1325	1450	1525	1550	1525	1450	1325	1150	925	650	325	0	0	0	0	0	0
195	675	975	1225	1425	1575	1675	1725	1725	1675	1575	1425	1225	975	675	325	0	0	0	0	0
190	700	1025	1300	1525	1700	1825	1900	1925	1900	1825	1700	1525	1300	1025	700	325	0	0	0	0
185	725	1075	1375	1625	1825	1975	2075	2125	2125	2075	1975	1825	1625	1375	1075	725	325	0	0	0
180	750	1125	1450	1725	1950	2125	2250	2325	2350	2325	2250	2125	1950	1725	1450	1125	725	325	0	0
175	775	1175	1525	1825	2075	2275	2425	2525	2575	2575	2525	2425	2275	2075	1825	1525	1175	775	325	0
170	800	1225	1600	1925	2200	2425	2600	2725	2800	2825	2800	2725	2600	2425	2200	1925	1600	1225	800	325
165	825	1275	1675	2025	2325	2575	2775	2925	3025	3075	3075	3025	2925	2775	2575	2325	2025	1675	1275	825
160	850	1325	1750	2125	2450	2725	2950	3125	3250	3325	3350	3325	3250	3125	2950	2725	2450	2125	1750	1325
155	875	1375	1825	2225	2575	2875	3125	3325	3475	3575	3625	3625	3575	3475	3325	3125	2875	2575	2225	1825
150	900	1425	1900	2325	2700	3025	3300	3525	3700	3825	3900	3925	3900	3825	3700	3525	3300	3025	2700	2325
145	925	1475	1975	2425	2825	3175	3475	3725	3925	4075	4175	4225	4225	4175	4075	3925	3725	3475	3175	2825
140	950	1525	2050	2525	2950	3325	3650	3925	4150	4325	4450	4525	4550	4525	4450	4325	4150	3925	3650	3325
135	975	1575	2125	2625	3075	3475	3825	4125	4375	4575	4725	4825	4875	4875	4825	4725	4575	4375	4125	3825
130	1000	1625	2200	2725	3200	3625	4000	4325	4600	4825	5000	5125	5200	5225	5200	5125	5000	4825	4600	4325
125	1025	1675	2275	2825	3325	3775	4175	4525	4825	5075	5275	5425	5525	5575	5575	5525	5425	5275	5075	4825
120	1050	1725	2350	2925	3450	3925	4350	4725	5050	5325	5550	5725	5850	5925	5950	5925	5850	5725	5550	5325
115	1075	1775	2425	3025	3575	4075	4525	4925	5275	5575	5825	6025	6175	6275	6325	6325	6275	6175	6025	5825
110	1100	1825	2500	3125	3700	4225	4700	5125	5500	5825	6100	6325	6500	6625	6700	6725	6700	6625	6500	6325
105	1125	1875	2575	3225	3825	4375	4875	5325	5725	6075	6375	6625	6825	6975	7075	7125	7125	7075	6975	6825

Sellers Payoff Table

Quantity

Price	1	2	3	4	5	6	7	8	9	10	11	12	13	14	15	16	17	18	19	20
205	1975	2850	3625	4300	4875	5350	5725	6000	6175	6250	6225	6100	5875	5550	5125	4600	3975	3250	2425	1500
200	1950	2800	3550	4200	4750	5200	5550	5800	5950	6000	5950	5800	5550	5200	4750	4200	3550	2800	1950	1000
195	1925	2750	3475	4100	4625	5050	5375	5600	5725	5750	5675	5500	5225	4850	4375	3800	3125	2350	1475	500
190	1900	2700	3400	4000	4500	4900	5200	5400	5500	5500	5400	5200	4900	4500	4000	3400	2700	1900	1000	0
185	1875	2650	3325	3900	4375	4750	5025	5200	5275	5250	5125	4900	4575	4150	3625	3000	2275	1450	525	0
180	1850	2600	3250	3800	4250	4600	4850	5000	5050	5000	4850	4600	4250	3800	3250	2600	1850	1000	50	0
175	1825	2550	3175	3700	4125	4450	4675	4800	4825	4750	4575	4300	3925	3450	2875	2200	1425	550	0	0
170	1800	2500	3100	3600	4000	4300	4500	4600	4600	4500	4300	4000	3600	3100	2500	1800	1000	100	0	0
165	1775	2450	3025	3500	3875	4150	4325	4400	4375	4250	4025	3700	3275	2750	2125	1400	575	0	0	0
160	1750	2400	2950	3400	3750	4000	4150	4200	4150	4000	3750	3400	2950	2400	1750	1000	150	0	0	0
155	1725	2350	2875	3300	3625	3850	3975	4000	3925	3750	3475	3100	2625	2050	1375	600	0	0	0	0
150	1700	2300	2800	3200	3500	3700	3800	3800	3700	3500	3200	2800	2300	1700	1000	200	0	0	0	0
145	1675	2250	2725	3100	3375	3550	3625	3600	3475	3250	2925	2500	1975	1350	625	0	0	0	0	0
140	1650	2200	2650	3000	3250	3400	3450	3400	3250	3000	2650	2200	1650	1000	250	0	0	0	0	0
135	1625	2150	2575	2900	3125	3250	3275	3200	3025	2750	2375	1900	1325	650	0	0	0	0	0	0
130	1600	2100	2500	2800	3000	3100	3100	3000	2800	2500	2100	1600	1000	300	0	0	0	0	0	0
125	1575	2050	2425	2700	2875	2950	2925	2800	2575	2250	1825	1300	675	0	0	0	0	0	0	0
120	1550	2000	2350	2600	2750	2800	2750	2600	2350	2000	1550	1000	350	0	0	0	0	0	0	0
115	1525	1950	2275	2500	2625	2650	2575	2400	2125	1750	1275	700	25	0	0	0	0	0	0	0
110	1500	1900	2200	2400	2500	2500	2400	2200	1900	1500	1000	400	0	0	0	0	0	0	0	0
105	1475	1850	2125	2300	2375	2350	2225	2000	1675	1250	725	100	0	0	0	0	0	0	0	0

Japan (yen)

買手受取金額表

数量

価格	1	2	3	4	5	6	7	8	9	10	11	12	13	14	15	16	17	18	19	20
205	385	539	662	755	816	847	847	816	755	662	539	385	200	0	0	0	0	0	0	0
200	400	570	708	816	893	939	955	939	893	816	708	570	400	200	0	0	0	0	0	0
195	416	601	755	878	970	1032	1063	1063	1032	970	878	755	601	416	200	0	0	0	0	0
190	431	631	801	939	1047	1124	1170	1186	1170	1124	1047	939	801	631	431	200	0	0	0	0
185	447	662	847	1001	1124	1217	1278	1309	1309	1278	1217	1124	1001	847	662	447	200	0	0	0
180	462	693	893	1063	1201	1309	1386	1432	1448	1432	1386	1309	1201	1063	893	693	462	200	0	0
175	477	724	930	1124	1278	1401	1494	1555	1586	1586	1555	1494	1401	1278	1124	939	724	477	200	0
170	493	755	986	1186	1355	1494	1602	1679	1725	1740	1725	1679	1602	1494	1355	1186	986	755	493	200
165	508	785	1032	1247	1432	1586	1709	1802	1863	1894	1894	1863	1802	1709	1586	1432	1247	1032	785	508
160	524	816	1078	1309	1509	1679	1817	1925	2002	2048	2064	2048	2002	1925	1817	1679	1509	1309	1078	816
155	539	847	1124	1371	1586	1771	1925	2048	2141	2202	2233	2233	2202	2141	2048	1925	1771	1586	1371	1124
150	554	878	1170	1432	1663	1863	2033	2171	2279	2356	2402	2418	2402	2356	2279	2171	2033	1863	1663	1432
145	570	909	1217	1494	1740	1956	2141	2295	2418	2510	2572	2603	2603	2572	2510	2418	2295	2141	1956	1740
140	585	939	1263	1555	1817	2048	2248	2418	2556	2664	2741	2787	2803	2787	2741	2664	2556	2418	2248	2048
135	601	970	1309	1617	1894	2141	2356	2541	2695	2818	2911	2972	3003	3003	2972	2911	2818	2695	2541	2356
130	616	1001	1355	1679	1971	2233	2464	2664	2834	2972	3080	3157	3203	3219	3203	3157	3080	2972	2834	2664
125	631	1032	1401	1740	2048	2325	2572	2787	2972	3126	3249	3342	3403	3434	3434	3403	3342	3249	3126	2972
120	647	1063	1448	1802	2125	2418	2680	2911	3111	3280	3419	3527	3604	3650	3665	3650	3604	3527	3419	3280
115	662	1093	1494	1863	2202	2510	2787	3034	3249	3434	3588	3711	3804	3865	3896	3896	3865	3804	3711	3588
110	678	1124	1540	1925	2279	2603	2895	3157	3388	3588	3758	3896	4004	4081	4127	4143	4127	4081	4004	3896
105	693	1155	1586	1987	2356	2695	3003	3280	3527	3742	3927	4081	4204	4297	4358	4389	4389	4358	4297	4204

売手受取金額表

数量

価格	1	2	3	4	5	6	7	8	9	10	11	12	13	14	15	16	17	18	19	20
205	1217	1756	2233	2649	3003	3296	3527	3696	3804	3850	3835	3758	3619	3419	3157	2834	2449	2002	1494	924
200	1201	1725	2187	2587	2926	3203	3419	3573	3665	3696	3665	3573	3419	3203	2926	2587	2187	1725	1201	616
195	1186	1694	2141	2526	2849	3111	3311	3450	3527	3542	3496	3388	3219	2988	2695	2341	1925	1448	909	308
190	1170	1663	2094	2464	2772	3018	3203	3326	3388	3388	3326	3203	3018	2772	2464	2094	1663	1170	616	0
185	1155	1632	2048	2402	2695	2926	3095	3203	3249	3234	3157	3018	2818	2556	2233	1848	1401	893	323	0
180	1140	1602	2002	2341	2618	2834	2988	3080	3111	3080	2988	2834	2618	2341	2002	1602	1140	616	31	0
175	1124	1571	1956	2279	2541	2741	2880	2957	2972	2926	2818	2649	2418	2125	1771	1355	878	339	0	0
170	1109	1540	1910	2218	2464	2649	2772	2834	2834	2772	2649	2464	2218	1910	1540	1109	616	62	0	0
165	1093	1509	1863	2156	2387	2556	2664	2710	2695	2618	2479	2279	2017	1694	1309	862	354	0	0	0
160	1078	1478	1817	2094	2310	2464	2556	2587	2556	2464	2310	2094	1817	1478	1078	616	92	0	0	0
155	1063	1448	1771	2033	2233	2372	2449	2464	2418	2310	2141	1910	1617	1263	847	370	0	0	0	0
150	1047	1417	1725	1971	2156	2279	2341	2341	2279	2156	1971	1725	1417	1047	616	123	0	0	0	0
145	1032	1386	1679	1910	2079	2187	2233	2218	2141	2002	1802	1540	1217	832	385	0	0	0	0	0
140	1016	1355	1632	1848	2002	2094	2125	2094	2002	1848	1632	1355	1016	616	154	0	0	0	0	0
135	1001	1324	1586	1786	1925	2002	2017	1971	1863	1694	1463	1170	816	400	0	0	0	0	0	0
130	986	1294	1540	1725	1848	1910	1910	1848	1725	1540	1294	986	616	185	0	0	0	0	0	0
125	970	1263	1494	1663	1771	1817	1802	1725	1586	1386	1124	801	416	0	0	0	0	0	0	0
120	955	1232	1448	1602	1694	1725	1694	1602	1448	1232	955	616	216	0	0	0	0	0	0	0
115	939	1201	1401	1540	1617	1632	1586	1478	1309	1078	785	431	15	0	0	0	0	0	0	0
110	924	1170	1355	1478	1540	1540	1478	1355	1170	924	616	246	0	0	0	0	0	0	0	0
105	909	1140	1309	1416	1463	1448	1371	1232	1032	770	447	62	0	0	0	0	0	0	0	0

Spain (pesos)

Tabla de Pagos al Comprador

Cantidad

Precio	1	2	3	4	5	6	7	8	9	10	11	12	13	14	15	16	17	18	19	20
205	88	123	151	172	186	193	193	186	172	151	123	88	46	0	0	0	0	0	0	0
200	91	130	161	186	203	214	217	214	203	186	161	130	91	46	0	0	0	0	0	0
195	95	137	172	200	221	235	242	242	235	221	200	172	137	95	46	0	0	0	0	0
190	98	144	182	214	238	256	266	270	266	256	238	214	182	144	98	46	0	0	0	0
185	102	151	193	228	256	277	291	298	298	291	277	256	228	193	151	102	46	0	0	0
180	105	158	203	242	273	298	315	326	329	326	315	298	273	242	203	158	105	46	0	0
175	109	165	214	256	291	319	340	354	361	361	354	340	319	291	256	214	165	109	46	0
170	112	172	224	270	308	340	364	382	392	396	392	382	364	340	308	270	224	172	112	46
165	116	179	235	284	326	361	389	410	424	431	431	424	410	389	361	326	284	235	179	116
160	119	186	245	298	343	382	413	438	455	466	469	466	455	438	413	382	343	298	245	186
155	123	193	256	312	361	403	438	466	487	501	508	508	501	487	466	438	403	361	312	256
150	126	200	266	326	378	424	462	494	518	536	546	550	546	536	518	494	462	424	378	326
145	130	207	277	340	396	445	487	522	550	571	585	592	592	585	571	550	522	487	445	396
140	133	214	287	354	413	466	511	550	581	606	623	634	637	634	623	606	581	550	511	466
135	137	221	298	368	431	487	536	578	613	641	662	676	683	683	676	662	641	613	577	536
130	140	228	308	382	448	508	560	606	644	676	700	718	728	732	728	718	700	676	644	606
125	144	235	319	396	466	529	585	634	676	711	739	760	774	781	781	774	760	739	711	676
120	147	242	329	410	483	550	609	662	707	746	777	802	819	830	833	830	819	802	777	746
115	151	249	340	424	501	571	634	690	739	781	816	844	865	879	886	886	879	865	844	816
110	154	256	350	438	518	592	658	718	770	816	854	886	910	928	938	942	938	928	910	886
105	158	263	361	452	536	613	683	746	802	851	893	928	956	977	991	998	998	991	977	956

Tabla de Pagos al Vendedor

Cantidad

Precio	1	2	3	4	5	6	7	8	9	10	11	12	13	14	15	16	17	18	19	20
205	277	399	508	602	683	749	802	840	865	875	872	854	823	777	718	644	557	455	340	210
200	273	392	497	588	665	728	777	812	833	840	833	812	777	728	665	588	497	392	273	140
195	270	385	487	574	648	707	753	784	802	805	795	770	732	679	613	532	438	329	207	70
190	266	378	476	560	630	686	728	756	770	770	756	728	686	630	560	476	378	266	140	0
185	263	371	466	546	613	665	704	728	739	735	718	686	641	581	508	420	319	203	74	0
180	259	364	455	532	595	644	679	700	707	700	679	644	595	532	455	364	259	140	7	0
175	256	357	445	518	578	623	655	672	676	665	641	602	550	483	403	308	200	77	0	0
170	252	350	434	504	560	602	630	644	644	630	602	560	504	434	350	252	140	14	0	0
165	249	343	424	490	543	581	606	616	613	595	564	518	459	385	298	196	81	0	0	0
160	245	336	413	476	525	560	581	588	581	560	525	476	413	336	245	140	21	0	0	0
155	242	329	403	462	508	539	557	560	550	525	487	434	368	287	193	84	0	0	0	0
150	238	322	392	448	490	518	532	532	518	490	448	392	322	238	140	28	0	0	0	0
145	235	315	382	434	473	497	508	504	487	455	410	350	277	189	88	0	0	0	0	0
140	231	308	371	420	455	476	483	476	455	420	371	308	231	140	35	0	0	0	0	0
135	228	301	361	406	438	455	459	448	424	385	333	266	186	91	0	0	0	0	0	0
130	224	294	350	392	420	434	434	420	392	350	294	224	140	42	0	0	0	0	0	0
125	221	287	340	378	403	413	410	392	361	315	256	182	95	0	0	0	0	0	0	0
120	217	280	329	364	385	392	385	364	329	280	217	140	49	0	0	0	0	0	0	0
115	214	273	319	350	368	371	361	336	298	245	179	98	4	0	0	0	0	0	0	0
110	210	266	308	336	350	350	336	308	266	210	140	56	0	0	0	0	0	0	0	0
105	207	259	298	322	333	329	312	280	235	175	102	14	0	0	0	0	0	0	0	0

Thailand (baht)

การผ่อนชำระ

เริ่มต้น ภคภ	1	2	3	4	5	6	7	8	9	10	11	12	13	14	15	16	17	18	19	20
205	28	39	48	55	59	61	61	59	55	48	39	28	14	0	0	0	0	0	0	0
200	29	41	51	59	65	68	69	68	65	59	51	41	29	14	0	0	0	0	0	0
195	30	43	55	63	70	75	77	77	75	70	63	55	43	30	14	0	0	0	0	0
190	31	46	58	68	76	81	85	86	85	81	76	68	58	46	31	14	0	0	0	0
185	32	48	61	72	81	88	92	95	95	92	88	81	72	61	48	32	14	0	0	0
180	33	50	65	77	87	95	100	103	105	103	100	95	87	77	65	50	33	14	0	0
175	34	52	68	81	92	101	108	112	115	115	112	108	101	92	81	68	52	34	14	0
170	36	55	71	86	98	108	116	121	125	126	125	121	116	108	98	86	71	55	36	14
165	37	57	75	90	103	115	123	130	135	137	137	135	130	123	115	103	90	75	57	37
160	38	59	78	95	109	121	131	139	145	148	149	148	145	139	131	121	109	95	78	59
155	39	61	81	99	115	128	139	148	155	159	161	161	159	155	148	139	128	115	99	81
150	40	63	85	103	120	135	147	157	165	170	174	175	174	170	165	157	147	135	120	103
145	41	66	88	108	126	141	155	166	175	181	186	188	188	186	181	175	166	155	141	126
140	42	68	91	112	131	148	162	175	185	192	198	201	202	201	198	192	185	175	162	148
135	43	70	95	117	137	155	170	184	195	204	210	215	217	217	215	210	204	195	184	170
130	45	72	98	121	142	161	178	192	205	215	223	228	231	233	231	228	223	215	205	192
125	46	75	101	126	148	168	186	201	215	226	235	241	246	248	248	246	241	235	226	215
120	47	77	105	130	154	175	194	210	225	237	247	255	260	264	265	264	260	255	247	237
115	48	79	108	135	159	181	201	219	235	248	259	268	275	279	281	281	279	275	268	259
110	49	81	111	139	165	188	209	228	245	259	271	281	289	294	298	299	298	295	289	281
105	50	83	115	144	170	195	217	237	255	270	284	295	304	310	315	317	317	315	310	304

การชำระเพิ่ม

เริ่มต้น ภคภ	1	2	3	4	5	6	7	8	9	10	11	12	13	14	15	16	17	18	19	20
205	88	127	161	191	217	238	255	267	275	279	277	271	261	247	228	205	177	145	108	67
200	87	125	158	187	211	231	247	258	265	267	265	258	247	231	211	187	158	125	87	45
195	86	122	155	182	206	225	239	249	255	256	253	245	233	216	195	169	139	105	66	22
190	85	120	151	178	200	218	231	240	245	245	240	231	218	200	178	151	120	85	45	0
185	83	118	148	174	195	211	224	231	235	234	228	218	204	185	161	134	101	65	23	0
180	82	116	145	169	189	205	216	223	225	223	216	205	189	169	145	116	82	45	2	0
175	81	113	141	165	184	198	208	214	215	211	204	191	175	154	128	98	63	24	0	0
170	80	111	138	160	178	191	200	205	205	200	191	178	160	138	111	80	45	4	0	0
165	79	109	135	156	172	185	192	196	195	189	179	165	146	122	95	62	26	0	0	0
160	78	107	131	151	167	178	185	187	185	178	167	151	131	107	78	45	7	0	0	0
155	77	105	128	147	161	171	177	178	175	167	155	138	117	91	61	27	0	0	0	0
150	76	102	125	142	156	165	169	169	165	156	142	125	102	76	45	9	0	0	0	0
145	75	100	121	138	150	158	161	160	156	145	130	111	88	60	28	0	0	0	0	0
140	73	98	118	134	145	151	154	151	145	134	118	98	73	45	11	0	0	0	0	0
135	72	96	115	129	139	145	146	142	135	122	106	85	59	29	0	0	0	0	0	0
130	71	93	111	125	134	138	138	134	125	111	93	71	45	13	0	0	0	0	0	0
125	70	91	108	120	128	131	130	123	115	100	81	58	30	0	0	0	0	0	0	0
120	69	89	105	116	122	125	122	116	105	89	69	45	16	0	0	0	0	0	0	0
115	68	87	101	111	117	118	115	107	95	78	57	31	1	0	0	0	0	0	0	0
110	67	85	98	107	111	111	107	98	85	67	45	18	0	0	0	0	0	0	0	0
105	66	82	95	102	106	105	99	89	75	56	32	4	0	0	0	0	0	0	0	0